Waking Up In
NASHVILLE

Also by Stephen Foehr available from Sanctuary Publishing:

Waking Up In Cuba/Dancing With Fidel
Waking Up In Jamaica
Taj Mahal – Autobiography Of A Bluesman

Printed in the United Kingdom by MPG Books Ltd, Bodmin

Published by Sanctuary Publishing Limited, Sanctuary House, 45–53 Sinclair Road,
London W14 0NS, United Kingdom

www.sanctuarypublishing.com

Copyright: Stephen Foehr, 2002

Photographs: Courtesy of the author and © Dave G Houser/CORBIS,
Bettmann/CORBIS, Mark E Gibson/CORBIS

Cover photograph: © Hulton Archive/Getty Images

ISBN: 1-86074-434-6

Waking Up In
NASHVILLE

Stephen Foehr

Sanctuary

Contents

1 Tootsie's

The guy on my left wore a spotless black Stetson, a virgin hat unsoiled by sweat or the sweet stench of cattle. No cowboy would wear such a hat, except, perhaps, to a High Funeral. The brim was so wide it looked like a hang glider jammed over his ears. One strong breeze and he'd lift off onto the high lonesome highway in the sky.

To his left sat White Lies in a Western shirt with swaying fringe and snap buttons popped open by her cleavage. She drained her third whiskey, hoping to find a song hook. She thunked down the empty glass and asked for my fish-scaling knife.

'No fish on this table,' I said.

She laid her hand open flat on the table. 'Give me the knife.' She lowered her head, like a bull ready to charge. I gave her my knife. She sawed the fringe off the front of her Western shirt. 'Now I'm Contemporary Country,' she declared.

To her left, hunched over with elbows on the table and a three-day beard that was more despondency than chic, was Willie Nelson. Only this Willie Nelson wrote songs by ripping up Valentines and piecing them together to spell Love. And he couldn't carry a tune, which is often true of the famous Willie. But that Outlaw Willie wrote about love and courage and despair from the bottom of a hole he had dug with a misery spade. Our Willie, whose name was Bill 'Buddy' Nelson – but why call him that – our Willie wrote his songs from the depth of commercials.

'That's the language of the common man,' he argued. 'Just listen to the top 40. Nashville is not about music but the business of music. I'm going to make it big here, I just know I am.'

The four of us met, at first by coincidence and then by unspoken design, at the table in the back left corner near the restrooms at Tootsie's Orchid Lounge, Nashville's historic watering hole for down-and-out songwriters. Kris Kristofferson, Willie Nelson, Harlan Howard, Roger Miller, and Jim Reeves are famous alumni of Tootsie's, where they groused, drank, pitched songs to each other, plagiarized overheard conversations and refashioned them into hit songs, and listened to the singer in the window.

I'm not a songwriter. I don't even like country music, for which I feel guilty. Country music calls itself 'America's true music', and a case can be made to support that self-congratulatory trope. But which case? That country music is a touchstone to some elemental American characteristics that have shaped the values and attitudes of the nation? Or that the music reflects the commercial, shallow, pop culture that is the United States' chief export? I came to Nashville to wake up my sensibilities to the nature of country music. Is country really as bad as I think, or is there something more to the music than I realize?

Singing in Tootsie's front window, on the small stage to the left of the door, is a rite of passage for many fledgling country singers. I had heard lots of bad Garth Brooks wannabes come from that stage and some terrific Patsy Clines. As White Lies reshaped her country-and-western image, I heard a voice in the window that was country born, country bred, and country true. The woman at the mic sang the sound of crops dying and the sadness of her farmer running off with the barmaid and the wisdom of knowing that she would survive the pain of betrayal.

After the set I offered her a beer. She accepted a Diet Pepsi. 'I'm Jill King.' Her voice was country South, long vowels with a twist of twang, and her handshake firm. She was a short woman with a tumble of dark hair and a smile that said she saw the world as an amusing place, until proven otherwise.

'Where did you learn to sing like that?'

'At the church my great-granddaddy helped build in Arab, Alabama.' That's A-RAB. 'I was three years old and I've been singing ever since. I grew up on gospel and roots country.'

Arab is a one-stoplight town surrounded by farmland. Like a lot of small rural communities, it is inbred. Everybody knows everybody, and secrets might as well be bed sheets hanging on the line for all to see. Looking out for each other by knowing what each other was up to, for good or worse, was called being neighborly. That made the town friendly, if all you were doing was stopping for a cup of coffee and a chat. But living there, that was like living inside a country song, Jill told me. That was all about frustration, and suppressed emotions, and being polite when what you wanted to do was rip out the eyes of your gossipin', backbitin', two-timin', narrow-minded, self-righteous neighbor, gouge their eyes out of their head with your dull fingernail clipper. But the town was also about good people helpin' each other out with farm work, and being truly sorrowful at a neighbor's loss, and taking comfort in the shared fabric of the daily community life.

'I got some good songs out of that town,' Jill said.

Her mother is a schoolteacher, so education was always important in the household. Her parents sent her to Vanderbilt University in Nashville, which was fine with Jill. She wanted to get out of Arab, and a good education was important, but most of all Nashville was Music City USA, the capital of country, and Jill, above all, wanted to be a country singer. Singing was the only thing she'd always wanted to do.

'I sing my heart to a roomful of strangers because for some reason I was given the ability to touch people.' Jill looked around Tootsie's, crowded with tourists from Kentucky and Indiana and Michigan, and smiled. 'These people aren't any different than the folks I grew up with. We know each other's experiences. I make my voice vibrate inside me like a heartbreak moment or a joyous moment of those experiences. That's a gift I have. Singers have done that for me when I needed it. It sure helps me to have those voices and songs to listen to and touch me and make me a richer person. If I can do that for other people, giving back to music what music has always done for me, then it's worth the risk of showing strangers my heart.'

At Vanderbilt, Jill studied English literature and geology and art and the music business. One of her professors, Cecelia Tichi, who has written books on country music, recognized Jill's true interest. She gave Jill an independent study assignment: write a song around a story or a chord of the story or a theme of the story. That's when the mule got hitched to the wagon. After graduation in 1995, Jill took a couple of part-time jobs. She became a demo singer for songwriters. She performed at writer's nights that give exposure to new talent, which are held in various small venues around town. She put her English degree to work by writing songs and singing them in Jack Sawyer's guitar bar, off Nolensville Road, a little dive decorated in dark and grunge. In the back room was a dusty guitar busted over a mannequin's head and a sign that said, 'He played cover tunes.' That set the tone for the place. Nancy Griffin, Will Rambeaux, Kim Richie, Dave Berg all hung out there. Jack's was their Tootsie's in which to practice beginner's chops.

Jack's dad was an electrical engineer and his mother a concert pianist with a strong interest in opera. Jack kept classical records on the jukebox, which he'd play to signal closing time. Playing another country song wouldn't get anyone's attention. If an aria didn't send people packing, he'd fire a pistol into the ceiling. That was a cowboy thing, and country music people understand the cowboy thing.

'Jack Sawyer was a guy in the trenches who has given more songwriters hope in this town than he'll ever be given credit for,' Jill said. 'He'd give the shirt off his back to any songwriter who couldn't pay for a drink. He'd help us link up with each other.'

Jack ran the bar so he could be around his kind of music, which was his basic mistake. A bar is a business and, as with all businesses, the bills have to be paid. Jack gave drinks to his friends. He forgot to collect debts because his friends didn't have any money. And everyone in the bar who played music was his friend. When the bar was threatened with closure, the musicians threw a benefit to raise money. That kept him going for a few months, but he still gave away drinks. The bar was finally forced to close its doors.

'Jack's writing a book about the experience,' Jill said. 'He should probably just write a song.'

Although an artist at heart, Jill is a pragmatist in her head. While at Vanderbilt, she did a marketing internship at MCA, one of the major labels on Music Row. In the meetings, she learned that the labels view artists as part of a business plan. The creative person and his or her songs are products. Marketing plans are developed to position the product. If the artist didn't exactly fit that position, well, he or she could be 'stylized' to fit. For Jill, this was as important a part of her education as learning to write a song.

'That let me see how an artist has to give and take.' We had moved outside Tootsie's to enjoy the afternoon sunlight. Jill does the 2–6 shift Mondays and Thursdays. She doesn't get paid, but the tips are good. 'That give and take can be a hard thing to do when you're talking about your own creativity and passion and maybe the core of who you are as a person. It's very hard to give and take that, especially if you want to sing and you want to be who you are and you realize that there are compromises, just like the marketing people have to make compromises with the artist.

'I've heard of a label signing somebody and saying, "We like this about you. It's what makes you so special. Now we're going to make you like Shania Twain or you're going to be the next George Strait. We need you to dress like this and do this and sing songs like this." The whole machine starts turning creativity into a formula that the label knows worked in the past. It's not based on popular demand. The public no longer dictates what types of songs will appear on a CD. The public doesn't choose what songs they'll hear on the radio. That's done by national program directors of the commercial radio chains. My working in the industry was a real eye opener.'

To be a well-rounded artist, Jill wrote her own business plan, actually two business plans, one for making it as a singer and another for making it as a songwriter. Since 1997, she's been a full-time songwriter for Gate-to-Gate Publishing, a two-person office on Music Row financed out of San Antonio, Texas, by David Leibowitz. Jill writes the female songs. The other writer, Scott Randall Rhodes, writes the male songs. She got the title cut 'For All It's Worth' on the new Michael Mason album. It will probably come out as a single, she told me. 'That's a big plus for us. If our songs do well, then that gives us an open door. Then we can say, "We'd like to write with a known name." We can point to our resumé with that cut. That's part of the business plan.

'I've got a plan for whatever obstacle might come up and how to proceed.' She snuffed out her cigarette in preparation for her second set in Tootsie's. 'I have to work hard to make it happen and not be turned off by how the music business does this or that. That's the reality of the workplace I'm in. What I have to do is find a way to inch up the ladder to where I can sit down and talk with a label somebody.'

She has a plan as to how to make that happen. She's working on putting together a showcase where she'll sing her songs to label executives, producers, A&R (artist and repertoire) representatives, marketing people, friends and family. The invitation list is 400 names long. She has to find a way to pay all the expenses. That requires another plan.

Before she went back inside Tootsie's, Jill looked over my shoulder and pointed with her chin. 'Somebody up there will notice me.' I turned to look. About two miles away, as the crow flies, on a ridge line overlooking downtown Nashville, is Music Row, home of the major record labels where the business of country music is done.

We went back inside Tootsie's. Jill stepped up on the stage and called out for a request. I walked to the back and asked Our Willie to come with me.

'Why?'

'For inspiration.'

'I got all the inspiration I need right here.' He waved at the autographed photos edge-to-edge on the three walls of our hide-away: Alan Jackson, Merle Haggard, Keith Whitley, The Oak Ridge Boys, Willie Nelson, Buck Owens, Rodney Crowell, Bill Monroe, Judy Rodman, Eric Heatherley, Jo-El Sonnier. Publicity photos of country music's famous and not so famous covered Tootsie's walls. Some photos were in ornate frames, especially the older ones dating back to the 1940s and '50s, covered with sheets of Plexiglas to protect them from the scribbling of bar patrons. Tootsie's walls are like reading a personnel directory of country music.

'So what have you written today?' I asked Willie.

'I'm working on something,' Willie mumbled into his beer.

'That's right. Willie and I are co-writing a song,' chimed in White Lies. Her real name is Amy. A Chicago native, she wanted everyone to believe that she was Southern fried with green beans on the side. She said 'fer' instead of 'for'. But when she got excited, or tired, or drunk, her broad flat Chicago 'A' came through like a klaxon blast tearing a hole in chamber music. She insinuated that she grew up rural and poor and tragic, none of which was true, as I later discovered. She wanted you to believe that she was a survivor of heartbreak, which is probably true, given her escape into booze. I called her White Lies not because of the false biography but after one of her songs, 'White Lies Are the True Color of My Baby's Blue Eyes.' I never called her White Lies to her face and suppose I should stop doing so now. From now on she'll be Amy.

'Come up to Music Row with me,' I told Willie. 'It will give you a goal, a vision of the home you're searching for. Besides, you need some sunshine.'

Willie peered over the top of his sunglasses. 'Sunshine. I'll be the sunshine through your rain cloud.' He tapped out a beat on the table. 'Write that down. Maybe we can use it.'

'I already did. It's called, "You Are My Sunshine". I forgot who cut it. Some ol' crackerjack Southern politician, I think.' Amy didn't crack a smile. In fact, I rarely saw her smile, even when we had happy times. She wasn't dour or sad or depressed, at least not unduly depressed. I once asked her if she ever found smiling to be enjoyable. She said that if you smiled too much it gave people ideas. She had learned that as a little girl.

The wisecrack about 'You Are My Sunshine,' co-written by former Louisiana Gov Jimmie Davis (a contemporary of Jimmie Rodgers), who made it his campaign song, finally dawned on Willie. 'I don't need this disrespectful bullshit. Come on.' He got to his feet and walked to the front of the bar. I nearly ran into him when he stopped abruptly beside the band. 'You know these guys? The house band? The drummer is Richard Stickley. He plays for Loretta Lynn. When she goes on the road, we have to find another drummer. Larry Nutter there, he played guitar behind Kitty Wells and George Jones. And on bass guitar, Larry Barnes. He's a regular at the Grand Ole Opry. They come down here to play because they love the music. Can't leave it alone.'

I dropped a dollar in the tip jar and waved goodbye to Jill at the mic.

2 Music Row

Willie and I drove up to Music Row, taking the Demonbreun Street bridge over 'The Gully' where the railroad tracks separate Down Nashville, the flats along the Cumberland River, from Up Nashville on the high land. We hit the traffic roundabout, the only one in Nashville, the gateway to Music Row, and went around twice to admire Owen Bradley waving from his metal piano. Music Row exists because of Owen Bradley – and cheap real estate.

The Nashville music business was scattered around town in the 1940s. The WSM radio station's studios were downtown in the National Life Building. Acuff-Rose Publishing was out in Melrose, a suburb. In 1947, three engineers from WSM – sponsor of the Grand Ol' Opry – established The Castle Studio in the downtown Nashville Tulane Hotel. The studio, a former dining hall, was divided into a recording room, a control room, and a area for the acetate lathes to cut the music directly on to lacquer discs, as tape machines hadn't been invented yet. This was a state-of-the-art studio with eight input microphones, twice the number of any other recording console at the time. It was Nashville's only dedicated professional recording studio, where Hank Williams recorded 'Your Cheatin' Heart'.

The Castle closed in 1954 when WSM management told the engineers that the studio presented a potential conflict of interests with their duties to the radio station. They had to decide between the studio and the station.

Bradley, a staff pianist, bandleader, and engineer at WMS and the then head of Decca Record's country division, needed a place for his studio. He left the downtown commercial area and explored the slightly run-down residential section of large stately houses that bordered Vanderbilt University. In 1956, he bought an old house on what is now the corner of 16th Avenue and Music Row South (the MCA building presently occupies the site) and converted the second floor into a recording studio. He later added a military surplus Quonset hut to enlarge his recording space. His Studio B and the Quonset hut became the foundation stone for Music Row.

Publishing houses, record labels, recording studios, and agent and management offices gradually moved into the neighborhood. During the 1960s and '70s, many of the big Victorian houses were converted into office space. United Artists built the first, and only, high-rise tower on 17th Avenue in the mid-'70s, expecting to reap rental rewards. The octagonal-shaped building, dubbed the Lipstick Tube, struggled for years to become profitable. In the 1990s, MCA Records, Sony, Warner Bros/Nashville, and Capital Records Nashville built office buildings as their headquarters on Music Row.

Architecturally, Music Row is a mixed message, an accusation made of country music itself. The old houses say 'down-home', 'family', 'country living'. The sleek office buildings say 'commercial', 'efficient', 'bland style'. Area carpets, fresh flowers, fireplaces in conference rooms, and the warmth of dark wood paneling decorate the offices to give a homey feel. It's like big city country. It's schizoid. Part of the country music business wants to project a modern façade, so hides the essence of country behind glass-and-brick walls. Another part of the industry wants to be seen in its living room while pretending not to be a big business, with all the inherent ambitions and cutthroat practices apparently necessary to be successful in today's big business world.

Country music is caught in the same paradox. On one hand, it wants to retain the traditional image of 'aw shucks, we're just plain folk who play music' and on the other hand the industry manufactures a slick product that relies on technology as much as human talent to reap millions in the pop culture market.

Our Willie and I found a parking place and walked over to pay our respects to Owens's monument, a full-sized bronze casting of him sitting on the bench at a grand piano. He wears what appears to be a Greek fisherman's cap. The statue has a big smile on its face and the left arm is raised from the keyboard, gesturing toward Music Row.

Music Row is actually three parallel streets, 16th, 17th, and 18th Avenues South, also known as Music Square East and Music Square West – the square is a rectangle, six blocks long and three blocks wide. A few years ago, Nashville's then-mayor Beverly Briley proposed taking out 16th and 17th Avenues and creating a new Music Row Boulevard. That would have meant mass destruction of the houses that give the neighborhood some character. The proposal was vigorously opposed. As a compromise, 16th and 17th Avenues were converted into parallel one-way streets, which did nothing to give Music Row an identifying signature.

Our Willie and I walked down 17th Avenue past the large ASCAP (American Society of Composers, Authors, and Publishers) building; past the modest Sony/Tree building. We were the only people out; traffic was sparse.

'This looks like a ghost town.' Our Willie muttered. 'Where's the bustle? Where's the hustle? Where are the stars?' A red-and-white banner congratulating a singer for a number one hit was being lowered from the front of the Sony building. 'Here today, gone tomorrow,' said Our Willie. 'That's some inspiration.'

I must admit Music Row was a disappointment, at least from a tourist's perspective. There was nothing to see besides office buildings interspersed with houses – some two-story brick, other single-floor bungalows – converted into offices. There were no piazzas, no glamor, no sign of life.

We continued down the street to the Starstruck Entertainment building, owned and created by Reba McEntire, country music's reigning queen and one of the more powerful women in the industry. Christine Kreyling, in her essay 'Architecture of Music Row', tagged the building as the equivalent of big hair architecture. I thought of it as neo-country. The building sits atop a broad flight of stairs, forcing you to approach as if you are entering a Greek temple. On each side of the double glass-door entrance stand two tall deco-gothic Corinthian columns of gray-rose marble. The building's façade is made up of bands of off-white pre-cast cement with rounded corners separated by rows of blue-black windows. A small free-standing building is off to the left side. Country is represented by bronze sculptures of a mare and a foal by the reflecting pool in front of the building fronted by a wall of dark glass. Flowerbeds of yellow daffodils and purple violets and red tulips give a garden touch.

'I don't hear any music,' Our Willie complained. 'This is Music Row, right? The heart of the Nashville country music industry, right? And it's dead still. Doesn't that tell you something? I'm going back to Tootsie's and the honky-tonks on Lower Broadway.'

He turned heel and walked off. 'I thought this is where you aspired to be, in the commercial heart of country music,' I called after him. He didn't reply.

For a moment I though of Willie Nelson when he turned his back on the Nashville music industry and returned to Texas, but that comparison gives Our Willie too much credit.

A couple of days later, I returned to Starstruck for an appointment with Tony Brown, who is considered to be one of the boldest and most important producer/label executives on Music Row. *Entertainment Weekly* regularly placed him on its list of Power 101 people.

Tony Brown was a musician (piano player for Elvis Presley) before he joined RCA as a song plugger and then producer. He was, for 18 years, the president of MCA Records (a division of Universal company) in Nashville. He signed and/or produced Steve Earle, Lyle Lovett, Nanci Griffin, Wynonna Judd, Vince Gill, George Strait, Alan Jackson, Trisha Yearwood, and many other top acts. On January 2, 2002, he and Tim DuBois, former president of Arista Records, formed Universal South Records, a quasi-autonomous label within the larger company – this means that Tony and Tim make the creative decisions and the parent company pays the start-up costs.

Tony Brown, together with all record label executives, has a problem. The music industry has tanked. Record sales are down. Production costs are too high. Profits are being shrunk to vanishing point. It's the bottom of a cycle, yes, it's the end of a cycle, the industry mavens repeat, as if in prayer, for that means an upswing is inevitable – maybe. Their optimism is based on hope. They acknowledge that the current pop country trend has just about played out. They hope a new country voice will emerge to pull the industry out of its doldrums. They are waiting for a hero.

Tony is 53 years old, 5' 3" (1m 60cm), with a slim build. He has brown eyes, a dark goatee, and thick dark hair, which is longish on top with blonde highlights. He speaks in a soft North Carolina drawl; to listen to him is a pleasant experience, something like having warm honey poured into an aching ear. His official job title is senior partner of Universal South Records. His job description is to 'find new acts and make them stars,' he told me as we sat in his second-floor office. 'We also intend to make money.'

And how does he find new acts?

'The same way we always find it. Either you're pitched a CD by a friend of the artist, or by the artist, or by a musician who wants to turn you on to somebody, or by an attorney, or a publisher. Someone you trust says, "Check out this artist." If that artist doesn't have a CD, you call up friends in the business to see if they've heard of this person.'

Tony and all other record executives rarely, if ever, go out to find talent. They don't travel into the hills the way early musicologists did to find that authentic voice. That is not time or money efficiently spent. They let the talent come to them. That's the way it's been since the 1920s.

On a late June day in 1922, Henry C Gilliland and AC 'Eck' Robinson walked into the Victor Talking Machine Company in New York. The staff was accustomed to odd-looking characters, this being New York, but Gilliland and Robinson made them stare in dumbfounded astonishment. Gilliland, an Oklahoma native in his late 70s, wore his authentic Civil War Confederation uniform. What was this? A one-man invasion by a grizzled vet? The Civil War had been over for only 58 years, so it was a living memory. Beside him stood his friend Robinson dressed in the full regalia of a Texas cowboy complete with the iconic Big Hat, but an authentic cowboy hat as he was from Amarillo, Texas. Vaudeville, are we seeing vaudeville here? This is a recording company, not a theater. You two hicks are lost, so get lost.

Then Gilliland stated their business. You want to do what? Gilliland and Robinson held their fiddle and guitar. Not sure if they were being joked or if they were looking at the Real Stuff, the engineers agree to let the two play. If nothing else, it would give the technicians some real-time practise on the new-fangled technology they were pioneering. Gilliland and Robinson recorded 'Sally Goodin' and 'The Arkansas Traveler', two popular, at least in their part of the world, foot-stompin' instrumentals. The records were released but did not become big sellers.

Around the same time, Fiddlin' John Carson was making a name for himself in his native Georgia. He had been playing at fiddle contests and political rallies for at least six years. He had a reputation as one of the best fiddlers in the Appalachian style. On September 9, 1922, he appeared on WSB in Atlanta, probably the first radio station to offer live country music. Ten months later Ralph Peer, an opera lover and the recording industry's first A&R man, came to Atlanta. Peer worked for General Phonograph Company (Okey Records) and Victor. An Atlanta record salesman convinced Peer to record Fiddlin' Jack. The salesman ordered 500 copies, then another 500 when the first batch sold out. Peer realized the potential and put the record in Victor's national catalogue. He then invited Carson to New York to record 12 more sides.

The Gilliland/Robinson and Carson recordings are considered to be the first commercial records of country music.

In 1924, Marion Try Slaughter, a former Texan with aspirations of operatic stardom, scored the first million-units country seller with the event song, 'Wreck of The Old '97', recalling a famous train crash. Slaughter recorded under the name Vernon Dalhart, a combination of two north Texas towns. The following year his 'The Prisoner's Song' also sold a million copies. Dalhart was the 'star' of the first five years of recorded country music. However, none of his subsequent recordings did well. He died on the job as a night watchman.

Samantha Bumgarner and Eva Davis recorded a banjo and fiddle duet for Columbia Records in 1924, followed by the solo act Roba Stanley and the cowgirl singer Billie Maxwell.

In late July 1927, Ralph Peer, who knew there was gold in the Southern Appalachian Mountains, left New York on a scouting mission to the railroad city of Bristol, Tennessee. He didn't have enough acts to fill his recording sessions in New York and was searching for undiscovered talent. A true music industry man, he had worked out a deal with the record company: he would work without pay in exchange for publishing rights of all the material he recorded. These copyrights became the foundation for his music publishing company, the Peer-Southern Organization. The real money in recording lies in the publishing. Peer spent much of the 1920s and '30s on field trips throughout the South recording musicians.

In Bristol, Peer (aged 35) rented the second and third floor of a former furniture store, draped blankets over the walls and called it a studio. He set up the recording equipment by running an electrical line to a steel needle, which cut grooves on thick wax disks. To re-record on a disk, the wax was smoothed out with sandpaper.

To attract talent, he placed an ad in the local newspaper offering $50 (£32) a side and 2.5 cents (1.5p) royalties per song to anyone he recorded. Fifty dollars could be a year's income for the farmers scratching out a living up in the hollers. They played fiddle for the neighbors to dance on Saturday night, why not play for this Yankee and take his money? Peer was deluged with long-distance calls of inquiry and people arriving by buggy, on foot, by bus, horseback and train.

A (Alvin) P (Pleasant) Carter heard about the offer and wasted no time. He borrowed his brother-in-law's car, bundled up his wife, Sara, their two kids, seven-month-old Joe and eight-year-old Gladys, and her 18-year-old cousin Maybelle, and headed down the mountain. Maybelle was eight months pregnant but that made no difference. She could sing real good and played the guitar. Sara played the autoharp and sang lead with her mountain-pure alto. AP played the fiddle and sang. They drove all day, forded a river, and fixed eight flat tyres on the trip from their hamlet, Maces Springs, Virginia. They arrived at dusk, tired and sweaty, but dressed in their Sunday best clothes, set the kids down, and made history. They recorded four songs, including the old Scottish folk tune 'The Storms Are on the Ocean', which they had sung all their lives.

On the afternoon of that same day, a Mississippi crooner named Jimmie Rodgers spent two and a half hours recording 'The Soldier's Sweetheart', an old-time ballad, and the 1860s vaudeville number 'Sleep, Baby Sleep'. In one day, Peer recorded the Carter Family and Jimmie Rodgers, the foundation blocks of early commercial country music. The Carter Family's music stemmed mainly from the white Appalachian country, a descendant of the English/Celtic ballad tradition. Rodgers blended black blues with vaudeville and his original inflections and high-pitched yodeling, pushing country music toward the future. These two branches remain elemental in today's country music.

During those historical Bristol Sessions, Peer also recorded the Tennessee Mountaineers and the Ernest Stoneman Family. Stoneman, a carpenter, made $100 (£64) for the day's work. In ten days, Peer heard 19 groups and recorded 76 songs, from gospel to string bands to old vaudeville and traditional Anglo-Celtic ballads. The wax disks were shipped back to New York on dry ice to keep them from melting during the journey. There, a copper plate was made from the wax original and vinyl 78rpm records were pressed by the thousands. The first release from the Bristol Sessions was 'Home Sweet Home' by the Stoneman Family with George from Iron Ridge playing the banjo. The Carter Family went on to fame and Jimmie Rodgers became the first true country star. He is now revered as the 'father of country music'.

Victor's 'New Southern Series' from the Bristol Session was an immediate hit, selling hundreds of thousands of records to a public that was feeling the initial tightening of purse strings as the first storm clouds of the Depression approached the nation.

As country music muddles through its own current mini-Depression, Tony Brown, together with the other label executives on Music Row, is trying to crystal ball what will turn the country music industry in an upswing. Will ol' timey music be the new way? Is the latest trend going to be back to the Appalachian sound of the Carter Family? Is the wave of the future the surprise number one hit soundtrack *O Brother, Where Art Thou?* Ralph Stanley's plaintive singing of the old ballad 'Man of Constant Sorrow' reignited his career and won him a Grammy. There was a time when Stanley couldn't even get arrested on the streets of Nashville, let alone get a meeting with a record executive. People made fun of him behind his back. Now he's the toast of the town.

If an artist (or a style of music) hits big, there is instantly a slew of imitators trying to cash in. Label heads try to cookie cut the young and hungry into the hottest trend as fast as possible, and plenty of raw talent is willing to be shaped and baked for their three minutes of fame. But Brown, and most other record executives, think that O Brother is an 'indication' rather than a 'turn signal'. Bluegrass, which is the strong flavor of the soundtrack's mountain music, is a cultivated taste, like grits with ketchup. If you grew up on it, you got the taste, but it's a particular taste. Bluegrass, a folk mountain music with banjos, fiddles, and nasal vocals is a niche music, not a support column for a sustainable national market trend.

'If a big artist is contemporary and hits big, a lot of artists will follow that direction.' Tony sat behind his U-shaped desk checking his e-mail on the computer. The desk is not cluttered, just covered with stacks of unheard CDs waiting for his attention. His office is very modest for the co-head of a record label, with none of the status accouterments of a famous producer. He turned away from the computer. 'If a big artist hits traditional, usually a male artist, it doesn't mean that country music is going traditional.' The success of O Brother is regarded as a flag that the consumer is tired of the slick predictable pop country sound. That's an indication, not a trend setter. Consumers voted with their dollars not necessarily for something, but against something. However, the artistic acclaim and commercial success of O Brother is having an impact on the thinking on Music Row.

'It means everybody goes, "Oh, that's what they like,"' Tony said. 'So it's follow the leader. It's a pack mentality in our industry. But I don't see all of us meeting in our offices going, "We've gotta get traditional." We talk about maybe this is a chance to sign some traditional acts. That doesn't mean we have to go back there. It does mean that we've gotta pay attention to the music's roots. If we ever lose all our traditional acts, we lose our format. If everybody became as contemporary as Faith Hill or Shania Twain, then we would no longer be country format.'

The Dixie Chicks is more of a marker for the future than O Brother, according to Tony. 'The cool thing about The Dixie Chicks is that those records are very country. They may be edgy, but they are very country. The Dixie Chicks sold more records than Faith but less than Shania. Image-wise, they fit into the pop culture. Music-wise, they carried the torch for traditional music. Faith and Shania went, on purpose, for the crossover sound and it paid off for them. Not every artist can do that. Lee Ann Womack had a crossover song called 'I Hope You Dance', but I'm not sure she's a crossover artist like Faith or Shania. Why not? All football players can't be quarterbacks or tight ends. Country music will always have a bit of both traditional and contemporary. If we start losing the Lee Ann Womacks of the world, The Dixie Chicks, Alan Jacksons, George Straits, and Garth Brooks, then that's when we're in trouble. But we haven't yet.'

So, what are you looking for next in country music, Tony? What type of artist are you looking for to make a star?

'It's intangible. I look for the voice. I love great singers. I've worked with Wynonna Judd, Trisha Yearwood, Vince Gill, Reba McEntire, George Strait. Those are spectacular singers. I've worked with Steve Earle, Lyle Lovett, and Marty Stuart. They're not singers but when they sing their songs, the end result is the same as when Wynonna belts out that big R&B voice she has. I look for an artist who can move me. Everyone wonders why Garth Brooks is so big. Like him or not, the guy communicates when he sings. I look for an artist that connects.'

Tony and Tim's company, Universal South, has signed five artists. Tony brought four of them with him from MCA: Allison Moorer, Dean Miller, Holly LaMar, and the Russian group Bering Strait. The fifth artist, Joe Nickols, is the new act on the label. He could have been a problem.

The other artists had a long relationship with Tony and Tim. The two have stood by their artists, supported them, and kept the faith. Allison Moorer is widely respected as a talented authentic country singer – only her albums have not sold well. She has not broken out. Why doesn't Tony drop her, people ask. Because I believe in her, Tony answers. Tim DuBois has stood behind Bering Strait for four years and they've yet to release an album, not for lack of trying but mostly because of bad luck. They've been dropped from five labels because of internal company strife, unfortunate timing, misaligned stars, unpredictable economics, whatever. All the choices are on the standard record industry checklist of why deals don't work.

Tony and Tim's original release schedule was first Dean Miller followed by Allison Moorer, Holly LaMar, and Bering Strait. Joe Nickols was slotted into fifth place, which might have happened a year or more in the future. Now, Joe Nickols will be the first release, which pushes back the time schedule for the others. They have waited years, paid their dues, did the rounds, sung the dives, and it looked like Universal South was the White Knight to finally lead them out of the dark woods and into the light of public recognition. They trusted Tony and Tim. They were friends, real friends, not air-kissing friends. And now they were told this 'WHO?' is getting first shot.

It's not that Joe Nickols hasn't paid his dues. He's not some *nouveau chanteur* with a tight butt and ruggedly handsome good looks, although he's not bad looking. He was singing in a barbecue place, Rippy's, on Lower Broadway, across the street from Tootsie's, when Tony heard about him. He wasn't even in Tootsie's front window. Rippy's is a tourist place with open sides, so all the traffic noise invades. In the corners are television sets tuned to sport channels. People talk loudly, clank silverware against plates and occasionally cheer their teams. It is not a singer-friendly environment.

He had been signed by Giant Records, a Warner Brothers label, but was about to be dropped before he even released a single. A top guitarist Tony had known for years brought him Joe's CD. 'Listen to this guy, Tony. He's got something. It's in his voice. You can see the life he's singing about.'

Tony listened and then did the nearly unheard of – he went to Rippy's to hear Joe live. This isn't quite like Ralph Peer traveling to Bristol, but in Nashville's terms it was damn close. He was sold on the voice before he saw the guy but he wanted to see the stage presence. Some artists have a natural stage presence. They get a buzz being on stage and that energy goes back to the audience. Others get up there and stumble around a few times, looking at their feet, never making contact with the audience. But they keep at it, start gaining confidence, start enjoying the risk of making a fool out of themselves in public. It's not given that every artist is 'road ready,' to use Tony's term. In Joe Nickols, he saw a truly traditional artist who looked like pop culture. He saw a road-ready opportunity.

'Wait,' I said. 'Back up. Why does a record company, say Warner Brothers, sign an artist, pay some kind of signing fee, pay for a demo record, pay for the studio time, pay for the engineers and musicians, invest a chunk of money, maybe even foot the bill for an entire album, and walk away without a release? That's like putting cash in a bag to take to the bank but deciding to burn it instead.'

Tony looked at me as if to say, what, you're a virgin?

'It happens a lot,' he said with a shrug, 'especially in pop music. You make a record and somewhere along the way either the A&R who signed the artist has left the company or has been fired. Unless there are other people in the company who are into the artist, that artist becomes so-and-so's act and he's gone. There's no one in the company to fight for the artist, to look after them, and protect their interests. They're orphaned. Or the artist records and by the time the record is finished everybody is not as excited about the person or the product as they had been. So the decision is made to fold the tent rather than continue the process.

'Say you spent $150,000 [£97,000] to $200,000 [£130,000] cutting a record. That's normal. Once you go to the next level, which is doing the album cover and putting in the marketing plan and doing the video, you are stepping from $200,000 [£130,000] to $500,000 [£325,000]. So if the excitement isn't there and you feel that you need to bail, you just fold the tent and move on. There've been a lot of great records lost that way, and some have been picked up by other labels. A label will fold a tent and somebody will say, I'll buy the record from the label. Sometimes the label won't sell it. Then the artist has to start all over again.

'You can make a record, finish it, turn it in, think it's done and maybe a promotion person will say, 'We don't have a first single. So they send you back in to cut a fresh single. So what normally happens, you go, "Well, if I'm going to cut one more song, I'll cut three more songs." Those three songs the marketing people, producer, whoever like better than anything on the album. Then starts the process of, "Well, go cut four more songs." Two years later, you're still recording. Maybe after that you've put together this great record. Then once in a while, after two years, everybody is either bored or decides to move on.

'Meanwhile the artist is trying to make a living. The artist usually doesn't make a dime on a recording. In Nashville, it's common for a new artist to get $50,000 [£32,500] advance. They get $25,000 [£16,000] when they sign the deal. They get $25,000 [£16,000] when they turn the record in. If the record is never finished, they don't get that backend payment. All along the way the musicians are getting paid for sessions every time they go in. The engineers are being paid from $100 [£65] to $200 [£130] an hour to $1,200 [£780] a day. In the end, an engineer may have made $60,000 [£39,000] to $70,000 [£45,000]. Everybody is getting paid but the artist. Of the artist's $25,000 [£16,000], his attorney probably got $5,000 [£3,000] to $10,000 [£6,500]. His manager got a 10–15 per cent commission. After taxes, the artist puts maybe $10,000 [£6,500] in his pocket and, if the record sells, he has to pay back the advance before receiving royalties.'

Back to Joe Nickols. Why isn't there a palace revolt by the four other artists because you decided to let Joe jump the queue? 'It was a business decision,' Tony responded. Those in the business understand the business, even if they are artists. If they don't, then they are artists without a business.

Tony cut a demo of Joe's new song, 'Impossible', which was not expensive, and sent it out for radio preview. The song started performing like a hit, even without promotion. 'We didn't spend a nickel to get air play and it climbed to number 36 in the charts,' Tony said. He couldn't keep the glee out of his voice. That was like found money.

'We reversed our thinking even though we promised the other acts that they would be out before. Well, we really didn't promise them. But, we had to deal with them. The psychology of being in the record business is almost as important as, or close to, the business side. You can be a great businessman but if you don't have good relations with your artists, they won't perform. They won't make records for you. They won't tour. We told our artists that we changed our mind because it was better for the label and what's good for the label is good for the artist – especially at a new label. As an artist, you should want the label to come out hitting a home run. It serves you well if we do that. Nobody said anything. They accepted it as part of the business.

'When I was at MCA, a few times the artist actually manipulated us. They used their power as an established artist to say I will or will not do this and you will do this for me or I'll be pissed off and won't perform. And we caved in. Most of the time the decision backfired on the artist. Then they accused us of it being our fault.

'Jimmy Bowen, who was the head of RCA when I started and my mentor, always said, "The artist is always right." If you can convince them to change their mind, that's one thing. But at the end of the day, if you don't make them feel that they are right, then you've got a problem. So I take the tack that the artist is always right. And if I think that they are wrong, I do my best to convince them to change their minds regarding touring or recording a song or doing interviews.

'I've heard artists do interviews that destroy all the success because they said something on air and record sales drop. Some artists are great on stage and are not good when they open their mouth. That will be their Achilles heel and can stop them from going all the way. But I love artists who speak their mind. They shouldn't be programmed, but saying careless things can cause unnecessary problems. I love an artist who is quotable, like Steve Earle. Oh, my God, what is he going to say next? But it is always something profound. Recently, when he was asked about what Nashville was like when his *Guitar Town* came out, he said, "That was during the great credibility scare of the '80s."

'When a person decides to become an artist, I don't know if they understand that they are giving up their life for a few years. They are beginning an artist's life, as a brand new artist or as a veteran who decides they want to be a star – when they get a record deal, both these artists are basically not going to have a private life. Interviews, day after day of promoting, of going back and working on the album, cutting new songs. They don't have private time. And when they do start to make it, then the hardest part is just beginning.'

Tony saw that up close when he played on the road behind bands. He played on Rosanna Cash's first album, produced by Rodney Crowell, and was also part of the touring troupe. After a performance he could sleep late, not having to be at the next sound check until 5pm. But Cash had to be at a radio station at 6.30am. She gave interviews all morning, did a greet-and-meet lunch with people that could help her career, and did more interviews in the afternoon. She'd get back to the hotel just when Tony and other musicians were returning from a movie, or waking up. They'd all go to the sound check, eat dinner, and do the show. After the show the musicians could return to the hotel or party while Cash stayed to meet with radio people and the press for an hour. Then she'd crawl back to the hotel and do it all over the next day.

'I've seen what artists have to do,' Tony said. 'Now, when I sign an artist, I try to look deep into the artist's eyes to see that even if the person has the gift, the talent, the charisma, do they have that little extra thing that makes them able to pay the price of what I will demand of them as a recording artist.'

Tony has personal experiences on how the demands on a professional musician can wreak havoc with a personal life. He is now on his third, and he swears his last, marriage.

His first marriage dissolved because he was on the road with the gospel groups up to 300 days a year. He was never home, which placed a strain on the family life. One day he came back from a road trip and found that his wife had taken their two children and moved to Colorado. She left a note.

When he married for the second time, he swore not to make the same mistake. He quit the road, mostly because he felt so guilty over the first marriage. He stayed in Nashville but spent all his time in the studio producing records. He loved it so much that he never went home. It was being on the road but without having to ride the bus. The marriage lasted 13 years, until his wife finally called it quits.

He stayed single for seven years. He took stock of his mistakes and made efforts to manage his time better, to take time away from the business and make room for friends – another relationship. He met and wooed Anastasia, a divorced mother with a five-year-old son. She had her own management company, so they had a common understanding about the business. She presently supervises the selection and rights for music in films.

'I never work on weekends now,' Tony said. 'I cherish my weekends with my family. I reserve all holidays for home and take my weekends at home. Family is very important. My partner at Universal South, Tim DuBois, feels the same way, so there is nobody putting a gun to my head to stay in the office.'

3 The Song

When I left Tony, I wanted to dash to Tootsie's and shout to my friends, 'Run!'

But Amy and Our Willie thought of themselves as songwriters, not performers, so perhaps Tony's description of a singer's life didn't apply to them. I wasn't sure of Hat, who had introduced himself as Hank, 'Like Hank Williams or Hank Snow.'

'Been in town long, Hank?' I asked on our first meeting at Tootsie's.

'Not long.'

'Plan to stay long?'

'Depends.'

'Depends on what?'

'How it goes.'

That's been a typical conversation with Hank.

When I arrived at Tootsie's, the three of them were at our usual table. Amy and Our Willie were scribbling on napkins, which was odd because Tootsie's doesn't hand out napkins. Hank sat with his back to the corner in a protective posture so he could scan the room.

'Lookin' for bounty hunters or chicks?' Hank scowled and tilted his hat further down over his eyes, his signal to zip your lip, he wasn't talking.

'Did you read about the squirrel fight in today's paper,' I asked Our Willie. A man, 23, and his girlfriend, 18, had gotten into a fight. He tried to drive away from their home, taking their pet squirrel with him and she jumped into the moving car and punched him in the nose, causing blood to flow onto his shirt and his car's upholstery, which really pissed him off so he struck back and there they were punching, slapping, clawing at each other, shouting and cursing, as the car swerved from side to side down the road as the tears from the stinging nose made it difficult for him to see and he was warding off her blows at the same time trying to backhand her, grab her hair, put a fist in her eye and that made the car swerve even more violently from side to side, which is what attracted the cops' attention. That and the squirrel going apeshit seeing its parents, so to speak, duking it out, this squirrel in frenzy, bounding from the front seat to the back seat, back seat to the front seat, a flying streak of fur, probably rabid from the cops' quick look as they went past in the opposite direction seeing this couple trying to fight off a wild crazed squirrel trapped inside their car. The cops pulled a sharp U-turn and gave chase, their patriotic red, white, and blue top lights flashing and siren screaming, and by the time they got up behind the erratic car the woman was trying to bail out and the man was either holding her back or pushing her out, it was hard to tell, and she kicked out the glove box on the dashboard, perhaps to get a foothold to prevent from being tossed from the car or to cause spiteful damage. And the squirrel was frantically scrabbling at the rear window trying to escape, baring its two sharp front teeth at the cops who now knew for sure they were dealing with wildlife when the car suddenly stopped, the woman having managed to jerk the gear lever into Park position, which nearly stripped the transmission of the car moving at 30mph (50kph) and slammed the driver against the steering wheel, knocking the breath out of him so he couldn't fight anymore.

She was charged with domestic assault and released on a $1,500 (£1,000) bail.

I thought it would make a terrific country song. The story had all the classic elements: love, hate, home, man, woman, family (the pet squirrel representing a child), a vehicle (poetic license allows the car to be changed to a pickup), jail. Whiskey probably was involved, or could be implied with artful writing. All that was missing from a classic country song was a train, so they could stall out on a railroad track.

'Remember Steve Goodman's perfect country song about this guy being drunk in the rain the night they let his mama out of prison and he took the pickup to get her but a big damn train ran over mama? Remember that song?' I asked Our Willie and Amy. 'Think of that song when you rework this into a number one hit.' I handed them the clipping from *The Tennessean*.

'We got something already,' Amy said without looking up.

I sneaked a peek at Our Willie's napkin.

I wake up every morning
A rented man in my own home.
She's in the kitchen being a short-order cook
With nothing on the ticket.
I wake up every morning
Tied to the marriage bed
A rented man in the Loveless Motel.

'Hank's going to cut the demo.'

'So, you're a singer.' I flashed Hank an encouraging smile.

'Workin' on it.'

'Well, praise the Lord.'

'That, too.'

If country music were not already in dire peril it soon would be if this trio ever got a shot. I needed assurance that good taste and talent might prevail.

'Excuse me,' I told my friends and went to the payphone. I called Gretchen Peters, whom I had known years ago when she was a teenage folk hippie going to high school and writing songs and making a local reputation for herself.

Gretchen is now one of Nashville's premier songwriters. George Strait, George Jones, Randy Travis, Bonnie Raitt, Trisha Yearwood, Patty Loveless, the Neville Brothers, Faith Hill, and Martina McBride have cut her songs. Her song 'Independence Day', recorded by Martina McBride, won the 1994 Country Music Association (CMA) Video of the Year. The song won the CMA Song of the Year award the following year and received a Grammy nomination. In 1996, Patty Loveless took Gretchen's song 'You Don't Even Know Who I Am' to number one and it won a Grammy nomination. In 1999, Faith Hill's version of her 'Secret of Life' went to number one on the Gavin charts.

She co-wrote three songs with Bryan Adams for the score for Dream World's animated film, *Spirit*, released in Spring 2002. One of the songs, the soundtrack's first single, 'Here I Am', produced by Jimmy Jam and Terry Lewis and sung by Adams, became a worldwide hit. Gretchen does not pitch her songs. Singers and producers call her and politely inquire if a 'Gretchen Peters' song might be available. If she really wants a song recorded, she cuts her own CDs, the two most recent being *Gretchen Peters* (2000) and *The Secret of Life*, first released on Imprint in 1996 and reissued on her own label, Purple Crayon Productions, in 2001. Both albums were produced with Green Daniel, her husband. She does perform live in the United States but is best known as a songwriter, whereas in England she is well known as a performer.

'She's down at Sony/Tree,' her teenage daughter told me. 'Maybe you can catch her there.'

I called. She was in a meeting of Nashville's Academy Awards committee, of which she was a member, as was Tony Brown. I left a message that I was on my way and headed for Music Row.

We met in the lobby of Sony/Tree, a homey space with Persian rugs and a matronly mother figure behind the reception desk to enhance the ambiance of home and family. A very large vase held 10lb (4.5kg) of freshly cut flowers. 'This place smells like a funeral home,' Gretchen said, as we walked into the conference room. The conference room had solemn dark wood paneling in Pretentious Masculine Library style, sans books. The whole room said, 'Hush. Behave yourself. You are in an Important Place and make no mistake about it.'

Gretchen took a chair at the head of the conference table. Green excused himself to find us some coffee. I asked if the Academy Awards meeting related to her Hollywood work. 'No, I'm just a film fanatic, seeing at least one movie a week,' she answered. Films are an artistic energy boost to her because independent films, even some Hollywood movies, are more provocative, intelligent, and artistic than the records being produced by Nashville.

'Maybe that's not true,' she said upon reflection. 'Maybe that's just my perspective. But even in Nashville, a mainstream conservative place, you can find an art film.' Her words were an indictment against the low aspirations of the country music industry. Even Hollywood delivers better stuff than Nashville, her tone said. What does that say? Bow your head in shame. 'Nashville is suppose to be a songwriters' town, so how are the wordsmiths treated?' I asked.

'You can't be creative in an atmosphere of fear,' she answered. 'There is an atmosphere of fear in Nashville because the music industry as a whole is down. People are afraid of losing their jobs. That's across the board, from the executives to the songwriters upstairs.' She gestured with a slight lift of her head to the floors above us where the writers on contract sit in cubicles churning out songs from nine to five. Gretchen also has a publishing deal with Sony/Tree but she does all her writing from her home studio 30 miles (50km) outside of town. She avoids Nashville as much as possible.

'When I first arrived in Nashville, in the late 1980s, that time, and the early '90s, was a golden opportunity for songwriters here who really had something to say,' she said. 'We were allowed to say things on serious subjects. Now the commercial radio powers and the major labels have methods to prevent anything with the possibility of being provocative from getting on the air. They've become craftier at preventing challenging issues or points of views from getting out.'

Radio's agenda, its entire purpose in life, is to sell ad time for a profit. This has nothing to do with cultural or social responsibility, even though the airwaves are public property leased by communication corporations. Thoughtful, provocative music, or any music that might offend or challenge, has a hard time getting airplay on mainstream commercial radio, which is the majority of the stations. That doesn't prevent songwriters from writing such songs, but it does prevent the songs from finding a public forum. Songs that challenge the social system, economic injustices, the self-serving policies of those in power are being written all the time but the songwriters, including Gretchen, have faint hope that they'll be recorded or, if they are, played on the radio.

'Culturally, it's a travesty.' Gretchen has a soft melodic voice but when it stiffens with indignation or anger, you can hear the starchiness of her values. 'It's emblematic of our whole culture, where you're talking about books, films, fast food; anything we sell to the public debases the culture.

It's not that new a thing. I just think it's picked up speed. It's flat out abuse.' Her voice became starchier, stiffer, like a board to whack someone with. 'I think that the audience in the US is used to being entertained to death. We've become so passive because entertainment is constantly forced down our throats. If we value culture, we will break out of this commercialization. The question is how do you get people to value culture? I have my days when I feel optimistic about fighting it and then I have my days when I really wonder about how that's ever going to happen.'

Can the artist subvert the commercialization of art? If the artists are increasingly dependent on commercial avenues (radio is a prime example), is their work being squeezed off to the margins, *de facto* out of the public's reach?

'There are tons of artists in this country doing the subversion,' Gretchen said, 'but what's happening is that as the avenues are fewer and fewer, like the number of independent stations, the number of voices heard gets smaller and smaller. With few voices being heard it becomes harder and harder to subvert the commercial power.' Now her voice has the tensile strength of an ironwood board with the heft of a club.

Then her voice softens. 'The most sad thing that has happened in the last few years, from a songwriting point of view, is that country music used to be adult music,' she said quietly. 'Now the country you hear on the radio is teen pop music. It used to be about real adult subjects. The Merle Haggards were, and are, doing songs for people in their 40s and 50s. You hardly hear a Merle Haggard song on the radio now. To write true country, you have to have some miles on you to get the real feel for the heart and sorrow and acceptance and heartbreak and joy of the music – or you have to be an advanced soul. For Nashville to try to cater to the teen market completely negates that entire emotional history of country music. Kris Kristofferson was very adult, like Faulkner. Those songs had a literary thing about them. That has really suffered. Not to say that those songs aren't being written, but they certainly aren't given voice in the market place.

'Country is more suburban than rural now. It's like Disneyland. Disneyland is not a place. It's a representation of a place that we think we remember from our childhood. It's not real and neither is a lot of country music. Some of these people are singing about growing up and sitting on the front porch with grandpa and the train going past, but it's not real. They didn't grow up that way. They grew up listening to Aerosmith.

'I don't suggest that we have to go back to writing songs about what Merle wrote. We can't do that. But country music is really folk music. It's folk music in that it's about our lives. It's not about rebellion and youth and about all the things rock 'n' roll was about. It's about every man and woman and their lives. It's truthful. I think that's what we've gotten away from and instead we've got what's marketable.'

She acknowledges that many Nashville songwriters struggle with writing about the nostalgic past of the idyllic rural lifestyle, of a simple life without crack houses, drive-by shootings, and white-collar criminals who loot corporations. The pastoral America sung about in some country music no longer exists, has not existed for over 70–80 years, but the country music industry still sells the image and the image sells records. There is just one little glitch for Gretchen and many other songwriters and singers in Nashville – such music is not authentic.

'I think it's disingenuous in songs where Daddy is on the farm,' she said. 'They don't sound sincere. It doesn't feel authentic. That's what I want in music. America is a suburban country now. You write about farm nostalgia and people who grew up in the suburbs can't relate. That's the struggle really. That's the nut of it in terms of the whole traditional versus non-traditional argument. How many coal miners' daughters are there? The argument, I guess, is that some people think country should never change. It should be like a museum piece. I completely disagree with that. The music will die if that ever happens. The old music will always be there. There will be, and are, great very traditional-sounding artists coming along, and to come along in the future. But you can't stifle something to the point where it's not about your life anymore.'

Gretchen doesn't deliberately set out to write provocative songs, or country songs. She writes about real life issues, which can be provocative. Country artists have recorded most of her songs, so she is known as a country songwriter. 'I hate those categories,' she said. 'I think that, in the record stores, all records should be alphabetical and do away with the categories. Where do you put Joni Mitchell? In folk? In jazz? In country, sometimes?'

But her songs have hit some raw nerves. 'Independence Day', recorded by Martina McBride, caused a stir and has become an anthem for women to fight back against domestic abuse. The song is written from the point of view of an eight-year-old girl growing up in a small town who witnesses her drunken father beating up her mother. She knew her father was a dangerous man. The people in the town knew the situation but turned a blind eye. The mother was proud and stood her ground but knew she was on the losing end. Finally she rebelled and burned down the family house. She lit up the sky that Fourth of July. It was Independence Day, a day of reckoning. Let the weak be strong, right the wrong, let the guilty pay. The daughter was sent to the country home but she was not resentful of her mother for making her homeless. Rather, she sang her mother's praise and cherished the lesson of her mother's revolution.

'Independence Day' was written six months after Gretchen quit smoking. 'That had something to do with the tone,' she admits. She was gaining independence from a nicotine habit. Written in between the song's lines is her struggle against the tobacco industry that profits from the health abuse caused by their product.

Since then Garth Brooks did a song and video, 'Let the Thunder Roll', about domestic abuse. The Dixie Chicks released a song, 'Goodbye Earl', about women killing the abusive Earl.

'Breaking the boundaries has been a tradition of country music,' Gretchen said. 'The most memorable songwriters and performers have done it. Merle Haggard. Loretta Lynn when she did "The Pill". The list of examples is as long as the history of the music.'

Green returned with coffee. He is a big man with a thick thatch of dark hair and a full beard, both turning white. He grew up 100 miles (160km) north of the Tennessee state line in Kentucky and has always been a country music fan. While in high school, he'd come to Nashville with his buddies to watch records being cut in the studios. He learned his way around the soundboard and how to produce. When he graduated, he came to Nashville and straight into the country music and radio production business.

'I was in love with this industry, in love with how Nashville worked and the music that came out of Nashville at the time,' he said as he settled into a chair across the table. 'That was Tom T Hall, Kris Kristofferson, Roger Miller, Mickey Newberry, Harlan Howard, and so on. Those guys were artists, true poets. Nashville was like the country Greenwich Village.'

Green has always been Gretchen's business manager, producer, loyal critic, musical advisor, and biggest fan. They met in 1978 when Green was running a studio/publishing operation in Golden, Colorado, west of Denver. Part of his job was to produce radio jingles. Succeeding in the Colorado music business was like being a ski instructor in Arizona – to survive you needed to do many different things. He began a management agency and tried his hand at songwriting. 'I should have been doing other things,' he admitted, 'because songwriting is terrifically hard to do.'

One day his partner brought in a tape of a wonderful clear pure voice. 'Who's this?' Green asked.

'Oh, some little folk girl up in Boulder, Gretchen Peters,' replied his partner.

'Get her down here with her guitar,' said Green. 'Put up two microphones and keep loading the pancakes [reels] of raw tapes until she runs out of songs. Let her record every song she ever wrote.'

'I didn't know who she was but I knew she was really something special,' Green recalled. 'She had written a song, "Daddy, You Don't Understand", kind of half-folk, half-bluegrass but so perfectly crafted and the sound of her voice was such a perfect match to the lyric. I did a deal with her on a handshake.' Gretchen was 19 at the time.

One of Green's other clients got a Nashville deal. Green started putting together a record producer network in his visits to the city – and started passing around Gretchen's tapes. He gave a tape to Tony Brown, then at RCA. 'That's it! That's it!' Tony exclaimed. 'She's like a cross between Dolly Parton and Emmylou Harris.'

Despite Tony's enthusiasm, he couldn't get Gretchen a record deal. This was the rhinestone cowboy era in Nashville, when songs like Barbara Mandrell's 'You Can Eat Crackers In My Bed Any Time' were in demand by the record companies. Gretchen's songs didn't fit into that box. Still, the quality of her work, as much as her singing voice, caught the ear of record executives. Judi Gottier at Famous Records thought Gretchen was 'a killer, some of the most incredible stuff I've heard in Nashville for a long, long time,' according to Green. Gottier played Gretchen's tapes to Barry Beckett and Paul Worley, both starting to stretch their wings as producers.

Beckett had played on albums by Paul Simon and the Allman Brothers, and later played the piano part on Vince Gill's 'When I Call Your Name'. He produced country acts for Warner Brothers before going independent. Worley was in charge of the 'Creative' department at the Tree Publishing. In 1991 he signed Gretchen to her original deal with Sony, where he was an executive and producer of Patty Loveless records.

Green landed Gretchen an 18-month 'exploitation deal,' that is a song-by-song agreement to publish songs that have been recorded. It was not a full publication deal, which was to Gretchen's advantage.

'Any other publishing deal, the company pretty much want your shirt, your arms, your legs, everything you write over the course of the deal, not just what gets cut,' Green explained. 'They want the songs for their catalogue, whether they do anything with the songs or not. It's just fodder for the companies and it keeps the material out of the hands of the competition. Our exploitation deal was a good thing. Exploitation in this sense pushes the song, rather than ripping off the artists.'

Gretchen was becoming an entity in Nashville, even though she didn't know it. She still lived in Boulder. She made visits to Nashville, sleeping on friends' floors while making personal connections within the music industry. The first two years of Green and Gretchen's relationship was strictly business. But Cupid had his finger to the wind and felt growing heat coming from them. In 1981, Green and Gretchen married.

'Between 1981 and 1987, we stayed in Boulder,' Green said. 'I was working radio. Gretchen had a day job at Rocky Mountain Records and doing band gigs at night. I'd be getting up in the morning to do the radio gig and she'd just be coming home from a show. We had our daughter during this time. I don't how in the world we ever did it. It was because we loved it so much. We always believed we were going to make it in the music industry. There was no question. We didn't know how but we were sure that we would. I was sure of her ability.'

They moved to Nashville in November of 1987 with their three-year-old daughter without jobs in hand. Two months later, Gretchen signed her first songwriting contract with Goldline/Silverline for $14,000 (£9,000) a year. Nearly two years later, her song 'Traveler's Prayer' was cut by George Jones on his *Friends in High Places* album. However, it was not her first Nashville song released – Highway 101 recorded 'I'll Paint The Town' after the George Jones session and put it out first. George Strait recorded her 'The Chill Of An Early Fall' in 1990 (released 1991) and several months later Randy Travis recorded 'High Lonesome'.

'Two or three years is a normal length of time for a beginner to get recorded in Nashville,' Green said. 'People don't consider you a real songwriter until you've been here for awhile. When other people start talking about you, then you've arrived. Now she is absolutely one of the elite songwriters in Nashville. She's even been called the best songwriter in Nashville. A lot of people look at her that way. She has the track record. Her songs span bluegrass, pure real country, pop, ballads. She has consistently been there. We went through a period for a long time that every time we did a demo session, one of those songs would get on a record.'

The Nashville Chamber Orchestra commissioned Gretchen to write two orchestral pieces with Conni Ellisor, the Julliard-trained violinist and composer for the orchestra. The second work-in-progress is called an operetta but the final form is not set, Gretchen confided.

'We're in the stage of just figuring out the subject matter we want to tackle,' Gretchen said. 'There are no boundaries. The idea is to put Conni and me together, coming from such different backgrounds, and see what happens. I wouldn't ever call myself a classical composer by any stretch of the imagination, but I think it will be interesting what hybrid we compose.'

Over the years, Green has not taken Gretchen's music in any direction that it wouldn't have gone naturally. But he has moved her business of songwriting along in a direction. Ten years ago you'd never hear the term 'business of songwriting' in Nashville. There was no business for songwriters. They were on their own without publicists or agents or managers. Green was possibly the first person to hire a publicist for a songwriter when he brought in Cathy Gurley to represent Gretchen. It was unheard of. A songwriter was just a songwriter, not an artist and certainly not in need of publicity.

'People looked at me like I was crazy,' Green said. His shaggy, casual self filled the high-backed leather chair. 'I firmly believe that when somebody sees your name over and over as a songwriter, not as a co-writer, your stock goes up as an artist. The greatest writers have been solo writers, like Leonard Cohen, Tom T Hall, Jimmy Webb, Joni Mitchell, Bruce Springsteen, Dylan.

'All you have to do is get that first olive out of the bottle and then they all fall. The first one is the hardest one. I tried to see to it that if Gretchen wrote a song and it got cut, it was in the newspaper. I wanted other people to know about it. It didn't take very long until people were referring to a 'Gretchen Peters' song. Then the buzz got going. So-and-so cut a Gretchen Peters song. George Jones cut a Gretchen Peters song. When we got that going it wasn't too long before people began to recognize a Gretchen Peters song.'

Gretchen wrote great songs and Green did a good job with the glad-handing and the business so she didn't have to deal with it.

'I think that the worst thing in the world is for an artist to have to represent her or himself,' said Green, the business manager. 'It's not what they do. They don't think that way. They end up getting taken advantage of or just don't look good.'

People in the Nashville music industry are basically honest, Green pointed out, but not to the point where they volunteer to give the artist an extra $20,000 (£13,000) a year. You have to know what to ask for. A lot of brand new songwriters don't get legal representation. First, there's only a handful of real good entertainment attorneys in Nashville. If a songwriter is not hot, then it's hard to get top legal representation. The attorney's bill for negotiating a song deal might run from $10,000 (£6,500) to $20,000 (£13,000), with no guarantee that the song will ever earn that in royalties. Even an artist can see that is not good business.

Yet, a songwriter who represents his or herself is a fool indeed. How many songwriters know how negotiate the controlled composition clause, for example? The controlled composition is, in a nutshell, a contractual clause that states the record company pays only 75 per cent of mechanicals to artists/writers instead of 100 per cent. This is a standard clause with all the record labels.

'It's nothing more than extortion and collusion against the songwriter,' Green charged. 'Mechanical royalties are those collected by the publisher on behalf of the publishing company and the writer from the actual sales of records. If you are an artist and wrote the song, the controlled composition clause says that the label will withhold 25 per cent of the mechanical royalty. Why? Because they can and because new artists are currently powerless to change the terms.

'The controlled composition clause is really famous, or infamous, in Nashville. It started a few years ago when the record labels decided, "Well, there's always songwriters and these guys are making money from their songs, and since we, the labels, are expending all this money to launch an album, we need a little break when we sign an artist who writes. So, what we're going to do is take the songwriter/artist and every song he/she writes for his own record, instead of paying the full 100 per cent statutory rate of 8 cents (5p), which is set by the US Congress, we will pay the songwriter/artist only 75 per cent."

'What for? Because the labels aren't making enough money. They need money. And, they reason, if you wrote ten of the songs on the record, the reduced mechanical ain't nothing to you. Look how much money you're making! It could be roughly half of the normal artist's income per unit sold, and it's not subject to recoupment by the label. They could do it, so they did it.

'And the labels still withhold money from the artist for shrinkage and breakage of records that don't break anymore. CDs don't break. But no money is given back. Fact of the matter is that it's cheaper to make and market CDs than it ever was to make cassettes or LPs. But still they withhold the money at retail. They don't say, "Well, we're making a better profit margin on the CDs so we'll give you back a bit." Forget about it. It doesn't happen. The artist is the primary source of the material. They should be getting the primary slice of the pie.'

Gretchen had heard Green's rant many times. She calmly finished her coffee and sat back. 'Things are getting better,' she said when Green paused for a breath. 'I hear songs on the charts about high schools or youth that are, for lack of a better word, more suburban. The songs are about things that anybody who grew up in suburbia can relate to.' If Green agreed, he didn't say anything. 'We songwriters have been complaining. Songwriters are legendary at complaining, ask any publisher. That's what songwriters do. Every now and then they write but mostly they bitch. People have been saying for the past four or five years, "My God, they're recording such forgettable songs. I have great songs and I can't get them cut." That sort of thing. Now, in the last six months, people have been saying, "It's getting better. They're recording better songs. They're taking chances."

'There's a definite attitude that things are turning around because, I think, nothing is really working right now. It's kind of a good thing when nothing is working because it means that some amount of experimentation has to happen. Something has to give. Someone has to do something different to shake up things.'

Green glanced at his watch. 'We've got to get back out to the house. Why don't you come out in a few days? We can tell you a lot more about the music, and the business of music, in Nashville.'

I agreed. I wanted to ask Gretchen about Leonard Cohen.

4 Exit/In

I went to the Exit/In for the weekly Tuesday night Billy Block's Western Beat Show, the best deal in Nashville – 12 acts of diverse, eclectic country music for $5 (£3). A large, beefy, polite man stood, as usual, outside the entrance. He will say good evening and open the door, if you give him a chance. He will also toss your sorry ass in the gutter if you cause trouble.

He said 'Good evening' and I let him open the door. He did it for good manners as much as because it was his job. One of the charming, if perhaps facile, characteristics of the American South is good manners. Youngsters are raised to say 'Yes, Sir' and 'Yes, Madam' to their elders. This becomes such an ingrained habit that it carries on through adulthood and extends to other adults. Southerners perform courtesy genuinely, even when it is a masque for mean-spiritedness. When people in New York want to get rid of someone they say, 'Fuck off'. People in Los Angeles say, 'Let's have lunch'. People in Nashville say, 'God bless you'. This lends a veneer of civility to everyday life that takes the edge off, deflates hostility, and reminds people to be pleasant to one another.

The Exit/In, a long-established club where U2 and other top acts have played, is in a nexus neighborhood. There are several of these groupings of club(s), restaurants, bookstores, and other shops scattered about Nashville, often in unlikely locales. Some are in strip malls, like the famous Bluebird Café; others on out-of-the-way quiet streets buried in a residential neighborhood, like the Radio Café; and others in a more visual and accessible location, like the Exit/In.

The club is roughly midway between the West End and Lower Broadway, the west and east ganglia of Nashville's entertainment corpus. The short block of Ellison Place has restaurants, a tattoo parlor, a pool hall, an ice cream soda fountain, a used clothing store and a used bookstore. Across the street from the Exit/In, partially hidden behind a pizza joint, is The End, a dive bar where you can hear punk rock and punk country, sometimes at the same time from the same band, such as the Shackshakers. Next to the Exit/In is the Sherlock Holmes Pub, a favorite hangout for musicians, especially after their shows at the Exit/In. The Nash Grille, adjoining the club, is a quiet and tasteful restaurant.

I paused just inside the door to let my eyes adjust to the dim light. The club is a large, high-ceilinged rectangular box with a full stage at the far end. The walls and ceiling are painted black. An outline of a guitar in red neon lights runs the length of the ceiling from the stage to the rear bar. Tables are available but more people stand than sit during the shows. A blank space is left open in front of the stage for people to fill with dancing.

Billy was on stage playing drums for the first warm-up act. He is a professional drummer, an impresario, a cancer survivor, father of two young sons, devoted husband to Jill, and an enthusiastic promoter of non-mainstream country. His show is a great place to hear new acts, performers with enough juice to be on the club circuit, or someone breaking out with a new CD. The show is taped for delayed broadcasting on Billy's eponymous syndicated radio show.

I planted myself in the best spot in the house, right behind the soundman in his open sound booth with a shelf to put drinks or elbows as an invitation to spend the evening, which I did. The soundman, a large, solid, fleshy fellow in a florid tropical shirt and baseball cap, was my nearest neighbor so I introduced myself. 'Frank Sass,' he said in reply. I later learned that Frank had been repeatedly voted as the best soundman in Nashville in a citywide poll of clubs. He was also an avid freshwater fisherman – trout or catfish, it didn't matter as long as it takes his bait – and absolutely gaga about his 18-month-old daughter.

I had come to hear Emma Fox from Liverpool, England. The buzz on Emma was that she was a comer. What does it mean to be a 'comer' in Nashville? Is it like being a jellybean in a jar, waiting to be discovered as the most piquant of the new flavors? Or is it more like digging a ditch with your guitar until someone thinks you've earned enough blisters and offers you a hand up?

Emma Fox lived the first eight years of her life in the hometown of another country music fan, Ringo Starr, who was responsible for making the country song 'Act Naturally' a Beatles hit. According to Ace Collins in his book, *The Stories Behind Country Music's All-Time Greatest 100 Songs*, when the Beatles were finishing their 1965 album, they needed an additional song. Ringo's star was ascending at the time so Paul McCartney asked him to sing a song. Ringo, to everyone's surprise, did a version of Buck Owens' 'Act Naturally', twanged with a British accent. Twenty-four years later, Ringo and Buck cut the song together and it spent four months on the country charts.

Johnny Russell and Vonei Morrison wrote the song in 1963. The love song started when Johnny had to break a date with a girl. She asked where he was going and he jokingly replied, 'They're going to put me in the movies and make a big star out of me.' Actually, he was driving from Fresno to Los Angeles to do a session with friends from Oklahoma. Vonei pitched the song to Buck Owens, who didn't like it. But Don Rich, his guitar partner, loved the song and sang it over and over and over. Owens finally agreed to record it and got a one number one hit.

Emma listened to her parents' country records as she was growing up. Her dad was a Buddy Holly, Tammy Wynette, Johnny Cash fan; her mother grooved on soul. When she was six years old, her parents took her to an Everly Brothers concert. She became a singer during her school years in the Lake District because other kids, especially girls, bullied her. She had always been creative, singing in school plays since the age of four, but did not make her defiant statement until the age of ten. The school's musical director needed a lead singer for the school's play. No one volunteered, so he lined up the kids and had each step forward and sing a line. Emma stepped up and belted those snotty-nosed little bitches with her voice.

'I was a sensitive girl. I don't want anyone to feel like the shit I did at school,' she says of that time. 'That shaped me. Maybe that's why I want to stand up and be admired on stage. Singing was the one thing that I did. It was like, "Fuck you lot, you can't touch me. I'm just going to sing now."'

Emma tooted on the sax a bit and studied voice to learn more about music. She started a course in performing arts and music at the University of Newcastle-upon-Tyne. She became the lead singer for a band doing covers, pop, standards, country, whatever the crowds would pay for in the local pubs and halls. An opportunity to audition for a pop project came up but it was a studio gig. She had never been in a studio. No matter. A smart girl, she caught on quickly about tracking and the different ways of singing in a studio versus live performances, like how to do her own backing vocals.

She wanted to be admired, to be a star. So after a semester at the university, she quit. Any frog can be noticed in a small pond. She moved to London and ruefully learned that it's difficult for a frog, even a talented frog, to get noticed in a large pond full of talented striving frogs. She did some studio sessions as a background vocal singer, even did some television work, but mostly she got hungry. She'd spend an hour on the train going to a studio gig, then an hour in the opposite direction to see a club owner who wasn't there, whole days spent crisscrossing London on the Underground, not even getting to see the sights. She had never been to London before so, like any tourist, she wanted to see Big Ben and Westminster Abbey and the Tower of London.

She started writing songs and doing a solo acoustic act in every place but the street corner. Her music was folk and country with a catchy pop commercial edge. Not that anybody actually listened in those pubs. After a few gigs in East London clubs, where fighting was considered a social gesture, she became a hardened veteran at reading the crowd. By the fourth song she could judge in which part of the club the fight would erupt and plan her escape route accordingly.

One night, she got caught in a mêlée outside a club down a dead-end alley. There she was, a woman with her guitar, and 40 drunken louts whaling on each other. She turned her face to the wall and waited until the blokes stopped amusing themselves. 'That's it,' she said. 'I've got to find another way.'

People had always told her that she sounded American country, probably an early influence of her parents' records. You ought to go to America, they told her, go to Nashville. That's where they play country and western. I'm sure that you'll be a hit, deary, an English girl looking like you and singing like them. 'Oh, right,' Emma thought. 'I'm struggling to keep myself together financially here in London so how am to fly across the Atlantic and then halfway across America.' But she's always been determined, so she started saving money. Her dad, a big country fan, also hankered to visit Nashville. 'Why don't you and me go?' asked Emma. Her mother, not well enough for the rigors of the trip, gave her blessing.

She didn't know a soul in Nashville and had no idea who she wanted to know. Even if she did, how did she contact them? She planned to be in Nashville only two weeks, not much time to make cold calls, especially to busy producers. She phoned every single contact she had in London. Who do you know in Nashville? How can I get to know someone in Nashville? Can you get me a contact? Within three weeks, she had 14 meetings booked.

Nashville is called the five-year town because conventional wisdom has it that it takes five years of paying dues before you're given a nod. The people in power want to know that you have the fire in the belly before they'll ask you on the team. 'All right, maybe she has the tenacity of a pit bull but can she hang on?' they'll wonder.

Emma was bowled over by Nashville the moment her feet hit the tarmac. She knew this was the place where she could pursue her dream. Her music had been a bit off beat in London. It was pop but not real pop because it had this funny American country sound, so the managers didn't know quite what to do with her. Audiences liked her but she hadn't gained a real following. But in Nashville, in Nashville she could do the music she loved and respected for one simple reason – that was the kind of music they did in Nashville.

Only, no one had the faintest idea who she was. Well, then, she'd introduce herself. She had put together a homemade press kit: a photo, biography, a demo disk, and copies of songs she had written. She handed out this calling card in every meeting with producers, songwriters, record people – never the top record people, the ones who can make the decision on the spot, but at least with people inside the record company's building. Everyone was nice and encouraging and charmed and was charming right back. 'All this way from England, are you? For a two-week visit? And you want a recording contract? Do you know the story about the fishes and the loaves? That's quite a story, isn't it? About a miracle? Almost unbelievable, don't you think? We don't believe in miracles in Nashville. You're here two weeks you say, all the way from England. You got to see the sights while you're here. Take a couple of snaps to remember your trip.'

Then she met her guardian angel, so to speak.

She had been given Garth Fundis's name. She knew that he had produced Trisha Yearwood, Don Williams, the late Keith Whitley, and Alabama, but she didn't really know who Garth Fundis was, not really, because Garth is a quiet guy who prefers the shadow to the spotlight. Here's a story, a true story, about who Garth Fundis really is:

In April 2002, Garth Fundis engineered the removal of the powerful president and chief operating officer of the National Academy of Recording Arts & Sciences (NARAS), C Michael Greene. NARAS is the Grammy Awards. Greene dominated the Grammy organization during his 14-year tenure as president. He took the organization from 14 employees with assets of $4.9 million (£3.1 million) and 3,500 members in the mid-1980s to 120 staffers, more than $50 million (£32 million) in assets, and 17,000 members in less than 20 years. He was a major LA player, a ring to be kissed, if not on bended knee then at least with a deferential bow. And he was a leader with an autocratic style that expected the NARAS employees to bend to his will, and that included the nonprofit trade group's board of directors who were nominally his boss.

Garth Fundis became the volunteer chairman of the board of directors in July 2001. On July 25, he received a letter from an attorney, Gloria Allred, putting the academy on notice that she was filing a sexual harassment lawsuit against the academy and Greene. Allred claimed that Greene had allegedly battered and sexually harassed Jill Marie Geimer, a Grammy executive in charge of the academy's human resources department. Greene denied the allegations but the academy paid Geimer $650,000 (£422,000) on Fundis's recommendation. Fundis then learned of accusations that Greene had allegedly harassed and forced out two other NARAS female executives in the mid-1990s. Fundis ordered a private investigation.

When the private investigators' report reached Fundis, he called an unprecedented meeting of NARAS's 38 trustees. The investigators had interviewed Greene, so he knew what was in the wind. His attorneys threatened to sue the academy if any of the report's information became public. Fundis didn't blink. He would present the findings to the board and they would vote on Greene's fate. Greene's attorneys had not succeeded in bluffing Fundis. They opened negotiations and two days later Fundis made the stunning announcement that Greene, although cleared of any wrong doing, would lose his $750,000 (£480,000) a year job. He was given an $8 million (£5 million) golden handshake severance package and a six-month deal as an independent consultant.

'Garth deserves a medal for this. He went into that life-sucking vortex of the old academy and stood up and did the right thing – and emerged with his reputation and soul intact,' Adam Sandler, a former vice-president at the Grammy organization, was quoted in the press.

Fundis was described as a 'very soft giant', a shy man who acts on his beliefs. That was the man Emma phoned, like a salesperson making a cold call. She got his answering machine. She left a polite, but 'pushy' message. He didn't return the call. She called him again and reached him. Fundis agreed to see her on a Saturday morning at his studio.

'So me and my dad drove to the studio,' Emma said of the meeting as we chatted backstage after her Exit/In set. 'I was thinking maybe he had a studio in his house. But it was Sound Emporium [*O Brother, Where Art Thou?* was recorded there] and I thought, "Yeah, okay, it's a lot bigger than I thought." I walked in and there are gold discs all over the walls. I had never been in a studio quite as professional as this. I told myself, "Don't start getting all nervous. What have you got to lose?" My whole attitude was shit or bust, what the hell, this is a once in a lifetime experience. I'm getting the opportunity to have my dreams.'

Fundis asked her to sing for him. While she warmed up in a side studio, he went out to the car and invited Emma's dad in. They were having a chin wag when Emma appeared for her informal audition. Emma played original songs for the famous producer. Then she sang Crystal Gayle's, 'Light Brown Eyes Blues'. Fundis laughed and told her that he knew the song – he had engineered the Crystal Gayle recording sessions.

'I didn't know he had done those sessions,' Emma exclaimed. 'I would have never sung that song if I had known who he really was. He said that I was pretty darn good. I met with him again the day before I was to fly back to London. He played the devil's advocate, you know, trying to see how much I wanted my dream, how hard I was willing to work. Then, at the end, he said that if I came back, he'd do some demos of me and help me get a start.'

Emma returned to England, closed down her London life, and moved to Nashville. Fundis found her a lawyer to apply for a work permit. Applicants must leave the country while the permit is being processed, so she returned to London. Seven days later, perhaps a record, she received the permit and flew back to Nashville. She found jobs cleaning people's houses, bartending at Tootsie's, and being a nanny. She got around town on a bicycle.

She's been in town for a year and a half now. Things are starting to look up for her. She drives an old car. She sings in clubs around town. People are starting to notice her. She has a new guy in her corner, Don Cook.

Don Cook is as legendary a producer as Garth Fundis. He put together Brooks And Dunn, the hottest duo in country today. He is a songwriter, one of the most successful in Nashville. He has his own company, DKC Productions, a small imprint label within the Sony family. The label's first act was Wade Hayes, who had a number one hit, then left Sony. Cook has offered Emma a production deal.

'This production deal is a God send,' Emma told me. 'I won't have to work five jobs to survive. I can concentrate on my music. I work six days a week at the moment with the three jobs and rehearsing and performing. I drink a lot of coffee. I'm tired. When I sign this, I could probably give up all my jobs but I'll just give up one at first. I like taking risks, but risks with calculation. I like to survive.'

All the production deal means is that Cook will produce her demo. Granted, it is Don Cook, but even with that promising break Emma is on the bottom rung of the Nashville stairway to heaven, a couple of steps behind Jill King. She's just another starry-eyed hopeful off the bus determined to set Nashville on its ear. They arrive by the hundreds every week, guitars in hand, eager with enthusiasm. You see them strumming in the clubs for tourists where the industry people never go. They play on street corners of Lower Broadway for spare change. You run into them in the lobbies of record companies as they ask the receptionist to send their demo up to a producer. You meet them pulling caffe lattes in the coffee bars, even those who have gigs, those who have toured with known names. They all think of themselves as 'comers'.

Don Cook has a ginger-colored mustache, a round face, and was dressed in an open-throat shirt and slacks when we met in his office, a mini-suite at the end of a second-floor corridor in the Sony/Tree building. The office is comfortably large and well appointed, but not showy, with a terrific sound system. Framed gold discs of his hit songs and pictorial art are on the walls. When I commented that he was a business executive with a keyboard and soundboard as part of his desk, Cook replied, 'My job is to create music all day long. It's a miraculous way to live. I get lost in the music. I love it. I go on vacation and I take people with me to write. It's the most energizing thing in my life.'

We sat in two high-backed comfortable armchairs around a small round table in front of his desk.

'I've spent my whole life working in recording studios, at least since I was 14. I love it. It's the most comfortable place for me in the world,' he said. 'There are times when I kind of get tired of it because I've been at it so long. Since I don't play a musical instrument well enough to call myself an expert, the studio is like an instrument for me, which I can play a lot better than I can play a musical instrument. I know what I can make sound good in the studio. I have the perception that you walk up to the plate and swing for the bleachers every time. I just try to do stuff that I think is really good. I put all my passion and energy into it. Sometimes it's good and sometimes it's less than good.'

A major turning point in Cook's life, musically and personally, was 1990. He had more cuts as a songwriter at the end of 1989 and 1990 than at any time in his career. Eleven of his songs were in the charts as singles – but none of them rose above 35. He had a George Jones single that didn't even chart. 'I felt like at that time I had personally destroyed the career of George Jones.'

That year, the relative closest to his heart, his grandmother, passed away. 'That just tore me up. At the end of 1990, right after my grandmother's funeral, I met this guy Ronnie Dunn. He came out to the house to write with me. I was standing out in front of my house, and he got out of his car and I said, "That's a country star." He just looked like a fully realized, fully formed country star. Kix Brooks was there with me because we were going to write a song that day. The three of us wrote Brooks And Dunn's second number one record. The following February 1991 we recorded their first album. We were just some guys trying to make a record we'd be proud of and wanted to listen to.

'I went from absolute despondency to an incredible sense of wonder and inspiration in the course of about seven months. I had the worst times in my career and the best times. I rode the emotional rollercoaster so many times I had wind burn. That old cliché about the darkest hour before the dawn, well, there's a certain amount of truth to that. But most of the time it's not that clear-cut. That period of time ended my life as a contractual staff songwriter and my life as a producer and publisher began.'

But Cook's fundamental bone is being a songwriter. 'I just love to write. I'll write about anything. In songwriting, you learn to focus your thoughts in kinds of musical forms and patterns. Language becomes a rhythmic thing, rather than just a way of communicating. Production and songwriting have acted as great places for me to escape to when I get tired of one or the other. It's wonderful that when I get frustrated with one, I can retreat to the other. It's not only a great place to hide, but it's a great motivator for the other. One feeds the other very nicely and that works in both directions. There's nothing like hands-on studio production to show you that you need to create better material to work with in a better way. But songwriting is my favorite part.'

As a songwriter, Cook is concerned about the same themes that have concerned him all his life – relationships. 'Most of my stuff is about real people. I don't write many philosophically directed songs. Country music always had a social element but that's because it's relationship music. It's story music. It's even philosophical sometimes, sometimes funny. It's got a serious dance component. All those things together conspire to keep it alive.'

Cook, a Texas native, admits that he's not really a country boy. 'I'd like to believe that I am, but I'm really not. I am a redneck but not a country boy.' He is not one of those Southern cracker reactionary isolationist cartoon rednecks who take pride in their ignorance, the kind of ignorance that mistakes injustice for comedy, except when it happened to them or theirs. Then the perceived injustice is cause for self-righteous violence. Cook started in folk music, the social protest songbook of the 1960s. The music of rebellion, of serious social change, set his guitar humming.

'I don't know if country will become the new protest music. If a blue-collar, bad-ass populist hero emerges from the country ranks, the music will become the music of social cause. That is one of the opportunities for country music right now. If it is just a pure entertainment form, then it won't. Rap has been filling those shoes for a while and doing it real well. Right now, country is the musical equivalent of comfort food. Country music is generally not the music of rebellion. It's got a different purpose.'

If there is a hero out there on the horizon, a 'primary hero', to use Cook's term, then neither he nor anyone else in the country music industry sees that person. But they hope that the primary hero, or heroes, male or female, will walk into their office in the next five minutes. The time is ripe. The industry needs to be saved, wants to be saved, even from itself.

'What has to happen is that one artist has to emerge, an artist who connects with millions of people. The *O Brother, Where Art Thou?* concept connected with a lot of people, but it didn't spawn one particular artist that connected. An artist with an image who connects is more marketable over a longer period of time than any concept that connects. We need the person. The rootsy music has been really successful and it's really important to this format. Great singers and talent have come out of that genre, like Keith Whitley and Ricky Skaggs.

'Every generation of listeners rediscovers the roots music. The rest of the music in that format is generally derivative. Rock music was the same way. *O Brother* is an example of an audience discovering the roots of where much of the pop country came from. The country audience is tired of top 40 country, the watered-down version of the real stuff. They like the purer version of it. Whether they become life-long fans of that type of music remains to be seen.

'Every eight to ten years the industry looks for a new set of primary heroes behind which everybody can march,' Cook said. 'We all hope that we are having a part in creating one of those acts.'

Country music, like every other musical form, is cyclical. The 1990s pop country cycle is winding down, a cycle turned by the likes of Garth Brooks, Tim McGraw and his wife, Faith Hill, and Shania Twain, the most successful female country performer in terms of worldwide popularity.

The difference between the 1990s and other cycles is the number of records sold. In the '70s and '80s, there were not many country multi-platinum-selling artists. In the '90s, Garth Brooks sold ten to 15 times platinum. Artists on the next tier down routinely sold 500,000 to a million records. The base level of units sold has pushed the market to new heights. The inevitable new cycle will build on that base and reach even greater record-breaking sales, so the thinking goes. The historical pattern shows that the audience size never drops back to the previous levels. The audience is always larger at the end of each cycle than it was before the cycle started.

'I feel we've been in the end period of the down part of the cycle for a while,' Cook said. 'It's time to retool, a time to reconfigure, to think about new strategies for doing business and creating music. When a cycle ends, the music tends to drift back towards the traditional roots. We're seeing that with *O Brother*. But the music never goes back as far into the traditional as it did before the cycle started. Now is a time to think about new combinations of creative teams. It's very exciting, you know.

'New heroes in the music business are made in these times. Everybody is a hero when the format is blazing hot. It's like when the stock market was beyond Thunder Dome. Everybody looked like a financial genius. But when things are not going well nobody looks like a genius. The new heroes are the people who can make money now. Whoever makes the music that connects will make the money. That's the next hero.'

But it will take more than a new musical hero to make money. The country record industry, all of the music industry, must re-examine how it does business. In the 1980s salad years, when money was rolling in, the labels spent freely. When water is abundant, you can be generous in nurturing the flowers. That's what the labels did; they spent record amounts to produce and market an album. But semi-arid conditions now prevail in the industry.

'We can't spend $500,000 [£325,000] to make an album and market and distribute it,' Cook conceded. 'I think we need to spend $100,000 [£65,000] on five albums, or $50,000 [£32,500] on ten albums apiece. I think with the advent of a lot of the inexpensive recording technology, that will happen.'

But there is another element outside the record industry that exerts a dominant influence – commercial network radio.

'Radio has to open its door to more material,' Cook said. 'Radio has to find a way not to kill off new material before the listening public gets to vote. Unfortunately, right now, research and marketing conglomerates and consultants kill records before anybody gets to say whether they like them or not. That's not a good situation. If I was in the radio business, trying to survive, I'd do anything I could to keep the doors open, to keep the people on the staff employed. But today's strategies can be self-defeating. Radio plays it safe with the same old rotation of songs that their market surveys say people listen to. But eventually the music can get to the point where everybody turns it off. Then the advertisers start considering putting their dollars predominately in other media choices. That's within the realm of possibility at any time now.

'I don't think radio is necessarily the villain, or the only villain. Radio doesn't play anything that we don't give them. However, they may not play things we do give them. But what's blocking those other things from being played is the very other things we gave them. They don't create their own music. They just play what we give them.

'Radio is not in the music business. Their goal is to sell advertising. We're in the music business. What we have to do as an industry is give consumers better product for their money. The music is there. It's just not getting to the people very much.'

Cook's BCK Productions allows him to look at music and talent that is more left of center. But, he acknowledges, the music he produces, the talent he promotes, will be filtered through the mainstream music machine process, which includes the commercial radio networks. So what kind of artist is he looking for that might be a bit left of center but can still get through the mainstream machine filters?

'I'm very excited about the possibilities for Emma Fox. She is a wonderful artist. She has all the requisite parts necessary to go the distance. She has a great sense of songs. She has a tremendous level of energy. She is truly tenacious and relentless, which is exactly what we love to see in an artist. She will work way past anyone else's point of exhaustion to get the job done. That's really what it takes to be a successful artist. It's my belief that most of the dominant acts that really reach a huge audience connection, those acts are blessed with an incredible sense of ambition as well as talent. I don't know many cases of artists that kept their careers on a backburner and reached that kind of promise. Most top performers are incredibly tenacious, incredibly ambitious, and have persistence as much as talent.

'There are a lot of people with talent. What persistence does, I think, is it couples with your talent and puts you in more situations where you get to show your talent, where you get to combine your talent with other peoples' talent, where you get to discover new things about yourself. That's what persistence brings out. But, of course, you have to have the real talent. If you don't have the real talent, you're not going to connect.

'It doesn't work just being in the right place at the right time. You might have one hit as a writer by being in the right place at the right time. But that's not how you're going to be an act like The Dixie Chicks or Alan Jackson or Tim McGraw. That's not how it works.'

Cook is so confident of Emma's potential that he has invited Peter Asher, the producer and founder of Peter Asher Management, who handles Linda Ronstadt, to make Emma their Nashville project. When Emma was in England visiting her folks at Christmas, Asher was also in London. He invited her to lunch and they hit it off beautifully.

'I think it's turned into a real workable relationship,' Cook said. 'I think Emma has a shot at being one of the primary heroes. It's an evolution that will take two or three years.'

As I left the office, Cook called out, 'You should check out my bookstore, Rhino, down on Granny White Road. I love books as much as songs, and I love the people who write both. All writers have the same fears and phobias and insecurities. It's just great. It's very heartwarming to discover that. They never get over the fears. NEVER EVER. The most phobic crazy people in the world are songwriters. And they are the most interesting. My writing partner, Fred Koller, who looks after the bookstore, is one of the most interesting. You'll enjoy him.'

5 Country Rocket Science

Joe Galante, the chairman of the RCA Label Group, is one of the most important men in the country music industry. He is universally regarded as an excellent record man and a stellar businessman. He introduced focus groups and market surveys to country music. He has never forgotten, in the 30 years he's been in Nashville, that he is an accountant from New York. His job is to discern which way the winds of country music are blowing and then adjust RCA's sails to go in that direction. He fiddles with the mainsail of business models. He changes the jib (to stay nautical) of which artist(s) leads RCA's country music into the future.

The RCA Label Group – Arista Nashville, BNA Records Label, and RCA Records Label – occupies the most imposing office building on Music Row. The mock-Italianate palazzo is classically stated in beige brick, but with dark windows placed asymmetrically for a neo-modern wink. A high double gate of black iron leads to the interior courtyard, which serves as a parking lot divided by a flowerbed. The building, on a slope overlooking the other labels, can be interpreted as a visual representation of Top Dog lording over the pack, but that is probably a stretch. Joe Galante doesn't cast himself in that role. However, the metaphor is there to be read. Perhaps it may more aptly apply to another tenant in the building, Clear Channel Entertainment, which owns the majority (1,200 of nearly 2,000) country radio stations nationwide.

Galante's fourth-floor office is buried deep within interlocking grids of narrow corridors lined with open cubicles. I tried to remember the receptionist's instructions – right turn, right turn, left turn or was it right, left, right – as I negotiated the maze, feeling a bit like Alice in Wonderland.

If his assistant, Donna, hadn't flagged me down, I would have surely missed the correct turn. She greeted me in the standard Southern manner, as if I was a favorite cousin arriving at a family picnic. She showed me into Galante's office. He wasn't there.

The office was surprisingly small for such an important executive. Although he has a corner view of the city spread out below, Galante cannot see it from his chair; the computer screen obstructs. He can see the television across the room, which was tuned to an all-news channel with the sound off. A sofa for informal chats was at the far end of the room, 20' (6m) from his desk. I heard him outside discussing in detail with Donna which airlines he should take to and from a West Coast meeting. Efficient time management, even at the inconvenience of switching carriers in mid-trip, was time saved.

He entered the room carrying a paper cup of tea he had fixed for himself. Galante is a small man, perhaps 5' 6" (1m 68cm), slight in frame, with prominent ears, a bony jawline, and intense eyes. His well-trimmed brown hair was combed to one side in a style reminiscent of Midwest 1950s. He wore a tan lightweight jacket, unzipped. He made a beeline for the desk without shaking hands. 'Let's start. Ask me a question.'

'What's your plan to increase the country music market share?'

'I don't have a plan to increase the country music market share. My plan is to increase *our* share, RCA's, by having three labels and to increase the depth of the roster of artists. A lot of labels in this town have one star and that's it. We have three separate companies and I make sure we have a number of stars on each of those rosters. By doing that, we're going to have a greater share of the market.'

'Do you find similarities between the current condition of the industry to the downturn in 1989–90?'

'I don't know if it's 100 per cent sure that we're in a similar place as 1989 and '90, when we came out of another downturn and into an upswing. There were conditions ten years ago in the country from a political standpoint. Everything about the Reagan era was coming through. It was a good time. There was a sense that pop radio, particularly rap, was so black in its message and that was driving people away from that market. Country music gained in popularity as more rap was being played on the radio. People were switching the dial to a music they could listen to. Well, guess what? We're now 12 years later and pop radio is really black but people are actually going out and buying the music. I think there is a real shift in terms of the difference of the youth and the young adults from 1989 to 2002. Now they're not turned off by that music. So we don't have the opportunity we did ten years ago, when people were feeling disenfranchised by pop radio and had to find something else.'

(In the early 1990s, when Garth Brooks, Shania Twain, and Billy Ray Cyrus pulled in the younger audience in large numbers, Music Row placed its emphasis on targeting pre- and early teens. That strategy is now seen as a failure for building a long-term fan base. RCA signed 3 of Hearts, a trio of Nashville high-school girls. The music was lightweight bubblegum with none of the mature life experiences that are the hallmark of country music. The act quickly disappeared. Atlantic Records went for the youth market with Tracy Lawrence, John Michael Montgomery, and Neal McCoy. The youth market is fickle for country music. When Garth Brooks released a pop album of his alter ego, *Garth Brooks…In The Life of Chris Gaines*, the younger audience hooted and turned their backs, although the album did sell 2 million units. Brooks, Faith Hill, LeAnn Rimes, and The Dixie Chicks have a substantial youth audience, but they established themselves first on adult country radio. The core country listener is a 34- to 36-year-old female, the same market as the early 1980s.)

'What is your forecast for the country music market?'

'We have a pretty solid market. Could it go up? Yeah. Do I think that it will go back up to 18–19 per cent of the market? I don't think so. But that doesn't do anything to our, RCA's, business model. I think there are some people [labels] in this town who need to go away. I don't think there is enough business to support everybody. Like in any situation, the big get bigger and they survive. The little guys who can't compete go away. There are some major companies who can't compete and they'll go away.'

(The country music genre peaked in 1992 with 17.4 per cent of the market share of US music sales. In 2000, the market share slipped to 10.7 per cent, its lowest mark in a decade. Sales in 2002 continue to hover at 10 per cent of music of all genres purchased by consumers 35 years or older. Country music did register a 1.2 per cent lurch in popularity when a clutch of patriotic songs was released following the World Trade Center attack. Alan Jackson, Aaron Tippin, Brooks And Dunn, Lee Greenwood, Hank Williams Jr, Craig Morgan, Charlie Daniels, and Ray Stevens put out flag-waving red, white and blue songs. David Ball's 'Riding With Private Malone', a Vietnam War-era song written before the September 11 attack, became a major hit.)

'Do you believe a primary hero is needed to turn the industry into an upswing?'

'I've always had a contention about a primary hero. Country music has always done its best when it doesn't have a primary hero. We do best when there is a plethora of heroes. A problem that we have in this town is that we focus on one. We stay too long on one person. The time we did best was the two-year period when we got Vince Gill, Alan Jackson, Garth Brooks, Clint Black, Travis Tritt. All those guys came within two years of each other. That was great. That's what we have to focus on. How do we get six of these guys? When the Latin thing happened in pop three years ago, then you had all those acts coming through. All of a sudden it moved an entire genre forward.

'We were sitting here thinking, you know, if we can get one star, everyone will turn to us. Bull. When we don't have a Garth record, our numbers drop through the bottom. You can't move a genre by one act.'

'What artists do you see as the plethora heroes?'

'Kenny Chesney [RCA], Toby Keith [UMVD], Sara Evans [RCA], and Lee Ann Womack [UMVD]. On the next level, you have Phil Vassar [RCA], Andy Griggs [RCA], Carolyn Dawn Johnson [RCA], and Blake Shelton [WEA/EMI]. We have a number of these people getting there. Kenny Chesney is bringing in the youth. His audience is anywhere between 18 to 30 years old and mostly female. I don't think there is another artist in town that does that, not in the depth he does.

'I think Kenny Chesney is the poster child of country music for the wellbeing of country artists. He's not being a pop act but he's certainly appealing to that same audience. I've been to a Garth Brooks show. Kenny has the same crowd. Actually, Kenny's is more female than male.

Garth had more male. That's the only difference between Garth and Kenny. Garth was 60:40 male/female and Kenny is 30:70 male/female.'

Chesney's new album, *No Shoes, No Shirt, No Problems*, made its debut at number one on the all-genres *Billboard* 200 chart, selling 235,000 units. At the 2002 37th Academy of Country Music Awards, Phil Vassar won the New Male Vocalist award; Carolyn Dawn Johnson was the New Female Vocalist. Toby Keith, who had the patriotic hit 'Courtesy of the Red, White & Blue (The Angry American)' following the September 11 terrorist attack on the World Trade Center, was nominated as a finalist in six categories but went home empty-handed. The song warns terrorists that 'You'll be sorry you messed with the US of A' and includes the phrase 'We'll put a boot in your ass.' That line got the Keith song booted from the ABC July 4 patriotic television special as being too angry.

Joe Galante first came to Nashville as an accountant and marketing man. He quickly rose through the ranks, returned to New York briefly, and was sent back to Nashville to head RCA's country division. His epiphany with country music came when he sat in on the early Waylon Jennings recording sessions at Tompall Glaser's Hillbilly Central studio. Jennings had left the RCA studio because he couldn't get the sound he wanted.

'It's 150 per cent correct that I started to love country music when I heard Waylon Jennings recording at Hillbilly Central,' confirmed Galante. 'I went, "Whoa, this is what I'm supposed to be doing. I love this. This is great."'

Galante identifies with the Jennings and Nelsons because, as he said, artists and executives have similar chemistry – in some instances. Some of both groups make it the hard way, surviving the dues-paying years. That gives timbre and vibrancy. There are some executives, and artists, who make $10 million (£6.5 million), like those in the dot.com businesses, who 'don't know what they are there for in that moment,' Galante said. 'Was that executive just brilliant for the moment or brilliant for the decade? For me, the artist that has the vibrancy and timbre is the artist who lasts more than a decade. I think that so much of what we do in our system rewards short term and not long term, both from an executive standpoint and from an artistic standpoint.

'I'm working on a long-term process. I'm not interested in my next quarter. I'm interested in my next year. And the next two years. And the next five years. That's how we're running this company. Is it more advantageous to go by steps than leaps? Well, it depends on how desperate you are and how long you've been in the doghouse. Maybe steps are better in the long term. I don't think American business, for the most part, is thinking long term. Everybody is thinking what is the next quarter and how do I get through that?'

RCA Label Group does have a track record for long-term development of its artists. Chesney, who was working parking cars for a restaurant before being discovered, has been on the label for eight years. The investment is paying off big time this year. Martina McBride was signed in 1992 and her first two albums did not make waves. She sold T-shirts to make a living. Sara Evans, a former demo singer, is now doing her third album and garnering attention. Carolyn Dawn Johnson was a waitress and a bartender before RCA nurtured her career. Phil Vassar was a bar owner for years, a wannabe star as a bar player, before RCA gave him his shot. Alan Jackson toiled as demo singer and songwriter before becoming RCA's top act.

'When we find somebody, we stay with them,' Galante said. 'I'm not flipping them like hamburgers. On a general basis, I think it is true that artists are turned out if they don't hit first time. There are people who can get lucky on a single. There are some companies in Nashville who can develop artists, but not everybody can. That's one of the things we're supposed to do, be an artist development company. Anybody can get lucky. Any schmuck can show up one day, put out a single and he gets a million units sold and everybody goes, "You're brilliant." Well, do it the second time, the third time. As a producer or label executive, do it on a couple of acts. Then you're brilliant.'

'So what does it take to be brilliant?'

'You get the right team around you – the artists, the managers, the staff, the producer. So little is talked about A&R but, to me, our success is because we've got a great A&R staff. All of us work together. We make tough decisions. If things don't go right and we don't see the future for the artist, we let them go. We've all made roots records that we absolutely love and we've got nowhere with them. It's a tough conversation to have about having a record you want out there but how much are you willing to lose in the effort. I hate those conversations. I still go back and look at records I've been involved in and say, "Why not? Why didn't that work?" I never have the answer.

'If money was the answer to our problems, we'd have stars everywhere. The one misconception that everyone has is that you can spend your way out of a problem. That's not true. I keep coming back to Kenny, to Martina McBride, who with each record carve a little wider space and develop their artistry. They will be here ten years from now, just like Alan Jackson. Alan Jackson never wavered from what he did. He wasn't flashy at the beginning. He had some mainstream hits but he's on the same path.'

(Jackson's 'Where Were You (When The World Stopped Turning)' was a mega number one crossover hit following the September 11 World Trade Center attack. He had a number one debut on the pop album chart with *Drive*, the first in his career.)

'I think there are those people who can do that,' Galante continued. 'The question is, "How do we create the next Alabama that lasts ten years? The next Reba McEntire? The next George Strait? The next Waylon and Willie?" Think back to when those guys were characters. The Outlaws didn't come because someone made up a colorful name. That's what they were, outlaws. The law was always chasing them because they were doing things that weren't legal. It's a little different today. Then, you could be that and be under the scrutiny of the media and it wouldn't ruin your career. Imagine what would happen to Waylon or Willie if they were starting now and doing the things they did back then. I'm not sure they would have survived.'

I had a final question. 'Many in the music industry claim that since deregulation of the airwaves, commercial radio networks dedicate a bland non-offensive music for their stations. Do you think the radio networks have a stranglehold on the music industry and that regulation should be reinstated?'

'If deregulation is what the market dictates, I don't think we can fight those forces. I don't look at the radio thing as the issue. It's part of the problem but not the problem. I can't blame everything on radio. Radio delivered 235,000 units sold on Kenny Chesney. My problem is that there is a lack of creativity at radio. The staffs are multi-tasked to the point where they don't listen and are not creative in their jobs. They have so much on their plates they can't think about being creative. And people are given promotions that don't have the experience to lead a station or a group of stations. They're guessing. We guess too but we have some tools to help us.'

As I was leaving, Galante asked if I had been treated well in Nashville? Was I able to speak with everyone I wanted? 'Alan Jackson's management/PR firm had been stonewalling me. Last week they finally said no to an interview, citing too many demands on his time.'

'I think we had something to do with that,' Galante said with a smile.

Country music has lost its base because it can't relate to the audience and because the audience can't relate to what the music is now saying. This is not rocket science.

Merlin Littlefield was warming up for a stemwinder.

'Country music has always been a 40-year-old plus audience. They've lived life and have been through things that real country has always been about – loneliness, separation, heartbreak, loyalty to country, home and family. It's autobiographical music.'

Merlin was trying to stay calm but country music is his passion and he is a passionate man. He leaned back in his chair, as if to get away from a fire and cool down, but then came aggressively forward to make a point.

'In today's country, you get these frivolous nonsense ridiculous country songs that, first of all, have no soul and, second of all, have a lyric content that can't relate to anybody in the niche of country music. This was partly due to corporate thinking that they had to capture the youth market.'

Merlin shifted in his chair, a precursor to the bounce that was building as he got more and more exercised about the condition of his beloved country music. 'I was there with some of the top honchos sitting around the board table and heard them say, "Now we're going after the youth market, the upscale market. Country music fans are not just driving Chevrolets and Fords. They driving BMWs and Jaguars." Well, that's a bunch of crap. Give me a break.'

Merlin nearly came out of his chair but grabbed the arms to keep himself in place. 'That thinking did not work and it's still not working. Country is a working man's music. Just like the blues. That's what country music people do. That thinking is like going to Wynton Marsalis and saying, "You know, you're going to have to be a little more commercial, a little cuter. You can't dress like that anymore and you have to be something that you're not." Give me a break. Get out of here.'

Merlin's eyes blazed with the fire you sometimes see in a preacher's eyes when he enters the God zone, where the vision of Truth burns so bright as to vaporize impurities in the soul, in country's soul; burns so intensely as to liquefy the devils incarnate who have taken over Music Row, even if they are his friends; the Damned be damned, some things are sacred, not to be despoiled for lucre.

'You can't do that to country,' Merlin exclaimed. 'You can't make it hip dandified. You can't make *country* country club. Country music is a working man's music. You're not going to change the fans. The fans are going to be there and they are going to find the real music either in a movie or make their own CDs or buy traditional, but not this new music. The country fans are still there, even if they're not buying as much of the music as they used to. Who can blame them? There have always been alternatives to country music. The Everly Brothers were a prime example of "We can be pop, too." Elvis was another prime example of being country and being pop. There are always those exceptions but fans of basic country music are still there. The fans still like it. All you have to do is give it to them. IT'S NOT ROCKET SCIENCE.'

Merlin came out of his chair as if to grab the lapels of the misguided and shake sense into their corporate skulls. He promptly sat down lest his staff see him through the open door of his office. Merlin is the director of personnel for the Tennessee Department of Corrections. He has held that post for only three years. Before that he had spent 35 years in the music business, 19 of those years as the associate director of ASCAP Nashville, the songwriter's organization. Merlin knows all the players on Music Row.

Merlin is a dignified looking man, a Texan, tall, with handsome white hair, brilliant blue eyes, and the erect carriage of an ex-Marine. An arm clad in a long-sleeved white shirt protruded from behind his desk, his hand palm up.

He graduated from TCU with a major in radio/television/film, which is evident in his flair for presentation. He also earned a major/minor in criminology and sociology, so when he says, 'When you want to study a society, look to the arts. The arts reflect society; society does not reflect the arts,' he's not just pontificating with hot air.

After university, he went back to school, the Marine Corps officer's school. His working career began as the nighttime intake director for the Dallas County Juvenile Department as he prepared to enter the Southern Methodist University law school.

But, on the morning of March 6, 1967, after he left the juvenile lockup, he went to the Dallas office of Capital Records and asked for a job. 'I was tired of school. I didn't want to go to law school. The music business sounded like me,' he explained.

He wanted a job in sales. 'We don't have a job in sales,' the Capital people said. 'We've got one in promotion.'

'What is that?' Merlin asked.

'You go to radio stations and promote our records so they get played on air.'

'I can do that,' he said.

'We'll call you,' they said. And two days later they did. Merlin was one of three people being considered for the job.

'Do the others have experience?' Merlin asked.

'Lots of experience.'

'Well, too bad for you,' Merlin replied.

'Why's that?'

'You've got to break them of their learned habits. You can train me to what you want and how you want me to do it. I'm very trainable. I'm a real good dog.'

Merlin got the job as the new district promotion manager for Capital Records. He became the promotion manager for the entire mid-United States, while managing a successful group, Wetlock. Then RCA hired him as their mid-United States promotion manager. While at RCA, he bought into a management company in Austin. Michael Martin Murphy, who had the hit 'Geronimo's Cadillac', was a client; BW Stevenson, with the hit 'My Maria', was a client, as was Ray Benson and Asleep At The Wheel, Bill and Bonnie Herne, and the Texan troubadour Steven Fromholz.

He sold his share of the management company and went to work for Stax Records in Memphis, who wanted to expand into country music. Then he moved to Capricorn Records in Nashville just when pop was coming into country with the Marshall Tucker Band.

One Friday afternoon, about 5 o'clock, Lyle Lovett walked into his office with a 15" master copy tape under his arm. He introduced himself and asked if Merlin would like to hear the tape. Merlin, who knew of Lovett but had never met him, fortunately had a tape player that could handle the master.

'I listened to it and said, "My God, this is incredible. Where did you cut this?"' Merlin recalled.

'And Lyle said, he said, "I cut it in Arizona with the house band from Mr Lucky's." And I asked him who wrote it. "I wrote it all," Lyle said. I started shopping it around town, playing it for people. I told Joe Galante that MCA was going to sign Lyle if he didn't get his butt on a plane to Texas. Joe was very interested in Lyle but he didn't get there quick enough. MCA was the first one to the trough on that. But a lot of times they didn't know what to do with Lyle.'

Merlin's professional duties began to crowd into our conversation. His secretary had questions about his upcoming trip to Washington DC at the request of the Department of Justice. Phone calls put on hold couldn't be held back any longer. People needed to talk to him, needed answers, direction, and advice.

'Look, meet me tomorrow at BMG, up on Music Row, for a showing of a rough cut of a film I had a hand in,' he said, clicking on his e-mail while simultaneously taking another call.

The next afternoon we met in a conference room at BMG, along with Tony Brown. Red wine was served in Waterford cut crystal goblets while we waited for the others to arrive. Tony and Merlin, old friends, caught up on news about the business. Mark Collie arrived, the man who nearly single-handedly, and at great personal cost, got the film made. He could not, despite his nearly heroic efforts, have made the film without Merlin.

The film, *Alive at Brushy Mountain*, is set in the Tennessee prison Brushy Mountain. Merlin arranged permission for Collie and his crew to perform in the prison and to film interviews with the inmates. Collie's agent, Ken Kragen, the super agent from Los Angeles, arrived, as did the cinematographer, and several marketing experts. The purpose of showing the rough draft was to get these people on board and coordinated for the release of Collie's record and the film.

We moved into the private theater and the show started.

Alive at Brushy Mountain is meant to be a vehicle for Collie, a songwriter and performer who bears an uncanny resemblance, in appearance and voice, to Johnny Cash. In fact, he once played Cash in a short film. But the full-length movie, scheduled for release in October 2002, is more than a documentary prison concert film. Collie did perform a concert inside the prison, with a guest appearance by Tim McGraw. But the heart of the film is about the music made by the prisoners and their personal stories. The prisoners, even the murderers, were shown as humans loved by others, who have aspirations for a better life, a better self. The audience, entertainment industry veterans who have seen and heard every heart tug the business can produce, were visibly moved, some to tears. Collie had spent two years of his life, lost his marriage, and most of his money to get the film made. Now he wanted support.

After the showing, Merlin and I went for a drink at the Vanderbilt Plaza, the favorite hotel for the big name acts who come to Nashville. For all his strong feelings about how country music and its fans have been betrayed by the corporate executives, Merlin finds more opportunity in country music, and the business of the music, now than at any time in the past ten years.

'Things have to change and change creates opportunity,' he said. 'I've met with every major label in the past six weeks, my friends. I like to talk to them. Everybody says it's a hard tough market place out there. If you're going for the great big one, the Faith Hill or Garth Brooks or Alan Jackson, if you're going on a massive scale as everyone's been programmed to do all these years, yeah, that will be a tough market. What the market is today, with the extended niches of entertainment, it's going to be much more difficult to have another Garth Brooks or

Faith Hill. I'm not saying we can't, it's just going to be harder because of the diversity of entertainment options, like 500 channels on cable television or the Internet or Digital Satellite radio.

'The corporate music business is definitely going to have to restructure their economics. I was talking to the marketing director at Capital last night about that. I said, "You don't have to spend more than $75,000 (£48,000) or $100,000 (£65,000) on an album. Technology is so good today that you can cut that stuff and it sounds incredible." Even an educated ear, and I have an educated ear, can't hear the difference between a $25,000 (£16,000) album and a $500,000 (£320,000) album. My friend T Bone Burnett did not spend an outlandish amount to produce *O Brother, Where Art Thou?* It cost $25,000 (£16,000) to produce that group Nickel Creek and they sold 600,000 albums.'

Then Merlin suggested something that is an anathema to any businessperson – shrink your market. That's right. Plan to deliberately reduce your market share. Forget the global reach. The unquestioned doctrine of bigger is better that has held sway over business, all business, for the past half decade has been proven fallible. Corporations that went on a merger binge, those would-be empire builders, are looking anachronistic. World-Com, DaimlerChrysler, AOL, Time Warner, United Airlines, JP Morgan, Chase, Arthur Anderson: 'all have got worse as they've got bigger, losing market share to smaller, more nimble competitors as they sag under their own weight,' to cite James Surowiecki writing in the *New Yorker*.

Up to a certain point, the more records you produce, the cheaper each record becomes, at least in theory. The price of CDs has not dropped despite the enormous increase in production of CDs. But a company doesn't need to be a behemoth to reap economics of scale. A 1998 study found, according to Surowiecki, that smaller banks were more efficient on a per-customer basis than their much larger rivals. They have lower expenses and higher profits. 'Smaller supermarkets are as cost-effective as larger ones,' wrote Surowiecki. 'As technology gets cheaper, the little people can afford it.'

The message is, think local, stay in your niche for a healthier and more profitable business. 'We're in a niche society,' Merlin said. 'The

Japanese proved that 30 years ago when they started beating up our car industry. But country, and the music business, didn't get it for a long time. Those huge monster stars in the music, I don't think we're going to see them any more. There might be a few who break out. But the labels are losing money and they don't have zillions of dollars to spend on an album. They have to learn how to identify and market and produce new acts in this smaller nichey society. Everybody got used to platinum and multi-platinum albums. You can make money on gold albums if you don't spend a million dollars putting it in the marketplace. The country music business has to shrink its market.

'I think that country is a big market and you can still make a lot of money in it. Let's cut to the chase. The majority of people in Nashville in the country music business are not holding hands and lighting candles and saying, "Let's do this for the fun of it." Hell, no. They want to make money. The chance to make money is there and has been for a long time. There is still a lot of money in the format and a lot of relationship with the audience. The industry has pretty well killed it off in recent years, but it's still there. It will come back. Thank God for Alan Jackson. I've never seen anybody misunderstand their customer as much as the music business. Not even relate to their customer. Not even go out and ask, "What do you think about it?"'

'So, Merlin, what do you see, musically, that might come from this opportunity of change?'

He reached for a handful of peanuts in the bowl on the table. 'Country gospel.'

Well, nail me to a cross. Talk about a niche market.

'Christian country music is the fastest-growing segment of the country music business. Christian country is just Christian gospel music, and it's got good musicians and good songs. [Merlin has won a Dove Award, the Christian music equivalent of a Grammy, for liner notes on a Christian album.] With some artists, it's hard to tell where the line is between country and country Christian music. That music has a lot of soul. It relates to the customer. It reflects what has always been there. It's still under the media's radar because it's not big enough yet, not splashy enough. It's related to O Brother, which is a little more bluegrass, but the lyrics content are shared and relate to the true country fan. It relates to the true country fan more than commercial country music does. Absolutely.

'It's a way of life. The Y generation is going to accept that. Not the X generation. They took life on their own terms, backed up in reverse, and ran over themselves. They wandered all over the road. The X-ers were rebellion and it wasn't an effective rebellion. They blew themselves out and continue to do that. Let's study the customer. The Ys are closer to the baby boomers. The Y generation has a better grip on themselves. They found out that the X's crap doesn't work. The Y generation is more loyal to their parents. They talk to their mom and dad and say how much they love them. They go to church, they are relating to God and Jesus and are saying no. They are more in touch, and I hate to use this word, with their soul.'

Merlin sat back with a smile, confident the industry would prove him right.

6 Women At Work

'It's like a velvet painting,' Amy said. Rain blowing in from Kentucky streaked the warm black night with silver highlights. 'The sound reminds me of a filigree of bluegrass notes plinking down, don't you think?'

'Write that down for a line in your and Willie's song.'

I was having a hard time seeing the street signs in the pouring rain. We were searching for The Station Inn because Amy wanted to hear Gail Davies, a Nashville songwriter, producer, and performer who is mentioned as a deserving candidate for the Country Music Hall of Fame. Davies was performing again after taking ten years off to raise her son, Chris Scruggs.

'No, it's too corny, like a velvet painting.' Amy peered out the windshield at the warehouses on each side of the street. 'Are you lost?'

'Probably.'

'Gail Davies has a line in one of her songs about the jagged edge of heartbreak. That line is my life. Livin' on the jagged edge of heartbreak makes me feel the most alive.'

'I get that same rush from a cheatin' heart, a cold, cold cheatin' heart. I like to hold my cold cheatin' heart in my hands, hold it out there for all to see, and then stuff if back into my chest. Makes me feel like a superior cowboy.'

Amy looked at me with one eyebrow cocked. 'You got potential, same as a cow has for hamburger.'

'What's that supposed to mean?'

'Don't eat with your mouth full.'

'What?'

'Don't take something alive and make it dead. Don't be crude by showing us what a mess you're making chewing on life. Being smart-Alecky is not the same as having a sense of humor. Any good country song knows the difference.'

'I think we're lost.' The warehouse district had given over to residential areas and gas stations. It didn't look like a place to find one of the best-known clubs in Nashville for country and bluegrass. Emmylou Harris has played The Station Inn. Sam Bush performs there.

'Told you so.'

I turned around in a gas station and started back toward downtown Nashville. 'It's supposed to be on 12th Avenue South.'

'You want to ask someone?'

I kept driving, trying to read the tiny green-and-white street signs. 'We just have to drive along 12th Avenue South and we'll find it.'

'We've already gone up and down 12th Avenue South and we didn't find it.'

'Then we'll do it again.'

'You're a huntin' dog with no sense of smell.'

On the third pass I found the club in a dip in the road across from an unlit warehouse. The low cinderblock building looked like a plumbing supply outlet. The small blue-and-white sign, The Station Inn, was difficult to spot. I had expected something more imposing, more self-announcing for a 'must call' stop for national and local 'real' country acts.

I pulled into the gravel parking lot and found a slot between two pickup trucks. 'We're gonna get wet.' Amy gripped the door handle. 'One. Two. Three.' She rolled out the door like a running back following a block through the line and dashed for the entrance. Wet is wet, I figured, and took a more leisurely approach.

Inside, the club was one room with a low ceiling painted black, including the exposed heating ducts. It was utilitarian, a bit scruffy around the edges, with no pretenses or posturing, so you're not distracted from the music on the stage. Neon beer signs added splashes of color but not a festive mood. The tables, all to accommodate four, were aligned edge-to-edge in long parallel lines. The chairs were a mishmash of molded plastic to slatted wood, remnants from garage sales. It was possible to touch the performers' boots without getting out of your chair, the tables were so close to the stage.

Amy glanced over the room for any familiar face. 'If you want something to drink, you have to go to the bar. You can sit here all night and not have a thing and nobody will bother you. It's a music place, not a drinking place or a pick-up place or a dance place.'

I went to the small bar in the back corner and asked the lady in a sweatshirt and jeans for two beers. She was so homey I almost called her Mom.

The band assembled on stage in bits and pieces; fiddler, banjo, mandolin, bass guitar, dobro, and rhythm guitar – a classic string country band. They dressed casual, as if wandering in from their living rooms, except the rhythm guitar player. He wore a white small-crowned 'city' Stetson, a crisp white shirt with red suspenders and a red tie. His long hair was neatly twisted into a single braid that splayed out at the end into a pompom, the kind that poodles wear on the tips of their tails. His goatee gave a rakish hint that the personality of a bon vivant and lover lay behind his stolid, unsmiling stage mask. During the set he played with one leg forward, knee bent, as if starting a cross-country race. He was a small, wiry man and played with great intensity, very muscular, like an athlete. He drove his shoulder hard into the down strokes, yet his picking was delicate and intricate.

When the band was tuned up and lined up, Gail strode to the center mic. She wore black jeans and a loose black cotton over-blouse. Her short hair, dark brown with blonde overlays, framed her shiny face and welcoming smile. She is 54 years old and doesn't hide it. She's been in the music business for 40 years, scored 18 hit records, toured with George Jones and Neil Young, and frequently performs in England and Scotland. Her song 'Someone is Looking for Someone Like You' has been translated into seven languages. George Jones told her that he wants it for his next album.

She launched right into song and didn't stop singing for the next three hours. She did her all-time hits, like 'Grandma's World', 'It's A Lovely, Lovely, World', and 'Blue Heartache', which drew from traditional country, soul, jazz, and bluegrass. She sang old standards and the duet she once performed with Ralph Stanley on the *Clinch Mountain Sweethearts* album. She field tested new songs for her next album. 'Now you all tell me if you like these songs,' she said. 'That will help me decide which ones to put on the album.'

A Nashville producer told me that when Gail steps into a studio to record, you had better be ready. She has such a natural voice and feel for the music that she lays down a song in one take. She has a pure country voice, strong and clear with no false twang.

She called her son up on stage for a couple of songs. 'This is Chris Scruggs.' Her voice brimmed with obvious pride. 'Grandson of.' She didn't have to supply Granddad Earl's name. The Scruggs family does not acknowledge Chris as one of them because Gail refused to marry the father, Gary, one of Earl's sons. Gail was very pregnant and the marriage was all set to go, until four days before the date. Then, according to Gail, Gary said he didn't want her performing after marriage and motherhood. Many people in the Nashville country music business have learned that you don't tell Gail Davies what to do or not do. She has a reputation for doing things her way. She called off the wedding and went her way.

'This is family night,' Gail announced as she introduced the bass guitarist, her younger husband Robert Price, an Englishman with a degree in jazz from the University of Leeds. Then she called her brother on stage, a well-seasoned singer/songwriter with credits on *Three Dog Night* and the *Nitty Gritty Dirt Band* albums. 'He walks with a limp because he has a steel plate in his hip,' Gail explained as Ron took his place for a duet. 'He fell out of Dolly Parton's upper-story window. You want to tell us that story, Ron?'

'I have a plate in my hip,' he replied laconically.

'At least you got it by falling out of the window, not in. That way you had already been there.'

The full, and more prosaic, story is that he was washing Dolly's windows at her sister Rachel's request. The ladder slipped and he fell. At the hospital he was just another guy with a broken hip until Rachel, who closely resembles Dolly, came for a two-hour visit behind closed doors. The nurses, mistaking the sisters, elevated Ron's status from patient to celebrity.

★

Gail Davies and her two brothers grew up in Broken Bow, Oklahoma. Their mother had been loved, and left, by a guitar player on the Louisiana Hayride, a radio show that once rivaled the Grand Ole Opry. The family was so poor that dinner was often peanut butter mixed with syrup and served on a cold biscuit. The mother tailored flour sacks into Gail's dresses. Gail cut her professional music teeth in Los Angeles as a background singer at A&M records. She sang behind Joni Mitchell on *Court & Sparks*, and with Stephen Bishop and Hoyt Axton. The studio engineer, Henry Lewy, seeing her interest in producing, taught her how to work in the studio. She had such an educated ear that she was allowed to sit in on a John Lennon session.

She moved to Nashville in 1975 when, as she put it when we met later, 'women were living in the music world Dark Ages. They didn't have much say in the sessions. They were barefoot, pregnant, and in the vocal booth. They were never behind the board. A guy from New York who was very unpleasant and difficult to work with produced my first album. He would take my guitar away from me and start playing my songs for the band. I protested. I had written the songs and I knew how they were to be played. He said that the band didn't want a woman telling them what to do. "Fine," I said. "If that's the case, these are not the players I want on my sessions." That's when I decided to start producing.'

Gail Davies says that she was the first female record producer in country music and there is no reason to dispute her claim. 'I had to stand up to a couple of guys in this town and back them down so they hate me. It's a popular theme to trash me here. It's a fish that turned into a whale story. It used to break my heart but I think it's funny now. Sometimes it still pisses me off but it also strengthens my resolve,' she told me over coffee at Fidos, a couple of days after the gig.

Fidos is one of several anti-Starbucks coffee houses around Nashville. Located a block from Vanderbilt University, it's a hangout for the artistically inclined, students, and the intellectually curious. The tables are salvaged veterans, as the scars and gouges testify, and the chairs are found objects. The floor has an incline, which separates the upper wood from the lower cement. The atmosphere encourages the patrons to act naturally. Two guys with superb biceps and impressive dreadlocks quoted their poetry to each other; young female students with exposed navels quizzed each other for a biology exam; writerly looking fellows in slouch hats worked on laptops; and there were the indefinable ones who looked as if they had missed two nights' sleep. They stared out of the window as if hoping to remember why.

Gail has an issue, to put it mildly, with how the male Nashville music establishment manipulates the music and the artists. She knows both sides of the coin in her capacity as performer and producer. The Nashville session musicians gave her problems when she did her second album, so she called her rock 'n' roll pals in Los Angeles: Leland Skalar, Billy Payne, and band members for James Taylor, Phil Collins, Little Feat, Journey, and Steely Dan.

She has not endeared herself to Nashville's corporate music powers by challenging their pronouncements. When her second album didn't sell as expected, the label's (Warner Bros) executives suggested that she get a new producer. She was the producer. Four of the songs on the album made it to the top ten. The producer did just fine, she told them. Perhaps you need a new sales team.

'As a producer, I don't try to steer anything toward radio,' Gail said. When she talks, she looks the person straight in the eye, demanding their attention. 'I think radio sucks.' The country music industry (the music industry as a whole) has a vampire/victim relationship with commercial radio. Who is sucking on whose vital fluids is a perpetual debate, but music executives willingly expose their necks. It's the price of doing successful business, they say.

'I don't make music to be a filler in between radio advertisements. I try to bring out the best of what the artist has to offer. The corporate music, they want to copy what is hot at the moment. That's their offering to radio. When the Judds came out, everybody started signing girl duos. That's another problem here in Nashville, the inability to appreciate uniqueness and make that work.

'You have to be able to hear somebody and know if they are good or not, regardless of whether they have a hit record or not, or a skinny butt or not, or an image consultant or not. To me, one of the success stories of the year is Leslie Satcher. She wrote a great song, 'Box Letters from Old Mexico'. A lot of people have recorded her stuff. She's beautiful but a bit heavy, not the popular in-demand image of a skinny waif. It's amazing that she got a deal. Today, Patsy Cline could not get a record deal. She was too overweight, too homely, and too outspoken.'

When Gail was a staff producer at Liberty Records, part of Capital Records, she worked with the then 15-year-old Mandy Barnett, now an established star who appears on the Grand Ole Opry. The experience is one reason Gail is an independent producer. The inexperienced Barnett didn't have a style, so the record company went searching for one to fit her.

'Jimmie Bowen, then the head of the label, kept saying, "Find me a hit. Find me a hit,"' Gail recalled. 'Who knows what a hit is? If he knew that, he'd be making hits every day. Eventually, Mandy evolved into her style, which is heavy ballads, torch standards, but then we were trying to find her material. We recorded some Gretchen Peters songs when she was just an up-and-coming writer and hadn't had any big hits yet. To me, the biggest problems in country music today are the record producers. They're not encouraging individuality and uniqueness with young performers, or helping them find their own style. The clones are easier to work with, to mold.

'It's all gotten so corporate that it's almost impossible to do a major album and keep individuality. Dwight Yoakam is one of the few who have done it but he also keeps his distance from Nashville by being based out of Bakersfield, California. In Nashville today, artists are like employees of the record label. If they piss off the record company, they're gone because there are thousands of others to take their place. The value of the individuality of the artist has diminished. That is subversion of the art, which is why we have the watered-down version of country music today.

'Waylon Jennings once said, "Nashville is hard on the living, but they love the dead." Once you're dead, the record companies can work with you. You are manageable. They can take your catalog and work with it. Once you're dead, the labels can package the artist's music any way they want.

'Every artist that lies down and says, "I'll do whatever you want me to do. Go ahead, screw me over, rip me off, steal my publishing, don't pay me royalties," every time they do that, they make it impossible for any of the other artists. It's like crossing the picket line. The Dixie Chicks sued their record label for money due. They stood up and said, "We're not going to take it," and other artists put them down for doing it. I'm damn proud of them.'

Gail's recent project is an independently produced tribute album to Webb Pierce, *Caught In The Webb*. She did the critically acclaimed album for love of country music, as did the performers, including George Jones, Willie Nelson, Emmylou Harris, Dwight Yoakam, RB-549, Allison Moorer, Matt King, Charley Pride, Kevin Welch, Dale Watson, and Mandy Barnett. Proceeds from the CD go to the Minnie Pearl Cancer Foundation and the Country Music Hall of Fame and Museum.

As we finished our coffees, Gail said, 'Some say that it's a lot better for women in this town. But show me how many women producers there are in the top 100 *Billboard* country charts, other than Alison Krauss, who is brilliant. There's just no room for women in this town unless they are willing to put on a gingham dress and say, "Yes, sir, I'm so happy to be here and you're so big and strong." I want to be seen as a human being first, a woman second, and a Caucasian last.'

Women have always had to fight for respect in the country music business. In the early years, the unspoken rule was that a male had to front groups with women players. In the Carter Family, Sara and Maybelle were acknowledged as better musicians than AP, especially his wife Sara, but he had to be the stage patriarch. The fundamental Southern Christian audiences wanted reassurance that a man controlled the show, not independent, self-assured women. Such women would be bad role models for the women kept on the farm. The Carter Family's handbills pointedly advertised that their program was 'morally good' and suitable for family entertainment. When Rachel Veach joined Roy Acuff and His Smoky Mountain Boys and Girls in the 1940s, the mandolin player, Beecher Kirby, took on the role of Rachel's on-stage 'Bashful Brother Oswald'.

Women have always had a principal role in country music: in the songs they were beaten, scorned, jilted, betrayed, and deserted. Men were the subjects and women were the objects. If a woman caused pain in the heart of a man, then she was mean and cruel and he the loving victim. If a woman left or betrayed a man, she was a bitch who deserved what she got, which sometimes meant justifiable murder. About the only positive female image in those old ballads were women as little girls or saintly old mothers, in other words, powerless females.

Women were painted in pastels of romantic and domestic sentiment from the days of Old English ballads, a source of early Appalachian country music. The good, true, all-enduring woman remains a popular image in the genre. In the early 1800s, as the Industrial Revolution changed social and cultural values, this sentimental portrayal reflected male society's passing from the remembered rural idyll of independent farmers to the regimentation of the factory and the machine. In the early 2000s, the sentimental portrayal of women and the rural idyll is nostalgia. The themes of nostalgia, domesticity, and home have always been, and remain, central to country music. Many of today's country songs speak of a simpler, more dignified and fulfilling rural place that has been paved over by suburbia.

But the war of the sexes has also been an old and enduring theme in country music. Porter Wagoner and Dolly Parton, during their long association, used the musical male-female give-and-take found in folk songs, such as 'No Sir, Yes Sir', and 'Reuben, Reuben'. Johnny Cash and June Carter Cash, and Conway Twitty and Loretta Lynn also recorded such duets, although such records fell out of favor in the 1980s. The female used the songs as a prop for women to challenge male supremacy and exert her own prerogatives. Now, no such prop is necessary. Gail Davies is an example of the unapologetic female in the country music business, as are The Dixie Chicks, Martina McBride, Joy Lynn White, Lucinda Williams, and scores of others.

But the strong female in country music has always been cut at the knees by the inevitable addendum, 'But you know, she had a powerful man behind her. She couldn't have done it without him.' Which was often true. The men did the business deals because the men running the music business wouldn't deal with the women. It just wasn't done and that was largely accepted on both sides. Loretta Lynn made a bold declaration for women's sexual independence with her song 'The Pill', but she wouldn't have been anything without her husband pushing her career, the snipes say.

Dolly Parton was given her big break by Porter Wagoner and rode his coat-tails for years, the snipes say. But Dolly finally realized that she was more important to Wagoner's career than he was to hers. When she declared her independence and struck off on her own, Wagoner didn't talk to her for years. Tammy Wynette had George Jones to open doors, so say her detractors, with George leading that choir. When their marriage broke up, George had Tammy so convinced that she had no career without him that she didn't even try, until friends convinced her to go solo. And she launched a successful career.

People in Nashville say that Reba McEntire, probably the most successful woman currently in country music, couldn't have done it without her first husband, Charlie Battles, paving the way. But her career really took off after she divorced Charlie. Her current husband, Narvel Blackstock, runs the day-to-day business of her Starstruck Enterprises, founded in 1988, that encompasses three music publishing companies, real estate holdings, a publicity agency, a concert booking and promotion agency, a management company, a construction company, and other entertainment offshoots. Blackstock has never claimed to be the engine of his wife's success.

Kacey Jones is another of the rare female producers and head of a record label in Nashville. She is a great admirer of Gail Davies. 'I have a lot of respect for her for being a female producer in this town when nobody else was. She was competing in the same arena with all those hairy-legged men. I am in a similar boat. There are very few female producers in Nashville. The hairy-legged men like it that way. "Oh, God, don't let the women in." I didn't feel prejudice as a female artist until I became a producer. But, it must be said, there have been some male producers in this town that have been very complimentary to me.'

Kacey's albums as a recording artist include *Men Are Some of My Favorite People* (Curb Music), *Ethel and The Shameless Hussies* (MCA), and *Never Wear Panties to a Party* on IGO (Irritating Gentile Optimist), her own label. She does not wear gingham dresses. Her latest project as a producer was *Pearls in the Snow, The Songs of Kinky Friedman*, on her Kinkajou Records. Kinky Friedman and the Texas Jewboys rode the outlaw trail in the 1960s with Waylon Jennings and Willie Nelson. He has since become a novelist of mystery stories, whose main character is a Kinky derivative. He is also a terrific, but underrated, songwriter. Willie Nelson, Dwight Yoakam, Delbert McClinton, Marty Stuart, Lyle Lovett, Tom Waits, Asleep At The Wheel, the Geezinslaw Brothers, a duo from Austin, Chuck E Weiss, Guy Clark, and Lee Roy Parnell appear on the CD to pay respect and honor to Kinky.

Getting a record produced can be difficult enough for a woman, but then she must deal with distributors. 'The bullshit starts to rise when dealing with distributors,' is Kacey's succinct summary. A New York distributor refused to pay her for records sold. She called everyone in the company for a year to collect the money and was always passed from one voicemail to the next. One day, a male friend was in the office. 'Tom,' she said, 'I'm going to call these people again and pretend to be a secretary. When the right person gets on the phone, I want you to say, "This is Kinky Friedman calling for Scott Cohen. Then I'll take over."' When the elusive proper male took the call, Kacey told him that if she didn't have the money within 24 hours, she'd sue him. He made excuses and still didn't send the money. So she put a collection agency on him and got paid.

'It's very hard for an indie [independent] label to get distributed and not get screwed,' Kacey said. 'I'm going to court in June in an attempt to settle a dispute with a distributor that has owed Kinkajou Records over $100,000 (£65,000) since 1999. In the past three years, I've had to threaten two other indie distributors with legal action and/or a collection agency. They all promise not to screw you, so you ship 'em your product, they sell it, they put the money in their pocket, and then you spend the next year and a half trying to collect from them. It's a time-consuming, frustrating pain in the ass. Some of these crooks go so far as to file bankruptcy, then next thing you know, three months later, they've opened shop again under a new name. Same thieves, different shingle.'

Is the Nashville country music industry really as chauvinistic as the women claim? I went after a third and fourth opinion. Susan Nadler and

Evelyn Shriver own, with George Jones, Bandit Records. Susan went from prison in Mexico to senior vice president at Times/Warner before taking the helm of Bandit. Evelyn left her public relations firm in New York and founded the most successful PR company in Nashville. Randy Travis was her first client. She represented the top country acts in town from 1986–92.

'Nashville is basically a good ol' boy redneck town regardless of what year we're in,' Evelyn said. The two women are plain-talking straight-shooters. We sat in Susan's office as they told me their personal experiences as the female heads of a Nashville record label.

'It's really difficult for women in Nashville,' added Susan. 'The reason being that it's a man's town, just like New York is pretty much a man's town in the music business. You have your Michelle Anthony and Sylvia Rhone, those are the standout women in the music business, although they are in the pop music industry. Women in Nashville really can't get past the all-male network. It's a lot like the movie business in LA. You have Sherry Lansing and a few women in positions of power, but typically it's a guys thing.'

'With all the female acts I represented,' Evelyn said, 'the record companies had no huge aspirations for them. They weren't perceived as ever being able to headline the shows. They weren't perceived as record sellers. The labels were happy if a girl could sell 100,000 units and open for George Strait. That was as far as the ambitions went. Eventually what happened was that the women artists were left to their own devices. They were never a priority and everything here comes down to whether the artist is a priority. If you are, the labels put money behind you. You, too, can be a superstar.

'The labels put out female singers' records because the male headliner had to have a female opening act. Then, lo and behold, women started making really good music. They started coming into their own as artists. They were doing far more significant material than most of the male acts during the '80s big explosion. Trisha Yearwood, Lorrie Morgan, Wynonna Judd and her mother Naomi, Reba McEntire – these women become headliners. They busted their ass in terms of their live shows.

'At that time, any halfway decent looking guy who could wear a hat and tight pants and sing in a traditional country voice was good enough. The music suffered. It became plastic, hollow country music. The main male headliners stood on stage strumming a guitar. The women had dancers and costume changes and hired production people to put on ten times the show that the guys did. Reba caught a lot of flak for doing that but it didn't matter. Her fans loved her.

'By that time, the trend of the moment was away from the drinkin' and cheatin' songs. That was embarrassing for Nashville to have that as the heritage of country music. They didn't want honky-tonk, or cheatin' songs, or the drinkin' songs. So they constantly tinkered with the plastic cowboys they had put together. We are still experiencing that particular moment in country music. The labels left the women alone and the women started making some pretty decent music. They were very good artists. The women jumped out in the forefront, which caught everyone by surprise. All of a sudden, they were selling millions of records and headlining.'

'But you have no females running a label,' Susan joined in. 'You have only one female manager who is really successful, Nancy Russell who manages Alan Jackson and Trisha Yearwood. Evelyn and I were the first women ever to run a label and we were closed out. There's no female booking agents, no female labels. Men just don't want the competition from women. They thought it was not a woman's field and that women should stay out of it.

'That attitude still predominates. The biggest artists are predominately men. The women don't make as much money on the road. They don't make as much money with the concessions. Talk to Shania or Faith and they'll tell you. [Both were unavailable for interviews.]

'If you're a woman and you're successful, you're called a bitch. If you're a man, you're called successful. I'm not a feminist. I'm not here with sour grapes. I'm delighted to be a woman. Always have been, always will be. Love men. But this culture has not evolved that much. Women are now realizing that we can't have it all, despite the promises. A man can – career, family, the support to back him up at home and in the work place.'

Susan and Evelyn were not novices in the record business when they started Bandit. Susan was managing Lorrie Morgan, who was selling platinum at the time. Sylvia Rhone, the CEO of Electra, a Fortune 500 music company, wanted to change the management at Asylum Records, a branch of Electra. She was convinced that Susan and Evelyn were right for the job. Susan didn't want to work for a corporation but was persuaded to give it a try. Ten days after quitting their jobs, Susan and Evelyn were running Asylum Records.

Rhone's insight and faith paid off. Asylum was in big debt but within the first year Susan and Evelyn changed the red into black for a million-dollar (£650,000) profit and won two Grammys for the label – one for *Cold Hard Truth* with George Jones and the other for *Trio II* with Emmylou Harris, Linda Ronstadt, and Dolly Parton.

Warner Brothers absorbed Asylum and essentially closed down the label. Asylum was stripped of its staff and Asylum artists were not given priority resources. Susan and Evelyn basically resigned. George Jones wanted to keep the Susan-Evelyn-George team together. Asylum had sold 800,000 copies of his album and he got a royalty check for the first time in 25 years. So he offered to finance a fourth ownership in a new record company, with Susan and Evelyn in charge.

A joint venture was formed with BMG and with Joe Galante, then head of Artista/RCA. Although undercapitalized, the newly minted Bandit Records produced an album, *The Rock*. The single off the album, a duet with George Jones and Garth Brooks, had the unfortunate timing of being released when the September 11 World Trade Center attack sucked the wind out of all other events. Bandit rolled with the punch and came out with a George Jones gospel album. Raul Malo, formerly the lead singer with the Mavericks, is producing a Spanish children's album for the label. But Susan and Evelyn are not naïve about the reality of women in the music business. They are diversifying by developing opportunities with HD Ready, a high-definition television company. They are repositioning Bandit to be principally an industry-ordination-talent acquisition company.

Susan acknowledges that the partnership with George Jones and Joe Galante flies in the face of her opinion about the male Nashville music business. 'Joe Galante is a friend and Joe is smart,' she said. 'He knows that George Jones is one of the last remaining icons in country music. Joe is a fabulous man and I appreciate everything he did for us. We brought in the talent and they made the album, and they paid for everything. But when you do a joint venture, unless you have a multi-million selling album, you don't make that much. The joint venture didn't give us the autonomy we needed. We have to investigate our own avenues.'

Historically, many of the country artists who have an enduring reputation are females, Evelyn pointed out: Tammy Wynette, Loretta Lynn, Patsy Cline, Kitty Wells. Historically, they are the heart of country music.

'Susan and I have worked with a lot of these women, particularly Tammy Wynette,' Evelyn said. 'She had always been an opening act and not the headliner, even though she far surpassed the men she opened for, even when she married George Jones. She was imbued with the mentality that she could never be a headliner. When she and George divorced, she believed that she could not go on in the business because she had never fronted a show. But she stepped out there and became a huge superstar, a bigger star than George Jones.'

'Contemporarily, the biggest female stars are Shania Twain, The Dixie Chicks, and Faith Hill,' Susan added. 'Shania might be the most powerful because she has her own publishing. I really don't believe that Mutt Lange [her husband and producer and the producer of AC/DC] is the power of Shania. I think that Shania is a very smart, self-possessed woman. If Mutt could have done it on his own, he did not have to marry her to have those songs come out. Shania was a very big component and her input helped Mutt enormously. I think Shania is very very talented. She has her finger on the pulse of what young women internationally follow.

'Reba is a strong and savvy businessperson in this town. She knows the market and, as a performer, is carrying the whole ball-and-chain of her organization. Reba came close to the fate that has befallen Wynonna. Wynonna has R&Bed herself right out of the country format and R&B hasn't embraced her. She has no format now. She can't get played on country radio. Reba came close to doing that by becoming too pop. Faith might have 'popped' herself out of country, too. But Reba backed up and then did a successful Broadway show. That took the onus off of being too pop. Because of her Broadway success, Nashville had something to be proud of that was happening in New York. The Nashville music industry flocked to embrace her. They conveniently forgot that they drove her out of Nashville.

'And no one doubts the business acumen of Dolly Parton. She is one very smart blonde.'

7 Willie's Coming To Town

I went to Tootsie's to find Jill King. I wondered about her sanity. What would possess any woman to walk willingly into the lion's den of the Nashville country music industry – and pay for the mauling out of her own pocket. Jill had estimated that her planned showcase might cost $2,000 (£1,300) to $4,000 (£2,600). Was the woman a megalomaniac or merely optimistic? With dream chasers, it's a fine line between self-delusion and self-confidence.

Jill hadn't arrived for her set but the crew was at our usual table.

'Howdy, Hank.' He tipped his hat.

'Amy.' I hadn't seen her since our foray to hear Gail Davies. She flashed me a smile. I became aware for the first time that she was pretty, in a worn way. The crow's feet around her eyes became laugh crinkles when she smiled. She had done something with her dirty dishwater blonde hair, put a wave in it and feathered in some highlights.

'Willie. How's the song coming along?' He seemed more lively in the eyes than usual and he sat up straighter.

'Have you heard?' he asked. I swear to God he seemed on the verge of excitement, shifting from cheek to cheek in his chair. Either that or he had to take a piss.

'Heard what?'

'Willie's coming.'

Willie Nelson was scheduled to play the Ryman Auditorium and the Grand Ole Opry in a couple of weeks, with special guest Keith Richards. It had been all over the papers, so what's the news? *The Nashville Tennessean* was running a contest for free concert tickets to whoever wrote the best verse based on Willie's song 'To All the Girls I've Loved Before'. One reader, Will Wright, had submitted:

Taxman knocking on your door
For assets you can't hide off-shore.
IRS came along, even sold off Willie's bong.
Better than living in cell block four.

Our Willie leaned toward me so we couldn't be overheard, not that anyone was listening. 'Willie's coming here,' he whispered. 'To Tootsie's. A special show in the upper back room after the Ryman. I got it from a good source. Only those in the know will get in.'

'How did you get in the know,' I whispered back.

'Wanda.'

'Wanda?'

'Wanda. She's knows Willie. There are pictures of her and Willie on the wall in the upper back room. She told me that Willie has done it before, sneaked in a surprise show here as homage to his days at Tootsie's. Wanda said he might do it again.'

'Who is Wanda?'

'She's up there in the back room with Conrad. Come on, I'll introduce you.'

He led the way up the six wooden stairs. Whereas the downstairs room was long and skinny, with the bar taking up nearly half of one side, the upper room was a box. The bar was next to the door and a stage was at the far end. The entire wall behind the stage could be lifted up, like a garage door, to facilitate getting equipment from a band's van in the alley onto the stage. The room was furnished for standing room only, not sitting. Our Willie guided me to the one booth where two people were sitting and made the introductions.

Wanda was Wanda Lohman, the first waitress Tootsie had hired when she took over the bar. Conrad was Conrad Preice, a songwriter who has made Tootsie's his second home since he arrived in Nashville in 1967. Conrad's song 'Back On My Night Again' was recorded by Ronnie Milsap and went to number one. Charlie Pride, Johnny Cash, and Hank

Williams Jr have recorded his songs. Conrad's dark mustache was flecked with white. He smiled a great deal and was robust and energetic. His whole presence said, 'I'm so darn glad to be alive and here with you I could burst out in song,' which I thought he was going to do a couple of times during our conversation.

Wanda had dyed champagne-blonde hair attractively styled in soft waves. She was missing a few teeth and her face sagged, but her once youthful beauty could still be seen. Wanda filled me in on some history of Tootsie's. Tootsie's real name was Hattie Louise Tatum born August 23, 1915, although no one, not even Tootsie, was sure of the exact date. She moved to Nashville in 1941 from Hohenwald, Tennessee. She was a good-hearted soul, always willing to lend a helping hand to any songwriter down on his or her luck.

'She was the kind of person who really had feelings for the musicians,' Wanda said of her friend. 'People here that she knew were hungry or whatever, she'd slip $5 [£3] in their pocket or run a tab for them. The guys over at the Opry, they'd come over and pay off that debt once a year so she wouldn't lose any money. When Tootsie died [February 18, 1978], Tom T Hall, that famous songwriter, you know, he came by and paid off the tab, about $800 [£500]. He said, "Miss Tootsie's gone and I don't want to owe her nothing." He took that cigar box with all the tabs in it and he laughed and he said, "You know what I'm going to do with it? I'm going to frame them and anybody who comes in I'm going to say, Look what I got."'

The bar had originally been named Mom's, after the elderly owner/operator. When Mom decided to retire, Tootsie and her husband, Jeff Bess, bought it in 1960. They owned a couple of other bars and Jeff had a radio show called Big Jeff and the Radio Playboys. Tootsie was a singer/comedian with the band. One of the bars they owned was Ship Ahoy, out on Franklin, that Wanda frequented because she loved country music. The two women became friends. When Tootsie and Jeff divorced, Tootsie took Mom's as part of the settlement and offered Wanda a job.

Tootsie asked a painter to redo the bar's front. He painted the whole façade orchid blue/purple, her favorite color, so the bar became Tootsie's Orchid Lounge.

'The place hasn't changed a real lot since we took it over in the 1960s,' Wanda said in her very Southern rural drawl. 'Then, downstairs there were three or four booths along the wall where the tables are now. There weren't many pictures on the walls back then. When Tootsie took over, the Opry stars started bringing their pictures and she put them up on the walls. There was a jukebox here in the upper room, where the stage is now. Otherwise, the place looks about the same.

'When Tootsie took over, if a young artist wanted to get up and sing, we let him or her sing two or three songs. When Tootsie first started a band upstairs here, she said, "I don't care what they look like or what you think they sound like. If they want to sing, let 'em do what they want. If they're not good, be nice and get them down." That way it won't hurt their feelings and they'd give her free publicity wherever they went. Tootsie said, "You don't know what you're going to hear." Look at Willie. This is where Willie got started in Nashville as a singer and songwriter.'

I asked her if was true that Willie might do a surprise performance when he was in town.

'He's done it before. Once, when he was in town for the Country Music Awards, he called Tootsie that Friday night and told her to fire her band for a couple hours because he was going to bring his whole band down. She came up to this room and told the band to go away for two hours. So Willie came and set up. Tootsie told me not to let anyone in the back door, that one there going out to the alley. This old drunk got in somehow and he was yelling, "Willie, Willie, sing this. Sing that."

'I said, "Shut your mouth. He'll sing everything he knows before he gets down."

'And Willie stood there for two hours and sang straight. When he got through, he gave all the fired band $100 [£65] and he gave us waitresses $100 [£65] each.

'He said, "We've taken y'all jobs tonight."

'We said, "Come back any time."'

Wanda laughed, her eyes bright with the remembering. 'I met Jim Reeves right here in this room. Dated him for three years. He's still my buddy. I wish he hadn't died.'

I asked about the story of Willie getting drunk one night at Tootsie's and becoming so despondent that he went out and laid down in Lower Broadway, hoping a car would run over him and kill him.

'Yeah,' Wanda said. 'He was drinkin'. He got drunk. He told me he was going to kill himself. "They don't like the way I dress or sing here in Nashville so I'm goin' to kill myself," he said.'

Back then, Willie wore suits with white shirts and ties. He had an IBM haircut, trimmed with a neat part on one side. He was a responsible family man with a wife and three small children to support. In the late 1950s, before he came to Nashville, he had been a Sunday school teacher at the Fort Worth Metropolitan Baptist Church. He was no outlaw, or perhaps a suppressed outlaw. Even while teaching the Lord's way on Sunday morning, he played the bars at night learning his chops as a songwriter and singer – and maybe earning a little money. The church's preacher thought that a bar musician was a bad image for Willie's young flock. Willie was given an ultimatum: Stop playing in the beer joints or quit teaching Sunday school. In Nashville, Willie never taught Sunday school.

When he lived in Houston, he taught kids to play the guitar at the Buskirk School of Guitar, while picking up licks and chords himself from the owner, Paul Buskirk. At night he played the club circuit. He chronicled this crazy, hard-on-the-family life in the song 'The Night Life', which he sold to Buskirk for $150 (£100). He needed food for the children and gas for the car. Back then, he wasn't so much the iconoclast wearing outlaw colors. He was a working man, a working artist, trying to get by and do right.

'So Willie went and laid down in the middle of Broadway,' Wanda said, picking up the story. 'My husband Louie was up here in this room working the bar. Tootsie told him to get Willie out of the street. So he did and slung him in that doorway over there leading up to the office.' She gestured to the stairs tucked away in a back corner. Kris Kristofferson, when he was a poor down-and-out Nashville songwriter, slept on the office floor and on hot summer nights moved out onto the roof.

'I said, "Willie, you don't want to kill yourself."'

'He says, "Yeah, they don't like the way I sing here in Nashville."'

'Louie said, "Just straighten up. You're drunk." And so he did. A couple of years later, me and my husband walked in and Willie and Kristofferson were standing at the end of the bar drinking.

'Willie said, "I'm sure glad this man saved my life." We all drank that night but we didn't go and lie outside in the street.'

In his book, *Willie: An Autobiography*, with Bud Shrake, Willie wrote of the incident: 'I got so drunk and discouraged that I laid down in the street in the snow late at night in front of Tootsie's and waited for a car to come along and run over me... I knew I could become broke and desperate again in the time it takes to snap your fingers. Anybody who went through the Great Depression – when broke and desperate described nearly the whole country and certainly the farm folks of Central Texas – grew up knowing financial security is an illusion.'

Tootsie's became a favorite hangout for songwriters because performers from the Grand Ole Opry, then located in the Ryman Auditorium across the back alley, would nip over between acts for refreshment on Friday and Saturday nights. 'We songwriters found out that the singers were here so we all came down and said, 'Hey, we've got a song for you.' We'd leave them tapes or play them a song,' Conrad joined in. 'The back door of the Ryman is just across the alley there from the back door here. So they could sneak over here real quick, have a couple beers, and run back over and sing their songs. The show was in different segments, like it is today, so they knew when they had to go back on.

'It was right out that back door where Loretta Lynn hit her husband, Mooney, and a girl with her pocketbook. That was back in 1966. She finally got tired to women flirting with her man, and him flirting back. That's where she got the line, "If you want to keep your arm, get your hand off my man." That's what she told that girl. Loretta is not big, maybe a bit over five foot [1m 52cm], and petite. But she's fiery. She'd stand up and fight for what she thought was right. In many ways, she was country music's first recognized political voice.'

Conrad arrived in Nashville the classic way – by bus. He was a rock 'n' roller in Texas when he was offered a piano gig in Cherry Point, North Carolina. He started driving but his clutch gave out at his mom's place in Oak Ridge, 200 miles [320km] from Nashville. He took a Greyhound the rest the way in to meet the band. The old bus station was, and the new station is, a few blocks from Tootsie's, the only place he knew about in Nashville. He hauled his suitcase the three blocks and sat down to hear Jack Greene sing his number one song at the time. Greene had just come from performing that night at the Grand Ole Opry. After his song, he walked across the street to do the Midnight Jamboree at the Ernest Tubb's Record shop, which is still there. Conrad trailed after Greene and met the man who wrote Greene's hit song. He was hooked.

'They say that anyone who rides the Greyhound bus here is destined to make it,' Conrad said with a big smile. 'Nashville has been good to me.'

The nostalgic heyday of the singer/songwriter era at Tootsie's was in the early '60s, when Harlan Howard (died March 3, 2002, at the age of 74), Kris Kristoferrson, Willie Nelson, Hank Cochran, Faron Young, Webb Pierce, Tom T Hall, Terri Clark, Eric Heatherly, Ray Price, and Roger Miller made the bar their workroom and clubhouse. Waylon Jennings, Hank Williams Sr, Patsy Cline, Mel Tillis, Jack Greene, Del Reeves, Roy Acuff, Jim Reeves, and Charlie Pride were among the famous that drank at the bar. Kristofferson, a 1958 Rhodes Scholar, came to Nashville on his way to join the faculty at West Point as an English teacher. He grew up the son of an Army Air Corps officer and he himself was an Army helicopter pilot who played in local clubs on the side. The army seemed to be his career path, until that fateful two-week vacation in Nashville. He must have had an epiphanic moment for he resigned his army commission and got a job as a janitor at a record company. He let his hair go from military shaven to long-hair hippie. He grew a beard and wore scruffy clothes. For three years his music career went nowhere. A turtle riding a train standing still was going faster than Kristofferson's career. It got so bad that he left Nashville and signed on as a helicopter pilot for a Texas oil exploration company.

One day, while sitting in his helicopter between flights along the Gulf Coast, he read an interview with Frank Sinatra. Sinatra bemoaned that if he didn't have a woman with him for a night, he'd take a bottle to bed to help him through the long and lonely hours. Inspired by Sinatra's plight, Kristofferson wrote his big break-out song while sitting in the helicopter's cockpit, 'Help Me Make It Through the Night'. The song, recorded by Sammi Smith in 1970, went to number one and won the Country Music Association's Single of the Year in 1971.

But that's ahead of the story. Kristofferson's pal, Roger Miller, brought him back to Nashville when he recorded 'Me and Bobby McGee', later made famous by Janis Joplin. Still, Kristofferson wasn't high rolling and Willie wasn't doing any better.

'Willie would sing here, just as the unknowns do now,' said Conrad, 'and go around pitching his songs. He used to joke that after playing his songs for publishers, he should hold up a sign that said, "What else you got?" That would save the publishers the trouble of asking, in other words, passing on his songs. He pitched his song, 'Hello, Walls' to Faron Young right here in Tootsie's. The singer Hank Cochran heard Willie playing here and took him down to Pamper Music, a publishing company where Hank worked. He told the honchos at Pamper, "Give him half my weekly salary if necessary because I think this guy's got something." Hank and Willie started writing together and Hank is credited with helping him get noticed by the right people. By 1963, Willie had hit it big as a songwriter.'

But the relationship between Willie and the Nashville music establishment remained uneasy, like two dogs not sure of each other. Willie would write only the type of songs that appealed to him, and that could range anywhere from jazz to swing to ballads to honky-tonk. The record executives wanted predictable hits on a regular basis. When Willie's Nashville house burned down, he took it as a sign to move back to Texas.

Before we left the upper room, Wanda took me along the photo-crammed walls, pointing to pictures of herself with Willie. Then she led me over to the bar. 'That one,' she said. 'That's Hank on his wedding day.' In a simple black frame was a picture of Hank Williams Sr, in a conservative suit, standing next to his new bride, Audrey, in a black-and-white dotted dress.

Back downstairs, Jill King had finished her set. I bought her a Diet Pepsi and asked how her plan to finance her showcase was going. 'Fine,' she said. 'My daddy wants to put up some money. And pay for a video. He thinks that if his little girl gets on Country Music Television she's got it made. I told him, "Whoa, you don't know the scope of that bill. Let's just think about the showcase." He's comin' in next week to talk details and see the banker. I've got to get a budget ready.'

Jill sounded a bit anxious, perhaps not as happy as she could be about her daddy opening his wallet for his daughter. The showcase was, I found out, as much about the family and healing as it was about her music career.

The past six years have been a standoff between Jill and her parents. They have hardly been able to speak to each other. While she attended Vanderbilt, they wanted her to come home every weekend, sometimes even midweek. If she didn't make the trip, they came to see her. Her parents' demands were intrusive as she tried to establish, for the first time, a life of her own. She was meeting new people, was in the university's Broadway revue troupe, and was working hard on her double major. Her world was blooming.

'I was able to explore the world on my own terms with the lessons Mom and Daddy taught me,' Jill said. 'And they did not like it. They could not let go of me and let me have that time. I'd always been the person who'd come and always be there.'

When Jill was 14, her ten-year-old-brother was diagnosed with cancer. Her parents were devastated by their son's life-threatening illness. Jill became the golden child of health and wellbeing. She tried to be the perfect daughter. 'I'd come home from school and try to be happy and help make it better. I'd try to fix it all and not give them any reason to be upset with me. While growing up, I never did anything that my mother or father disapproved of, ever. I figured that for the first 18 years I'm under their roof. They're my parents and they know more about what's right or wrong than I ever will. They raised me well. Our life was happy. I did pageants when I was little and played basketball in school and cheerleading. I didn't drink or smoke or cuss or anything all through high school. I'd say "sugar" or "flip". I didn't go out on weekends or anything like that.'

When Jill graduated from Vanderbilt, her parents wanted her to return home. They offered to build her a house on their 80 acres (32 hectares) of farmland across the road from her childhood home. They wanted to pick out her husband, at least that's how she felt. They had the perfect picture of her married, raising their grandchildren right across the road, Jill and her mother having morning coffee together, and every Sunday the families would share dinner. That would be her life. They insisted on it. Even her brother insisted on it.

Jill had other ideas. Her parents had instilled in her that she could do anything, be anything she wanted, as long as she was responsible, really believed in it, and felt morally okay with the choices. Jill wanted to be a country singer. They had encouraged her childhood singing, that was cute. But being a professional singer, that would take her away from Arab, further away from them.

'At one point, my mom told me that I couldn't sing anymore. She said that she didn't care anything about it and that I wasn't ever going to make it. That was devastating. My mom had always been my greatest supporter. My dad has always been, "Well, if you want to sing, that's fine."

'I said, "Look, I only get one life. I know you're my parents but I really believe in my singing and writing." I stood them off to where I was almost living in my car. I was working three part-time jobs, trying to get a publishing deal, working on writing songs. If anything happened that was wrong, or anything personal, I wouldn't call them. If they didn't want to share my joy in what I was doing, then I didn't feel it was responsible for me to ask them to share in anything hard for me. I've always wanted to maintain contact with them, but set boundaries. I had no idea how to set boundaries. The whole time I lived under their roof we never had any conflicts or differences of opinion of what I should do.'

And she had to deal with the unspoken rules of Southern culture. There is duplicity about the South and that duplicity can be seen in how the family is presented, she explained. It's always a picture-perfect front, civil, gentle, warm, and friendly. Yet, behind the façade hid the frustration and dysfunction and anger and strain of hard times people go through. Southerners can use good manners as a shield to deflect scrutiny that might find fault lines in the polite smile. If they behave impeccably, then maybe no one will put a magnifying glass on them.

Her mom and dad had that Southern make-everything-look-perfect-to-the-outside-world mentality. The man is the head of the household and the wife obeys the man.

'Seeing my mom follow my dad, obey my dad, sometimes when it was so hard for her, that's influenced my life and my music,' Jill said. 'My father is a good man but he would be strong, so strong at whatever cost if he thought he was doing the right thing. Whatever it took to make mother or me or my brother fall in line, then that's how it was going to be. Sometimes it wasn't so pleasant and didn't feel so good, having the expectations and demands that you felt were really not what you needed to be doing, and being forced to do them. So a lot of my songs come out of seeing my mother just say "Okay", because that was her role in the marriage. And then seeing both of them trying to do that same thing to me. I have a big thing about being independent. A lot of my songs are about women becoming independent and strong, even if it causes them pain. The outlaw, the individual, the seeking freedom and independence found in all country songs are the women found in my songs.

'I was raised around a lot of very gentle Southern women who would sugar coat any displeasure they had with your opinion or what you were doing. You could just hear this subconscious jab in their voices. You could tell in the cut of their eyes that they were sizing you up. My mom is very good at it, all these subcurrents layered in. I was used to that. I'd go up North and it was cultural shock. Up North, the people say what they don't like about you and why. Northern women think it's ridiculous for a woman to think, to act like a man can run them. The Southern woman says, "Oh, well, I think it would be more than fine to do this but you know Johnny, he won't let that happen and I've got to take care of him." It's not even defined as anger, but you can hear this bubbling under the surface of emotions that are not expressed. You can feel it. It's almost an art form. There are country songs that are just like that art form.'

Jill's 'Lovely Little Town' is a song about her hometown and all the parts that eat away at you every night, if you live there. She doesn't consider it a backstabbing song, just well-meaning mischief. She balances that with the song 'Down the Fields to Hay' about her grandpa and his life on a small farm. She praises the good things about the country and the good values of being raised in a small Southern town. They are songs about Southern country life, a life that is largely disappearing from the American landscape.

Her brother passed away last October. He was 24 and had just gotten married when he suffered a relapse of the cancer. That event started a shift within the family that is bringing her father to Nashville to buy into his daughter's dream. Jill sees the reaching out as an effort not to lose another child. As her brother succumbed to cancer, her parents' world revolved around him, closed in smaller and smaller around their tragedy. They sought solace in the Pentecostal God, a strong presence in the South. Jill is spiritual but, she states, not religious. As her parents became more rigid in their fundamentalism, she became more open in her world views. They butted heads on almost everything, so it was better not to talk. That way they could avoid a potentially fatal breakup. The façade could be maintained and nobody would know how deep the fissures ran. But now a rejoining might be possible.

Jill had a dream about her brother after he died. They had reconciled before his death and in her dream he was on her record and traveling with her. It was like he was saying that it was okay to be what she wanted. The week after the dream, she went down to Tootsie's and got her gig.

'That's what brought back my love for performing,' Jill said as we sat at the bar in Tootsie's. 'Part of my dream was stagnated because of the situation with my family. So a lot of my songs revolve around emotional sacrifices, or getting your mental state in order, or the good things about growing up and the hard things about becoming an adult, or being independent of your love partner or family or friends or society, and to live as true as you can to yourself and learn your own lessons.

'My goal is to be known as an artist. I want to have a career like Emmylou Harris, Willie Nelson, Dolly Parton, Kris Kristofferson. I want to be a person with an identity outside of the songs I select, and yet also within the songs. I would hope to be defined as a person who sings a song as my art. What I'm wanting to do is look like myself, the best self I can look like, get up there, and sing the fire out of every song.'

'When's your showcase?'

'In less than three weeks.'

8 At Home With Vince Gill

I had a hell of a week and wanted to brag. I took the chair next to Our Willie and said, 'Guess who I had coffee with.'

'Listen to this,' he replied and started to chant/croon:

I woke up this morning
For breakfast at the Loveless Motel
My baby's the short-order cook
Pretending sunny side up
Makes it all right.

Chorus: Loveless Motel, Loveless Motel
Place I call home
To lay my head
On a broken heart.

I got up and left, walked to the front of Tootsie's, listened to the band for one song, walked back to our table and sat next to Amy.

'Guess who I had coffee with.'

'I see this as a cheatin' song,' she said. 'A man cheatin' song. But maybe he doesn't really know who he's cheatin' on, himself or his woman. Give it some mystery to be resolved in the last verse. Listen to this.

I woke up again
Renting my heart
Where my baby lives

He gave me the room number
But not the key
For the Loveless Motel.
Think I'll check out
Pay my bill
For a room in the Loveless Motel
With a broken heart.

I got up and left.

I bumped into Hank coming through the front door. 'Guess who I had coffee with.'

He pushed the black cowboy hat back on his head and put a hand on my shoulder. He looked me in the eye, like a preacher deciding whether or not this sinner was worthy of a dipping in holy water. It was friendly, even loving, for Hank. 'Come tell me about it.' He led the way back to our table.

Amy and Our Willie were arguing about his Loveless Motel chorus. 'You got an idea,' she said, 'an idea slidin' on ice, if you know what I mean. It's goin' somewhere but it doesn't know where. We've got to grab that idea to stop it from slidin' into a dark hole in the ice, if you know what I mean.'

'The only thing slidin' is your bullshit,' Our Willie said. 'This song's about the Love Less Motel. Get it? The Love Less Motel is this man's home, a loveless home. Nobody's fault. Both are trying to act the loving home part, cookin' eggs for breakfast, being sunny side up. Get it?'

Hank sat down between them and said with calm authority, 'Guess whom Stephen had coffee with?' Both looked at him as if a dead uncle had suddenly appeared at the dining table and announced he was taking back the inheritance he had bequeathed them.

'Vince Gill,' I said quickly before they recovered.

'The Grammy winner?'

'The mandolin player?'

'The golfer?'

I nodded cool and casual. 'He called and invited me out to the house for coffee.'

No big deal, my smugness said. Why wouldn't the 12-time Grammy winner (his latest Grammy was in 2002 for a country instrumental performance of 'Foggy Mountain Breakdown' with other country music notables), the winner of 17 Country Music Association awards (more than anybody else, including Performer of the Year, Singer of the Year, Song of the Year), the repeat host of the Country Music Associations Awards show, why wouldn't Vince Gill ask me to drop by for a chat? Happens all the time.

I decided not to mention that I had been pounding on his management's door for two months requesting an interview. And had been largely ignored. My sudden success must be credited to a little insider help. Tony Brown, a very good friend of Vince's, put in a phone call. Within two days, I was given Vince's cellphone number. We played phone tag and he touched me first. But, hey, why make the miraculous sound prosaic? When I answered the phone, Vince had said, 'Glad we finally linked up. Why don't you come out at nine tomorrow morning?' and gave me directions to his house in Belle Meade, the Beverley Hills of Nashville.

Vince and his wife, Amy Grant, the Christian/pop singer, live in a large quasi-colonial brick house at the end of a street. Child and adult bikes filled the racks at the side of the house. The dark green paint on the front door needed retouching. That detail reassured me. When meeting a superstar – two, in fact, as Amy has her own long successful career (four Grammy nominations, a string of multi-platinum and gold albums, *New York Times* dubbed her 'the Michael Jackson of gospel music') – one is never sure what one will get. A glossy PR image? A haughty ego in expensive clothes? A too-cool-to-care character who merely tolerates you?

After ringing the bell, I heard Amy call out, 'Coming.' She answered the door in what were apparently her sleeping clothes: loose cotton pants and T-shirt. She didn't wear makeup and her hair looked early morning. The baby, Corinna, had been up since 3am, she explained, and neither she nor Vince had gotten much sleep. I followed her into the kitchen where Vince stood, a big solid man, dark shadows on his unshaven cheeks, wearing yellow LSU (Louisiana State University) mesh athletic shorts, a T-shirt of a golf tournament he sponsored, and a black baseball cap over his shock of thick dark hair.

We exchanged a soft handshake. 'Nice to meet you,' he said.

'Would you like some coffee?' Amy asked. We did break-the-ice chitchat while she ground beans and set coffee to brew. She handed me a filled cup and excused herself. 'I'm going to catch a nap before the baby wakes up.'

Vince and I settled on a sofa. The dog, Chester, introduced himself, and then waited by the door for Vince to let him out into the backyard. When Vince sat down again, I asked, 'Do you take risks?'

'It's necessary to take risks in order to keep your creativity sharp. The experience of life will keep that edge as much as anything.' His speaking voice has same tenor tone as his singing voice. 'To be able to have a career, you have to be willing to go to where it's going on. A lot of times that means taking the plunge and going there – and be willing to starve.'

Vince took his first big risk when, as an 18-year-old, he packed his jeans and T-shirts in a van and moved from his parents' home in Oklahoma City, Oklahoma. He had graduated from high school with no thought of going on to college. Music was his life; he knew that but didn't know how it all might work.

He was already a skilled and talented bluegrass player with a budding reputation. Someone called and asked if he wanted to be in a band. So he left home and drove to Louisville, Kentucky, where he had never been, to play with people he had never met.

'I was willing to step out there. That was a risk. Life is going to lead you more than you're going to lead it. You are going to react to life more than plan it. Then, another phone call took me to Los Angeles. I had never been there. Okay. I'll pack up all my stuff and move to Los Angeles and see what that's like. Just being open-minded enough and willing to go into experiences of life, take a risk and see what's on the other side of the fence. That has always paved the way for me.'

In 1979, he was a member of Pure Prairie League, a very successful hot bluegrass group. His lead vocals on 'Let Me Love You Tonight' helped to make the song a hit. His instrumental skills on the banjo, guitar, and mandolin were appreciated as much as his singing. Mark Knopfler, founder of Dire Straits and a highly regarded world-quality guitarist, tried to recruit Gill for his band. Vince stayed with Pure Prairie League for three albums, during which he wooed, and eventually won the hand of Janis, half of the duo Sweethearts of the Rodeo.

'I take risks as a songwriter,' Vince said. 'That's where I lay it on the line. As a songwriter, I just try to be honest. If that has to include life as it really is, that's what it is. My own songwriting is mostly from life. But also being a great songwriter is having an imagination. Being a great songwriter doesn't always have to be telling the world all about yourself.

'It's an odd thing being a songwriter and an artist. If I were just a songwriter, nobody would try to put two and two together and say it is my life. But being somewhat public makes you a target for everybody's thought process of what the songs are about. They always try to make them autobiographical. Sometimes they are and sometimes they aren't. It's kinda hard to say two years later what a song was about. I don't have a good enough memory. One song I've written for this new record in progress is called, "I Have a Feeling". That is probably going to be conceived as part of my past life. But it's really about going to see the film *Oceans 11*. That's where I got the idea to write the song.'

Vince is a bit sensitive about reviewers and critics interpreting his life through his songs, although compelling comparisons can be made. He admits to wearing his heart on his sleeve, as is apparent in songs on *The Key* album (1998), called one of the best albums in country music history for its raw emotional power and the traditional country sound reminiscent of the 1950s. The title track was written in honor of his father, who died in July of that year.

In 1982 he signed with RCA and made 'three or four albums nobody wanted to hear,' he freely admits. While he commercially struggled, Janis's career was going great guns. Vince wrote a song, 'Everybody's Sweetheart', which a reviewer pointed out must be about his wife being more in demand than Vince based on the line, 'I used to be first in line/but now I've fallen way behind/she's everybody's sweetheart but mine.' The song, 'I Still Believe in You' was seen as a musical apology to Janis after an argument. 'Never Knew Lonely (till you)' was seen as being about the heartache of being on the road and away from his family.

Maybe he's sensitive to the second-hand guessing about his life in song because of the personal risk he took in the very public friendship with Amy while they were married to others. Rumors of an improper relationship between them made tabloid headlines. Amy went on record about the relationship: 'A lot of disparaging things were said about my very public friendship with Vince. One of the reasons that the friendship was so public was because it never occurred to me to hide it. I would hear rumors about, "You guys were seen doing this, you guys were seen doing that."

'I just said, "Not true."'

Still, they became targets for pundits' boards about country stars posing with loyal wife and dog, while appearing with someone else's loyal wife. This was an image that defied country music values of honoring family, loyalty, and the union only God could sunder. Their public friendship could have put their careers at risk. In 1997, Vince and Janis divorced after 17 years and one daughter. Two years later, in 1999, Amy divorced her husband, Gary Chapman, a songwriter who wrote *My Father's Eyes*, which became an Amy Grant standard. Vince and Amy married in 2000.

And now Vince is taking a professional risk – he's producing, for the first time in his career, his own album.

'There is a switch in mentality from being the artist and being the producer,' he explained. 'I find it difficult to remain objective when I'm the one actually performing what I hear. I've done a little bit of producing on two or three projects and discovered that if I'm not performing on a piece I hear it differently. When you've been part of creating an album, playing and singing the cuts, you can't help but listen for your contribution. Whereas, if you don't play, you can hear everything in its entirety. The hardest thing is to separate yourself from listening to yourself all the time. That's a challenge of this new project. It's all original songs I've written. We still have about half the album to mix and are going to record a few more things. I hope to have it out in the autumn but it doesn't even have a title yet.'

Vince admitted that being a producer has been part fun and part lonely. He loves comradeship. As an artist, he likes input, the involvement of the other players and the studio personnel, including the engineers. 'I love it when the others have an idea to try,' he said. 'The floor has always been open with me. That seems to be the smartest way to do it. Make people feel great and trust them. Being a great producer is sometimes getting out of the way and not being a control freak by having to put your stamp on every note and every part.'

Vince has always been a risk taker with his music. When he made *The Key*, radio programmers told him that they didn't want records of him singing traditional country music. But he hoped that the album might spark new interest in the type of country music heard in the Texas swing of Bob Wills. He wanted people to hear the country shuffle in Ray Price's voice and vocal riffs of Lefty Frizzell. The Depression-seared reality of Merle Haggard was not getting airplay and he wanted people to notice. He took a risk for the music and lost the commercial roll of the dice. Despite the critical success of *The Key*, it didn't get much airplay and did not sell well.

He took the risk for the fans, as he did on the heavily traditional *When I Call Your Name* (1989) album and the more new country *High Lonesome Sound* (1998).

'The core country fan is middle aged and is always the one that gets the short end of the stick, in my opinion,' Vince said, getting up to let the dog back in. 'They're just as crazy about George Jones and Merle Haggard as they ever were. But they don't have the opportunity to hear them, certainly not on the commercial radio.'

He got up again to let the dog back out. 'Country music always has taken risks in order to survive,' he said, sitting back down. 'Nothing stays the same. Country music has never stayed the same. I think it's a huge myth that a lot of people would like you to believe, that country music has stayed the same. It's always changed, taken risks, since its conception, since the Carter Family and the roots of Jimmie Rodgers. Roy Acuff was different than the Carter Family.

'Then came the '50s and Eddie Arnold in his tux and crooning. Then the music got twany again, then cosmopolitan again. Ricky Skaggs, in the early '80s, brought a bluegrass element to country that was seen as new and fresh. Travis Tritt came along in the late '80s and gave it another traditional sound. And today Alan Jackson has given the music a traditional thing.

'Now, I think, country music is taking a nap. Getting out of that nap is going to be the result of what this generation of artists has learned and what they know. All they can do is what they know. They know the records of the Eagles, the records of the '70s and '80s. Those kinds of pop influences are going to be part of their music. But, at the same time, you look at the country records of the '70s and '80s and they weren't all traditional. It just keeps evolving. The only thing that scares me is if there comes a day when the back-to-the-roots thing goes away. Then I think the music is in trouble.'

One of the reasons country music is taking a nap is 'that everyone is scared for their job, so they're somewhat safe and cautious,' Vince said. 'Economics is dictating how the music business is run. Economics dictates how our country is run. It costs so darn much to break a new artist, about a million bucks [£650,000] to sign an artist, produce a record, make a video, go promote it. If you miss a few times, you're dead. This is not working. But it has taken a while for the music industry to figure this out. Some people in charge are slow to come to that understanding. The new technology has a lot of ability to do a lot of damage to the big companies. They're walking on thin ice.'

And what will wake them up from their nap? 'The fringy stuff is what's going to pull us out of the sameness,' Vince answered. 'Artists like Steve Earle, Mary-Chapin Carpenter, Lyle Lovett made everybody see how country music can be a little different. Something will come along that will turn everybody's head because they are getting bored with mainstream country music. We could very well be seeing a ground swell of under-the-radar country music. The artists in that movement are being creative by going back to traditions yet making the music sound new. Nickel Creek is a big part of that. Alison Krauss is a big influence. She has single-handedly bridged the gap. She had a big country hit but decided not to go commercial country because she liked to explore in a new way. I feel that I was part of the mentality 25 years ago. I was out playing bluegrass in bands that weren't mainstream. We were doing what was necessary without commercial radio.'

As I was leaving, I asked Vince about his golf game. He's a foamer, one of those avid fans absolutely mad for the sport. He's a driving force behind Vince Gill Tennessee PGA Junior Golf Tournament. He sponsors charity fundraising golf events, enlisting the help of numerous country music famous names. He works tirelessly for charities, especially those that help children and the sick. This work has won him as many, if not more, plaudits than his musical accomplishments.

He laughed and downplayed his golfing ability. (He has a golf handicap of one.) But he did acknowledge a secret desire to be a professional golfer. 'I'm on the downside of my musical career now. Still, it's no different than when I was 18. I'm still trusting my ears and trying to write a great song and get it on tape as good as I humanly can and to improve.'

Tony Brown waved me into his office and I thanked him for his helping hand with Vince. 'He's the nicest guy in town,' Tony replied, 'and an example of a musical survivor. He gives a lot of quiet help to young musicians, like paying for scholarships and helping their careers, without taking public kudos. He remembers how tenuously his Nashville career began and how important it is to persist.'

It is arguable that Vince Gill has his career thanks to Tony Brown. Tony signed him to RCA and produced Vince, who had some small hits but nothing big, nothing that said 'potential big star'. When Tony left RCA and became the president of MCA, he kept in touch with Vince. When Vince left RCA, Tony signed him to MCA. 'If you really believe in the artist and believe he is a star, you stay with the artist,' Tony explained. 'It's a gamble. Sometimes it pays off and sometimes it doesn't.'

Vince recorded the album *When I Call Your Name* with Tony. The first two singles off the album were stiffs. Critics said that Vince's tenor voice doesn't work in country music. A deep voice is country, that manly sound. Tony's reaction was, 'You're wrong. This guy plays great guitar, he writes great songs, he looks great, he sings great, and he's a great guy.' But both Vince and Tony knew that without a great record, Vince would have a great non-career.

'After the first two singles failed, we decided to put out a third single off the album,' Tony said. 'Both he and I knew that if this didn't work, he didn't have a chance at all. This had to be a hit.' They released 'When I Call Your Name' and held their breath. It was make-or-break time for

Vince's career. The song won the Country Music Association's Song of the Year. Vince went on to sell 30 million records and won Entertainer of the Year, twice.

'Sometimes it's your turn, but only if you deliver the goods,' Tony said. 'I know a lot of people who are better than the majority of the stars today, but their turn never came because they never delivered that record.'

Tony had a career as a musician before his career as a record label executive. He knows how the pressure to produce a commercial hit can mess with an artist's mind. He also knows how an artist's ego can mess with a label executive's mind.

'Lots of times, artists want things on their terms only,' he said from behind his executive desk. 'They insist on singing only the songs they want to sing, without regard of the market place. If they write songs and they write a bad song and you tell them that, they get mad at you. And sometimes they don't even know when they have a hit. Vince's song "I Still Believe In You" was the last song on the album because he hadn't written the second verse when we had finished tracking the album. I told him to finish the song. "Why?" he asked. "It isn't any good." I told him it was a hit in the making. "You think so?" he said. "Then I'll finish it." He didn't think it was a hit, but he was wrong.'

Tony admits that there is some frustration wearing two hats, that of the musician and the label executive. As an executive with a musician's soul, he finds the business reality of what makes the machine work very disillusioning.

'The reality is not pretty,' he said with a shake of his head. 'Sometimes you don't need to tell an artist how you managed to get their record played on air. It wouldn't serve any purpose. Then, when an artist gets arrogant and starts pointing fingers of blame at you for his lack of success or the level of success the artist thinks they deserve, then you want to say, "Oh, if you only knew how much I love you and how much I put up with because I think you're incredible."

'The psychology of this business, especially of being in my chair, is almost as important as anything. If you ever destroy an artist's spirit, they're not going to perform for you. They may not perform for anybody ever again. If you upset them to the point where they won't perform for you, but they might for someone else, then you've made a bad business decision. It's a fine line where you have to go suck it up and occasionally take some grief from an artist just because.

'Being a musician, I have a lot of empathy with the artist and their spirit. I totally understand them. There are times when I'm on their side. I try to straddle the fence and say, "Look, I'm going to say this and do this. This is my strategy. Go with me on this."'

Tony began his music career in the style of Southern Gospel, which is basically a piano player and four guys singing four-part harmony. He was born in 1946 in Greensboro, North Carolina, but grew up in Winston-Salem. His father, an evangelical preacher, set his two sons learning the piano early. Tony was six when he started lessons. He would watch during his older brother's lesson, then execute his lesson flawlessly. One day the teacher made him play first. Tony looked at the sheet music and couldn't play a note. He had learned by ear and couldn't read the music. His mother mistook his sudden inability as a lack of interest and he didn't take lessons again for seven years.

When he was 13, he came back to music by accident, or fate. His father had hired a lady to play piano at his services. 'She was an amazing piano player,' Tony recalled. 'She heard me messing around on the piano one day and said, "Do this," and I did. She figured out that I could play by ear, so she taught me a song. I played it the next night with the family at church. I learned that maybe there was something to this playing thing.'

So did his father, who sent him to the Stamp School of Music in Dallas, Texas, when he was 15. The intent was not to train Tony for a professional career but rather as a piano player for the church. The Stamps Quartet was famous in the 1930s and '40s on the gospel circuit. Learning under their tutelage would keep Tony close to the fundamental base and away from worldly bright lights. He took six weeks of lessons in music theory but was, by his admission, too lazy to pick it up. But the piano teacher recognized that Tony had a gifted ear. She taught him how to play in all the keys – he had mastered only three – and some cool riffs and tricks of the keyboard. Then she made a deal with his dad.

'Let your son stay with me for one year and I'll give him free piano lessons,' she proposed. Tony would live with her family in Bastrop,

Louisiana. The lessons were free because her family had a gospel group and Tony would be their piano player. He'd be in good hands, she promised, God-fearing Christian hands of good people.

'She taught me all the cool licks and stuff, how to dazzle people with a cool piano piece,' Tony said fondly. 'That was my teaching.'

He graduated from high school in 1966 and got his first gig – playing piano in a band on weekends, and painting houses during the week for the guy who ran the band. His first real professional job was with the Traveler's Quartet in Winter Haven, Florida. Then he joined the Klaudt Indian Family group, a real Native Indian family troupe. He was given an Indian headdress to wear on stage.

'But I'm not an Indian,' he protested.

'But you're in showbusiness,' he was told.

He quit after two months.

The next gig was his real start on the path to a musical career. He joined the Stamp Quartet with JD Sumner, his hero. He stayed with the group for seven years.

New opportunities opened as Southern Gospel grew within the contemporary Christian world. Tony joined the Oak Ridge Boys, then a strict gospel group, and stayed with them for three years.

'They signed with Columbia and decided to go country, having decided that the Statler Brothers were not that good and that they could kick their ass,' Tony said with a smile. 'I, disillusioned, quit the Oak Ridge Boys and joined a house band that Elvis Presley had started. He was a gospel music fanatic and wanted a group of people to play those songs in his house when he was around. So he hired three guys to sing and me to play the piano. We were on call 24 hours, seven days a week. We'd go to his house in Palm Springs or to Graceland in Memphis or Beverly Hills. We knew every song he could possibly know. Eventually that led to us opening his shows in front of the Sweet Inspirations, his normal band. That gig finally fell through, which was not surprising to me because we were not a very good group.'

Tony stood in the wings at Elvis's shows and watched the hands of Glen D Hardin, the piano player of the Sweet Inspirations. Tony learned every song of Elvis's shows by ear. Glen D had a side gig recording with

Emmylou Harris. He told Tony how exciting it was to play with her, how great she was, and that if she toured with the new album he might go with her. He had been with Elvis for a long time and wanted a change. The day came that Glen D left and Tony stepped in, without a rehearsal, to play before 20,000 people. He became Elvis's piano player and stayed with him until the 'King' died.

Out of a job, Tony went to Nashville and became a song plugger. A song plugger is a very specialized niche in the music business. A plugger's job is to get into a producer's or label executive's or artist manager's office, play them a song or two, and get out without pissing them off. The objective is to sell them a song, or at least be welcomed back for another pitch. Whether the person loves or hates the song, the plugger's job is to leave that person feeling very comfortable with the meeting.

A plugger doesn't have to be a musician, doesn't even have to be able to hum. But a plugger has to know how to play the charm chords. A plugger is first and foremost a people person, then a music person, who can properly insert a demo into a CD player. A plugger has to fervently believe in a song, believe with evangelical zeal, believe with the conviction of a super salesman. They have to be sincere, trustworthy to have the goods, deferential when necessary, and kind but honest. Above all, a plugger has to be likable. In many ways, a successful plugger is like a good hunting dog that reliably points the hunter to a bird in hiding. But a plugger's two most valuable assets are a thick hide that rejections bounce off and unfathomable optimism. The vast majority of songs that a plugger presents are rejected maybe eight to ten times a day. But the plugger has to smile sincerely and say, happily, 'Okay, next time I'll slay ya. Next week I'll come back and we'll record a song, by gum, just you wait and see.'

Tony was a successful plugger. The same traits make him a successful producer and a successful record executive.

When he first came to Nashville, Glen D was in town playing with Emmylou. When he left to play for John Denver, Tony took his place as he had done with Elvis. He worked with Emmylou for three years and did weekend gigs with Rosanna Cash, Rodney Crowell, and Emmylou's Hot Band members. This period was pivotal to Tony's future career in the music industry. Through the Emmylou experience he met Vince Gill, who was Rosanna Cash's guitar player. Through Crowell he met Guy Clark. Through Guy Clark he met Lyle Lovett and Nanci Griffith. As a record executive, he signed Gill, Lovett, and Griffith to contracts.

'I started learning about how relationships musically shape who you want to be,' Tony said. 'I found out that I was really shaped by singer/songwriters: Guy Clark, Town van Zandt, Rodney Crowell, Rosanna Cash, Vince Gill, and Emmylou, who was influenced by the West Coast Country sound. The labels hired me because they thought I had a connection to that element, which at that time, 1980–4, was the happening thing. I was hired because I had an in with those people. I learned quickly that your relationships are not only how you expand your musical knowledge but also how to expand your ability to raise your profile.'

Being a musician has given Tony an edge as a record executive. 'Coming out of a music background gives me a little one up on Joe Galante, the head of RCA, or someone like Joe. I used to work for Joe, now I'm his competitor. If it got down to us vying for the same artist, the one up I have is that I can talk to the artist on the level of a musician. Joe could talk on the level of his brain as a record man, and his track record proves how successful he has been. To be the head of a label, you have to have some gut instinct, or something, to be able to spot talent. You don't have to be a musician or have a music background to run a label. Joe comes from a business background but he surrounds himself with competent people who have the gifts he doesn't have. Joe surrounds himself with great A&R people.

'I can talk to the artist differently than he does. That doesn't make me better than him or, because he's a genius businessman, make him better than me in the record business. My partner, Tim DuBois, has a bit of both Joe and myself. He's a songwriter and producer with an MBA. That's a hard combination to beat. I think being a musician makes you a better, well-rounded talent scout.'

9 The Others

Phil Lee is an Others. The Others are practitioners of Risky Country; risky because their music is a roll of the dice on the financial craps table and risky because they may cause unpredictable mutations in country music.

The Others consider themselves purveyors of the country music that has always claimed to be America's music. That music is not about wrapping oneself in red, white, and blue bunting at the sacrifice of critical thinking. It's not about playing feel-good songs to put people in the mood to buy tyres. It's about the ordinary miracle of making a life out of a baloney sandwich on white bread and being nourished. It's about wearing your heart on your sleeve without fear or shame. It's about not getting above your raisin', a Southern expression for getting too big for your britches and forgetting your roots.

The Others share a key trait – live the life you celebrate in song. Don't pretend you drive a sexy tractor when all you have is a riding lawnmower. Don't pretend you come from a working background when your experience with hard labor is parking cars. If you sing about romance, be a romantic. Sing about the values you live. Sing out against whatever or whoever places corporate greed and authoritarian power above humanistic values. Be respectful of everyone's right to be who he or she is. Don't sell out.

Nashville is hub of the under-the-radar Others movement, little noticed by the media and mostly ignored by the major labels. The movement's elders are Dwight Yoakam, John Prine, Steve Earle, and Lucinda Williams, who won a 2002 Grammy for Female Rock Vocal Performance for her

'Get Right With God'. Nashville's Others includes Phil Lee, Joy Lynn White, Lonesome Bob, Matt King, Duane Jarvis, Buddy and Julie Miller, John Stirrat, Allison Moorer, Tim Carroll, Todd Snider, Amy Rigby, Gillian Welch, and Billy Joe Royal. Robbie Fulk is a founding member but he left Nashville for Chicago. Dale Watson and David Baerwald are part of the Texas branch. Hank Williams III divides his time between Nashville, Austin, and the road.

This is Phil Lee: put two toothpicks together, stick on a tuff of gray cotton and top with a black fedora or beret. Picture a shrimp that stands 5' 6" (1m 68cm) on tiptoes and weights 135lb (61kg) on a heavy-gravity day. This slip of a man wrestles an 18-wheel Peterbilt long-haul semi-tractor through traffic at high speed. Phil Lee. Conjure up the charm and chutzpah necessary to survive being the Hell's Angels' in-house musician. Phil Lee. Dream, as a poet, the scene of Phil Lee stroking his electric guitar and doing his little Chuck Berry hop when he looks beyond the stage lights and spots a woman in a banker's power suit. Before the last note of his song fades, he's at that table making a fool of himself, as a puppy does when sucking up. He wants to marry this woman and he doesn't even know her name. After a traditional Southern courtship, with Phil Lee inventive twists, he does marry her.

Phil Lee is a prototypical Others; the Others are Phil Lee, with individualistic variations in their colorful behavior. The Others don't want to be tagged with a definition. They are individuals within the country genre who don't want to play cookie cutter music. That's it. They do not consider themselves as outlaws, but they feel like outsiders. They prefer the insecurity of their independence to the relative security of a major label contract. Some Others, such as Joy Lynn White and Matt King, have gained critical acclaim on major labels. Buddy and Julie Miller have written top 40 songs for Brooks And Dunn, Lee Ann Womack and others. Some Others, such as David Baerwald, are on small labels, like Lost Highway, within the larger corporation (Sony). Dale Watson is on a small independent, Audium. Lonesome Bob is his own label.

Phil Lee's 2001 CD *You Should Have Known Me Then* (Shanachie) was called 'Best of the best country album 2001... If combining the social conscience of Woody Guthrie with the twisted fury of Jerry Lee Lewis sounds good to you, you can't go wrong with *You Should Have Known Me Then.*' (Jim Patterson of the *Associated Press*). And rollingstone.com said, 'If there's such a place as honky-tonk heaven, you can bet that everyone there is sitting around waiting for Phil Lee to pay a visit.'

At one time, during his LA drugs-and-death period, Phil Lee stumbled zonked toward the gates of honky-tonk heaven, but he pulled back. He attempted to give up music as part of his self-redemption effort and became a trucker. That didn't work, of course. He'd been playing music since he was a teenager in his hometown of Durham, North Carolina. His band opened for the farm news on the television show 'Homer Hopper and the Daybreak Show'. Clyde Moody, who played with Bill Monroe, was a regular on the show. Phil played drums behind such ol' country boys, and then would drive to high school and play student. On the weekends, he performed with bands on the back of flatbed trucks, opening for mobile home sales. Such work is an honored tradition. Jerry Lee Lewis did the same type of gigs. He once played on an open truck right through a Texas dust storm.

Phil Lee was a country drummer who loved rock 'n' roll, or a rock 'n' roll drummer who grew up listening to country. He could play it either way. In 1971, he moved to New York City and played in a rock 'n' roll band with country overtones. Beverley D'Angelo and Rob Stoner, who played with Bob Dylan during his Renaldo and Clara days, were band mates. He had a rock band called The Road Band that played the matinee at the Five Spot, the legendary jazz club.

'All these old jazz guys – Mingus, Sun Ra – would come in and yell at us, "This is a jazz club. You guys are assholes. Get out of here,"' Phil recalled as we talked at his home in East Nashville. 'They were pretty mean. But we got to go in the club at night free and listen to Ornette Coleman and hang out with him. He didn't seem to like young white people who were playing at the club.'

We sat in the upstairs room where he keeps a drum kit and several guitars. On the floor was a futon covered by a blue blanket, the corners neatly tucked in. Five feet (1.5m) away stood a cardboard target bristling with throwing knives. I imagined Phil lying on the futon with his wife, Maggie, throwing the sharply honed knives.

'Phil, baby, you feeling a little tension right now?' *Thunk* goes a knife.

'No, darling wife, why would you think that?' He cradles a flat-bladed knife in the palm of his hand.

'Phil, baby, if you're feeling a bit stressed out, there are other ways to dealing with it.'

'What would that be, darling Maggie?'

I met Maggie. She's an accountant in a bank. Her salary is the couple's main income. Sometimes she gets seriously tired of Phil coming home after three weeks on the road and having only $700 (£450) to show for it.

'I'd throw the money down on the table and say, "Babe, check it out"' Phil said.

'She says, "In America, that's not making it."

'"Well, it's better than coming home $1,500 [£975] poorer," I'd say. But it goes against everything she knows about how to make money work for you.'

When they are strapped for cash, Phil takes a quick trip hauling freight. Last week he did an afternoon job for $120 (£78) from Nashville to Jackson and back carrying body parts, 'spare feet, eyeballs, kidneys, arms, that sort of thing they didn't need any more,' he explained. 'I took them from the Jackson hospital to the Nashville hospital with the state's only incinerator licensed to burn up human flesh and bone.'

Maggie is a knockout. No wonder Phil fell for her from the stage. She has red hair and peaches-and-cream complexion and a smile that makes you laugh for the sheer joy of being in its presence. It's like having healing hands laid on you and all your cares vanish. Phil says that she can appear as a perfect 1940s Southern wife, doing for her man what a modern woman might consider kowtowing. But look out for her one-line zingers.

'She's as sharp as my throwing knives,' Phil said, 'and can cut you as cleanly. All with a smile. We've been married four years and have never had an argument. She calls me "Buggy" because that first time we met, in the club, when I was doing my hypercharm act, anything to get her to notice me, she looked at me as if I was some odd insect trying to crawl up her nostril. I can't believe she agreed to marry me. When I started courting her, I didn't do the rock 'n' roll star routine, "Here, baby, hold my guitar while I fuck you." No, I did it right. I was the Southern gentleman. You know what finally got her to say yes? I took her for a ride in the cab on my Peterbilt.'

By the mid-'70s, having had enough of New York, he returned to the South and wandered about playing music and writing songs. In 1975, he moved to San Francisco, then down to Los Angeles, where he stayed for ten years. He switched from being a drummer to being a guitar player and did the clubs, Whiskey Go-Go, the Roxy, and everything in between on the LA club circuit.

'I was doing the same kind of music I do now,' he said. 'I got a lot of blank stares because the skinny-tie people were popular, like the Knack, the Germs, the Dead Kennedys. I was basically playing country music. I was feeling brave because back then there weren't the categories like alt country or Americana. It was either country or pop.'

He got a gig with Neil Young – driving an equipment van during the making of one of his videos. 'I got to see that those guys have the same problems that I was having,' he said, 'like problems with girls. I couldn't believe that. I said, "You're Neil Young. You can't be having those problems."

'He said, "Yeah I do, until I tell them I'm Neil Young." He kinda shakes. I saw him last year and he looks like he's been taking care of himself.'

One of Phil's songs, 'When I Close My Eyes I See Blood', was in *Cruisin'* with Al Pacino. That was his entrée into the film world. He lived with an actress, Rainbeaux Smith, who was in tits-and-knives movies like *Revenge of the Pom Pom* and *Caged Heat*.

'She was a cult figure,' Phil remembered fondly, by the smile on his face. 'Made tons of B and C movies. I'd be watching TV movies at four in the morning, not able to sleep, nothing to drink, and she'd come on television in *God vs Philly* or something. I'd say, "Don't take your clothes off." There they'd go off and then a big rock would come down and kill her. That was her role. She was knockdown gorgeous. Posed in *Penthouse*. Her real name was Cherl. She was a flower child and the drummer in my band. She had a thing about exposing herself to the bass player. We'd be on stage playing and I'd look back and she'd be flashing him. Anything to drive me crazy. Towards the end of our relationship, she ended up being a stripper. She was crazy as hell and dangerous by anybody's standards. She tried to kill me – twice. Once with a knife.

'Those were crazy wonderful days. Sort of like a season in Hell. I looked like death on a stick. I looked like Ozzie pretty much, had that demeanor. Hobbling along. When I played, people would guide me by the arm to the microphone. "Here you are, Phil. Don't fall over."

'One day I said, "Okay, that's that," and got the hell out of there. Either that or I was going to die.'

He returned to North Carolina and found steady work with the Hell's Angels. It started with a gig at a house party, then another party, and then a party or two nearly every weekend. There were benefits to raise bail money to get a member out of jail or pay attorney fees. Everybody was going to jail so there was plenty of work and it paid fairly well.

'They were a fun bunch,' Phil said. 'They were just people but with them you had a limit. They wouldn't mind knocking the hell out of you if you overstepped that line. Common sense basically dictated your behavior. Sometimes there were people with no sense of tact or diplomacy. They got what they deserved.'

But he had to put distance between the Hell's Angels and himself. If you hang around that fire too long, you might be the next log on the blaze. And he was sick and tired of the music business. He didn't want to talk to anybody who looked like a musician. It just wasn't fun any more. So he decided to get a job. But what's a 40-year-old guy with zero skills and a bad attitude to authority figures, such as a boss, what's he doing to do? Who would hire him? He decided that he needed an independent outsider's job that paid steady. So he went to truck driving college. He'd ride around and hang around, just like being a musician.

'I figured I'd be the strangest character there, but that wasn't true. We had a transvestite, Renee. She was the best at backing the rig up. We had a jet pilot guy. He quit after a week. That school was tough. Eight weeks, 11 hours a day. It was hell. Most of the time we were walking behind the truck as the instructor told us stuff. It was hot.

'When I got my truck-driving diploma, my family was so proud of me. Now I did something that they could understand. A week or so later

I got a call from Sneaky Pete of the original Flying Burrito Brothers. He had heard some of my stuff and wanted me to come back out to LA and help get the Burrito thing going again. Okay, great, I don't have to drive a truck after all. I fly out there and we record four or five songs, do publicity stills, but it didn't work out. So I did truck driving. Trucking is a lot like playing music. You really gotta drive all the time. Around 1998, I settled in Nashville and got pretty much back into music.'

Phil Lee took a job on Music Row as a songwriter and discovered that he was an Others. 'I tried to write what was acceptable and didn't even come close. And they let me know it. It was like that cartoon of a guy in hell and he's whistling a happy tune while mopping up. Satan is saying, "You're just not getting it. You're not with the program." That was me on Music Row.'

His song '3 Faces in the Window' is a case in point. The song was inspired by Baudelaire's poem, 'The Eyes of the Poor'. The song's narrative is about a couple eating in a high-price restaurant. The faces of three hungry, homeless people press against the window, watching. The woman of the couple becomes extremely uncomfortable under the scrutiny of the needy and asks the man to run them off. The subtext is about how much you can misread the person you're in love with. The man wants to invite the hungry trio in and feed them. He realizes that the woman he is with, the woman he loves, does not share his fundamental values. It's a love song.

'The Music Row people liked it,' said Phil, 'until the song leaned into art commenting about society. They got almost mad, "How dare you take our money and bring us this kind of stuff." Music Row is quick to reject anything that has an edge. And it doesn't have to be, "I'll slit your throat for a fuckin' dime," or "I beat the wife and kids." It can be over a word like "eat", as in "I'd like to work so I can eat." When I play "3 Faces" live, people get it just fine. Gillian Welch and David Rawlings sang it with me on the *You Should Have Known Me Then* CD. That song is the difference between Risky Country and Music Row. It's like day and night.'

An increasing number of country musicians are joining the Others, whether they identify themselves as such or not. There are pockets of musicians and fans in Los Angeles, Houston, Seattle, Washington DC,

Minneapolis, Charlotte, North Carolina, and St Louis. The Nashville Others all showed up in town at more or less the same time in the mid-1990s. Nashville was Country Central with recording studios, good engineers and technical personnel, and a plethora of high caliber musicians. Nashville's location made it convenient to travel to Illinois, Missouri, Florida, North Carolina, and New York where people were clambering to hear the music.

But Phil Lee, and the Others, admit that they will always be on the fringe, a cult, like folk music or bluegrass. Being an Others is like being in the American Communist Party in the 1950s: you're doing something you shouldn't be doing, according to The Establishment. But, like the ideals of ideologues, there will always be an audience for left-of-center music. The demand for the Others' music is growing.

'The success of O Brother shows that people are damn tired of what they are being force fed,' Phil pointed out. 'There is a market for this Risky Country. Music Row is trying to downplay it, saying, "It's a fluke, like O Brother. It will blow over." But the record executives on Music Row have no idea which way to turn. What they are producing is no longer working and they know it. They're looking for something. The band Pinmonkey is sort of a missing link. Pinmonkey's lead singer, Mike, was my lawyer's secretary. The drummer, Rick Schell, has done work on my records. They were just like us, just bopping around. They had this harmonic sensibility and kinda rocked it up. To my way of thinking, they were basically a bluegrass band, like the Darlings with electric guitars. That a label got behind them points to the fact that singing is making a comeback. The labels are signing top-rate singers, and that's a good sign.'

The Pinmonkeys started as a casual jam session between Music Row writers and session players. After six months, they still enjoyed themselves enough to play at Billy Block's Western Beat Roots Revival at the Exit/In. The audience clapped and cheered and jumped and jigged, getting in the spirit of the country-bluegrass-alt-country-rock music. The band decided to cut a demo of their favorite songwriters, including Gillian Welch, David Rawlings, and Duane Jarvis, a core of the Others writers. Capitol, Sony, and MCA checked them out. The band played for RCA's Joe Galante in his office and he signed them.

But the band members had some second doubts. Would a record deal be detrimental to their careers? Nashville is a songwriters and music business town. Singers and performers are down on the food chain. Singers like Maura O'Connell and Mary-Chapin Carpenter and Emmylou Harris are given esteemed respect because of their voices, but they are the exceptions. Singers are as common as dirt in Nashville. So the band members worried that breaking out as performers might be held against them as songwriters. On the other hand, they had an opportunity to help encourage the changing attitude at the country mainstream labels. If you like us, you oughta to hear our friends. You, Mr Music Business, oughta take a risk on them, too.

'I'm not taking these risks to shock anybody or be cute,' Phil Lee said. 'I'm trying to be Phil Lee and to amuse myself. I'm 50 years old. It's not going to happen that I'll become America's sweetheart, like some of these country music poster boys. The risk is that at age 62 I'll end up on a corner with a sign that says, "Help me". But I know that my records will be lying around for a long time after I'm dead. So the whole idea is to make the best music we can and hope for the best. You have to believe in yourself beyond all reason. The label executives are not paid to take risks. We are not being paid, so what the hell, why not take the risks? What are they going to threaten us with, poverty? We already own that.

'There is an attitude, a value judgment in this country, that says, "If you're so good, why are you broke?" The value is not, "I heard this record and I thought it was great." In America, it's all about making money. But that's not our focus. We take the risk to try to make the country music art form more than it is. That's what artists do, push the boundaries to create. Johnny Paycheck, Hank Williams Sr, those guys were way out there. But they were trying to make money, too. It's nice to be able to pay the rent.'

Joy Lynn White often plays with Phil Lee, and Duane Jarvis, on the house circuit. The house circuit is a nationwide network of private homes where folk and country musicians are invited to play in the host's living room for a small group of invited guests. The trio is each other's band on the road. Such small groups, performing in intimate venues, favor a stripped down sound, as opposed to the wall of rock sound heard in country concerts as well as rock concerts. The simplified string band sound is a result, in part, of economics. House circuit musicians don't make much money and can't afford to carry the expenses of a band. But the sparse band is also a conscious effort to achieve an old country sound.

Joy Lynn is one of the most seasoned of the Others. In the early 1990s, she had two major releases on Columbia. Her videos were on television. The label spent a lot of money on her in complete confidence that they would see a profitable return. An internal shakeup at Columbia led to her being dropped, along with Rodney Crowell and Shelby Lynn. She has performed with Iris DeMent, Kim Richie, the Mavericks, Buddy Miller, and Dwight Yoakam, who sang a duet on her last album. She sang with Lucinda Williams on her latest album, *Essence*. She has toured England, Scotland, and Holland many times as a solo act, the latest in early 2002. Joy Lynn White is widely admired in the Nashville music scene, both on Music Row and off the Row, as a real country singer.

We met at the Bongo Java coffee house across the street from Belmont College. The street is another of those micro-nooks in Nashville: the anti-Starbuck coffee house, a used bookstore, and several restaurants offering exotic world cuisine at affordable prices. Bongo Java has a large wooden front deck with tables under the cool spread of huge trees. Inside is the atmosphere of someone's living space converted into a club's meeting room. Newspapers are scattered around, interesting art is on the walls, and people are engaged in conservations, often about a recording or publishing deal from what I overhear. In the back is a small one-table room with an overstuffed armchair and a window looking out onto greenery. That's where Joy Lynn and I sat and talked.

She was tired. She had just returned from her weekly 600-mile (960km) road trip to visit her mother in eastern Tennessee. Her mother is seriously ill with cancer and the prognosis is uncertain. And this when Joy Lynn is just starting to come back into the world. After her last record, her 12-year-old niece and her whole family was killed in a flood.

'After that, I shut down for awhile,' she said. 'Now I'm dealing with my mom who could die. We don't know if she's going to come through.' There is no self-pity in her voice, no poor-weary-me. She's been through hard times before and when she sings the worry lines and concerns are heard. When Columbia dropped her, she came to Nashville with no money and not knowing a soul.

'I'm not a rich girl. I just persevered,' she explained. 'I went in there and sang until people finally got it and gave me a record deal. That's success. I've been here 20 years. Now I'm a staff writer at Welk Publishing. My first album at Columbia, which went out of print, has been reissued on Lucky Dog. My independent record, *The Lucky Few*, is distributed through Mercury, so I'm back out there. Right now, I'm about to sign with Hi-Tone, a good label out of Oakland, California. Buddy and Julie Miller are on that label. Hi-Tone really look after their artists. They put promotional money behind you.

'I like where I am as an independent a whole lot better than being signed to a major label. I'm going to make records now the way I want to make them. I'm not going to try to be some pretty model girl trying to make happy songs for country radio. If country radio wants to play something I do, then, cool, play it. That would be great by me but it's not my goal in life. I don't even pay attention to radio and the music machine. It's too big a machine. Why am I going to worry about that and let that irritate the hell out of me? They're going to do what they are going to do.

'I want to leave behind a body of work that has some integrity. It's not all about making money all the time. Yes, I'd like to make money. I'd like to get my share of what should be given to me. But that's up to God.'

The music machine irritates the singer in Joy Lynn. She explained that recording technology, being what it is now, means that you don't have to be that good a singer. Your mistakes and shortcomings can be fixed in the studio. You don't even have to be able to tune your own instrument, or play it on the record.

'The labels market you on how you look,' she said. 'What goes on in commercial country radio is based on how young the singer is and how good they look, and if they can sing. The commercial music, they want you to think that everyone is happy in the world. Well, they're not. Let's hear some real stuff that is going on the way country used to be, like George Jones and Loretta Lynn and the good singers who actually sang. There was no Pro Tool technology back then so the computer put you on pitch. If you couldn't sing, you got out.

'Artists are not robotic types of people. They're weird and quirky. It used to be that's what record companies wanted because they knew they were signing real talent. Now, if you're weird and quirky, they think you're nothing but trouble. God didn't give you all that talent and then make you a real business-type person. It doesn't go together. Figure it out. I'm not saying that people should get away with being assholes and being so weird that nobody can talk to them. But, on the other hand, it's not the makeup of a real artist to think like normal kinds of people. I've always tried to be real normal but that's a hard thing for me to do.'

Is the house circuit really viable to make money and build a career? A lot of people in the industry, or what they consider the 'real' music industry, look down on the house circuit as a place for the 'weird and quirky'. They equate it with playing second-rate vaudeville theaters. Joy Lynn nearly snorted.

'The house circuit is huge. People out there are so hungry to hear real people get up and play with not a lot of stuff to mask the real art. It's just you, your voice, and a guitar. You can't hide when you're playing in someone's living room with 50 of their friends practically sitting on your knees. If you're faking it, if you're not being true, they'll know it. You can't duck out the stage door. You've got to talk to them afterwards, look them in the eye. People are starved for that.

'Look how well Iris DeMent has done. She's not a glitter star but she sure is well respected. She has a big following and she does the house circuit. I do it. I have a booking agent for the house circuit. I think the under-the-radar country music is a whole lot better than that music produced by the major labels. It's real. It's better songwriting because it's not songwriting trying to make a quick buck. The songwriters are fresher than the songwriters who have been here for years and get all the cuts on commercial albums. They basically write about the same thing over and over because it works on country radio. Nashville can make you feel like you're in this bubble where you think the only music being made is what the major labels on Music Row are putting out. If you really go out around Nashville and see what's going on, you'd be amazed at the intelligent writers that nobody knows about.'

Duane Jarvis is one of those intelligent writers whose name pops up in conversations. He co-wrote 'Still I Long For Your Kiss' with Lucinda Williams, featured on her Grammy-winning album *Car Wheels on a Gravel Road*. His songs were in the film *The Horse Whisperer*. He has toured with Dwight Yoakam and backed up John Prine. He lives in East Nashville, where he and his wife, Denise, run Cat's Pajamas, a bed-and-breakfast that caters to musicians. The idea first came to Denis when she and Duane lived in Inglewood, California. Many of Duane's musician friends crashed at their small house and she loved playing hostess to the ever-revolving cast of colorful characters. She then worked as an art production manager at Capital Records, until she burned out. When she and Duane moved to Nashville, she saw a large old house for sale and knew her next career move.

Duane and I sat in the living room of that house drinking tea and listening to his new CD, *Certified Miracle*. His two previous albums, *DJ's Front Porch* (Medium Cool) and *Far From Perfect* (Watermelon) garnered critical acclaim, so he decided to take a risk with the new album to firmly establish himself as a solo artist. He paid for the studio time out of his pocket. He put his money where his mouth was, even if it would take most, if not all, of his money. And instead of him playing on other people's albums, they would play on his. His friends Joy Lynn White, Buddy Miller, and Richard Bennett, who has done world tours with Mark Knopfler, joined him.

When the project was finished, Blue Buffalo Records in Germany licenced the European rights. The German edition of *Rolling Stone* gave *Certified Miracle* a four-star rating. The European success got the attention of Slewfoot Records, which released the record in the United States. There are ways to skin the Music Row cat.

Originally from Portland, Oregon, Duane came from a '60s rock 'n' roll-top-40-bubble-gum country background: Jimi Hendrix, Petula Clark, Roger Miller. In the early 1980s, he heard 'cowpunk', then popular in Los Angeles and the West Coast. Jason and the Scorchers from

Nashville, and who still play in Nashville, were pioneers in the punk-rock-country music.

'I met Lucinda in 1987 when she was playing in a punk rock club, the Roggie's, for about ten people,' he said. 'My attraction to country music was the simple, heartfelt song, and for the feeling that runs through punk rock and rock 'n' roll, the feeling that anybody can do it. It's not elitist music. The feeling about punk and rock and country is that anyone can pick up a guitar and learn a few chords, learn a song and sing it. That's the common denominator, the level playing field of those musics. They don't exclude people. You should talk to Hank Williams III. He has a lot to say about this.'

10 Punk Loves Country

Are punk and country kissin' cousins?

Do pierced lips pucker for a twangy kiss?

Can country's wholesome mouth suck on a studded tongue?

It happens more often than you might think, and not only in the umbrageous corners of the dance floor.

But we need not be so crude for there are legitimate All-American philosophical ties that bind punk to country – rights of the individual, freedom to be and say who you are, the unalienable right to question authority, the duty to rebel against stifling authority, and the civic responsibility to demand respect for the person regardless of color, economic status, choice of hairstyle or lifestyle or music. These rights are written into the United States Constitution and Bill of Rights. These rights are expressed in the words and scores of punk and country music.

Punk musicians are heavily into rebellion and individual expression. So are country musicians, from Hank Williams Sr to Waylon Jennings to Wayne 'The Train' Hancock. Dale Watson, Robbie Fulks, Jim Lauderdale, Buck of the Shackshakers, Lucinda Williams, Kinky Friedman, Alison Krauss, and Steve Earle are a small sampling of the country singer/songwriters who carry the banner of the spirit of true country music.

The punk musicians rebel against authority, against conformity, and against people's preconceived ideas: ideas that someone is a slacker if they have multi-body piercings and tattoos and hairstyles that resemble topography more than fashionable style; that they are somehow morally degenerate, riff-raff of no worth because they do not contribute in a meaningful way, for example, an economic consumer way. Punkers live the anti-image as part of the American tradition of rebellion. Their anthem is the music of 'I'm being who I am, of doing what I want to do and if you can't accept me for that fact, well, the hell with you.'

The old true country musicians expressed much the same attitude. Their rebellion came out by breaking social rules and proper images through hard drinking. Country music has always idolized the uncontrolled individual who preferred living a wildness that others wanted confined to jail. The musicians chased women in life and in song for romance and self-indulgence. They were seen as a threat to the good order of church and family.

That lifestyle put the musicians on the edge of society, in a place of no fixed address, metaphorically and literally. They slipped the handcuffs that keep most men, and women, working under rules not of their making. Old true country had the attitude of an outsider who lives by a code that defies conformity and who fights for the little guy. Old true country was a voice of a social class most often imagined as poor rural farmer. The old true country raised a voice of protest against the overclass, represented by bankers, who threatened to foreclose on the family farm and destroy a way of life.

The old country music spoke out against the hardships of life, the personal pain of injustice and the sorrow of loss, be it a baby who died, or lovers and friends gone away, or human values consumed in the pace of modern life. The hardcore punk speaks of the injustices inflicted on those who dare to be different, of the sorrow of being excluded from the general community, of the debasement of humanistic values by commercial forces.

Traditional themes of country – loneliness, alienation, the outsider, the individual without a peer group – are also found in punk music. The punk outlaw and the country cowboy suffer from the lack of acceptance and lack of understanding. In country music, the loner cowboy moves on despite the promise of a good woman's love. The punk version is of a kid who makes him/herself totally unacceptable to the corporate world, despite the promise of consumer goodies. This alienation has been, and continues to be, a major theme in both musics.

The hardcore punk rock has more apparent anger and angst. People overtly act out more now than in the time of old country. The technology of big amps, booming subwoofers, buzzes electric guitars, speaker towers and a wah-wah pedal amplifies loud anger into bellowing angst. The old country sound didn't have that technological volume, so it sounded more sorrowful and lonely. The heartache is more clearly heard in the strings. Country is more melodic than punk. Country is more melancholy in its emotions, whereas punk puts a hard edge of anger on its emotions.

Both country and punk are fast-paced music with high energy. In the Others Risky Country, a lot of energy is put into the rebellion against the sound-alike hit formula music and bubblegum pop. In punk music, the high energy is a release of aggression. It is also trance-inducing to take people out of themselves, to separate them from the solitary individual self and make them free to join the tribe dancing around them.

These common traits shared by punk and country were articulated to me by Michael McCanless, the fiddle player in Hank Williams III's band. Michael is, more accurately, the ex-fiddler player. On the band's last tour, Michael felt an unexplained tiredness, which he attributed to the wear and tear of being on the road. Two months previous to our meeting, he had been diagnosed with cancer in the throat and chest.

'At night, lying in bed, I can feel the tumors growing,' Michael explained to me as we sat in his living room. 'It is very hot. That causes the night sweats many cancer victims experience.' Michael is tall and sparse, not quite gaunt, except around the eyes. The sockets are wide and deep frames for his eyes' bright intelligence. His face is long and lean and his head shaven, except for the lank hair tailing off the back of his skull. He is fighting the cancer by traditional chemo treatments and less orthodox herbal and diet approaches, which are approved by his doctors at the Vanderbilt University hospital. The initial assault to his system has passed and now he feels energy to practice the fiddle. He speaks of playing on stage in a month or so.

Hank Williams III has two bands in one, the country band, Hank Williams III and the Damn Band, and the punk band, Three and Assjack. The same players play the same instruments in the same show in both bands. (Sheldon Hank Williams III always introduces himself as Sheldon, never as Hank Williams. The media calls him Hank 3 but his friends and family always refer to him as Sheldon.)

'We do two sets for every show,' Michael explained. 'We open with a 90-minute set of old-school honky-tonk, the hillbilly stuff, but contemporary so it's not going back to the old songs. It's not the music of his grandfather, Hank Williams Sr, but probably music his grandfather would like. A lot of bluegrass players insist on doing the songs the way they were done 50 to 70 years ago. You can't change a note, an inflection. You have to stay pure. Well, we're not about being pure. We want to have our own expression in this music, the style and tunes.'

The band takes a five-minute break after the country set and reappears as the punk band. They wear the same casual clothes and play the same instruments for a full set of hardcore heavy metal and punk.

How does a traditional country fiddle fit into a punk band? 'It works quite well if you have the imagination to conceive of it and the balls to do it – and the right effect pedals,' Michael replied with a laugh. 'I can make the fiddle sound just like an electric guitar, or nearly indistinguishable from it. Then the fiddle becomes another lead instrument, whereas in the country band the fiddle is a support instrument. I get some interesting music playing the country fiddle as an electric guitar in a punk band. This can be translated in terms of rebellion. Just the presence of a fiddle in punk music is a rebellion against any preconceived notion of what punk music is. And it's also a rebellion against the pop country stuff. This applies to every instrument, like the standup bass, in the band. We all play outside the box.

'Country is pretty predictable. What we are doing injects unpredictability into the music. Once you've gotten the sound, or style, in your head, once you've gotten your head around the idea that fiddle and punk music do go together, that changes how you think about the instrument in general, not only from a musician's standpoint but from an audience's standpoint as well. For me, when I'm playing the country set, the musical ideas I have in my head are not quite the same as they would have been if I hadn't been playing punk music. From the audience's standpoint, they're watching the show and looking at that instrument and thinking, "That instrument, it does more than just stay within the box."'

The country and the punk sets are bookends, opposite ends of the spectrum. But they embody the same rebellion spirit. One of the band's country songs has a lyric, 'If you don't like my hillbilly sound, well, hey man, go fuck you.' It's a song about demanding respect without compromising a person's sense of self. One of the punk songs, 'Tennessee Driver', tells about a guy whose car breaks down. He walks into a bar to telephone for assistance and the bar owner tells him, 'Hell, no!' because he has a Mohawk. It's a song about discrimination because a person displays his sense of self without compromise.

'The hardcore punk fans love the country music because it's genuine,' Michael said. 'It's authentic, spoken true from the heart. That is also true of punk music. It's honest music, music from the heart. It's not pretentious, not trying to fulfill someone else's idea of what good music is. This is music that we play because we like it and it's good music. You'd expect the country people to hate punk and the punk to hate country, but they don't. In both the country and punk, we move at a brisk pace. There tends to be more recognizable chord progression in the country. In the hardcore set, the progression is from pretty damn loud to screaming pure noise. By the time we get to the end of the set, we're doing tunes that really don't have a melody. They may have some riffs but lyrically Hank's screaming. He's not singing. He's screaming.

'In every show Hank does a spiel about how we're not out here trying to say that we're better than anyone else, because we're not. But we're playing the real country music the way it ought to be and not that pop country bullshit. He does rail against the commercialization of the industry. He encourages people to call up their radio stations and request the old-school singers, like Johnny Cash, and the new people, like Dale Watson and Wayne "The Train" Hancock. In that sense, he's trying to encourage a rebellion against commercialization by the radio stations.

'In this country, the United States, we don't have an obvious oppressor, like a dictator, that is easy to focus against. Instead, we have corporate policy. Part of corporations' policy is to be inconspicuous, to be subtle. It's all-pervasive, but you can't put your finger on it. In advertising, there is bias presented in creating the image of the lifestyle you're supposed to want. But how do you say where that comes from? It's very diaphanous. How can you rebel against it if you can't say what it is?

'I wouldn't say that there is any particular political statement in our music. If there were a protest, it would be more of the cultural nature, more against lack of acceptance, stereotyping, the looking down on the younger, alternative generation.

'It's certainly plausible that our type of country music might be the art form that will speak out against that diaphanous force that so shapes and influences our society. In order to bring that about, and bring it off, we, as musicians, need to educate ourselves as to the nature of our adversary. And to spread that education to our audience.

'It's not so much that we're trying to provide an answer. We're just doing what we believe in. That happens to be providing something for people to respond to when they have this lack of substance elsewhere. We don't see ourselves as crusaders, although we'd certainly like to promote greater enjoyment of the type of music we are doing. And not just for ourselves but in general. Crusading against the commercialization in our culture? That might be a bit big to bite off.'

Michael McCanless grew up in Oskaloosa, Iowa, a small town in the midst of rolling cornfields and pig farms. His parents were classical musicians, so their house was filled with symphonies and classical chamber music. He began playing music at the age of three and started formal classical violin lessons when he was seven. He was raised with a very strong sense of music for the sake of music, art for the sake of art. As a teenager, he played in local symphony orchestras and chamber quartets. He enrolled in college but quickly realized that physics was not his life's path. He increasingly spent more time on his music than on his science books. His musical interest expanded into bluegrass, Irish music and other folk music styles. It became poignantly clear that if he didn't start making money by playing music, he wouldn't have any money.

He decided to become a country fiddle player because that's where he could find a job. His first job, in 1983, was in a local top 40 honky-tonk cover band. They played only the country music heard on straight commercial radio country. But Michael kept experimenting with folk music. 'Why are you learning all those weird folk tunes?' the bandleader asked. 'No one is ever going to pay you to play that Irish music. Why don't you just learn the songs the way they're played on the radio?'

'In that one statement, he encapsulated the whole conformist idea,' Michael said. 'Why would I want to be an individual and express myself? It's going to be much easier if I just conform and be like everybody else. That was the very idea I was rebelling against. All my life I've held to the concept that you find your own ideas, make sure they are based on a strongly held moral and ethical standard, and stand by them.'

He knew then that he was born to old true country. Punk hadn't emerged but Michael would be there tapping his foot when it finally made the music scene.

'The whole idea of the commercial musical establishment, and corporate establishment in general beyond that, is the message: "Don't be yourself. Don't think for yourself. Be like everyone else. Just conform. Go with the ease path." Well, that's the attitude found in so much of the bubblegum commercial music, whether it's called rock 'n' roll or country or pop. It's everything being like everything else. The songs in the 20 rotation slots allotted on the big mainstream commercial stations all sound the same.'

Michael arrived in Nashville in 1995 and found work with various country bands, including the house band at Billy Block's Western Beat Show. His friendship with Hank 3 began when they occasionally jammed together and shared gigs. One night, Hank asked if Michael was free to play in his band that weekend. Hank was running a rotation of fiddle players until he found one he liked. Michael became part of the rotation schedule. He was not given charts or tapes from which to learn the music. There were no rehearsals. If you make it work, you can keep doing it, Hank told him. If it doesn't work, we'll let you know.

Michael's first challenge was to learn Hank 3's original music without ever having heard it, or having charts to read as guidelines.

'At the time, the steel player was Big Jim Murphy,' Michael recalled. 'He was a coot from way back. He was playing all these signature lines. That was my cue. When you hear a signature line more than once, you think maybe you ought to play it also. So I'd listen close, as it was all by ear. It got to the point where before he was done playing that line, I'd have a harmony laid down on top of it. All of a sudden, we were a section. As long as I paid attention to Murph and listened to what he was playing, then I knew what I should be doing. Pay attention. Watch yourself. Stay out of everybody else's way.'

Michael became Hank 3's permanent fiddle player.

'The hardcore stuff that Hank writes, and all the hardcore stuff is his original material, is pretty challenging,' Michael said. 'It goes real fast and has all these unexpected left-hand turns. You just have no idea as to what is coming. Some of the melodic lines are fucking insane. So the fingering patterns are quite a challenge. But I love a challenge.'

Previously, Michael had spent years playing in country bands where the fiddle player was told to stand in the background, play your little licks, stay within your little box, and don't dare step outside the boundaries of that box. In Hank 3's band, there was no box, no boundaries, no rules. Figure out something to do in this song that works. It's up to you. You can do whatever you want to. Michael found a musical home. All the creative freedom and artistic expression he had in classical music, but had suppressed during the cover band years, came surging back.

As musicians, the band said, 'We're not like anything else. We don't sound like anything else. This is us. We're doing this because we believe in it.' This was a proclamation of revolt against the country conformist commercial corporate radio establishment. They hoisted the hardcore flag of rebellion. They were not going to dress like other country bands or punk bands. They were not going to act like other country bands, or punk bands. As a band, they were making an individualistic statement against the conformity to musical forms and the fashion code of the punk world.

The band's Music Row label, Curb Records, didn't know what to make of Hank 3, his music, or his musicians.

'Hank's relationship with the label is contentious at best,' Michael said, confirming an open secret. 'They wanted him to be a nice clean-cut image boy. When he signed his contract with them years ago, he didn't have much experience in the industry. He started out in Branson, Missouri, doing a Hank Sr tribute show. He was just making his entry into the country music field and the record label was trying to shape him to a nice image. He's been doing the country show for at least eight years. By now, he's found his sound and what he wants to do. They don't know what to do about it.'

In January 2000, the band launched their hardcore sound and a year later recorded *This Ain't Country*. Hank 3 and the band were excited by their experience. However, Mike Curb, the founder and president of Curb Records, did not share their enthusiasm. He has refused to release the CD. This is a very sore point between Hank 3 and Mike Curb. Meanwhile, Hank 3 and band continued to forge ahead. They have developed enough new material for at least one more album.

'The sound is louder, faster, darker, more tending toward death metal,' Michael said. 'It sounds weird playing death metal on the fiddle but we do. We use more minor chords as part of the darkness in the musical sound. The subject matter tends to deal with darker aspects of culture.'

The lyrics of one song called 'And Now He's Dead' say, 'I used to know a guy/who was a drug addict/and now he's dead.' The song does not advocate death or drug use. It speaks to the dark elements that exist in life; subjects taboo in mainstream country music but nevertheless a real part of urban American life. This willingness to speak about issues that are relevant to the United States as a country, and not only to the regionalism of country music, is what makes the Others different in country music. Their effort to write and sing realistically about American society as it is, rather than ignore the warts or portray the ugly through a soft lens, is why the Others claim their music is the real American music.

'We are trying to get kids, in particular, to think that if you go out and put a needle in your arm, it can lead to death,' Michael said. 'The music has a lot of anger in it – anger against unfair treatment by the establishment to anyone out on the fringe. That includes not only punk kids but also people who are on the outside edge of country music as well. Just standing up and screaming your ass off saying, "This isn't fair. This isn't right. And I'm really fucking pissed off about it." That's where the darker stuff comes in.'

If Mike Curb doesn't like Hank 3's hardcore sound, a growing number of fans have embraced it. A dedicated fan base comes to show after show.

They load friends into vans and drive for hundreds of miles to initiate the neophytes to this not-your-father's country music. The fans are an amazing mix of hillbillies with cowboy hats, rock'a'billy greasers with sideburns, and the punkers with Mohawks. Mosh pits happen at every show, even during the country set.

Hank 3 fans are not so different from Grateful Dead fans. They are fierce in their loyalty. They have a distinct, if diverse, look. Pot is part of the culture. They like the country fiddle with the hard-rock electric guitar. The Grateful Dead never hid their country roots under rock 'n' roll shouts and glitter. Hank 3 injects hard rock into country.

The joining of country and hardcore rock fans is not seamless. The hardcore audience is enthusiastic in expanding their country music horizons. The country music fans, who have been raised and programmed by contemporary commercial radio, are not as open-minded to change. The music is attracting a growing number of young punkier, hard-rock fans, and still holding the country fans, Michael has observed.

'We sell out nearly every show,' Michael said. 'Texas – Austin, Houston, and Dallas – has been really really strong for us. The West Coast – LA, Orange County, San Francisco – has been enthusiastic. One of the best clubs we play in the country is in Minneapolis, the First Avenue club. It's a huge rock venue for about 2,000 people. We've had strong audiences in there.

'That's the market we're working in, the small clubs, the small venues where you can get right down with your audiences. When you're doing a big arena show, where the stage is 20' [6m] away from the very closest people and you've got 20,000 people, the people in the back can't see you any better than on a TV screen. The types of clubs we do are small, dark, and smell. The people are right there at the front of the stage. They reach right out and touch you. They grab a hold of your leg sometimes. You get that connection with your audience and that's the market we're targeting. We really don't want to be playing huge concert venues because you lose touch with your audience.'

Since Curb Records has refused to release *This Ain't Country*, Hank 3 sells bootleg copies of his own work to his audience. Fans are encouraged to tape the shows. Michael has helped fans set up their recording equipment.

'If the record company won't release it, how are you going to get the material out?' Michael asked. 'Well, you sell it directly to your fans. We do very small runs of these bootleg CDs. Once they have sold out, no more are printed. We go on and do a small run of the next one. So far we've got four bootlegs out. The first two are highly collectable items, highly sought after. We would much rather have distribution on a record label. But given that is not there, then bring it to the fans anyway. This is Hank's response when Mike Curb wouldn't release his hardcore record.'

Art subverts commerce.

'There is a lot of leeway between the tiny backroom independent label and the national or multi-national corporate record companies that have driven us into the dirt,' Michael pointed out. 'There is a lot of room to work with there. The most effective protest against commercial marketing is don't buy the damn records. You want to spend $20 [£13] on a good CD, get on the Internet, find your favorite artist, order directly from their website. There are all sorts of resources people can turn to and find this music. You can't just sit on your butt. You have to exert a little bit of effort. That is a musical version of casting your vote. You're casting your vote with your wallet. If you devote your money and resources to people who deserve support, in your opinion, that's better than yelling and screaming about how much you hate Faith Hill. Forget about Faith Hill. Literally. Forget about her. She'll go away.

'You can take what we do as plainly against the norms of the commercial music establishment, country, and hardcore. You can take it further. Instead of having a political dictator or political oppression in our country, we have a more subtle cultural oppression. Everyone is supposed to conform to the same ideas. That sameness comes from thinking you have leeway, until you threaten to tip over the boat. When you threaten the established power and profit structures with something radical, then the power of sameness is brought to bear.

'It starts as soon as a child sees images of society around them on television, in magazines. Images that are presented to us through advertising and television programming, they all encourage conformity. If you want to find acceptance and happiness in our society, they say, here's how you do it. The key words are "our society". Within the authoritative hierarchy there is, I'm fairly certain, the realization that people are more controlled if they don't think for themselves. It's a truism. If people don't analyze the information put in front of them, if they simply accept it, then you'll be able to manipulate them and control them.

'Well, fuck that. I've adopted, in my own life, the attitude that if you get in someone's face and argue with them about a certain set of ideas or ideology, you're going to end up yelling and screaming until you're blue in the face. No one's opinion is changed,' Michael said. 'The most effective form of persuasion is simple demonstration. You just live your life being who you are regardless of what anyone else says about it. That will attract more attention for you than yelling and screaming. Just by playing the music that we believe in, we get that response from the audience that the record labels won't have expected a few years ago.'

11 Hank 3

Sheldon Hank Williams III lives in quite a hilly, working-class neighborhood of East Nashville, not the up-and-coming chic East Nashville with gingerbread cottages painted in San Francisco pastels and latte shops that serve organic raspberry muffins and stores selling new handmade wooden antique toys and cozy restaurants with tablecloths. Hank 3's neighborhood is on the other side of the tracks, literally, from that East Nashville. In his neighborhood of modest brick houses there are no latte shops or upscale markets. Nobody is doing expansions and renovations to increase their property values. Hank 3's East Nashville a good place to go unnoticed.

Hank 3 lives in a small brick house with shade trees and a fenced backyard. Freshly potted flowers were on the doorstep, an appropriate female touch as the house belongs to his girlfriend. He led me down to the basement, clearly his territory, dense with broken chairs, a beanbag chair on the floor, a huge-screen television, speakers, guitars, a computer, punk/death paraphernalia filling the walls, and vinyl 78rpm records of his grandfather, Hank Williams Sr. Two large cats rubbed against me; a young Rottweiler nuzzled my hand to have his ears scratched.

'That's Trooper,' Hank 3 said, introducing us. 'I found him starving outside the Sony studio in LA while I was recording there. I had to bring him home. He's a very mellow dog. He's so mellow that the other morning a friend came over to get me and I was asleep, so my friend tried to rile Trooper up, get him to bark and cause a fuss, thinking that would wake me up. Trooper was in the backyard and my friend threw sticks at him, shouted at him, banged on fence and Trooper didn't make a sound. Some mean watchdog Rottweiler he is. The fuss trying to get Trooper to make a fuss woke me up.'

Hank 3 has the long lank jawline, skinny frame and scooped-out chest of his grandfather. He stands about 6ft (1m 83cm), the same height as his grandfather. He has a sweet and gentle smile, same as his grandfather. He little resembles his father, Randall Hank Williams, known in the music business as Hank Jr, whose full beard gives him a burly bear look.

'Here, you take the throne,' he said, motioning to a broken office chair. He flopped down on the floor and pulled out a Mason jar full of buds. I got down on the floor with him. He filled a small glass pipe and we went to work.

'What do you like about country music?'

He took a hit. The intent was not to get blurry stoned, only fluid. A hit or two, set the pipe aside, lit up a cigarette, leant back into the beanbag and chatted.

'I like the fans,' he replied, 'how they stick with ya through thick and thin, that's for sure. They'll go with you to your grave, almost. I like some of the dynamics of the music. You can make it hard and then bring it down a little bit. There are more heart-felt songs in country than in some other music. Johnny Cash always says, "Write a song for yourself and nobody else, then it's a good song." The true country poets out there really had, and have, a way with words and know how to paint a great picture. When I listen to country music, some of the voices out there blow me away. Junior Brown, Asleep At The Wheel, David Allen Coe, Webb Pierce, Wayne "The Train" Hancock. Those are some of my big loves. Most of my music is original tunes and tunes by Wayne the Train. He's the only guy who has more Hank Sr in him than I do.'

Hank 3's voice is more hillbilly than Southern gentile. Its strong distinct twang is not softened by a honeyed accent. The voice does not try to convince you of anything. It carries hesitancies, shades of doubt followed by firm opinions. When Hank 3 talks about his values, the values of his music, and what he believes in, the voice is strong and clear.

'What you do like about punk music?'

'I've always liked the dark side. I've found the hardest furthest thing from blues or country and fell in love with it. I used to be a drummer until

I was about 19. It's cool to play that steady slow beat, but when you have a drum going rapid fire' – he acts out on his thigh, hands flying in a complicated rhythm – 'it's like WOW, check this out. It was all about the beat for me. I don't know what it is but something has always pulled me towards the dark side, towards hard rock, anti-social rock. Musically, it's not hard for me to switch between country and hard rock. The country is getting warmed up and the hard rock is really trying to let go. The hard rock is more therapy than my considering if it's going to be a great song.

'Our music is really not for the girls. It's for the guys out there wanting to let some aggression out. I don't know what that is but it's helped me become my own person for sure. I just want to see what happens with it. I'm playing Russian roulette going on stage and doing an hour of country, taking a five-minute break, and then doing an hour of punk screaming my brains out.'

For Hank 3, punk and country share the same attitude about depression, sorrow, hatred, loneliness, and alienation. Just the energy is different. When he shouts the hardcore, the melodic vocals of country are the last thing on his mind.

'In hard rock, most of the time the vocals have been spacey and don't have to make sense,' he said. 'Half the shit I'm saying people aren't gonna understand anyway. With rock, it's all about the riff for me. But in country, you can understand what the singer is saying. That's the tradition of the music. The audience listens a little harder. They want to feel some kind of connection with the music. The rock stuff is all about aggression and conflicts – drugs, Satan, fast cars, anger, sex, and all that stuff. Country is not quite like that, a little bit, but not quite.

'I know that there are a lot of country people out there that don't understand why I play the hardcore and absolutely hate it,' he admitted. 'That's why I give them five minutes between sets. I try to be cordial to my fans. I say, "Thank you for coming out to the show. I appreciate it. But if you don't like heavy metal or hard rock, it's time to go. I'll see you next time."'

Hank 3 is a mixed signal. His thin brown hair hangs free to below his shoulderblades. Garish tattoo designs cover most of his left arm. The right arm has a more modest display, perhaps a work in progress. He was wearing jeans that drooped off his hips because he has no butt to speak of to hold them up. A thick silver chain hooked his wallet to a belt loop. At first sight, it would be easy to tag him as a hybrid hippie-punker-biker.

He is also a polite, courteous, Southern boy anxious to please – up to a point. He described himself as 'pretty insecure, shy, a nice guy, lookin' down at the ground a lot, you know.' When he said 'nice guy,' it was with the inflection that he was too much a nice guy, the nice guy people took advantage of, or tried to, because they thought nice guys have a soft backbone. His mother, Gwen Yeargain Williams, from Jane, Missouri, raised him in a single-family home. It was a strict, religious upbringing that tried to keep the Devil away. He was forced to go to church three or four nights a week until he was 18. His heavy metal and rock albums were banned and burned, which was like throwing gasoline on his teenage rebellious nature.

'I was the honky-tonk hellbilly and the hellraising started in the Missouri hills,' he said. 'I put my mother through a good deal of angst and worry. But she never turned me out or turned her back on me. She's always been a loving caring mother, always stood behind me 100 per cent.'

His father is a touchier subject. The relationship is not the closest, or always the warmest. Although both are musicians, they don't play or record together. His father bought Hank 3 a truck for his 16th birthday and, after Hank 3 drove it into the ground, got him a car for high school graduation. That's about the most praise Hank 3 can muster, and that his father always paid the child support on time. He and his mother were never on an easy streak. She worked minimum-wage jobs and, as a teenager, Hank 3 was a record store clerk, garage door installer, whatever job he could find.

Hank 3 has settled the $24,000 (£15,000) child support suit for the son that resulted from a 'one-night stand', as he describes the union. To pay the settlement, he agreed to headline a Hank Sr tribute show in Branson, Missouri.

Hank Jr is a notable hellraiser himself, known for his love of parties and Jim Beam whiskey. And, like Hank 3, he is a mixed message. For years he stayed in the traditional country image. Then there is

Thunderhead Hawkins, Williams' alter ego who sings the blues. This switching of identity is a Williams' family trait. Hank Sr called himself Luke the Drifter when he stepped out of his country crooner style to record recitation songs.

And Hank Jr, 52, has been stepping out musically. For years he played his daddy's songs in the same style. On his new album, *Almeria*, Hank Jr's rowdy id Bocephus (Hank 3 is sometimes called 'Tricephus' behind his back) sings about doing it in a truck, asking the woman if she's XXX-X-Tremely country? The album has the song, 'The F Word', a duet with Kid Rock, which says, 'In country music, we don't use the F word.' Hank 3 considers the message hypocritical, whether it's meant to be tongue-in-cheek or not. He can let fly a perfect mimic of his father's litany of F words when he has the mind to do so.

Besides his country band and his punk band, Hank 3 plays bass in a third band, Superjoint Ritual (Sanctuary Records), whose first CD, *Use Once and Destroy*, was released in Spring 2002. The band is based in Austin, Texas, where they record, which is why Hank 3 splits his time between the first and second bases of country music. (To stretch the baseball metaphor, Bakersfield, California, where Buck Owens and Dwight Yoakam are headquartered, is the third base.)

On Hank 3's *Lovesick, Broke & Driftin'* album (Curb Records, January 2002), the song 'Trashville' plainly tells his opinion of Nashville and the Music Row country business. He calls it a 'dirty town'. I used to think that country was in Nashville, he sings, but all he sees in Nashville is a bunch of 'backstabbers' who don't care about the music. He'd rather take his things and go back to Texas because playing country music in Nashville ain't what it used to be. He can take only so much of the putting people down. He's tired of the new stuff they tried to make him sing. It ain't country music to him.

Hank 3 wrote 12 of the album's 13 songs (Bruce Springsteen's 'Atlantic City' being the exception), and not one song is about happy times. Regrettable times, drinking to forget times, sorrowful times but not happy times.

'I always write country when I'm either mad or sad,' Hank 3 said. 'I rarely write when I'm in a happy mood.

A song in the old country gothic style entitled 'Curb & Me (A Bitter Tale)' might be on his next album. The history between Hank 3 and Curb Records is contentious. He's locked into an eight-album contract with Curb; to date only two albums have been released in six years – *Risin' Outlaw* and *Lovesick, Broke & Driftin'*.

Hank 3 has made it known, loudly and publicly, that he hated his debut album on the label, *Risin' Outlaw*. Curb, concerned about Hank 3's drinking, put him in rehab. But Hank 3 thinks the real reason for taking him out of circulation was his outspoken dissatisfaction about his first album.

'Curb wanted me to go to media school to learn to talk to the press, what to say or not say,' Hank 3 said. 'Curb asked me ten times to go to media school. I said, "Fuck you, no way am I going to do that." I just say what I feel, even though it gets me in trouble. It's just been me speaking the truth. That gets me the respect from people who know what's up. It also translates into the kind of music I do. If I compromise who I am, then I compromise the music. It just goes back to the underdog thing.'

He is much happier with the *Broke & Driftin'* album, which he produced. That album is a more focused and balanced effort. It has all the classic country elements – prison, worn-out dog and worn-out cowboy, trucks, repentance, whiskey, rambling, lovesick loneliness, outlaw attitude, individual independence, a good marriage and home broken by drunk nightlife, and the misunderstood outcast.

The album's melancholy song, 'Cecil Brown', is about 'small town people who didn't think much of me. It's about someone on my mother's side of the family who gets in trouble,' Hank 3 explained, but stopped short of claiming that it is autobiographical. He does admit to totally relating to it personally.

He has been fighting with Mike Curb, founder and president of the label, for two years to release his *This Ain't Country* album.

'I've only been around Mike Curb three minutes. The only time I've seen him ever since I've been on his label is when I walked past him in a plane's first-class cabin to take a piss when we were on our way to an awards show,' complained Hank 3. 'If they would wake up and let me do my Jekyll and Hyde country/hard-rock side, I could knock out eight albums in two years. All I want to do is four country albums and four rockers. I have enough material right now for that. It's awful. One day I might have enough respect to find the right guy to buy me out of the enemy. I've been doing everything I can do. Curb's finally comin' around to talking to a couple of other labels. I've already got the deal set up. He doesn't want me to be a rocker, that's all there is to it. I could have had album after album out if Mike Curb would get off his high horse. The point of it is spite.'

(Curb does have a reputation in the industry of being contrary with artists who go against his wishes. He holds them to their contracts, even when no work is being produced and everyone is losing money.)

'Talk to anybody that's been on Curb Records more than two years and see how many horror stories there'd be,' Hank 3 railed. 'You could write a book, *The Worst Label in Nashville, Curb Records*. Everybody would say it's been the biggest fuckin' nightmare ever done, every client from Merle Haggard to Dale Watson to Tim McGraw to LeAnn Rimes.'

However, the heavy profanity in the *This Ain't Country* album probably influenced Mike Curb not to release it. He has a reputation as a God-fearing conservative. Hank 3's most popular live song, 'I'm Going To Put The Dick Back In Dixie', was rejected for the album because Curb did not want to put an advisory label on any of his products.

But Hank 3's deepest resentment against Curb is for the creative time he has lost with the label.

'I've just had a lot of time wasted because of the record deal,' he complained. 'I'm out there having to work on the road all the time. I hardly ever have time to be creative in the studio on tape. When I'm creative in a studio on tape, it takes two years to get it released through Curb. I feel like I'm losing time. This is definitely a weird business. I love music, until I see the machine working.'

As part of his guerrilla warfare with Curb, Hank 3 sells bootlegged CDs of his music at his shows.

'I don't have an arrangement with Curb to bootleg my own records. That's just me doing it. If I made a million dollars [£650,000] tomorrow and had a number one hit song, they'd sue me like that.' He snaps his fingers with a quick angry explosion. 'But I'm doin' what I've got to do to live. Curb doesn't give the band and me any tour support. They never have. They've wasted my career since 1996. I've gotta do what I've gotta do because I've got fans out there in punk black T-shirts and fans out there in country shirts wanting to hear my music. The bootlegs have kept me alive. We're pretty much well received all over the country. But some places don't know what the fuck is happenin'. But a lot do. There is a growing fan base. We're doin' pretty good, having been able to stay on the road for ten years without any help. That says a lot.'

Hank 3 does have an agenda behind his campaign but it's not a marketing plan or a political agenda. 'I've never voted because it doesn't fuckin' matter,' he said. 'It's all a machine. If they want a guy for president, he'll be fuckin' president, you know. That's the way it fuckin' goes. I'm proud to live in a free country. If it boils down to it, I'd shave my head and go fight, like in a bad world war. Everybody's got to be a patriot and do their thing. But as far as politics go, I'm not into it. I don't agree with the way they treat people who have bad problems with drugs. That's my only complaint about the US. So much of our personal freedom has been twisted, absolutely. I see that going from state to state touring all the time. That's why I kinda live day to day. Just get through each day and be thankful. I'm walking and talkin' and seein' the sun here and there.'

His voice changed in timbre during this speech. The tone said, 'I believe in the virtue of honest work and respect for toil of common folk who are the salt of the earth. And I'll stand up for what is right without thought of the consequences to myself.' His attitude shifted, as if he had pulled up his T-shirt and exposed a strong stubborn streak, as one would reveal a scar earned in a fierce battle. If Hank 3 thinks you are unfair or dishonest to him, or anyone, he'll be in your face faster than a rabbit on fire. He won't be snarling at your throat, but staring in your eyes so there's no mistake of his challenge or his intent to fight the wrong. He's a good ol' boy in the best sense of the word, a man who simply wants to make his way, who stands loyal to friends, who doesn't hold himself above his raisin', and doesn't respect those who do.

Hank 3's agenda is to build a broader platform for country music to support his dream – the Hillbilly Lollapalooza Tour. In the old days, the days of Hank Williams Sr and his compatriots, musicians toured together and sang each other's songs. Hank 3 longs for that kind of comradeship.

'There's a place for that comradeship again. I'm trying to make it happen,' he said. 'I've been talking to guys to maybe do a Hillbilly Lollapalooza tour. I've talked to the big guys. I've talked to the underground guys. We'll call it Outlaws. I talked to Dwight Yoakam about it a week ago. Dwight is an outlaw in his own right. What he did was all on his own. Nashville kicked him out because he had that Bakersfield sound. He respects what's real and that says it all. He has stayed out of Nashville and the system, and he has been a commercial success. That's why I'm talkin' to him about the Lollapalooza Hillbilly Band and a couple of other guys with clout. They can make it happen. If we can get the right people, the right sponsorship, the right package, make sure that everybody gets paid right.'

According to Hank 3's vision, the tour would include George Jones, David Allan Coe, Dave Alvin from X and a band like the Blasters. There would be three or four young guys that people have never heard of, then some of the middle guys that some people will have heard of, then respected elders such as Coe and Jones. Add some headliners, such as Dwight Yoakam or Merle Haggard, and that's a good day festival.

'The underground guys will get together one day and try to get some comradeship happenin',' Hank 3 said. 'It's happenin' already with the Others. The savior of country music is going to be some kind of outlaw. It's not going to be some pretty boy dancing. I know that.

'Waylon and Willie and Johnny, when they're all dead and gone, then we'll look at country music and see what a bunch of faggots and pussies everybody is compared to what Johnny Paycheck was or Merle Haggard was. Now, the guys coming up out of college have these simple lives, man. The primary hero of country music will come from outside the system.

'The Shackshakers might be one of the saviors. They've been around at least ten years. They are the ultimate thing in this town as far as I can see. I'm so jealous. It's like that's what I want but that's not what I am. Musically, performance wise, energetically wise, everything about what they've got is what I've always wanted.'

In the early years of country, a hero, and anti-hero, in the music was the individual, the stranger, the outsider. The country heard on radio now pays lip service to that, at best. Hank 3 believes that his music, and the music of similar sympathies, is more true to the temperament of the pure country. 'It's more for the common people, I'll put it that way,' he said. 'It's not fake. It's not clean. That's what my music is about and there are a lot of guys doin' this music. There's a grassroots movement in country music. It's just that we're fed all this slick stuff. There's a lot of country music out there that is not heard on the radio. It's a shame because some of the best people you never get to hear.'

And as for his personal future, Hank 3 expresses confidence.

'Right now I'm pretty comfortable. I got a girlfriend who has a real nice house. Everything is good but I've never been used to having that much money. Money, or trying to play the game to get a lot of money, has never been an issue with me. Junior Brown, he doesn't need the radio and he's still out there doing shows because he loves his music. That's kinda what I'm about. But being on the road takes away from my creative time, as far as trying to get stuff on tape. If I died tomorrow, I'd not have very much documented. I've recorded as many shows as I can. But I would have never got to really explore my mind the way I wanted to in a studio with somebody there turning the knobs and pushing me and being creative.

'I want people to remember that, "Man, this guy was a kid that could go out and play his kind of country music and then go out there and completely freak out and do his rock." It's like punkers wearing Johnny Cash T-shirts nowadays. When I'm 70, I want the music I've done to have bled over into the underground a little bit. I want people to know that I was a little off the wall, a little out there. That's good for me.

'I want another good ten or 15 years. Really just to get out five to ten albums. That's all I hope for. Get out country albums and rock albums and I'll be a happy man. That's all I want to do – and work the road until I can't work no more, man. That's my goal. Keep on sticking with it. I've already played with about everyone I want to play with, all my rock heroes, all my country heroes. All the other guys I want to play with are dead. I've had my dreams fulfilled that way. I just haven't had my creative dreams filled.

'I'm 29 now. I've been doing this for ten years. That takes a toll. Physically, I'm starting to feel all the years of damaging my lungs come into play. It's holding me back a little bit, 'specially when I want to rock harder but can't because I'm physically almost at my peak on a hot summer night with 500 kids in the club and doing a two-hour show. One day I'll get it happening. I'll try to get on the straight and narrow. I'm feeling that huff and puff coming out a little bit more.

'I smoke pot from the time I get up to the time I go to bed. Cutting back on that would be getting on the straight and narrow. I see myself chillin' out to be able to get physically better to be able to rock out harder. But the pot, that lifestyle, that's what I sing about, that's what I know about. I don't want to be a hypocrite to it but I don't see myself doing it for the rest of my life. But, I might, you know. I might be like Keith Richards and do that crazy stuff.'

12 Folk/Punk/Country

Folk and punk and country music seem, at first blush, very odd bedfellows. Imagine Joan Baez and Sid Vicious and…let's not go there. That could be nothing but trouble. But those three music genres have, in their spirit, always gone looking for trouble. Folk music of Woody Guthrie and his fellow travelers in the 1930s threw rocks at the big bosses who fought the worker's right to unionize. They aimed lyrical barbs at the banks that foreclosed on farms. They sung about the powers used to humiliate and crush the soul of ordinary human beings, who were often belittled as the 'little guy'. Merle Haggard and his fellow country travelers wielded their music in the same tradition to give voice to the plight, travails, and good times of the 'folk'. The punk rockers screamed for the underdog, and howled in protest against the injustices and prejudices visited upon the individual.

Joan Baez, Bob Dylan, Janis Ian, and the folkies of the '60s were leading voices against the United States government waging an 'illegal' and immortal war in Vietnam. Kris Kristofferson and Tom T Hall were among the country music chorus questioning the war and translating the policies into human terms. They poked the giant in the eye with their guitars and words.

Folk and country music have a long history and love for a good tall tale. One songbook for the '60s folk revival was Cecil Sharpe's two-volume *English Folk-Songs From the Southern Appalachians*. Most of the songs can be traced back to English or lowland Scots sources. Two of many examples: 'The Jewel, My Joy', published in England in 1809, was a song about a military funeral that became the benchmark for 'The

Streets of Larado' and 'The Dying Cowboy'. Bob Dylan's 'Queen Jane Approximately' echoes the Celtic original 'The Death Of Queen Jane'.

Dylan's 1968 *Nashville Skyline,* recorded in Nashville, was the blessing from the pope, so to speak. Artists from folk to pop to rock followed him to Nashville, including Neil Young, the Byrds, and Linda Ronstadt. Dylan's recording was 'one of the single most important things that happened to Nashville as a recording center,' said Charlie McCoy, the musician who put Nashville on Dylan's radar. 'It removed the stigma that many artists saw in country music.' (McCoy is quoted by Dan Daley in his book, *Nashville's Unwritten Rules, Inside the Business of Country Music.*)

The urban folk revival made cult figures of Dock Boggs and Doc Watson, a true-blood country fiddler. The banjo picking and plain-speaking vocals of folk singer Pete Seeger have an Appalachian accent. The Dillards were country musicians who went to California and played the folk clubs, such as the Ash Grove, where Bill Monroe often performed. Taj Mahal studied Monroe's picking style by sitting on the edge of the stage and watching the master's finger patterns.

Woody Guthrie put new words to Carter Family tunes. Their 'Wildwood Flowers' became his 'Ruben Jones'. Guthrie's famous 'This Land Is Your Land' was a derivative of 'When The World's On Fire', sung by the Carter Family. Guthrie was a link in the chain for Dylan from the Appalachian Carter-type sound (even through Guthrie, son of a musicologist, was Harvard educated and learned the banjo in his college years) to the modern folk music.

Sara and Maybelle Carter were reunited at the 1967 Newport Folk Festival. Eck Robinson, credited with making the first country recording in 1922, appeared, in his 60s, at the 1965 Newport Folk Festival and collaborated with The New Lost City Ramblers.

'Folk singer' in the old old tradition means music learned at home from the folks passing the songs down from generation to generation. Sara Carter learned 'Wildwood Flowers' at the knee of her mother. The term was applied to the singers of 'old-time music' associated with Appalachia and became the template for the revivalists. Joan Baez, when asked if she was a folk singer, replied that if she was a 'folk singer' she would live on an old farm in the Appalachians, wear dated clothes and sing with a nasal twang, according to Brian Hinton in his book *Country Roads – How Country Came To Nashville* (Sanctuary Publishing, 2000).

Baez began her music career playing the ukelele and singing country songs like 'Your Cheating Heart'. But she re-recorded many of the Carter Family songs and made her fame and fortune as a folk singer.

Janis Ian, who won her core audience as a folk singer in the 1960s, told me that, 'Growing up on folk, you have to grow up on country. That's why I've always felt comfortable in Nashville. I heard Hank Williams and Jim Reeves as a kid.'

During lunch in her favorite Japanese restaurant, we discussed her science-fiction writing but the conversation kept drifting back to her music.

'Folk has always been, unless you're talking about the folk Nazis, has always been the music of the outcast, the disenfranchised, whether it was the Appalachian Mountains or minstrels,' she said, expertly using the chopsticks. 'The music has always had a high tolerance level for differences. Folk has always promoted the common man, which country does too, but country went more toward the real white Anglo-Saxon Protestant backwoods preacher. Folk has always embraced diversity, well, not always, but in general, particularly in this country. We've turned it into something very different than folk music in England.'

Janis won her credentials in the folk protest movement when, at the age of 14, she wrote 'Society's Child' about interracial marriage and American society's reaction. The song, which indicted America for its racism and hypocrisy, appeared when racial and civil protests were challenging the nation. Interracial marriages were illegal in many states. Only later did the US Supreme Court strike down laws criminalizing such marriages.

She became a target of racist hate mail. Government agencies took an interest in her, which was not new. When she was six years old, FBI agents tailed her from home to school. The surveillance was so routine that she thought all the kids had FBI agent escorts. Her father, a civil rights activist who openly embraced socialistic ideas, was under the government's scrutiny. The FBI had questioned him and his wife for years before Janis was born.

'Society's Child' was called subversive and banned across the country by radio stations. The conductor/composer Leonard Bernstein openly supported Ian and public opinion swung to her favor. The song went to number one and suddenly she was famous, appearing on national talk shows and hanging out with Jimi Hendrix and Janis Joplin.

But Ian believed in the socialistic ideals of her father. She did not pursue the spotlight and gave most of her money away to charities and friends. She wrote songs and played them on the folk circuit, building a loyal following, which she continues to do today. The music press didn't put her in headlines as they assumed that she was a 'has been' because of her under-the-radar work. When she won her first Grammy with 'At Seventeen', an anthem for disaffected teenagers struggling to be women, the press declared she was a 'comeback'. Ian figured that she had never gone away. She was still writing and singing about the negative impact of injustices and prejudices.

She became famous again for a while. She got married and, duped by her accountant, she was once again the subject of a government investigation. The marriage ended in a bitter divorce. Her accountant misled her about her taxes. The IRS came after her for seven years of unpaid back taxes. She sold her house, guitars, piano, publishing catalogue, everything to pay the bill and avoid jail.

She moved to Nashville in 1988 with little more than a guitar and the clothes on her back. Five years later, she made a 'comeback' with her Grammy-nominated album *Breaking Silence*. She also announced that she was a lesbian, which prompted *Rolling Stone* to pronounce 'Before Ellen came out and anyone who wasn't a Bible scholar knew who Lilith was…before Jewel even…there was Janis Ian.' Her response has been to speak out against spousal abuse and fight for the rights of AIDS victims.

Janis estimates that she has written 500 to 600 songs and that 280 to 300 have been recorded and released.

'I figure there are also about 400 cover copies of my songs have been released. After 38 years of songwriting, writing something else, like poetry and science fiction, looks really attractive. I wrote articles for *The Advocate*, to which I still contribute. I found that I really liked working in another form. So when Mike Resnick started on at me about writing science fiction, I found I really like that too. Between that and the articles, I think it brings a new scope to my songwriting.

'For me, the best science fiction is not about bug-eyed monsters. It's about what could be or what already is and we don't know. If I look at my songwriting, a lot of that has always been there, because I've always read science fiction. Songwriting starts from the imagination. If you only write about your own life, it's really boring. Most of us have pretty small lives compared to literature.'

Janis admitted that she is stunned by her ignorance about how to write short stories. She is such a prolific songwriter of quality that she assumed that might carry over into another writing form. She discovered that what she took as talent was actually experience in her craft. In writing a song, she knows what to avoid, what leads to a dead end, which corner is a wrong turn. She is just learning how to navigate fiction.

'Isn't it great when you discover something?' she asked with real enthusiasm.

She has learned, as an artist, that you have to be in control of your craft, yet simultaneously be released from the control. The more you write, the better you write and the more comfortable you are with writing. You learn more craft by not repeating your mistakes.

'I'm a big advocate of craft married to talent,' she said. 'You reach an age where talent is no longer enough. If you don't have the craft to back you up, you can't write to deadline. I could have never done any of the movies I did, or written songs for our people, or written lyrics in an emergency when someone desperately needed them. It's the craft that sees you through when talent needs a break.'

But, like Gretchen Peters, Janis is suspicious of songwriting schools. 'I think there is a tendency to lose sight of the heart in those situations,' she explained. 'Without heart, all the craft in the world is meaningless. As songwriting becomes more of a profession, and less of something that just outlaw delinquents go into, and people get songwriting degrees from songwriting schools, well, you tend to write from the head rather than the heart. Making people aware that they should change their heart to humanism is what the artists should be doing. In the best of all possible worlds, that is absolutely our job. But changing hearts is an individual project, one song at a time.'

Does she think that folk and country are still kindred spirits as they were in the times of Woody Guthrie and Hank Williams?

'I think that there is very much a country movement akin to the folk coffeehouse movement in the 1960s,' she replied. 'There is a grassroots movement going on just below the media and corporate radar screens. Country writers are very active in that. We, as a country, are ripe for a resurgence of a grassroots political movement, something like the '60s, if you can find anything to rail against that doesn't shoot you when you start.

'I think one of the reasons that the '70s became the "me" decade was because the '60s generation watched both Kennedy and King get killed. So the '70s generation figured, "Hey, you set that spark, they're going to crush you." You read stuff now about the FBI and CIA infiltrations, which has increased alarmingly since Bush declared his war on terrorism, and you realize how desperate those in power were, and are, to keep the status quo. They would stop at nothing. So I don't know if an effective people's political resistance could take root now.

'Why should someone take action against a system that provides so many goodies?' she asked rhetorically. 'It's like going into Vietnam and offering ideology instead of rice. Whoever had the most rice won.

'On the other hand, such suppression will spawn resistance sooner or later. I think a resistance attitude is popping. But things will have to get a whole lot worst regarding civil liberties and personal freedom for a backlash to happen. My generation found the '50s stultifying. Women weren't allowed to have their own credit cards. Men weren't allowed to cry or play with babies. That world was like a prison to my generation. I personally think that the major reason we wanted a revolution was not just because things were wrong, but because we had been promised in school and on television and by our parents that all the things we objected to were the way it should be. When we figured out that those people lied, it was a short step to believing that everybody lies. From there it's a short step to, "Then I'm to cram this truth down their throats." I don't know that these past two or three generations have anything near that big to rail against. Things today are not overtly repressive enough.'

Part of the grassroots movement in music is the house concert circuit.

'There is a whole world out there of home shows, living room concerts, little theaters in people's converted garages, regular clubs like the Bottom Line, where a folk and country singer can scrape out a living,' Janis said. 'If I had to make a living from Nashville or country music, I'd be dead. I'd have to work five day-jobs. But I make a very good living on the folk circuit and the concert circuit.

'Three or four years ago, we were all bitching that there were no clubs under 500 to 600 seats. Clubs that big, or bigger, are economically unfeasible for the under-the-radar performer. Well, living-room concerts sprung up. People started turning their garages into invitation-only clubs. I just did one in Fayetteville, Oklahoma. It had about 75 seats and you, the customer, have to subscribe to the entire season, which is six shows, at $25 [£16] a show. So the entrepreneur knows that they can pay the acts. It's a packed house every show once a month. You can make a living doing such a circuit. It's a great thing. It will be interesting to see how it pans out. The music business's death grip on the old way is loosening. There is nothing new to replace it, which is happening now in country. Something will come in to fill that vacuum.

'For the under-the-radar country performer, there is no other way to get your music out or to make a living. Because country artists are writers, the folk circuit is open to them. And it dovetails with folk singers moving to Nashville, such as Emmylou Harris. The folk clubs are a venue for the country artists, if you don't tell the promoter that you're a country singer. You present yourself as a singer/songwriter.

'When I first moved to Nashville, I described myself as an artist in the elevated sense to mean an "artist". I'd hear people say, "What do you expect, she's an artist." I finally asked someone about that. They said that artists are the singers. You can't expect much from the singers. In Nashville, there is a real line drawn between singers, who only sing, and songwriters. Some singers, like Maura O'Connell, are singers but it's okay because they choose really good songs. They have the hearts of songwriters.

'But, for the most part, country singers in Nashville are looked upon with a fair amount of contempt. Producers pick their songs. In the folk world, there was such a move on for people to write their own material that you assumed a folk performer was a singer/songwriter. That is not always a correct assumption in country music.'

Does she see any changes coming to the country music business?

'In the next ten years, as the bigger companies continue to fail and drown under the weight of their own infrastructure, you'll start seeing small companies either attached to a larger company, like Lost Highway's relationship with Mercury, or new small labels forming on a wing-and-prayer,' Janis replied. 'Given the choice, people will respond to real worth, like the music of *O Brother*. People will go for the real goods before they will respond to technological sales pitches, which is what much of commercial music sounds like.'

Janis sees hope for this change in producers like Don Cook and Allen Reynolds, and in executives like Don Herrington of Dualtone and Tony Brown and Tim DuBois at Universal South.

'Tony Brown is first and foremost a musician who is a label executive. That can make you schizophrenic, trying to be in two places at once. It's like being gay and not being out nowadays. Remember that Fireside Theater ditty, "How can you be in two places at once, when you're not anywhere at all." That's the crux of it for someone like Tony. I love Tony. He's a good man. He's got a conscience, a heart. He knows that a lot about the business is wrong. But he also knows that his bosses are only going to go so far. And everyone has a boss nowadays.

'That's where folk is different from country. Folk has always been anti-boss. I don't want anybody over me. I'd rather be out here on a railroad track. But look at country's individualistic artists. How many records do they sell? We paid homage to the outlaws, but Waylon died without a major label contract. Willie could not go to Columbia or BMG. The industry pays homage to such artists when they get old enough. They figure that you'll die without enough awards. But awards don't pay your bills. The industry is starting to pay homage to me because I'm past 50.

'Willie and Waylon are leaders, and we still don't give a shit. They are innovators, someone whose goal in life is to make something bright and shiny and new. You're not talking about people whose goal in life is to be famous. Greatness doesn't have to have nice clothes to dress well. Willie and Waylon and me and others are doing this because there is something too big inside to get out any other way. You can live a big life with a little soul, or you can have a big soul with a little life. They don't merge very well.'

'What are you working on now, Janis?'

'I have to finish paperwork on an insurance policy,' she replied without irony. 'I'm editing a poetry book. I go on tour from mid-May to mid-November. Next year I want to stay home most of the year, if I can afford it, and just write stories. In five years I don't want to be touring so much, given my age. In the past two years, I did 100 dates a year. I want to stay home and see if I can be a writer.'

13 What Is Country?

Traditional country. Classic country. Young country. True country. Rock country. New country. Alt country. Metal country. Gospel country. Kickin' country. Old-time country. Christian country.

Are these just marketing categories for country music or do they have real meaning to help understanding of the music?

I went to the Country Music Hall of Fame and Museum to search out sources of country music. The original Hall of Fame near Music Row has been torn down and the new structure, located downtown across the street from the ice hockey arena/convention center, opened in 2001. The old building was a somewhat modernistic barn-like structure; the barn was a reference to country roots. The new building is constructed of swooping cement; the industrialization is a reference to country's urban home.

The board of directors of the new Hall of Fame is very proud of their statement. They have every right to be justifiably pleased with the museum within the statement, a wonderfully interactive, entertaining, user-friendly exhibition and historical archive. Free-standing video screens show stars telling anecdotes about their life and careers in a personal and engaging manner. You can sample the sounds of the history of country music at various listening stations. Webb Pierce and Elvis Presley's cars are in a face-off on the third floor. The flamboyant Pierce had a white Pontiac Bonneville with chrome-plated, pearl-handle six-shooters for door handles. Silver dollars, in need of polishing, are glued to the dash. Attached to the grille is an impressive set of Texas long horns the width of the car. Elvis's 'Solid Gold Cadillac', a white limo, nice but not exceptional, is a conservative understatement in comparison to Pierce's showbiz. He also had a guitar-shaped swimming pool in his Nashville backyard. If the two cars were mobile, they'd be one second away from a head-on collision.

A wall of tall glass fronts the lobby, which runs the width of the building. Huge steel I-beams, painted dull red, support the sloping glass roof. The lobby's interior wall is a massive concave curve of pre-cast beige cement. Water pours out of the top of a lower wall faced with natural Tennessee limestone, like rain from a spout, into a small pool. This sterile display of stone and water is supposed to evoke nature, as is the parquet floor. The stone, water and wood are the only natural elements of country incorporated in the architecture. Static goldfish of shiny coins lay in the bottom of the 6" (15cm) deep pool. A black granite wall backs the pool. Etched into the granite are the names of the Hall of Fame sponsors: Ford Motor Co, Vince Gill and Amy Grant, and various record companies and local corporations.

The view from the lobby out of the two-story tall windows is of the skyscrapers of downtown Nashville. Directly confronting the Hall of Fame is the headquarters of Southern Central Bell telephone company. The twin spikes jutting up from each side of the roof bring to mind Michael Keaton's headpiece in the Batman movies. The building is popularly called the 'Bat Building'.

The slender twin spikes can also be interpreted as the gesture for being cuckolded.

Seen from this perspective, Mr Commerce in his big building is giving the horns to Mr Country (and country music is fundamentally male). Here was the deal: Mr Commerce said to Mr Country, 'With your beautiful voice and my business acumen, we'll make a great team. Let me control your music. Accept my proposal and I'll make you famous and both of us rich. I'll provide you with a beautiful house, expensive cars, state-of-the-art touring bus, boats, horses, whatever your heart desires. Without me, you'll live in a rented trailer, not even a double wide. You'll be a nobody driving a rusted-out pickup with failing brakes. Play the game my way and we'll both make out like bandits.'

Mr Country thought about the offer. 'But will you respect me? Can I trust you? Will you honor my art and my artistic soul?'

'Absolutely,' replied sincere Mr Commerce. 'Why, we'll even be seen in public. We'll have our picture taken together.'

The relationship was consummated. Mr Country gets adoring fans and a PR firm to guard his door. Mr Commerce consolidates little companies into big companies and thinks that it's more fun than sex. Everyone in the topping position knows that power is an aphrodisiac. Mr Country gradually starts to feel like the bride after the honeymoon, when she has been downgraded to chief cook and bottle washer. Mr Commerce waltzes in and says, 'Break a few of those country eggs, throw in a dash of spice to give it a new taste, and make me a hit omelet.' Mr Country protests that he is a chef, not a hash cook. Mr Commerce winks and says, 'Whip that up. I want it climbing the charts in six months.' As he goes out the door for a dinner date with sexy Miss Venture Capitalist, Mr Commerce waves goodbye, his first finger and little finger extended in the Sign of the Horns.

Metaphors are built out of the stuff of life, even bad overextended metaphors.

From the lobby, I walked up the ramp between the towering cement wall and the self-effacing stone wall to the second-floor rotunda. In the place of honor is Thomas Hart Benton's painting, *The Sources of Country Music*. The Hall of Fame's board of directors commissioned the 6' x 10' (2m x 3m) painting by one of America's most famous and respected regional artists in 1973. Benton's charge was to illustrate and educate about country music.

Norman Worrell, then the executive director of the Tennessee Arts Commission, and Woodward Maurice 'Tex' Ritter, the famous singing cowboy and member of the Hall of Fame's board, went to Benton's home in Kansas City, Missouri, to sound out the artist. At a panel discussion at the Hall of Fame commemorating Benton's birthday, Worrell recounted the visit.

'Benton and Ritter had an immediate rapport and liked each other,' Worrell said. 'They enjoyed Jack Daniel, cussing, and both were politically conservative. Ritter once ran for governor of Tennessee as a staunch Republican conservative who blamed the socialization of the United States on FDR's New Deal. Benton came from a very prominent liberal

Democrat family. His granduncle, and namesake, was Senator Thomas Hart Benton, who once got in a fight with Andrew Jackson and shot him. This was before Jackson became president. At that time, the Bentons lived in Tennessee, where Jackson was a powerful politician. After the fight, the Bentons thought it prudent to move across the state line to Missouri, where Uncle Tom was elected senator. The painter Benton became quite conservative in his elder years, so he and Ritter were on the same wavelength.

'After a couple of shots of Jack Daniel, we went out to Benton's studio behind the house. This was a get-to-know each other visit, not a business meeting, but I asked how much a mural would cost.

'He replied, "$5,000 [£3,250] a square foot [0.1 sq m]. How many square feet do you want?"

'I answered, "$50,000 [£32,500] worth." That would make the painting 5' x 10' [1.5m x 3m], so he threw in a couple of square feet for free.'

Benton was an avid country music fan. His grandfather was a fiddler. In the 1920s, Benton traveled throughout the Ozarks, Virginia, and the Appalachian Smokey Mountains making paintings and sketches of musicians. His paintings *Lonesome Road*, *Country Dance*, *Jealous Lover of Lone Green Valley* and the lithograph *Coming 'Round the Mountain* are examples of rural folk music in Benton's artwork.

In the early 1930s, Benton learned to play the harmonica and devised the fingering now in use to teach the harmonica. When he lived in New York's Greenwich Village (1932–4), he formed a string band with his art students, musicians, and businessmen from the recording industry. One of the student players was Jackson Pollock – before the two painters split over artistic disagreements. Benton didn't like Pollock's abstract work. Benton also recorded, with his son, a three-record set for Decca, *Saturday Night at Tom Benton's* (1941), defined as 'a folksong revival statement'.

In correspondence between Benton and the Hall of Fame board, the painter made it clear that 'THE FORM', as he printed out in block letters, was entirely up to his discretion. But he was open to suggestions about the content. Bill Ivey, former director of the Country Music Hall of Fame and Museum, who also spoke at the panel discussion, suggested the source themes include white Protestants, a Negro, a transmitting tower, a microphone, and a recording session or radio show to demonstrate that country music was already a commercial enterprise in the 1920s. Benton nixed the recording session. Ivey also suggested a train to symbolically represent the modern progress of the nation and country music in the 1930s, when radio was spreading the music across the country. Benton okayed the train. He had a childhood fascination with trains and placed them in many of his paintings.

'When the train came in, Benton's mind shifted from just country music to the cultural influences of country music,' Ivey told the panel's audience. 'The train shifted his thinking and focus.' It also solved an artistic problem. Until then, Benton had divided the painting's interior with artificial barriers separating different themes. The painting had no central focus point. The train, placed in the mid-distance in the painting's center, became the visual focus. The painting's figures look into the interior of the painting at the train and draw the viewer's eye with them.

Benton worked on the painting for two years. One evening after dinner, he went to his studio behind the house, as was his habit. *The Sources of Country Music* was finished, lacking only his signature. He was gone an unduly length of time. His worried wife, Rita, went to the studio. She found her 83-year-old husband lying dead by the right-hand corner of the painting, where an artist normally signs the work. He was wearing his spectacles, as if bending over to sign the painting when his heart failed.

'We had no idea of the progress of the painting when we heard that he had died,' Ivey said. 'After the funeral, we went into the studio and the painting was essentially finished, all but the final varnish and his signature.' The painting remains unsigned.

The painting is not a literal representation of the history of country music, but rather done in a nostalgic spirit of folk-and-rural, as was the style of Benton, Grant Wood, and John Stuart Curry, the triumvirate of Regional painting. But the painting does capture the traditional values and references of country music.

In the painting's foreground on the right edge is a cowboy strumming a guitar. Although it was agreed that none of the figures would resemble a specific individual, the cowboy is a deliberate visual representation of Tex Ritter. Ritter died while the painting was in progress and Benton asked permission to reference his friend. The cowboy is an important motif in country music, evoking the rugged, independent, self-reliant loner who could conquer frontiers with his bare hands. These characteristics continue to shape how Americans view themselves and explain a great deal about the nation, from its Darwinian economic system to its present foreign policy of, if necessary, single-handedly ridding the planet of bad guys as defined by Sheriff USA.

In Benton's sketches the original cowboy figure was smaller and on horseback, facing away from the viewer, gazing over a wide-open Western landscape dotted with cattle. The larger singing Tex Ritter cowboy links the Western to 'country and western music'.

Billboard magazine didn't create a 'country and western' category to chart the music until 1949, and has since dropped the 'western' out of 'country'. Bob Wills and his Texas swing is the notable exception of authentic Western in country music. The cowboy songs were largely a Hollywood creation.

Opposite the cowboy, on the left edge of the painting, are two women, one playing the lap dulcimer and the other singing a duet with her. They pay homage to Appalachian women and their enormous contribution to country music. Appalachian women traditionally collected ballads and other songs to exchange among themselves at quilting bees or sewing circles. The women took on an important social identity by being the keepers of the songs and stories. This oral history made strong bonds between kin and neighbor and community. The women were cultural workers; the men did the farming and commerce.

Since the 1950s, women have gained more prominence in country music as performers. In general, they aligned themselves with rural and working-class women. Loretta Lynn is the foremost example of this but she is not the only one. Dolly Parton is an authentic card-carrying member of the poor, working-class Appalachian heritage, and the most lyric poet of that Southern mountain culture. Parton's musical style is rooted in Elizabethan ballads preserved by isolated Appalachian mountain people, in the emotional religious music of Protestant fundamentalist churches, and in the country music on early 1950s radio. Benton includes all three motifs in his painting.

In her book, *My Sister*, Willadeene Parton wrote, 'For the first years of their life together, we were sorry for Mother because Papa's word was law; and the last years, we were sorry for Papa because Mother keeps breaking the law.'

In the painting are two fiddlers on the dance floor, one with a jug of moonshine at his feet. Only males, usually only white males, played the fiddle in rural music until the 1930s. The music played in the hills and hollers of the South was based around string instruments, such as fiddles and dulcimers, Celtic instruments brought from Europe, and the banjo, with African origins. The music from that region was dubbed 'hill-billie music' by the *New York Journal* in an article on April 23, 1900 and the term stuck.

A hillbilly is 'a person who lives in or comes from the mountains or backwoods, especially of the South; somewhat contemptuous term,' according to *Webster's Dictionary of American Language*. The hillbilly has been portrayed in American literature and films as an uncouth, primitive, uneducated, degenerate, stupid, poverty-smeared hick. Country music, by association, was tarred by the same brush and fought the image from its commercial beginnings. Most country performers did everything they could to disassociate themselves from the hillbilly image, from wearing cowboy outfits to the tuxedos of Eddie Arnold in the 1950s. Only on the Grand Ole Opry or the television shows *Hee-Haw* and *Beverly Hillbillies* did country musicians dress as hicks, and that was to exploit the image better commercially. Buck Owens' *Hee-Haw* hick character was authentic only in the music that Buck played.

The hillbilly image was class-antagonism, the North against the South, rich versus the poor, the civilized educated versus the ignorant. But the hillbilly also had a positive connotation as symbolized in the wild rose.

There are two conceptions of the rose as an American cultural symbol. One is of the hybrid tea rose, bred of civility, meant to decorate the gardens and flower shows of the upper class. This delicate beauty is protected by long traditions in a highly structured society. Then, there are wild roses. Wild roses live outside the orderly garden bounds of dos and don'ts, protocol, tradition, custom. Like the early European immigrants, wild roses leave their origins to seek growth and vitality in an untamed world. They seem to grow randomly and spontaneously, a perfect symbol for the American idealism of individual freedom. The wild rose is beautiful and tough, able to endure harsh conditions and still flourish, much like the music of the mountain people.

In country music tradition, the wild rose is counter to the carefully cultivated rose grown under controlled conditions. The hillbilly wild rose becomes, in this sense, a musical celebration of free spirit. The wild rose is identified with the idea of unbounded personal freedom and the vitality and beauty of the natural world. Country music has always prided itself on simplicity mistaken as natural performance. In the early years, the singers stood stiffly upright on stage wearing their Sunday-best clothes. They did not indulge in preplanned, artificial entertainment. They sang the music pure without the distraction of the performer creating showbusiness. This 'natural' style is carried on at the Grand Ole Opry. The style is lost in the arena stage shows of Brooks And Dunn, Tim McGraw, Faith Hill or Shania Twain, who followed the road opened up by Garth Brooks and Reba McEntire.

Brooks, who has a university degree in marketing, brought the antics of rock 'n' roll to the country stage. He understood how to be entertaining with flash and dash, but still be country, even when he sang Kiss songs. He is the most successful performer ever in country music history. Reba McEntire was the first female country performer to hire a choreographer for her shows. She brought on a troupe of background dancers and introduced elaborate costume changes between songs. On her 1992 'Fancy' tour, McEntire stepped out of an elaborate feathered creation that resembled a rhinestone angel nailed to the floor and emerged as a slick cowchick wearing Western boots, tight pants and a satin jacket embroidered with sequins. She currently has her own successful sitcom television show, 'Reba'.

In Brooks and McEntire, and like-minded performers, country is trying to have it both ways – delivering the authentic natural music of the simple folks who made their way in the New World, and brashly making that music sound like the unnatural New World. Part of the charm of old country was deluding oneself that the performer was just a neighbor convinced to play, somewhat reluctantly, a fiddle tune for you. Doc Watson carries that off, as does Ralph Stanley and Bill Monroe, although they are consummate professionals. The audience suspends disbelief that the old-time performers, even if they are youngsters, spend hours upon hours of practise time or take voice lessons. 'No, they are simply using their natural talents,' the fan wants to believe. The country of on-stage flashpots, complex lighting schemes, electric guitars and loud bands doesn't try to hide behind the gingham. The performers work hard at entertaining and are not ashamed to show it. But they want the audience to believe it is still country, even musically true to old-time country.

Country has always practiced the sleight of hand between appearing as an extension of the natural world, yet being accomplished art. Despite the videos and overwrought stage shows, country performers still want the audience to believe that they are essentially down home, certainly more down home than the drug-snorting, guitar-bashing, hotel-room-wrecking, groupie-orgy, self-indulgent rockers who perform as much for themselves, and the money bottom line, as they do for the people. Country performers are just folk, plain-spoken, straightforward folk; a rose gone a bit wild. That is an important marketing image in the country music industry.

Dolly Parton, Linda Ronstradt, and Emmylou Harris, on the cover of the Grammy-winning, platinum album *Trio* (1987), are festooned with the wild rose motif on their Western-wear costumes. In Emmylou Harris's quasi-autobiographical country opera, *The Ballad of Sally Rose* (1986), the major character, Sally Rose, has the identity of a mountain or country rose – a wild, wild rose, a hillbilly. Dolly Parton's 'Wildflowers' is a song about nonconformity, flight, freedom, individuality, and the American road. Individuals must leave the hometown and travel. The American Rose Society has bred roses named after several country music artists whose work connects them to the flower: Lynn Anderson, Minnie Pearl, Barbara Mandrell, Patsy Cline, and Dolly Parton. A rose is a rose. Be it Garth Brooks or Emmylou Harris, it is still a hillbilly country rose.

Hillbilly music produced an offspring – bluegrass. To read country music without considering bluegrass is to miss the long continuing gothic tradition of the high and lonesome sound, haunting tenors, twang, violent murder, ghosts, dark and dreary woods, lonesome graveyards, and a fascination with death, often by murder. Bluegrass alignment with the gothic is rooted in the British ballad evolving out of folk songs, instrumental pieces, and dances brought to America by Anglo-Celtic immigrants. The dancers in the center of Benton's painting refer to how the jigs transformed into the hoedown of American square dancing.

This hillbilly Appalachian association is continued in the painting by the preacher/choirmaster directing his two-woman choir and the little white church on the hill in the background. Church music was a vital factor in the development of country music. Many of the harmonies and melodies of early country came straight from the hymnals. Songs such as 'Amazing Grace' and 'Will The Circle Be Unbroken' remain perennial country favorites. Country music is laden with references to God and redemption. Fun and sin are staples of the music. You can't have one without the other, just as you can't have good without the bad. Otherwise, how would you know the difference? This simple folk philosophy makes country elegant.

The steam train, the symbol of modern industrial might that will pull the people out of rural poverty, is the center focus of the painting. The train, a strong motif in early country music, represented freedom and the open road and moving forward. It was strong and masculine, and often tragic, as portrayed in 'event songs'.

Event songs were in fad in country music during the early 1920s. Circulated throughout the American colonies before the Revolution, event songs were a descendant of the ballad broadsheets sold on the streets of London and Dublin. Event songs were mainly ballads that recapitulated controversial news or recent disasters. They didn't so much spread the news as comment on and put in perspective what people already knew, often adding a moral. They were an important subgenre of hillbilly country music and were fundamental to the success of the early country music record industry.

In 1924, two major event songs fueled the country music industry: 'The Sinking of the Titanic' and 'The Wreck of the Southern Old 97', later shortened to 'The Wreck of the Old 97'. Ernest 'Pop' Stoneman, a carpenter from Galax, Virginia, recorded for Okeh Records the retelling of the sinking of the Titanic in 1912. Vernon Dalhart's 1924 release of 'The Wreck of the Old 97' was country's first gold record in sales. It was based on the real wreck on September 27, 1903 of the express mail train running between Washington DC and Atlanta. The train, probably going too fast, flew off a trestle and crashed in a gorge near Danville, Virginia. The song has survived as a country standard performed by everyone from Hank Snow to Johnny Cash to the Statler Brothers.

Event songs brought an audience to the recorded country music industry. People became accustomed to buying the records as phonograph players became more readily available. A car battery was the only source of electricity in many rural areas. So, when sales of event songs faded after 1925, people still bought records of driving fiddle tunes by the Skillet Lickers and songs Jimmie Rodgers and the Carter Family.

In Benton's painting, the train itself is based on the event song 'Casey Jones', about another famous wreck that brought posthumous fame to the dead engineer. The engine in the painting bears the number 382, the number of the engine Casey Jones crashed in 1900. Benton was familiar with the subject. In 1943, he painted 'The Wreck of Old 97' based on the event song.

Benton paired up the blues and country in his painting by aligning a black banjo player with the white cowboy guitar player. The blues has been integral to country from the beginning of recorded music. Jimmie Rodgers, AP Carter, and Bill Monroe learned from, and traveled with, black musicians. An original member of the Grand Ole Opry was a black harmonica player. But blacks have never been part of mainstream country, despite the success of Charlie Pride and the country hit albums of Ray Charles.

The pose of the black man and the cowboy are almost identical in how they hold their instruments, the bend of their elbows and knees, the tilt of their heads, and angle of their hats. The black man holds a long-neck, five-string banjo. The five-string banjo is a bluegrass instrument, which directly links bluegrass to country in the painting. The minstrel four-string banjo was played in vaudeville or Dixieland jazz and not accorded the same respect as the five-string.

In Benton's early sketch, the black man wore clothing with ripped sleeves and pants. Some scholars think that the figure was based on a 1930s photo of the famous folk/blues singer Leadbelly. In the painting, the tattered clothes, which suggest poverty or slavery, were replaced by farmer's overalls, which suggest an independent freeholder. Benton had originally put the black man on the same value plane as the white dancers. The figure was eventually placed further back, perhaps to be associated with the riverboat and a group of blacks dancing on the riverbank. This somewhat ambivalent placement reflected the situation of blacks in country music. The minuscule black figures in the background welcoming the riverboat echo the slavery cotton heritage of the South, but also the contribution of the exuberance of black gospel to country music.

The Sources of Country Music contains the explicit and implicit traditional themes of the music. The common folk, religion, hope and optimism for a better time, enduring what you have to, and a brotherhood in music that overcomes skin color are plainly seen in the painting. Perhaps on the backside of the canvas, out of sight, are the other staple themes of country: heartache, loneliness, despair, hard times, failed hopes, abuse, violence, drinking and cheating, betrayal, and the antagonism of the working class against the wealthy and powerful overclass – and the way to seemingly escape all that.

Ever since the beginning of recorded country music, the music has been an avenue to escape the hardscrabble farm, the rural poverty, the limitations of poor education, and being at the mercy of outsiders who can close the coalmine or foreclose on the farm. Untrained backwoods musicians found wealth and fame through their music. This inspired others who plowed by day and fiddled by night. The success of country music made it an agent of social change.

Dolly Parton defined country music as 'just stories told by ordinary people in an extraordinary way.' Bill Monroe called it 'plain music that tells a good story.' Harlan Howard said it was 'three chords and truth'. The chords – one, four, five – are blues chords, and the truth, well, that's what gives country its diversity.

Country has long been associated with the South, in particular the Appalachian mountain region. But it's a fiction that country is pure white, Southern, and rural in its origins. Here is a summary list of people who historically have made up the South:

- Black, rural working class
- White, rural working class
- 'Old South' white aristocracy
- Urban black Southerners
- Urban Southern Jews
- Southern Appalachian white
- Urban/suburban white Southerners
- Louisiana Cajuns
- Southern Mennonites
- Cherokee, Choctaw, and Seminole Indians.

All of these peoples have influenced country music.

Country has always been a hybrid of many styles of popular and religious music. Within country music can be heard Irish and Scottish string music, Mississippi blues, Christian hymns, Celtic fiddle tunes, Western swing, big band sound, rock 'n' roll, jazz, Tin Pan Alley, vaudeville, and Mexican conjunto music. Traveling minstrel and vaudeville shows provided cornball humor and novelty songs. The country staple of the ballad 'heart' songs can be traced to Tin Pan Alley from the 1870s onward. Country absorbed accordion-dominated Cajun and polka forms, the folk songs of Woodie Guthrie, Burl Ives, and Leadbelly. English folk music, as embodied in 'Greensleeves', 'Black Jack Davy', and 'Barbara Allan', joined songs from the American working class like 'Tom Dooley', 'Home on the Range', 'The Wreck of the Old 97', and 'Casey Jones'. The commercial country music that emerged in the 1920s came from three major sources: Anglo-American folk music, old-time religion, and elements of 19th-century American showbusiness.

There was even gothic country that predated the 1990s Goth fad. Appalachian dead baby songs, such as 'Little Rosewood Casket' – 'There's a little rosewood casket/Laying on a marble slab' – is a typical gothic country song. The British ballad 'The Oxford Girl' became 'The Knoxville Girl' in which the girl takes an evening walk with her love. A mile from town, without warning, he knocks her to the ground and beats her unmercifully with a stick, drags her around by her golden curls, then throws her into the Tennessee River that flows through Knoxville. He ends up in prison for murdering 'that Knoxville girl, the girl (he) loved so well.'

In the song 'Banks of the Ohio', a man holds a knife to his lover's breast and pushes her into the river and watches her drown. He is then remorseful for killing the only woman he loved because she wouldn't be his bride. The moral of both songs is, 'Either, I [the male] have my way or you die.' Murder enacts a ritual misogyny. The woman who is the innocent 'true love' is transformed into a femme fatale and the man has the right, if not the Old Biblical moral responsibility, to rid such a temptation from other men.

Mainstream country has long reflected the 'dark side'. In Garth Brooks' 'We Bury the Hatchet', a couple digs up old hurts because they buried the hatchet with the handle sticking out, to better grab it up again and flay open emotional wounds. In Brooks' 'Papa Loved Mama' the man rams his rig into a motel room to kill his cheating wife and her lover. Updated story line with the same old result: man ends up in prison and the woman ends in the grave.

Randy Travis's 'Before You Kill Us All' is about a man whose woman is leaving him. He claims that if she does not come back, it will kill us all, implying murder, even though he was in the wrong.

Mary-Chapin Carpenter's 'He Thinks He'll Keep Her' depicts a woman revolting against a restrictive domestic situation. Wife tells husband that she doesn't love him anymore. Her independence is rewarded with a job in the typing pool – a warning also of what can happen to women in the patriarchal world. The domestic abuse and its repression is tame in comparison to violence and murders in 'The Knoxville Girl' and 'Poor Ellen Smith', 'Down in the Willow Garden', 'Pretty Polly', and 'The Fatal Wedding', but the theme is still the danger to women in a patriarchal world.

Rock groups have always found an affinity with country. Poco did country-rock fusion. Alabama brought together country, gospel and rock. Crosby, Stills, Nash and Young, Jackson Browne, Linda Ronstadt, Gram Parsons, the Eagles all incorporated country. The Grateful Dead went country with their *Workingman's Dead* and *American Beauty* albums. The Rolling Stones put country into their rock with 'Honky

Tonk Women', 'Dead Flowers', and 'Wild Horses'. The Beatles, Jimi Hendrix (who once lived in Nashville), Vanilla Fudge, Iron Butterfly, The Doors, Jefferson Airplane all recorded a country sound. Fourkiller Flats, Porter Hall Tennessee, the British group Mekong, Hank 3, and many others have found an affinity between punk and country.

Country crossover into other genres started when AC 'Eck' Robertson and Henry C Gilliland released 'Sallie Gooden' on RCA in 1922. They were accused by purists of abandoning the roots of the music. In 1927, the Blue Yodeler, Jimmie Rodgers, had a crossover success. In the 1950s, Eddie Arnold, Hank Williams, Tennessee Ernie Ford, Kitty Wells, and Elvis Presley had crossover hits. In the 1960s, Roger Miller, Merle Haggard, Johnny Cash, Charley Pride, Jim Reeves, Patsy Cline, and Loretta Lynn crossed the line. In the 1970s, Dolly Parton, Charlie Rich, Waylon Jennings, and Willie Nelson charted in both pop and country music. In the 1980s, Alabama, Randy Travis, George Strait, and Reba McEntire had dual hits. In the 1990s, Garth Brooks, Trisha Yearwood, Shania Twain, and Faith Hill became pop and country stars.

And that's a short list.

Crossover success is an old story. Bach borrowed from the pop of his day to model his suites on courtly dance music. Mahler used Jewish klezmer-style music in his symphonies. Stravinsky used jazz and tango references in several of his pieces. George Gershwin's *Rhapsody in Blue* (1924) brought the pop composer into the concert hall. Cross-fertilization of music is necessary for the evolution of music, whatever the genres. One simple example: Elvis covered Monroe's bluegrass 'Blue Moon of Kentucky' on the flip side of his first Sun Record's release. Monroe's original version was a slower tempo but Elvis revved it up. Since that time Monroe always played it at a hellbent pace.

So, what's country music?

14 The Hat Act

The Country Music Hall of Fame is a block from Tootsie's, so I walked over to find my three amigos. Only Hank was at our usual spot. On the table, resting upside down on its crown, was a new cowboy hat.

'Howdy, Hank.'

'Howdy.'

I picked up the hat to admire it. 'Nice. New?' I set the hat back on the table, resting on the brim.

'Never touch a man's hat.' Hank's vehemence startled me. He snatched up the hat, smoothed the nap, and carefully placed it back on the table, resting on its crown. 'A man's hat is personal.'

'Sorry, I didn't know your hat is part of your privates.'

'You obviously don't know the first thing about how to treat a cowboy hat, so just keep your hands off mine.'

Hank folded his arms across his chest as a buffer against whatever friendliness I might try to rub on him.

'What do you call a man who, when hearing a woman singing in the shower, puts his ear to the keyhole?' I asked.

He kept his arms folded.

'A true lover of country music.'

I thought he'd at least smile at that old chestnut, but his mouth stayed stern.

'You know why you never put a cowboy hat down on its brim?' he asked and, without waiting for an answer, replied, 'because the hat can lose its shape. It can be less aerodynamic.'

'We talking hats or airfoils here, Hank?'

'A man who lays his hat down on the brim doesn't appreciate his hat. The weight of the crown will flatten the brim, ruining the aerodynamics. Always set a hat on its crown, which is the strongest point. You can tell a man's character by how he sets down his hat.'

'Aerodynamics of a cowboy hat?'

'Cowboys invented aerodynamics.'

I tried to imagine some old cowpoke sitting on his horse working out the math of airflow and curvature of a wing's leading edge. Maybe he watched a hawk riding a thermal and held up his hand to mimic the bird, trying to get the feel of the wind. Picture this scruffy ranch hand, bored out of his mind watching a herd of stupid crud-chewing cattle, standing in his stirrups, his hand gracefully tracing patterns in the air.

'Hey, Hoss, you all right, there,' calls out his partner. But the cowboy, lost in the higher physics of his hat, doesn't answer. He appears to be engaged in some sort of air ballet. 'Hey, Hoss, you need to get out of the sun,' calls out his partner. I looked at Hank skeptically. 'Cowboys didn't fly airplane, at least not the old-time cowboys. They rode horses. So why would they invent aerodynamics? They didn't ride Pegasus or anything.'

Hank's look told me that he was educated enough to know Greek mythology, too, so don't get uppity with him. 'They needed to keep their hats on when riding fast to chase down a runaway steer. That's a damn awkward time to lose your hat. Or, if you lose your hat in a high wind on a blazing hot day, you could have sunstroke. And die. Out there on the plains, all alone, who's going to call 911 for you?'

I folded my arms and we had a face off across the hat in the middle of the table. 'Hank, you've been reading too much Louie L'Amour.'

'It works this way.' Hank's voice had the patient sigh of a teacher explaining two plus two to a particularly dense child. 'You tug the brim down low so it acts as an airfoil. You keep your head tilted slightly downward so the wind presses the top edge of the brim, forcing the hat down tighter on the head. If it's not working right, you can reshape the brim. Cowboys figured out how to get the right aerodynamics. When you see someone wearing their hat on the back of their head, the front brim riding high, you know they are no cowboy. They are poseurs.' Hank smirked, like, I know big words, too.

'Put on the hat, Hank. I want to check out the aerodynamics and see if they fit your face.' Some people can wear a cowboy hat as if they were born to the saddle; others look plain silly, completely out of place, an object of deserved ridicule.

Hank reverently lifted the hat by his fingertips and settled it on his head. He adjusted the brim to precisely his eyebrow line. The deep black, flat-topped hat looked the real deal on him.

'It's a Resistol 20x Black Gold,' he said, satisfied. 'The hat of choice by real cowboys and 90 per cent of rodeo riders for its durability. Stetsons are good and so are Serratelli, but Resistol is favored. A fellow named Harry Resistol of Texas and Missouri made that hat. There's the Borsolino from Italy and the Christy from England but they are more show hats.'

'20x?'

'The number of Xs tells the quality of the hat.' You know how some people's eyes fire up when they hit on a subject they irrationally love, like grown men playing with elaborate train sets or powerful cars? Hank's eyes got that glow. His eyes had the moist sheen of longing and romance as he talked about cowboy hats. I remembered that sensation from watching cowboy movies as a kid – Gene Autry, Roy Rogers, Cisco Kid. Watching those films, I knew that all I ever dreamed of lay just over the endless Western horizon. That horizon teased and satisfied at the same time. If I kept riding forward, I would find the treasure. The horizon kept unrolling, so I never got any closer to the edge. But the journey forward was satisfying; the thrill came from moving into new territory and knowing there was yet more new territory. I think it's a very American satisfaction, the restless in pursuit of destiny. It's a good itch Americans like to scratch. That's part of the reason country and western are symbiotic.

Hank leaned forward and spoke earnestly right into my face. 'The number of Xs signify the amount of fur to wool in a hat. The more fur, the higher quality of hat. Now a 2x hat, the kind most these tourist yahoos wear, they feel like cardboard. It's all wool. At the 3x and 4x level, you start to get a little fur blended in, rabbit or fox. Beaver is used only in the higher Xs, like this one.' He touched the brim of his hat. 'Beaver is the toughest fur, so it's the most durable. A hat with high beaver can be treated rough on the range and not lose its aerodynamic shape.

You can dunk it in a water trough and it's good as new.' Hank had the believability of experience.

'Now you get up to 200x, now that's a hat. It has a real nice shine, like a well-fed Black Angus oiled up for show. A 200x has 50 per cent beaver and 50 per cent mink. It's a very durable hat.'

'You wear a beaver-mink hat to chase cows?'

'Well, I don't wear it on the range.'

'You have one?'

Hank hesitated, perhaps from modesty. 'Yeah.'

'How much did it cost?'

'You know why hats are rated by the number of Xs?' Hank asked, dodging my question. 'About 100 years ago, when they first started making the hats, they were all beaver. The number of Xs showed how many beaver pelts went into a hat.' That sounded like folklore but good folklore so worth passing on.

'What's the most expensive cowboy hat you've seen, Hank?'

'A $17,000 [£11,000] Stetson. One of a kind. All ermine with a diamond hatband. It was just a show hat. No real cowboy would wear such a hat. Maybe a Hollywood cowboy or one of those Texas oil cowboys. But I've never seen anyone in Wyoming wear such a hat.'

'But cowboys in Wyoming wear beaver-and-mink cowboy hats?'

'Well, for goin' out and dancin'.'

'How much did it cost, Hank?'

He ducked his chin and mumbled.

'What?'

'$1,799 [£1,150], plus tax. But it will last me a lifetime. And it's a real working hat. The best fitting hat I've ever owned.'

'If it's a real working hat, and you never wear it on the range, what kind of work do you do?'

Hank smiled shyly. 'Well, now you know that a cowboy never takes off his hat, even in bed.'

My guffaw caused people at the neighboring table to stare, as if I had let loose a hurricane sneeze. I suspected that the whole hat discussion was a set-up for his punchline, his way to sidling up to male bonding without exposing vulnerability. A real cowboy, Hank.

★

The cowboy hat is the iconic symbol of country music, although there is no cultural link between the hat and the music. Texas country swing might be a connection but the Texas swing of Bob Wills has more affinity to big band jazz than to 'Home on the Range'. In recent years, the cowboy hat has become a banal symbol made risible by the 'Hat Acts', such as Brooks And Dunn, Clint Black, Garth Brooks, Ricky Van Shelton, Alan Jackson, and Billy Ray Cyrus. Marty Stuart, a former bluegrass prodigy, and Travis Tritt, a country rocker from Atlanta, mocked the Hat Acts with their No-Hats Tour. The tour's poster featured a red REJECT stamped across a cowboy hat.

Nevertheless, the cowboy hat and the Western look have a long history in country music. In the 1920s, rural Southern musicians wore cowboy garb to distance themselves from the hillbilly image. The hillbilly was the low man on the social totem pole, the uncultured hick from the hollow. The cowboy was a romantic figure, a manly man. The hick image was disliked by the authentic mountain people and by country performers. AC 'Eck' Robertson wore cowboy clothes when he went to New York to record the first country record. Country's first superstar, Jimmie Rodgers, wore cowboy chaps, shirt, bandana, and wide-brimmed cowboy hat. He recorded 'Yodeling Cowboy' and 'T for Texas'. He was also photographed in a railroad brakeman's hat (his work career began as a railroad brakeman), and in a fashionably smart Panama snap brim straw skimmer.

The hillbilly hick image was, to a large extent, a commercial ploy. Impresarios, such as George Hay, who shaped the sound and image of the Grand Ole Opry, impose the look upon the hill country musicians. The performers were cajoled, if not coerced, into wearing floppy straw hats and overalls. On stage, they went bare-footed and called themselves the Fruit Jar Drinkers or Possum Hunters. The image worked in the marketplace. In 1926, Dr Humphrey Bate's country string band posed as stolid middle-class bourgeoisie dressed in business suits. They held their instruments as a banker would a pen. In a 1928 photo, Bate's band posed in farm pants, work shirts, and shapeless felt hats against a painted backdrop of farm fields and a timbered cabin with a stone chimney. The hillbilly look proved durable to the 1990s, with popular television shows like *Hee Haw* and *Beverly Hillbillies*.

But country musicians, left to their own devices, performed in their Sunday best, or dressed up in the 'tuxedo' tradition. In the 1950s, Eddie Arnold appeared on television in formal wear suitable for Fred Astaire.

The hillbilly gal was a popular image for female country performers during the Depression, the era of the new radio barn dances. The barn dance show developed out of vaudeville, not from barn dances in the hollows. The most popular woman on radio in 1936 was Lulu Belle. Her real name was Myrtle Eleanor Cooper. She began her career as a 19-year-old who sang the songs from her native North Carolina. The producers of Chicago's WLS National Barn Dance, perhaps the nation's most popular barn dance radio show, renamed her for the market value of the back-mountain image. Myrtle Eleanor revamped her straightforward country music into Lulu Belle's showbiz Appalachian shtick fitting of the vaudeville tradition.

But the cowgirl, as well as the cowboy, look became more popular. Rubye Blevins, a singer from Hope, Arkansas, reinvented herself as Patsy Montana with a full Western cowgirl outfit, a fashion with no historical truth. In 1931, she joined the first singing-cowgirl group in Hollywood. Four years later, she wrote 'I Want To Be A Cowboy's Sweetheart', the first million-dollar (£650,000) selling country recording by a woman.

The cowgirl look for female country singers remained popular through the 1990s. Patsy Cline's first incarnation in the 1950s was as a cowgirl. Loretta Lynn appeared as a cowgirl in the 1960s. Emmylou Harris had the long skirt and boots look in the 1980s. Reba McEntire was a real cowgirl who grew up on her father's 17,000-acre (7,000ha) cattle ranch in Oklahoma. It was a family operation and as youngsters Reba, and her brother and sister, worked the cattle on horseback. Her father was a former three-times world-champion tie-steer roper. Reba competed in rodeo barrel racing. Her musical career kicked off when Red Steagall heard her sing the national anthem at the National Finals Rodeo in Oklahoma City. He urged her to give Nashville a try. In the 1990s, Tanya Tucker developed her own line of Western wear.

As the 1930s Depression dragged on, and poverty became a blight on the consciousness of the nation, the hillbilly image morphed into the cowboy/cowgirl look. The hillbilly was not seen as competent to deal with the complexities of a nation brought to its economic knees. The strong, self-reliant cowboy was considered a more appropriate role model to withstand the hardships with stoic resolve.

Americans wanted to be cowboys, not hillbillies.

Also, the cowboy movies of the 1930s linked country and western music genres, even though there was no tradition that connected Nashville to the West. In the late 1930s and early 1940s, the nation went on a Western jag, not unlike the urban cowboy rage of the 1970s. Country performers wore full Western regalia that no cowboy would wear, even if they could afford the custom-designed outfits. Singing cowboys, such as Gene Autry, Roy Rogers, Tex Ritter, the Sons of the Pioneers, and Foy Willing's Riders of the Purple Sage, dressed in the Hollywood version of Cowboy High Fashion. They sang sappy ballads about coyotes and horses and cattle and buffalo and lonesome prairies.

Almost none of the celluloid cowboys knew the real cowboy life, with the exception of Gene Autry. Born in Tioga, Texas in 1907, Autry was the son of a rancher and livestock trader. He grew up knowing cowboy skills, riding, roping and driving cattle. His grandfather was a preacher at the Indian Creek Baptist Church, where young Gene first sang. When he was 11, his mother bought him a guitar and he became an autodidact on several instruments. After high school, he took a job as a relief telegraph operator with the St Louis & Frisco Railroad in Sapula, Oklahoma. By this time, he knew hundreds of old standards.

His music career started big time with the hit 'I Left My Gal In The Mountains'. He rode his recording career into the movies in 1934, making *In Old Santa Fe*. Known as 'Oklahoma's Singing Cowboy', Autry made 90 cowboy movies from 1934 to 1954. After his movie career, he became a wealthy real estate/businessman who bought a professional baseball team, the Los Angeles Angels.

The popularity of the singing cowboys and their movies grew so that the country field became known as 'country and western'. Alabama-born Hank Williams cashed in on the trend and named his band the

Drifting Cowboys, complete with Western clothes. He recorded 'Cowboys Don't Cry' to reinforce the connection.

There were real working singing cowboys. Cattle drovers knew that cattle on a trail drive were prone to stampede at the slightest provocation unless they could hear a human voice.

'Some trail bosses didn't like to hire a fellow who couldn't sing. We boys would consider it a dull day's drive if we didn't add at least one verse,' quotes Wayne Gard in his book *The Chisholm Trail* (Norman: University of Oklahoma Press, 1954). 'On bad, dark nights the cowboy who could keep up the most racket was the pet of the bunch. We called him the bellweather, and he always brought up his side of the herd… In his long days in the saddle, songs helped to speed the hours and to keep him from growing lonesome. In the evening around the campfire, they gave a bit of diversion before the tired men hit their bedrolls. The hands on night guard used songs not only to keep the cattle quiet but to keep themselves awake… Methodist hymns were popular…although good old-fashioned Negro minstrel songs have been found equally effective in soothing the breast of the wild Texas steer…after the men had sung a few lullabies to the steers, they [the steers] all lay down and started snoring.'

Cowboy songs were being collected as early as 1908. One popular song was 'Goodbye Old Paint', attributed to the black cowboy Charley Willis around 1885. There was a black version of 'Yellow Rose of Texas', where the girl is not white but mulatto. But the songs heard in Western movies were not written or sung by range hands. Professional songwriters, like Fred Rose, wrote most of the songs. Rose, originally from Chicago, was a skilled Tin Pan Alley songsmith and eventually a major player in the Nashville music publishing business.

'Tumbling Tumbleweeds', one of the best-known Western songs, was written by Bob Nolan, a native of New Brunswick, Canada. In 1922, when he was 14, he and father settled around Tucson, Arizona. As a boy, Nolan spent many hours walking the woods of his native land. He continued his love of walking in the open spaces of the American desert.

Originally, the song was called 'Tumbling Leaves'. But Western radio listeners misheard and kept requesting 'tumbling weeds', a large globular dry bush blown along by the wind, a common sight in the southwestern

United States. Nolan, tired of explaining that the song's correct line was 'drifting along with tumbling leaves', changed 'tumbling leaves' to 'tumbling weeds'. Gene Autry cut the song and it became a huge hit, and is now a Western standard. Autry named his film *Tumbling Tumbleweeds* to cash in on the song's popularity. Nolan also wrote another Western classic, 'Cool Water'.

Nolan attended the University of Arizona on a track scholarship (pole vaulting). He majored in music and wrote poetry for the student newspaper, *Tumbleweed Trails*. After college, he joined a traveling Chautauqua troupe, reciting poetry and singing songs. In 1933, he founded the Pioneer's Trio with Tim Spenser and Leonard Slye, later better known by his movie name, Roy Rogers. In 1934, fiddle player Hugh Farr joined the group and the name was changed to Sons of the Pioneers. When Roy Rogers' movie career as 'King of the Cowboys' took off, the Sons of the Pioneers became his backup band. They were good enough on their own to be inducted into the Country Music Hall of Fame.

The historical cowboy period in the Old West was from the era of the long cattle drives, around 1867 to the late 1880s. Cowboys were working hands hired to drive cattle, mend fences, and do the grunt work around the ranch. It was a hard, physically demanding, uncomfortable, low-paying life. Wranglers were on the road months at a time on 1,000-mile (1,600km) cattle drives; round-up time required weeks of riding over rough ground searching for free-ranging cattle. It was a romantic life only in song and mythology.

By 1890, the cattle drives were all but over and with them the era of the Cowboy West. The disastrous blizzard of 1886–7 killed thousands of cattle. Fever hit the Texas herds hard and neighboring states passed quarantine laws to protect their ranching industry. The Texas herds were prevented from crossing state lines. That effectively put an end to the cattle drives along the famous Santa Fe or Chisholm trails, cattle drives that had been celebrated in song and in the movies. Although the cattle trials moved further west, overgrazing, falling beef prices, and settlers fencing off open rangeland for their cropland contributed to the end of the Cowboy Era. However, the cowboy lives on as a romanticized figure in country music.

To refer to country music as 'country and western' is an automatic tip off that you are out of the loop. *Billboard* dropped the 'western' years ago. Only in France and Japan do fans come to country concerts wearing fake six-shooters, a toy Sheriff's star, and a cowboy hat. Americans do not enjoy that kitsch because they know the lie of the Old West mythology.

The American West has been intentionally mythologized as a place of adventure and romantic escape. Cowboy songs are a pack of wish-fantasies, myth-images, and white-male conquest songs. The appeal of cowboys, and the songs, has been primarily their 'escapist lyricism'. For decades the entertainment PR machine has turned out a product called 'Old West' based on a mythic lie. Country and western became one more product of an image factory.

Primary point: the Conquest of the West. There is no nice way to conquer. Someone has land you want so, if you are the powerful conqueror, you murder, plunder, pillage, rape, rip asunder governing institutions, destroy a sense of cultural heritage and a people's identity. Those are the basic rules of conquest and they were applied to the American West.

Honor, compassion, justice, fairness, or nobility is not in the lexicon of conquest. The popular romantic image has never been the reality of the West. The conquest of the West was a commercial enterprise, and continues as such today.

Professor Patty Limerick of the University of Colorado and author of *The Legacy of Conquest: The Unbroken Past of the American West* (WW Norton & Co, New York, 1987) debunks the myth of the American Old West. The Old West, she states, was not a center of freedom and national destiny but a site of greed, ethnocentrism, and imperialism.

Pragmatic and often exploitative economics, as much as idealism, were a major force in the settling of the West, according to Limerick. Land speculators, greedy profiteers, dirt farmers, small-time entrepreneurs, and barons of commerce were far more influential in shaping the West than the Cowboy Nobility portrayed in Hollywood films – and country songs.

'Frontier had no clear meaning other than "where white people get scarce", regardless of how many other peoples lived there first,' Limerick has stated.

Some of those other peoples of the West, rarely honored in song or film, include the Pueblo, Navajo, Hopi, Pawnee, Lakota, Paiute, Ute, Comanche, Apache, and scores of other Native Americans. The Chinese laborers imported to build the railroads that linked, for the first time, America's East and West coast. The African-American cowboys, shopkeepers, farmers, and miners are never given their proper due. The Mexican and Hispanic populations, which were in the West before the Europeans arrived on the East Coast, may as well be invisible.

The white cavalryman, homesteader, trapper, miner, saloonkeeper, and land baron are enshrined as the conquerors of the West. However, none have become as synonymous with the Old West as the cowboy, the masculine ideal of personal competence and skill; a lone figure dependent upon no one else, neither family nor team members nor peer group. He signified freedom, self-reliance and self-sufficiency. The cowboy was All-American. Except for the black cowboy.

The black cowboy, and blacks in general, have been largely bleached out of the history of the West, and country music. Professor Michael 'Cowboy Mike' Searles, teacher of African-American history at Augusta State University, has this insightful explanation:

'The West became the mythological place where white men tested themselves,' he explained. 'The West was where the white man gained a sense of independence and all the notions and images of where a man could be man, could stand tall; where a man could live without fences, where democracy was born. The West was the true America, the America that is the foundation for all other Americas. The West is what distinguished the United States from Europe, if you accept the seminal Western historian Frederick Jackson Turner's argument that the East Coast was just an extension of Europe. The West was truly American and black folks did not have a place in that mythology. To be true American meant to be white. In the West, it meant to be white male. Black folks in the West, especially as cowboys, sullied that notion.'

The black cowboy was often given dangerous dirty work, like breaking wild horses for riding or taking on a mean bull. These difficult and rigorous jobs caused injury and death. 'If the blacks are out there as cowboys doing the hard and dangerous work, and the white cowboys are turning this work over to black men, what kind of man are these whites anyway?' Searles continued. 'People might ask, "You mean that you, as a cowboy, would relinquish any part of your manhood to a black man? So what if bustin' a bronc is a gut-wrenching experience that will tear your lungs loose and have you spitting blood, and break your bones, and leave you with a short life. That's what a man does." But if you turn that work over to a black man, that doesn't sound too much like the manly West, where a man stands up and does whatever's necessary and does it with flair. If the black cowboy rides the bronc that the white cowboy prefers to avoid, what has been said? Who is more the man?

'You want Roy Rogers or Gene Autry turning over, on the big screen, the hard work to a black man? Then, after the hard work is done, saying, "I'll take it now." That doesn't square with the image of independence, the self-made man. So you don't talk about those things. Besides, there was no market in telling that story. White America didn't want to hear that story.'

There were black cowboys in Appalachia, primarily in Georgia and South Carolina, where the cattle industry provided beef to the East Coast and the West Indies. These Southern cowboys were slaves before being made free men in 1865 after the Civil War. They carried a loaded gun and rode on horseback. They were often unsupervised, given the isolated and solitary nature of the work. Being armed and riding a horse gave that slave a sense of personal power that the field hand slave did not share. But the values of being a cowboy and of being a slave are incompatible. Being a black cowboy, slave or free, was often a conundrum.

'Probably nowhere do the blacks have as much independence and freedom as the black cowboy,' said Prof Searles, who specializes in the study of the black cowboy. 'How they operated in the society was an interesting dynamic within the person and the society. In every way, they could see themselves as cowboys, having met the idea of a self-made man. Yet, they could not be quite sure of how they would be treated. Would the next ranch they work extend the hospitality given to cowboys? Or would they find harsh feeling because sometimes ex-Confederates owned the ranches? Folks could be antagonized by their very presence. There were social taboos and restrictions, such as drinking out of the same bucket of water. Black cowboys got killed by white cowboys for talking back, although they, too, carried a gun, rode a horse, and did the hard work.'

Alexis de Tocqueville, in his *Democracy in America* (1833, 1840) interpreted the American tendency toward self-reliance as individualism. Individualists, he said, 'owe nothing to any man [and] expect nothing from any man; they acquire the habit of always considering themselves to be standing alone, and they are apt to imagine that their whole destiny is in their hands.' This remains the American ideal today. Tocqueville found this sort of individualism to be sad: 'It throws him back forever upon himself alone and threatens in the end to confine him entirely within the solitude of his own heart.'

Willie Nelson and Waylon Jennings' song 'Mamas, Don't Let Your Babies Grow Up To Be Cowboys' on *Waylon and Willie*, the Outlaws album, shared some of Tocqueville's observations. The cowboy is independent and self-sufficient, the exemplar of self-reliance, a deeply respected American value. But the song does not romanticize the cowboy. Rather, it urges mamas to block their sons' ambitions to be cowboys and instead raise them to be 'doctors and lawyers and such'.

The song presents the self-reliant psyche of the cowboy, 'He's not wrong, he's just different.' Being different means refusing to be conventional, being a loner, a man apart. The cowboy holds his thoughts and feelings inside. He's hard to love. As a stranger, the cowboy is slightly suspect for not being part of the community or the family. The stranger makes people uncomfortable because he/she is not bonded to the place or people, or necessarily beholden to the rules of the society. As a free agent, they are unpredictable and therefore a potential danger.

'Mamas, Don't Let Your Babies Grow Up To Be Cowboys' was written by Ed Bruce. The first hook came easily but the verses refused to show themselves. It's too autobiographical, he told his wife, the singer Patsy Bruce. She helped to finish the song and suggested the title line.

The cowboy's mythological ancestry can be traced to the frontier man of James Fenimore Cooper's Leather-Stocking series: *The Pioneers* (1823), *The Last of the Mohicans* (1826), and *The Prairie* (1828). Cooper, an aristocratic upstate New Yorker, created the hero Natty Bumppo. Bumppo wore buckskin leggings, a natural product. The cotton of his other clothes was homespun, not milled as in the English fashion. He took what he needed from the wilderness, not from the factory. He was a quiet loner, independent, who could live off the land. He was the antithesis of the gentry, of the English gentleman, of the Boston city dweller. This parallel between the natural self-reliant man and the tamed dependent man is evident in the friction between the Appalachian hillbilly and the Northern city slicker, between the cowboy and the townspeople. And it remains a theme in country music.

In post-Civil War America, the cowboy replaced the buckskin frontier man of Daniel Boone. Instead of deerskin moccasins, the cowboy wore tough boots. Instead of a fur cap of coonskin, he wore a ten-gallon broad-brim hat. The ten-gallon hat was part of his survival gear in which he could literally carry water to his horse or for himself, or which he could use to shade himself from the brutal desert sun.

It is doubtful that the ten-gallon hat was a beaver-and-mink concoction, like Hank's. Hank's hat (and all the hats of country music) is about style and image. No one in Nashville can better talk about style than Manuel. Manuel created the wild rose outfits that Dolly Parton, Emmylou Harris, and Linda Ronstadt wore on the *Trio* album cover. He put Johnny Cash in black. When Gram Parsons was looking for a way to blend Music Row and Haight-Ashbury, Manuel embroidered rhinestone marijuana leaves and poppies on his jackets and pants. He designed suits for the Beatles and put Elvis Presley in the wide-lapel white jumpsuits. He designed the customs for *Urban Cowboy*. When the Urban Cowboy look became passé and New Traditionalism emerged, he made a retro-1950s jacket for Dwight Yoakam. A Manuel jacket can cost $5,000 (£3,000).

Manuel's showroom, a converted deep-red brick house, is a few blocks down the hill from Music Row. We sat surrounded by his creations and discussed country music style.

'Imaging is kind of a discovery about yourself, what you always wanted to be. What your fantasies were, what you really wanted to look like.' He spoke with a faint accent of his native Mexico. 'I try to image off the individual. I must talk to that person and we must have conversations that are really true and useful. Without those conversations, it's impossible. I listen to the musician's music. I need to see them perform. I need to know their message if they want to do it the right way. I could make them look like Tom Jones or Elvis Presley but that is not my position. My position is to make, to discover in there, the person they always wanted to be on stage or off stage.'

Manuel had a three-month conversation with Gram Parson before he designed the famous marijuana jacket. 'Fifteen years later, after he died, I discovered that he was explaining to me how he was going to live and die. I was captured by the fact that we were young, both of us, and we were confessing to each other the things that we liked and I was going to make him look the way he wanted to look. He has become like a flag of dressing that way.

'It's really important that the performer carry an image. You can see the traces of the person, even when you see them at parties, the behavior. It's not the clothes but somehow the visual, the transparent, the feeling about them that shows the image when they actually entertain. I try to find part of their off-stage persona and put that into their on-stage image. It can be tricky. For that reason, I think it is very difficult for the average person to have an image. Imaging is a very difficult thing to achieve by the individual singer or entertainer. Sometimes they never get to the bottom of it and understand how important it is to them. I've had some kid come here and say, "All I want to be is some country girl or country boy."

'I say, "Then we're done with each other."'

'What do you mean?' I ask.

'If all you want to be is a country girl or boy, there you are. We're done. Now if you want to be an entertainer, you want to be a showpiece of the world, somebody people will look after and imitate, or at least not feel defrauded by paying $25 [£16] to go see the show, then we're talking different terms.'

The flamboyance of Manuel's colors and designs in his clothes reflect his Mexican background. He was born Manuel Cuevas in Coalcomán, Mexico, one of 12 children. His father believed that if you give a person a skill, he or she would always be able to find work. 'My dad was a champ at trading. He was a guy who could sell condoms to the pope. He was so smart. My mother's ambition was for her kids to be lawyers and doctors and professionals. We are all professionals; the majority of us are working in the trades. We all went to college. Most of the family lived in the United States, now many have moved back to Mexico and retired young.'

Manuel's learned skill was sewing. He taught his mother how to sew. He has made his own clothes and jewelry since he was eight years old. He is a skilled silversmith, woodworker, furniture designer, leather worker, and craftsman in wrought iron. His clothes are displayed in the Smithsonian Institute. The King of Morocco saw a picture of a Manuel jacket and called the shop to order the same one. Manuel told him no. I can make one similar but not the same, explained Manuel. I don't make two alike. His only outlet is the store in Nashville. If you want a Manuel design, you have to come to him.

'Like a songwriter writes a song on paper, I do it on fabric,' he said as we walked around the showroom. 'I don't look at magazines for what is happening in fashion. I just try to listen to my inner self and go forward. My mother said, "Don't look for your true self, it will find you." I think that's what happens. It will come to you.'

He pointed out various jackets, shirts, and dresses of intricate beadwork. He selects the materials and has special suppliers for the beads in an array of delicate shadings. Manuel designs each article of clothing, cuts the patterns, and constructs the complex interior structure down to the hand-sewn buttonholes.

He stopped in front of a jacket depicting a detailed visual description of the war of terrorism, showing American troops fighting in Afghanistan, tanks blasting away, explosions from bombs erupting.

'I've done a lot of political and social interpretations in my jackets,' he said. 'On September 11, I was scheduled to do the runway in Washington DC. So I did a jacket with the bald eagle and put 13 stars on each sleeve to represent the foundation of our country. On the back, I made a perfect architectural copy of the World Trade Twin Towers with a bit of smoke and on the bottom in script said, "Our flag is still here." And, in the center, I put the flag all the way across. People stopped the show and started singing "God Bless America" and crying. It was very moving.'

Another jacket honored NASA with rockets lifting off. Snakes, roses, crosses, and brilliant bursts of colors are favorite motifs in his clothes. He respects the American heritage, by which he means all the Americas, including the Indian cultures of the Aztecs, Incas, and southwest plains tribes. Their emblems and symbolism are found in his designs.

Manuel immigrated to the United States in 1955 and found work in Hollywood with the tailor Sy Devore, who made suits for Frank Sinatra and Bob Hope. He later worked for the legendary designer Nudie Cohen, a former boxer from Brooklyn. Nudie defined what we now think of as the rhinestone cowboy. He dressed Gene Autry and Roy Rogers in the 1940s and Hank Williams and Tex Ritter in the 1950s. Nudie did Porter Wagoner's outfits for the Grand Ole Opry, including the jackets adorned with glitter wagon wheels. In 1957, Nudie created Elvis Presley's $10,000 (£6,500) 24-carat gold lamé tuxedo.

Manuel worked for Nudie for 20 years and married his daughter. He left Nudie in 1974, after divorcing the daughter. He relocated to Nashville in 1989. He is a striking-looking man, short and solid, and wears his silver hair in a ponytail. He has the reputation of a bon vivant and ladies' man. He is seen frequently in the clubs with an attractive woman on his arm and a drink in hand. But there is a private side he does not display. He is a deeply spiritual man, attends Mass regularly, is quietly generous to young artists, giving fatherly advice in long behind-the-scenes conversations.

Part of his advice to newcomers is that developing a style is as important, if not more so, than developing the talent. Two people can sing equally as well and the only distinction between them will be their behavior, something about their image.

'Style plays a high percentage in entertainment,' Manuel said. 'When an artist develops an image, calculate 60 per cent imaging, 30 per cent packaging, 10 talent. Which sounds kind of weird but what the artist doesn't understand is that his or her imprint, that 10 per cent, represents 100 per cent of the artist. Imaging is the high point in the panoramic view of what is brought into the public. You must be able to package as well as image. My clothes are the image and the package.

'The distinction between a star and a performer is from here to the moon. It's difficult to become a star. But I'll tell you that one of the most difficult things for the star is to enter the galaxy of other stars. They have to learn another way of life. When people put my clothes on, you can see the change on their faces. But some are afraid of the transformation. They want to be themselves, be genuine. I tell them, "Yes, of course, you'll be yourself and you'll be genuine. But if you want to be a clown and not a comedian, then you've got to put some spots on your face and do things that children understand as clown. But if you want to be a comedian, then you move into another age, another image."

'Making clothes is not the thing. Anybody can make good clothes, pretty clothes. But to adapt those clothes to the clothes of the clown, of the king, or the beggar is another story.'

The same can be said of music. Wearing a cowboy hat does not make a country singer. The singer must make the music into the real article.

The Ryman Auditorium, the original home of the Grand Ole Opry, known as the "Mother Church of Country Music."

The bronze sculpture of Owen Bradley, a founding member of Nashville's country music business, marks the entrance of Music Row

Phil Lee, one of the "Others," in the country music underground based in Nashville

The state capitol building in downtown Nashville

Emma Fox, singer/songwriter from Liverpool, England working for her shot at big time country music

Wanda Lohman, a friend of Tootsie's, Willie Nelson, and Jim Reeves at Tootsie's Orchid Lounge

Shelton Hank Williams III, grandson of Hank Williams Sr., links traditional country and punk in his music

The Flatlanders – Joe Ely, Jimmie Dale Gilmore, and Butch Hancock – doing Texas country music in Nashville

Singer/songwriter Matt King writes of his gothic hillbilly background

Vanderbilt University, is one of renowned educational centers, and along with Fisk University, is the reason why Nashville is called the "Athens of the South."

Tony Brown, co-president of Universal South Records, and one of the most highly regarded record label executives in Nashville

Gretchen Peters, one of Nashville's esteemed songwriters, at her home studio

Lower Broadway is the country music heart and soul of Nashville, a strip of honky-tonk bars featuring superb live music

Michael McCanless is one of the "Other" country players who plays punk on his fiddle

Raul Malo, the Cuban-American country singer, formerly with the Mavericks, expects a strong Spanish influence in country music

The new Country Music Hall of Fame in downtown Nashville holds the history of the music

The Parthenon, the only full-size replica of the Greek original, features a 40-foot tall Athena

The original Tootsie, Hattie Louise Tatum, a keystone in the survival of honky-tonk Lower Broadway

Jill King, singer/songwriter, putting in her dues at Tootsie's and catching the breaks in Nashville

Chris Scruggs, grandson of Earl Scruggs, playing with the All Star Hillbillies at Robert's on Lower Broadway

The Loveless Motel is now a restaurant famous for its food and the place to see country celebrities

Gail Davis, a pioneer female producer in Nashville, who is also a top hit
singer/songwriter

15 Hazel Says

Manuel is one of the colorful characters on the Nashville country music scene. Another wonderful personality, and important person in the music business, is Hazel Smith. Hazel is a journalist, radio commentator, songwriter, and much-beloved mentor to country performers. She tagged Willie and Waylon as Outlaws, a name that has defined a genre of country music and a social movement within the music. I can't tell Hazel's story better than she told it to me in her living room. So, I'll just step aside and let her tell her tale in her own words.

'I was born in Casell County, North Carolina, 17 miles [27km] from town. My daddy was a part-time deputy sheriff and a farmer. He had us in the field working from the time we were knee high. I have two brothers. My mother worked in the fields, too. My dad's been long dead. My mother is 88 and she is in a home in Greensboro, North Carolina.

'Tobacco was our main source of income. The most my dad made in a year was $5,000 [£3,000]. Then we thought we were really in high cotton. We had field corn for cattle feed and gardens for us – corn, green beans, peas, sweet potatoes, and Irish potatoes. He had grapevines and peach trees and apple trees and pear trees and damson plum trees. We raised our own pork and cows to slaughter for beef.

'We got electricity when I was 16 years old. We got a freezer. Then we could slaughter a cow every year, because we had the cows there. Everybody was just poor. We lived on a dirt road. We didn't even have a radio. My Uncle Wade had a radio. We'd go up on Saturday night and listen to the Grand Ole Opry. My cousin Hassel would climb up the pole and wrap a Lucky Strip Green cigarette packet around the aerial so the signal would come in clear. Being a kid, I thought it was the cigarette pack, rather than the tinfoil that would make the Opry come in clear. Until I moved to Nashville, I thought that the Opry had static.

'I loved that music. I loved what Bill Monroe did. When I was a kid Bill Monroe was a really high boy. He had played around in North Carolina where I was from before he ever came to Nashville. He and his brother Charles had growed up not too far from home where I lived. When I was four years old, Mom and Dad had taken me to see the Monroe brothers. That would have been 1938.

'I would listen to the Opry. I remember so well when Hank Williams came on there for the first time. He did encore after encore. It was unbelievable hearing that man sing. I could picture that man in my mind but he didn't look a bit like I thought when I saw him. But I knew that he would have on a hat and a suit that would match. I was so excited when I saw him in a white suit with the music notes on it. Nudie was doing the designing then. Now it's a man called Manuel, who designs a lot of clothing for the country music people. I love to see them dress that way.

'I remember when I was in school and Kitty Wells and Johnny and Jack came to Cherry Grove school, just an elementary school. Kitty sang "Honky-Tonk Angel" and I thought that was the most powerful thing. Kitty Wells was to me the prettiest thing. I thought Patsy Cline was the most marvelous singer. I remember seeing her in Greensboro. She had been in that bad wreck so she was wearing a wig. You could see the scars up here on her forehead. This was in December, before she was killed in that plane crash in March. When that woman would sing it would send chills all over ya. I remember Faron Young was there that night. We would always go see the country music people.

'But I kept that love for bluegrass. I can remember that Merle Haggard came to Greensboro to the coliseum. I thought that was powerful. I got so that I loved the lyrics of songs. Carl Smith was real popular at the time that I finished high school. The songs "Hey, Joe" and all those things. Just marvelous, marvelous songs. He just looked like a movie star. I never thought about Hollywood. Hollywood was the furthest thing from my mind. All I thought about was Nashville and country music. I just loved it with my heart.

'Everybody up in my high school class was engaged or something by the time we finished high school. I finished high school two weeks before I turned 16 years old. I started school a year early. I was promoted to the second grade in April and I didn't turn six until May. My parents said that they sent me to school early because I begged to go but I know it was because I talk so much and I got on their nerves and they wanted me out of the house. That's what I always thought.

'I finally got married when I was 19. I know now that was relatively young but over in the country, when you're 17 miles [27km] from town, you have no telephone and a dirt road to the house, you know, the thing to do is get married. Or you can go to church. Or when they have some hillbilly show down at the schoolhouse you go to that.

'This was long before they ever got the coliseums and what have you. But eventually they came and that's where I saw Ernest Tubbs and the great Buck Owens. I remember going to Winston-Salem and seeing him and carrying one of my children and sitting there and just lookin'. I remember going to see Johnny Cash and June Carter before they were married. That was just the most powerful. Johnny Cash is the most charismatic of all the people, the most charismatic. I just loved seeing that show.

'The night I went to see Patsy Cline I was holding Terry, my baby at the time, and he peed all over me. He was a big ol' boy sittin' up in my lap. I didn't have half a brain thinking to get a babysitter. I just took the kids with me everywhere I went.

'As time went on, I continued to be a real big fan of all the country music people, learnin' to love the lyrics of songs. I started sort of writin' songs, thinkin' that I was a girl Kristofferson 'cause when his songs started being recorded I just...you know...Kris had such a tender way he handled sex so nobody even knew he was thinkin' about sex, that the songs were talking about sex. He was such a powerful poet and he did it numerically. His rhymn pattern was numerical. That was the most amazing thing that I had ever heard in my entire life. Like his song "Me and Bobby McGee". "Busted flat through Baton Rouge/waiting for a train/ feeling 'bout as faded as my jeans." Where did that come from? It was like Shakespeare, you know. I loved the lyrics of Tom T Hall, too.

I thought he was powerful. My son Billy especially has become really close with Tom T and has written with Tom T and his wonderful wife, Dixie. I'm very proud of that.

'But anyway, my marriage was somethin' I don't talk a whole lot about. I did not like being married. I don't think I'm smart but I felt that I could do things myself without somebody telling me what to do. I didn't like being bossed by nobodies, especially somebody that I knew that was orally abusive to me. So the marriage was over and I took my children, two sons, Billy and Terry, and moved to Nashville, that's what I did.

'I have to brag on Billy and Terry. Billy has had between 50 to 60 songs recorded by bluegrass people. Terry is probably the best bass player in music today. He plays upright bass with Mike Snider for the Grand Ole Opry. He's been on the Grand Ole Opry for about 12 years. I have five grandchildren; Adam is 18; Jeremy is 15; Tyler is ten; Karen is ten; and Trevor is three and a half. They are the joy of my life.

'We are all in the music business. The first thing I did in the music business was some part jobs. I bought my first job through an employment agency. I didn't know but two or three people when I moved here. I just keep working. Eventually I started writing for Pier, this was in the early '70s, and then I met Kinky Friedman. Kinky had that wonderful album *Sold American*. Kinky was just too clever for radio. Kinky's lyrics were just so clever that radio just would not play him. Glen Campbell eventually recorded his song "Sold American" but it was never the single it should have been. Because there was one line in there that radio refused to play. The line was "with the Singin' Brakeman screamin' through your veins". They thought that was morphine, you know the morphine that Jimmie Rodgers had to take, he was the Singin' Brakeman. That was the medicine he had to take before he died. [Rodgers died of tuberculosis.]

'I met Kinky and started doing some promotion with him through radio. I did some promotion for Tom T Hall at his office. In the meantime, Waylon, Waylon Jennings, moved to Nashville. The office was at 915 19th Avenue South, which was Tompall Glaser's sound studio, which became known as Hillbilly Central. The recording studio was upstairs. The office was downstairs. That building became a shrine for everybody and anybody who was somebody. In 1973, Waylon didn't like the way his recorded music was sounding. He wanted his records to sound like he sounded on stage with that back drum beat, the strong beat. That stuff that was unheard of in the recording studios in Nashville, Tennessee at that time. Everything then was pretty much surface and what have you. They were doing good. They weren't doing anything wrong, you know, but it was more countrypolitan I would say than what Waylon was doin'.

'I think it was the music more than the lifestyle that made them such outlaws on Music Row. This was hard drivin' music. It was fiddle and steel but it was the way they brought the drum in stronger and the bass in stronger. And it was the types of songs that they were singing. They were not singing syrupy sweet love songs. They were singing songs with lyrics that had substance. That was the difference.

'This was what Waylon wanted to do, and basically he was eventually able to do so on *Honky Tonk Heroes*, which was the first album he did the way he wanted to. During that time, I felt that the music needed a name. So I kept lookin'. We called it progressive and called it renegade and those names. One day I thought of outlaw. I opened this dictionary, I always kept it right under my desk, and when I turned to the word outlaw and there was a line in there that catch my eye, and that was "living on the outside of the written law". I thought that was exactly what they were doing with their music here. What they are doing is not what Music Row is doin'. They're doin' something outside of Music Row. So I thought outlaw was a good term.

'I said the outlaw to them. Tompall frowned. Waylon just grunted and looked at me like I did something bad or stupid. He shrugged. I don't think either one of them liked it but Tompall Glazer told me, "Go ahead and use it but don't tell anybody that it came out of this building."

'I said, "Okay." That was the deal we had.

'Jessi Colter, Waylon's wife, thought it was ridiculous, I'm sure. She was just this wonderful Christian lady and still is. That woman is just a saint, Jessi Colter. Anyhow, there was a radio station in Asheboro, North Carolina, one in Flint, Michigan, and one in Austin, Texas, they all started calling in "outlaw music" immediately and they were playing the music 24 hours a day.

'I sat down one day with an unelectric Underwood typewriter and typed up an article and called it "Hillbilly Central" and sent it to *Country Music* magazine in New York. The editor, she sent me money. That was the first time I ever wrote anything for anybody. I had never written an article in my life. But I did that and that worked. That was $100 [£65] a month for me, man. That was nearly enough to feed my children back then. I still write for that magazine 30 years later. This guy from the *Baltimore Sun Times* came down to Nashville. He's the first man who wrote a headline that said "Outlaw" in regard to the music. I will never forget the day that I got the paper. I had chills because I thought that we are doin' something and they don't know what we are doin'. It went around the world.

'Anyway, I worked with the Outlaws and I wasn't making a lot of money. Tompall started me on $75 [£50] per week. Jessi she thought that was pitiful so he upped me to $150 [£100]. Then when the Dr Hook people came in, they offered me $350 [£200] a week so I went to work for them. You know I wasn't there to decorate the place. I worked with them for eight years. I ran the whole operation. I knew where 45 people were 24 hours a day. I knew their phone numbers, their social security numbers, their cell numbers, whatever they had I had it all in my head. Birthdays, childrens' names, where they went to school, their social security numbers, the whole thing. I did that until Dr Hook eventually broke up.

'During that time, I had several songs recorded. That's how I made the down payment on this house. I happened to be on the B side of "When You're in Love with a Beautiful Woman" in the UK with a song I had co-written called "Dooley Jones". I had several songs recorded by various artists, like Brenda Lee, Tammy Wynette, Bill Monroe. Dr Hook recorded about eight of my songs I believe it was. The Whites recorded a song of mine. But it wasn't enough money generated that I didn't have to have a day job, you know. I kept my day job and kept writing for my magazine and all that.

'After the Dr Hook gig I was personal assistant for Ricky Scraggs and Sharon White. I worked out of their home for six years. After that time, this friend and I opened a management company. We did that until that played out. And then about seven years ago, because of my magazine writing, they called me from WFMF in Indianapolis and wanted me to come up and sit on a panel at a Country Music Exposé, they called it. The first year we had about 5,000 people came. It was a nice turnout. There were a couple of well-known producers on the panel. Both of these guys who produced records said that they would just as soon have a guitar vocal demo as have a full-blown demo to listen to the songs. They asked me what I thought and I said that is not the norm on Music Row. Those producers on Music Row want a full-blown demo and not only do they copy it verbatim, they use the same fiddle player that you used on your demo if it's a new player who just got to town.

'A man in audience named Charlie Morgan was laughin' at everything I said. When I came off the stage, Charlie he said to me, "Hazel, have you ever thought about doing radio."

'I said, "Well, Lordy mercy, you think about things."

'He said, "I think you'd be great on the radio doing the news. We can fix it up for you to give country music news."

'So I said, "Okay, let's try it." So we did it on Friday one day a week for a month. The ratings were so high they put me on five days a week. I've been doing that for seven years. I gave the country music news this morning from here in the house.

'Last Thursday, I found out something about Tim McGraw. He's a superstar married to one of the most beautiful women in the world, the very talented Faith Hill, and they have three lovely daughters and he could be anywhere in the world he wanted to be and he's got a beautiful home out in the rich section of town and he's got a bus that's the best you can buy. He could do anything he wanted but last Thursday he was at a place called Imiginatorium, a place for children to play, all kinds of animals, and children spend the day and have fun and learn. That, for me, that is a great man who will do that with his little girls. He spent his day at Imaginatorium with his daughters. Isn't that sweet! That gives you an idea of the kinds of stuff I dig and find that nobody else has, you see.

'Willie Nelson, he had left Nashville but whenever he came to town he hung out at Hillbilly Central. I can tell you a time when Willie Nelson, Kinky Friedman, and myself and about six other people were hanging out with Bill Monroe at his office. This was in the early '70s when the

Opry moved from the Ryman to the new Opry out on the edge of town. We were up in Bill's office and Willie said, "Bill, I suppose you were at the Opry at the new opening, weren't ya?"

'Bill says, "No, I wasn't there. I didn't want to be there. I was on the road. You know, Willie, I'm a Democrat and I didn't have no yo-yo." Well what happened there was that Mr Roy Acuff and President Richard Nixon were yo-yoing on the Grand Ole Opry stage.

'Billy, Billy, come in here and tell this man about how you met up with Waylon. Billy's a songwriter and musician. He was about 20 years old at the time of Waylon.'

Billy came in from another room, where he had been fixing up for his mother. He is a slight, handsome man with dark hair and a soft voice. He began by saying, 'During that time there were the Ronnie Milsaps and Barbara Mandrells and the music was having a pop thing going when Waylon first came in. He had questions about even being in this town because the music was going so weird like that. I remember going up there where the records were cut. I was in the studio when *Honky Tonk Heroes* was recorded. I was sitting there talking to Tompall when this guy came to the door, hitting both sides of the door, dressed in black, with black greasy hair and black sunglasses. He looked like such a derelict person I said, "Who in the hell is that?"

'Tompall said, "That's Waylon Jennings." They started cutting that music. It was on the edge, like Southern rock. It had a gut thing going to it. It was like real music. The damn songs were great. Shel Silverstein and Kinky Friedman and John Hartford were all coming through that same office. That was the sound around those people. Waylon said he wanted to do it his way because RCA wouldn't record him his way. Those guys were sitting there drinking whiskey. Ralph Looney playing steel with a bottle of whiskey. Waylon would be just raising hell. That music was creative. Waylon didn't have a thought about having a hit. They were there for the music. They cut Billy Joe Shafer songs and really cool stuff.

'People's ears are waitin' out there to hear something honest, which is the appeal of *O Brother, Where Art Thou?* The big money is with the commercial. You think that nothing will change it but something always has. I was with Randy Travis the night he went on *Nashville Now* television show and that was the night, 1985, the music changed. Randy Travis by no stretch of the imagination is not the greatest country singer to come along but, by God, he was singing George Jones and Merle Haggard and filling that void we're all hungry for. That's out there. But right now, it's real stagnant. If you talk to Tony Brown or Tim DuBois, they'll speak the same language we're speaking here. They know all about it. But they've got to fill those 25 to 30 slots the radio gives them.

'That Waylon came along and there was an audience for it. The college kids liked it. The true-to-life country fans that like good songs. You got the intellectuals who can't tear it apart because it's solid. It hit the ears out there. The hippies are going out to fill an open field and do a Woodstock – Willie and Waylon made them one.'

Hazel intervened, 'I can remember when Willie called the office one day, he called Waylon, and Waylon was listening and he told me, "I think Willie's lost it. He's telling me that he's got lawyers and hippies and doctors and college kids and dope smokers all sittin' beside each other in concerts down in Austin at the Armadillo World Headquarters." Waylon could hardly believe this was true, but it was true.

'I think that the term "Outlaw" was a term that the media could use and make it bigger and bigger. They still use it religiously. It will never die. And to think that I just came up with it in 1973. I hadn't even realized that's what I was doin' but I did. That's what I did. Another thing I did was type the lyrics to "Four Poster Bed" by Shel Silverstein to take it to Owen Bradley to produce it on Brenda Lee. I think that's a pretty famous thing.

'The Class of '89 was Garth Brooks, Clint Black, Alan Jackson, and Vince Gill but he was already around. All those guys have pretty much done well. Garth was pretty much a phenomena because he was able to find songs that people could really relate to, a song like "Friends in Low Places". Any person who heard that song and didn't like it was not a smart person. That was a country song if I ever heard it. It's a perfect country song.

'Even though Garth is not performing these days, he is still doing a lot of help for children. You take a man like Alan Jackson, who's very shy. He's hotter than a pistol these days with that song "Where Were

You When the World Stopped Turning", which turned out to be the anthem for the terrorist attack on America. Just this year Alan built a home down in Georgia for young people who have nowhere to go if they have a trouble with their parents or in their home. They call it Angel Home or something like that. That's a wonderful thing that Alan's done.

'I heard this story about a dying girl, 13, and her dying wish was to meet Alan. This was around Christmas time. Alan got her in his Lear jet and flew all around the Opryland Hotel, which is lighted up so beautiful that time of year. He took her up to Kentucky, where she lived, and come back and then took her in his car and drove her all over Nashville to see the Christmas decorations. When they got her back to the hospital, they asked her if there was anything else she wanted. She said that she wanted clothes. It was then that they realized the child had never any but pajamas to wear, they were so poor. And they went and bought her everything. She went to heaven shortly after that. But Alan gave her what she wanted.

'Vince Gill does not do one day of his life that he lives without doing a charity.

'Young Brad Paisley has started doing everything he can to help kids in the place he was brought up in the poorer part of West Virginia in the Appalachian area. Last weekend I was visitin' with him and he told me, "I'm so tickled you know last weekend we had my homecomin' two weeks ago and we done bought a piano for the school up there. We didn't have no piano at the school." Isn't that wonderful that they're able to do things like this?

'Let's talk about Dolly now. That's the smartest person that's ever been born in the state of Tennessee. She has a wing at the hospital up there in Sevierville, the Dolly Parton wing. Let's talk about what she does. When she started her book foundation, the dropout rate in Sevier Country was the highest one in the state. So she started giving every graduate in the country $500 [£300] to finish high school. She's almost put a stop to dropouts. Now, every child that is born in Sevier County gets a book a month from Dolly Parton from birth to kindergarten. The kids in Sevier County call her the book lady. Her husband, Carl Dean, thinks that is just great. He said, "All you've ever been known by is your singin', song writin', your hair, and your boobs. Now you're the book lady and I love that." Ya, Dolly Parton is the smartest person ever born in the state of Tennessee. And she is the best poet there is of her culture, no two ways about it. There's no man in country music stronger than Dolly. She can whip a bear with a balloon.

'Tom T Hall, let's don't leave him out. I told you my son Billy has been writin' with Tom T. He's got some wonderful songs and Harlan Howard. Harlan went to heaven here this last month. Harlan had over 100 hits, number ones and top tens. I knew when Harlan had died that he had lost weight. His wife told me that he had grieved after Waylon died because Waylon was younger than he was. I know we all have to go but it sure does hurt me. These are friends of mine you know. My good friends.

'Now, almost two years ago, Renee Bell, who was senior vice president of A&R at BMG Records, came to me. Let me tell you part of the reason she came to me. I had Joe Galante, who is the head honcho up there. I told Joe, "You're doin' good here at RCA since you came back from New York but you got one weak place."

'"Oh? Where's that?" he asked.

'"A&R. You need to hire Renee Bell."

'"Why?"

'"Because she has the same passion for songs and acts that you have," I said. By the way, Joe was a bean counter at RCA Records with Waylon on the label. He learned to love country music by listenin' to Waylon recording the same songs that my Billy heard him recording in the studio. That's where Joe learned to love country music. He didn't even like it until then. But at any rate, so Joe and Renee got together and Joe hired her at the table when they had lunch.

'Renee came to me and said, "You need to write a cookbook."

'"A cookbook!"

'"Yes, you do," she said. So I put it together. It's called *Hazel's Cookin' with Country Stars Hot Dish* (Dalmatian Press). I got Shania and Dolly and Reba and Vince and 58 stars. All these people. I'm real proud of my cookbook.

'I got this award from CMA in 1999 given for the journalist of the year. They really surprised me with that. My friend Fletcher Foster, who at that time was an executive with Arista Records and is now senior vice president and general manager at Capital Records, he was at the BMG building and we were going to supper. They got this room for events, the Chet Atkins Room, since Chet's gone to heaven. He said, "Have you seen what they've got in here?" and he opened the door. There were like 300 people there. I didn't know that I was going to get this award. I did not know this party was going on. There were flowers everywhere. Garth Brooks sent me 100 roses. Alan Jackson gave that Waterford crystal. Patty Loveless had a piece of crystal made for me. I had flowers over this house. We had flowers, I've never seen so many flowers, we had flowers that reached to the ceiling. My son Billy started cursin' the flowers.

'I said, "Billy, don't be cursin' me flowers."

'He said, "Mama, I've stuck thorns in my hands from all these flowers. My hands is bleedin' from all these flowers." Let me tell you something. When I die there won't be that many flowers. In '96, this girl was giving me a massage right here in this room when I had a heart attack. And, Maven, if you're reading this, I was hurtin' in the middle of my back in the spine. That's where the pain was. So you can be hurtin' in your toe and could have a heart attack. She realized that the pain was pretty abnormal so she called the cardiologist. She was his masseuse. She told him about the sweatin' and the pressure and the pain. He said get out here.

'Well, after about a week in intensive care, this nurse came in and asked if I was able to talk over the phone. I said I guess so. She said Waylon Jennings is on the phone and he threatened to dynamite the hospital if we don't put him through. That was a wonderful thing too.

'Vestal Goodman is the greatest gospel singer. Now listen, George Jones is the greatest country singer that ever lived and his song "He Stopped Lovin' Her Today" is the greatest country song. I was over at George's house at Christmas time and Vestal was over there. Let me tell you somethin'. When George had that bad car accident three years ago, like to have killed him, he was in the hospital. When he woke up, he asked for Vestal. Well, they found her over in Greensboro and took her to his hospital room and she prayed with him. Her prayer is what brought George around.

'Let me tell you something else. She went down to the bridge where he hit that bridge and she got them demons off of there. She wanted him to sing the song "Angel Band" in the studio. They went in there and George couldn't sing. Won't a word come out. She did an exorcist on that studio and George sang. He's been singin' ever since. Vestal is a powerful powerful woman. She still sings gospel. She was with the Happy Goodman Family, that is who she sang with, her and her husband and his two brothers. Her and Dolly are friends. She brings Dolly peas out of her garden.

'Now let me tell you something. You can write this down. Chuck Berry is a country songwriter. If he ain't writin' country lyrics, then I ain't got a brain in my head.

'Let me tell you another story. Grady Martin died this year. Grady Martin was a great innovative, unbelievable guitar player. He played on everybody's sessions. He was playing on "Don't Worry About Me" with Marty Robbins and something happened to the speaker. The guitar had this fuzzy sound in it. Well, Grady played a perfect break on it but the sound was odd. A tube in the speaker was messed up but Marty liked the break and they kept it on the record. So they started using that. They'd take the tube out of the speaker. Other people started using that in their sessions and recording. There was a soldier from up at Ft Campbell here in Nashville who started hanging around Grady about this time. He followed him all over town. He'd emulate what Grady did on the guitar. The Private First Class asked Grady all kinds of questions. That soldier wasn't allowed to go to the hotels but he went to Grady's house. His name was Private First Class Jimi Hendrix. He took the buzz to the world. That's where it came from, right off Music Row in Nashville. He'd play the juke joints down on Jefferson Street when he was in the army here.

'I don't think Garth will record any more. He really wanted that Chris Gaines project to happen because he thought it would work. It was a great idea for a movie. They never did do the movie. They may still do it. They were talking about it last time I spoke with him. Garth was pretty much country but he had the rock 'n' roll theatrics on stage. He would go into a transformation almost when he would go on stage. He loved the stage.

'What has happened to country music now that bothers me worse than anything else is that it ain't got no heart. I got this theory that they took a bunch of kids who had been to college and used them as interns and those interns ended up in the A&R department choosin' songs, "Oh, this sounds good!" That's not what country music is. Country music's supposed to say, "That feels good." It's supposed to make you laugh or make you cry. Country music.

'Louise Scruggs, wife of Earl, is a good friend of mine. She told me something one time that I think is kind of important. Earl is, you know, kind of shy when he talks. His banjo playing does his talking. His banjo does most of his talking and continues to do so today. Louise told me that she didn't do anything that Earl didn't tell her to do. She ran the business, booked the acts, kept the books and raised three sons. She's a tough gal and a fine lady. She was the first businesswoman in the music, no two ways about that. There's been others; Connie Bradley at ASCAP and Donna Hilley runs Sony Tree publishing. Another powerful woman is Francis Preston who runs BMI (Broadcast Music Incorporated). She's in New York now. But, like Dolly Parton, she took the country with her. Francis Preston started working as a receptionist at WSM radio. She doesn't have a college degree. She doesn't know how to type. She doesn't know how to run a computer and she runs BMI. She managed that because she's a smart smart woman.

'Bill Monroe is the love of my life, no two ways about that. My sons worked out on Bill's farm located on Allen Road when they were teenagers. It was at the end of the road and he kept the gate up and the gate was locked so people couldn't get in. Billy, come back in here and tell about you workin' on Bill Monroe's farm.'

Billy continued, 'We used to work out on his farm. Work with mules and stuff like that. He had a tractor he used to mow each side of the driveway and then parked it. Rest of the time we plowed with mules and go up on the hill and cut fence posts with axes. It was kind of a play farm.

'Out there working he wouldn't speak. He did a lot of hand motions, pointing his finger meaning a nail needs to go there. He wanted to save his voice. So he had some peculiar things. He had this bull that he had for so long. Instead of trading the bull around like you're supposed to for breeding purposes, he fell in love with this bull. He had him eight years. The bull was huge. His head was the size of a bison's head. Bill would go lay up against the bull, then crawl up on its back and ride 'em around. They were like buddies. That bull was called Bobo. When he died, Bill buried him out there on the farm and put a rock over him. Every cow Bill had had a name. He'd buy beef but he'd never slaughter a cow. He was that kind of man.

'Me, my brother, Bill and his brother, Birch, all four of us together built this barn shelter around his barn. Birch is the type of old man who would spend the entire day straightening rusty nails. He tried to get us into that but I wouldn't cross that line. One day, we were using wood so old that it was so hard it was like petrified. But we were going to use that. Birch, he was going to make this piece of woodwork. He laid it up for a rafter in the barn shelter and started nailing this nail in. But the wood was so hard that the nail would bend. He did it over and over and over this nail bending routine.

'Bill, Terry, and I weren't talking, just watching him. Never saying a word but smilin' at each other like we couldn't believe this old man was this stubborn. His face gets real red and he gets down off the ladder and goes to the dairy barn. Comes back with a brace and a bit, drills a hole in the wood and lets the nail slide down into the hole and hits it through. We took a break and Bill said to my brother, "Put a nail in this thing here."

'His brother asked, "What you want me to use, a hammer?"

'"Yes, of course use a hammer, although some people use a brace and a bit," said Bill. We'd cut our hands working. Bust a knuckle at least once or twice a day hammering nails. Bill did that. He didn't worry about that. We used old-style tools. Instead of a drill, we'd use a brace and a bit. Old saws and hammers.'

Hazel carried on, 'Bill had cancer of the colon. I can't remember what year it was. He thought he was going to die. He was right up here in the hospital about a fourth of a mile from my house, Nashville Memorial. He called me one Sunday morning and he was cryin'. I said, "You want me to come there to the hospital, Bill?"

'He said, "I wish you would."

'I didn't even take time to take a shower. He was cryin' and needed somebody to talk to. When I got there Earl Scruggs was there. Bill and Earl, that's two of the quietest people in the universe. Bill said to Earl, "Well, I'm glad you come."

'And Earl said, "Well, I had to come see ya."

'Bill said, "I got to have an operation."

'Earl said, "I heard."

'Bill said, "I got cancer."

'Earl said, "That's what I heard."

Then Earl started to say that he really appreciated that Bill put the banjo in his music. "If you hadn't put the banjo in, I'd probably stayed up in North Carolina like my brothers working in the cotton mill. I want to thank you for that. I don't know what I would have done if you hadn't done that."

'Finally I said, "Earl, don't you know Bill Monroe loves you?"

'And Earl started cryin'. He said, "And I love him, too. I love him more than anybody in the entire world. I always loved him like I loved my daddy."

'And Bill said, "And, yes, sir, I love you, too."

'It was two great men of music who worked together years before. Earl came in with the banjo and made what Bill had started even more wonderful. Something that will live much longer than we will.'

16 Lower Broadway

Willie Nelson was to play the Ryman Auditorium on this Friday night. I went to Tootsie's to check any buzz that he might sneak in a back room surprise. Wanda wasn't at her usual front window table. Strangers occupied the three amigos' table. The evening was early, so I decided to check the other honky-tonks.

Traffic clogged Lower Broadway for a mile from the top of the sloping hill to the riverfront. Ordinary cars, family sedans, cars that bounced up and down at the touch of a button, cars painted as harlots and proud to strut, candy-apple shiny low-rider pickup trucks, suburban SUVs, and stretch limos that looked like night crawlers with rigor mortis crept along bumper-to-bumper. Two overweight cops on white Harleys zipped between the cars, like cowboys on quarter horses, cutting offenders out of the herd. The single cool blue light mounted behind their helmets flashed a disco beat.

The street scene was typical for a weekend – on its toes, swinging from the hips, and stomping its collective boots. The sidewalk was New York on lunch break. I stopped dead to admire a woman with seething curls of very bright platinum. She wore a black Western yoke shirt beaded with spangly silver and red roses, skin-tight black satin pants, and shiny black alligator cowboy boots. I was so engrossed in this vision of the New West that I didn't see the biker type wearing a cowboy hat with horns that flashed on and off. We bumped. 'Excuse me, sir,' he said politely. An out-of-town family group in baggy shorts and T-shirts pressed against a storefront with the startled look of deer caught in a spotlight. Three Vanderbilt testosterone-charged males stood at the curb sending whoops and rebel yells across the four lanes of traffic. They reminded me of fly fishermen casting into a turbulent river to see if they could get a rise.

The people laughed a lot on the sidewalks. They acknowledged each other as distant cousins, although they were strangers, welcomed into a weird musical family. Boogie-woogie, country waltzing, rockabilly, twang rock, croonin' ballads, belt-shinin' heart songs, and boot scootin' came out the bars' open doors that didn't close until 2am. The music made the street happy.

On the corner next to Tootsie's is Legends, where everyone sits at a table or at the bar. The band on the front stage was playing predictable country when I walked in. A spinning mirrored ball above the front door sent bright dots of light around the room. Musical instruments hung on the upper wall below a single strand of white mini-Christmas lights. The back part of the open room was elevated four steps to give a better view of the stage. I preferred this space of tiny black, round-top tables and its own bar. The walls were covered with edge-to-edge album covers. Three signed guitars encased in protective plastic hung at eye level; one had Gene Autry's signature. There was a photo of John Lennon wearing a People for Peace armband next to a cutout photo of Elvis.

I spied no familiar faces and didn't like the music. Back on the sidewalk, I walked past Tootsie's, going toward the river, to the other honky-tonks – the Second Fiddle, the Bluegrass Inn, Robert's Honky-Tonk Grill, Jack's Bar-B-Que, and The Stage. This was the neon heart of Nashville's live country music scene, where bands play from early afternoon to early morning, rotating five or six live acts through in ten hours.

This historical strip was almost lost to sleaze in the late 1970s and early 1980s. When Tootsie died, her place closed. XXX moviehouses and rough bars took over the neighborhood. People avoided the place because it wasn't safe or pleasant. Steve Smith, an entrepreneur and lover of country music, bought, with a partner, Tootsie's and Legends. That was the beginning of the revival of Lower Broadway. The city decided to renovate the riverfront and designated Second Avenue, two blocks from Tootsie's, as the showcase. The old brick, multi-storied cotton warehouses were cleaned up and converted into restaurants and tourist shops and places for music. A Hard Rock Café moved in.

I glanced into the Bluegrass Inn's big plate glass window and saw an extraordinary sight – Jerry Lee Lewis playing the keyboard with his butt. I couldn't believe it. I went inside to check the reality. Chicken wire fencing separated the stage area from the front door entrance, creating a zone. A fighting zone? A jail zone? A musical roller derby zone? When I looked close, the keyboard player was not *the* Jerry Lee Lewis, but if there hadn't already been a JLL, this guy would have been him.

His dark blond hair was highlighted, in patches. He wore tight leather black pants and a shirt open to his navel. He pounded the keyboard with the heel of his cowboy boot, did trilling hand-over-hand runs up and down the keys, and hit atonal chords with his buttocks, all the while playing a recognizable tune. He was an incredible musician and a whoopingly delightful entertainer. He put a bottle of beer on the black keys while belting out a song, his band going 100mph and picking up speed. He swigged half the bottle without dropping a beat, then knelt on one knee. Evangelical boogie rockabilly straight out of the JLL songbook, I thought. He balanced the half-full beer bottle on his head and outplayed the boogie, outraced the rockabilly, and was chasing down the master, while keeping the bottle in a Zen state of calm. He leapt up, grabbed the bottle off his head, emptied it into his mouth, and landed in the splits right on beat. He sprung up on his heels and played with one hand while facing the audience and singing.

The guy was crazed, zoned out, staring through his own chicken wire. He turned back to the keyboard, pounded out the closing chords with both hands and flipped the keyboard over as the finale. The drummer rose out of his chair, slammed the final boom, and threw his sticks down, like a spent man dropping out of the saddle. The jaded audience treated this as a normal act, worthy of perfunctory applause.

'What was that?' I asked the bouncer.

'Brandon acting up again,' he answered.

Brandon Giles. I tried to talk to him but he hadn't returned to this world yet. I walked on to the Wildhorse Saloon, the palace of Second Avenue and also a showcase for country music – professional and amateur. It's too made-for-tourists to be as authentic as the Lower Broadway dives, but it's a fun place to dance and hear top acts. When I entered, the finalists for the Sing to Win contest were nervously preparing to go on stage. The Wildhorse sponsors the ongoing ten-week contest that attracts amateurs from the surrounding states. Each week, there is a winner and the ten winners compete in the finale, which was tonight. This could be someone's Big Break Nite. The winner receives a new guitar, a $100 (£65) gift certificate at a local music store, a backstage tour of the Grand Ole Opry and, most importantly, an invitation to open for a major act at the Wildhorse. The judges of tonight's contest were the Nashville editor of *Billboard* magazine, a representative from the Grand Ole Opry, and a talent agent. Tonight, a star could be born.

I sat through the entire show. A chunky 14-year-old boy in a Garth Brooks big-brim hat delivered a song in an amazingly strong and confident voice. He got my vote. Then a young woman from Louisiana sang Cajun country. I switched my vote to her. A handsome 19-year-old took the stage and I immediately liked his verve. He put just enough Elvis into his act to get the girls screaming but not so much Elvis to be called an imitator. He performed in the spirit of the Memphis Carl Perkins-Elvis Presley-Chuck Berry country school. He had the audience on its feet. I switched my vote to him. There was not a clinker among the ten performers. Half of them could easily be on the radio and you couldn't tell the difference from a signed act. The winner was a Tennessee woman with a big clear Patsy Cline voice and an authentic country accent.

After the show, free dance lessons were offered for the Texas Line Dance, Cowboy Stomp, Shake, Backdraft, Electric Slide, Rebel Strut and other boot scootin' steps. Dance music has been vital in shaping the stylistic patterns of country music, as Prof Bill C Malone traces in his book *Don't Get above Your Raisin', Country Music and the Southern Working Class* (University of Illinois, 2001). According to Prof Malone's research, immigrants from the British Isles, Europe, and Africa are the source of many Southern country tunes and dances.

The Old World dance origins are found in the celebrations of religious feast days, the planting and harvesting cycles, and secular holidays. The music and dance, whatever the source, shared the spirit of a hedonistic good time. The fiddlers and pipers of the British Isles were public performers who played the taverns and festivals for the same pay scale as present-day performers: money, sex, food, drink, shelter, and adoration. Musicians being musicians, the same can be assumed for their African brethren.

This spirit of 'Merrie Ole England' came to the New World and flourished. Much of this spirit can be attributed to the stiff-necked Oliver Cromwell, who, after leading a successful revolt that resulted in the beheading of Charles I, imposed his morals and government upon England. He banished musicians from the court and deprived them of church patronage. The musicians were forced to play for the people in the streets and in public drinking houses.

The Cromwellian restrictions, and the ensuing Puritan era, brought forth John Playford's *English Dancing Master*, a publication in 1651 that had a profound role in the development of country dance. The book originally described 104 dances, largely based on rural and peasant dances. In following editions of the popular book, the number of dances increased to 918. The dances included 'longways', in which men and women faced each other in two lines, the same as in present-day country line dancing. In other dances, couples were arranged in circles and squares, the very same formations of the American square dance.

The square dance caller was an American innovation that opened the dance to everyone. Playford's book was aimed at the middle- and upper-class clientele, who had the wealth to buy books, the education to read them, and the leisure time to dance whenever. The caller democratized the dance. He shouted out the movement and directed the dancer's various steps. Instructional books, and their economic/social implications, became superfluous. People had only to listen to the caller. The music was paced to the cadence of the caller and was also used to give speed to dance patterns. The square dances became the basic ingredients of musical culture in America and a foundation of country music. Many of the old fiddle-tune staples of bluegrass and country music follow the dance patterns.

The longways dances collected by Playford became fashionable with the French upper class after the accession of the Stuarts, the family of Bloody Mary, to the English throne (1603–49) and their Restoration (1660–1714). Relations between the French and English ruling classes normalized. In France, the longways dances were known as *contredanses* because the dance partners were lined up opposite each other, or in counter positions. 'Country dance' is not a corruption of *contredanses*, Prof Malone points out. He dispels the misinterpretation that the dances went from France to England. Rather, they went from England to France, although they did travel back across the English Channel with Frenchified names for the dance terms.

The French plantation/slave-owning class took the dances, now with French court overtones, to Haiti. The Afro-Haitians added to the *contredanses* a fast, five-beat syncopation called the *cinquillo*. When the 1791–1802 Haitian slave rebellion drove the French to neighboring Cuba, *contredanses* with an African beat took on a Spanish accent very similar to the familiar Argentinian tango. This rhythm is the foundation of modern Cuban music. The present-day *habanera* Cuban style of music and dance is the immediate descendant of the *contredanses*. This music is also basic to today's Puerto Rican music and the Dominican Republican and Haitian *merengue*.

The quadrille, where four couples are arranged in a square formation, is the basis of the square dance. The French *cotillon* (anglicized as cotillion) apparently derived from the quadrille. A *cotillon* was a peasant girl's petticoat, so the dance's rural connection appears strong. French dancing masters brought the dance to the American colonies, along with dancing instructions like *allemande, promenade, dos-a-dos*, and *chassez* (sashay). This language is used today in calling the steps to a square dance.

The square dance is associated with western as much as country, as is the hoedown (throw the hoe down and party). But other dances, and the dance music, belong to the South. The buck-and-wing, flat-footing, clogging, double shuffle are rural South, although they may have a common root in the Irish and Scottish jig. The buck-and-wing, a solo dance, is also a tap dance step seen in vaudeville. Clogging, and blazing fast fiddle playing that accompanies the dance, can be traced back to Cape Breton, a small island off Nova Scotia. Cape Breton was passed back and forth between the French and British, depending on which of the imperial powers controlled Canada at the time.

Cape Breton was the northern point of what the French called '*L'Arcadie*' (from the ancient Greek meaning 'beautiful land') that extended down to what is now Georgia. In 1758, the British got in the last boot and kicked most of the French out of Cape Breton. Longfellow commemorated their expulsion in his poem, 'Evangeline'. They migrated south, following the Appalachian mountain chain, which drops into the sea at Cape Breton. Many settled in the American Appalachian region, while others continued to the Louisiana Territory, then in French hands. The term 'Cajun' is a corruption of Cape Breton 'Arcadian'. They brought with them their fiddle playing and clog dancing, which the Cape Bretons are still famous for.

All this history was the unseen influence behind dances that were performed in the 1990s dance clubs – a big market for the country music industry. Songs, such as Brooks And Dunn's 'Boot Scootin' Boogie' were remixed specifically for the dance club market.

Marian George and Melanie Greenwood, then Lee Greenwood's wife, set off a worldwide country dance movement with their 'Hot Country Dancin'' videos. Melanie created the Achy Breaky dance for Billy Ray Cyrus's song 'Achy Breaky Heart', which was then the top country rage. Marian, a film producer, saw the video potential.

'Melanie created the dances and I put together a business proposal,' Marian told me when we met. 'All the labels turned us down. Billy Ray's label won't let us use the master. Billy Ray gave us permission to use his photos for the promotion. We got the publishing rights, funded it ourselves, licensed the master tracks from the label, and did a remake of the song. We took it to direct marketing and it was like riding a wave around the world. I went to England, Ireland, and Australia with it. We did a grand opening in a downtown Manhattan country club. In Dublin, people were lined up around the block waiting to get into the dance clubs. I was flabbergasted. The dance videos brought a lot of younger people and women to country music. Middle-aged ladies felt safe in the clubs. You didn't need to bring a partner, or you could have a partner. We did three volumes with songs by Dolly Parton, Lorrie Morgan, Marty Stuart, Patty Loveless. American line dancing was the newest phenomenon in country music in the last 15 years.'

After the Wildhorse show, I walked across the street to the Old Time Pickin' Parlor, where the serious bluegrass crowd hangs out and plays together. The original Pickin' Parlor was started by Travis 'Tut' Taylor, the legendary dobro player, along with Randy Wood and Grant Boatright. Neil Young, Bob Dylan, Sam Bush, Vassar Clements, John Hartford, Norman Blake, and Charlie Collins were some of the drop-in musicians who came by to play. From 1971 until it closed in 1976, the Pickin' Parlor was the place in Nashville for bluegrass and traditional music. Tut and his son Mark, a renowned guitar builder and owner of Crafters of Tennessee, opened the new Pickin' Parlor to create the same atmosphere of playing around the pot-bellied stove with amateurs and pros. The Pickin' Parlor is probably the most non-commercial music place in Nashville that captures the spirit of pure country mountain music.

I wandered over to the Ryman Auditorium, a couple of blocks away, to see if Wanda was around and had word on Willie. The Ryman is named after Thomas Green Ryman (1841–1904), a prominent riverboat captain. In front of the building is a bronze statue of Ryman at the wheel of a riverboat. He was a generous contributor to the construction of the Union Gospel Tabernacle, the original name of the building. When Ryman died, the building was renamed in his memory.

The Ryman is also called the 'Mother Church of Country Music', in part because the architecture reflects a church and in part because the building was the original home of the Grand Ole Opry. In the lobby is a life-size bronze sculpture, by Russ Faxon, of Roy Acuff and Minnie Pearl sitting on a wooden pew. Her right hand rests on his arm, as if she is telling a good joke. Roy has a fiddle tucked under his left arm and a bow in his hand.

I could hear the concert in progress. It sounded like the opening act; Pat Green (the young Texan and his band that are filling arenas) was still on stage. I walked to the alley stage door directly opposite Tootsie's back door. No one was standing around, not even a security guard. I tried the stage door. Locked. I took my search into Tootsie's. A country-rock band had the back room packed. I pushed down the stairs to the front, where a solo singer in a big hat was doing covers. Wanda still wasn't at her table and the three amigos weren't in sight. Maybe they knew something I didn't. Maybe they were backstage at the Ryman with Willie at this moment having a personal high moment. Back on the sidewalk, I trolled the honky-tonks again.

The term 'honky-tonk' describes a place of low-life drinking and dancing, and some times fighting, fun. The term was used as early as 1894 and by 1936 was commonly applied to Southern bars where 'nice' people didn't go. They were rowdy places where women of ill repute caroused with men of the road and with musicians. Gospel songwriter James Paris, at the request of Texan singer Al Dexter, composed 'Honk-Tonk Blues'. Honky-tonk is a wide brush that puts color into a number of musical styles. It didn't become an influential part of country palette until the mid-'60s.

I stopped back in the Bluegrass Inn to see if Brandon was coherent. He wasn't around but the Hillbilly All Stars were finishing a set. I recognized the guitar player, Chris Scruggs, who played with his mother, Gail Davies, at the Station Inn. The three string players and the drummer launched into 'Whiskey Boogie', which brought a couple dressed in retro-'50s jitterbugging in front of the band. The next number, 'Teenage Boogie', got another couple dressed out of the Eisenhower era to cut the rug, if there had been a rug on the well-worn linoleum floor. Chris and the band mates favored 1950s country, from boogie to ballads, but they weren't simply a nostalgic throwback. They didn't go back and look up a style, then try it out. They made the style present in the same way an old hymn can take on a new voice and spirit in a modernistic cathedral.

The band's front man was Joe Buck, the ex-Chicago rocker then called Gringo, who, with his wife Lala, owns the Bluegrass Inn. Joe's alter-ego fronts the Shackshakers so much admired by Hank 3. With the Hillbilly All Stars, Joe Buck adopts the persona of Howdy Doody as an Oklahoma hick. The other band members – steel player, standup bass, rhythm guitar, and drums – are the BR549 band that made a big splash in the mid-1990s. They were preparing for a summer European tour. The band did Bob Wills covers, truck driving songs, mournful love songs with a weeping fiddle, and out-of-the-mind blazing songs racing on the rails of the lap steel guitar. At the closing song, Chris said, 'It's Saturday night. Prophecy says to tip the band big on Saturday night. It's in the Bible and we do obey the Bible, don't we?'

After the set, I joined Chris, Chuck Mead, and Shaw Wilson, the guitar player and drummer for BR549, at a table to talk about their music.

'The music goes back to Merle Haggard, Johnny Cash, the golden age of real country music in the 1950s,' Chris said. 'Of the choices you have of the American music, or roots music or whatever you want to call it, the music we play is the real cream of the crop. There are lots of people in their 20s and 30s who are into it, as are the people in their 50s, 60s, and 70s who grew up listening to Bob Wills and Jimmie Rodgers. I was raised on the Everly Brothers, Webb Pierce, early rockabilly stuff. I played in a punk rock band when I was 13. The two guys who got me thinking about country were Dale Watson, who played with us when I was touring Europe with my mother, and BR549. They were playing in punk rock bands, then they heard Dwight Yoakam.'

Chuck Mead joined in: 'Back in the '70s, when Shaw and I were starting out, what we played was just new music. It didn't have the labels and divisions on it. We didn't even call it punk rock back then. It was just rock 'n' roll. The Clash, the Jam, the Ramones, X, Nick Lowe, Elvis Costello, and all those bands coming out of the late '70s. The music industry's PR and the media put that "punk" or "new wave" label on it, depending what record store bin they wanted it in.

'To me, what links country and that new music is the '50s and '60s garage rock. Nervous Norman recording "Transfusion" in his mom's bathroom and it's a hit. Do it yourself music. Ernest Tubb said, "I'm here to prove that anybody shoveling shit in a barn can hear me sing and say, well, I can do that." Of course you can. Just do it. That's the whole spirit behind the movement against corporate rock.

'It started with Iggy and the Stooges and the Dolls and that metamorphosed into the Ramones and Blondie. They went over to England and that's how a lot of the English bands got started. The big punk explosion in England really started in the United States. It was garage rock 'n' roll. Those guys were going back to Ernest Tubb's "anybody can do it". They said, "Let's make a lot of noise because it's fun noise and we can get our point of view across without putting together some pretentious concept album." The sense of individualism in country, the outlaw, and the sense of individualism in rock 'n' roll and in punk is about the same thing – being who you are and demanding respect for it.'

Shaw Wilson leaned into the conversation. His shiny combed-back hair and sharp sideburns made him James Dean-killer handsome. Simply by sitting still he suggested danger, delicious danger if you're female. 'I don't think Waylon or Willie or Johnny Cash set out to be a primary hero,' he said. 'They knew that they had a purpose. They knew they were that purpose. People recognized that and therefore the legend followed them. Nowadays, it's really hard to recognize someone with that caliber because so many musicians sell out so quickly. They take the brass ring because it's so hard to make a living as a musician. It goes two ways with musicians. If a musician really wants to make music and money at the same time, they take anything that is handed to them. The record people say, "Okay, you're coming into the cycle at this point. You're going to have a two or three album, or year, career. Let us help you make a bunch of money and then it will all go away." Or, you can be the type of musician who learns and grows. Alan Jackson and Ricky Skaggs are good examples. They played the number game for ten years. They did everything the label asked of them, against their better judgment. They made a name for themselves and then went back to where they started musically – Ricky Skaggs in bluegrass and Alan Jackson in honky-tonk. That's the stuff they love. They went through hell and fire, sort of, but like Waylon and Willie, they are outlaws because they are doing their thing.'

Chuck and Shaw are Kansas farm boys who grew up shucking corn and baling hay. Chuck's father, mother, and her two brothers were the Wines Family, a country-western-gospel-rockabilly band, part of the Hayloft Gang in the late 1940s and early 1950s. When he was 12, they needed a drummer and his music career began behind a kit.

'My high school friends laughed at me because I was buying Chuck Berry, Little Richard, and Elvis records and playing country western and rockabilly,' Chuck said. 'I was ahead of my time.'

Chuck and Shaw's fathers came from Pittsburg, Kansas and knew each other. But Shaw's family moved to Nebraska. His father wouldn't buy him a drum set. 'My dad was a huge country fan but he said that a drum made too much damn racket,' Shaw said. 'I had to work three jobs to save enough money to buy my first kit. I was self-taught by the time I was 22. I came through it organically.'

The two joined up as a guitar and drum duo known as Dos Cojones. They toured all over the country in an Aerostar van. 'It was more like Jack Kerouac and less like the Rolling Stones,' remembers Chuck. 'In May 1993, I came to Nashville at the urging of an old band mate. My goal was to work at Tootsie's Orchid Lounge. That's the job. Play in the window. I got a job at Tootsie's and met some musicians at Robert's, just a couple doors down.'

Chuck asked Shaw to join him. The band wasn't making much money but they were playing every night doing the music they wanted. Shaw arrived. Their friend Jay Dow joined as the doghouse bass player. A doghouse bass is an upright bass also known as a bull fiddle. In England, it's called the double bass with a three-quarter scale instead of a full size bass. It's called doghouse because it looks like a doghouse and the body is big enough for a dog inside. Donnie Herron joined the band. He is a bluegrass steel guitar player influenced by the French jazz violinist Stephane Grappelli and the Gypsy guitarist Django Reinhardt. The band's sax player, who didn't stay long, named the band BR549, after the mock phone number of the car salesman on the television show *Hee Haw* played by the comedian Junior Samples.

BR549 became the house band at Robert's Honky-Tonk Grill. They played original songs, Carl Smith, Webb Pierce, Johnny Cash, Charlie Pride, Roy Orbison, Carl Perkins, Elvis, and the old country not heard on mainstream radio. To make 'Mule Skinner Blues' BR549's 'Mule Skinner Blues', they'd took Jimmie Rodgers, added a little Bill Monroe, a dash of the Fenderman, Freddie Fender, a little bit of the Ramones, and that was their version.

The Vanderbilt college crowd discovered the band. 'We were doing something that nobody had done for a long time,' Shaw said. 'These 18-year-old kids who didn't know Johnny Cash told us, "I don't like country but I like you guys." Our music was otherworldly to them. We just laughed because we were as country as we could be.'

Fans formed lines around the block from Robert's to get into BR549's shows. Radio stations and the records labels took notice. Tim DuBois, then president of Arista Records and now partner with Tony Brown at Universal South, signed the band.

'We still owe him a phone call to say, "God bless ya and thanks for giving us a chance,"' Chuck said. 'He was never anything but honest with us. We always felt we were pretty well taken care of at Arista. He's a wise man, Tim DuBois. He's very creative, an intelligent hillbilly from Oklahoma who recognized what we were doing.'

BR549 toured for six and a half years in Europe, Australia, Japan, the United States, and Canada. During their eight European tours, they built a loyal following in Poland, Holland, the United Kingdom, Norway, Germany, Ireland, and Holland, where they had a number one hit, 'Even If It's Wrong'. Now the band is in transition. 'I call it road fatalities,' said Shaw. 'Nobody's dead but we're going through a divorce of the second reincarnation of BR549.'

Chris Scruggs, 19, also finds a direct tie between punk rock and hillbilly music, rockabilly music, and country music.

'I don't see much difference between someone like Hank Williams and Johnny Cash and someone like The Clash or X,' he said. 'It's all folk music, not the coffeehouse folk music, but music that is for the folk. Punk rock and country has the same basic message – simple, honest, made by people who aren't virtuosos who went to music school. It's for the people, about the people, whether it's the Ramones or Carl Smith. There is definitely a line there between those styles. It's a thick line in places but very thin in other places, as far as the basic entry level. In the past few years, there have been a lot of bluegrass bands with punk rock, like the Spit Lip Hayfield. They are a bunch of tattooed guys who play very fast punked-up bluegrass. The bass player, his bass is made out of a gastank for a '78 Lincoln. He put one string on it. He plays a one-string gas tank.

'A lot of people give traditional American music a hard time because a lot of it has only three chords. The basic chords are one-four-five, the basic blues chords. From a rock point of view, you play a chord progression and you write a song around the chord progression. In country, you write around the melody. When you write around the melody, you have only three or four chords because there are only eight notes in the scale. You're not going to have that many chords because the melody is doing the changing. So you don't have the monotone sound of an electric guitar and electric bass playing the same power chords to each other to get the melody. On a rock chart, the chords are jumping around. On a country chart, you hold on the four forever before going to the five/four forever because the melody is doing all the moving around.'

I asked if they had heard any rumors that Willie might play the back room at Tootsie's after his Ryman show.

'Anything is possible with Willie,' Chuck replied.

I found Wanda at the entrance of the alley between the Ryman and Tootsie's. She looked very spiffy, attractive, years younger.

'Where you been?' I asked, 'You been with Willie?'

'No,' she replied. 'It's not going to happen.'

'You don't want to see Willie?'

'I don't have to see Willie to know Willie. I'm too old to be hanging around the stage door. I'm going home.'

'You look awful nice tonight, Wanda.'

'Thanks, that's nice of you but I'm still going home,' she answered with a laugh.

17 Texas Country

Our Willie was coyly smug.

'Where were you all weekend?' Amy asked in a tone more querulous than expected from just a co-writer.

He wore a faded Armadillo Headquarter T-shirt I hadn't seen before.

'Hanging out.' Dramatic pause. 'And pitching.'

Amy eyed him suspiciously. 'Who with and where?'

Our Willie leaned back away from the table to give us a full look at the front of his T-shirt. Down near the hem was a scrawl of ink but I couldn't read it.

'Willie and Keith and Toby and Ray. The gang.'

'What are you talking about?'

Our Willie turned to me and casually said, 'By the way, Vince says hello.'

'You got in, didn't you?'

Our Willie allowed himself a satisfied smile, and then threw his head back in a hoot of laughter. 'More than that, my man. Much more than that.'

In a quick stroke, here's how Our Willie spent his weekend pitching his song to Willie Nelson:

Crafty Our Willie showed up at the Ryman early Friday afternoon and passed himself off as part of the sound check crew. He made quick friends with the real crew by introducing himself as a representative of a local guitar repair shop on 24/7 standby for any instrument emergencies. That got him a security pass. From then on, it was clear sailing. Not only did Our Willie stay for the Friday night Ryman show, but was backstage at the Saturday's Country Music Television live show at the Opryland's Gibson Bluegrass Showcase. 'And the big one,' Our Willie crowed, 'the special Sunday taping at the Ryman of *Willie Nelson & Friends: Stars And Guitars*.'

That where all the big stars showed up: Keith Richards, Jon Bon Jovi, The Dixie Chicks, Emmylou Harris, Lyle Lovett, Ryan Adams, Dave Matthews, Lee Ann Womack, Sheryl Crow, Ray Price, and Rob Thomas, who wrote several songs on Willie's new album, *The Great Divide*.

'Vince Gill played lead guitar on the show's opener,' Our Willie reported as an insider. 'Willie and Sheryl Crow sang 'For What It's Worth' and Keith did *Dead Flowers* with Willie, Hank 3, and Ryan Adams.'

'You could have read that in the papers,' interrupted Amy, clearly irritated. 'I don't think you were there at all.'

Our Willie turned a superior eye toward her. 'I was in his hotel room.'

'What hotel was that?' Amy challenged. When in Nashville, most of the big stars stay at the Vanderbilt Plaza. However, Willie had not and his location was a secret.

'The Hampton Inn,' Our Willie snapped back. 'At Green Hills. And we drank Whiskey River (Willie's signature bourbon), and he gave me this.' Our Willie tugged at the T-shirt, stretching out Willie's signature on the bottom. 'And best of all, I pitched the Loveless Motel song to him.'

'What!' exploded Amy.

'He said it showed promise. He liked my idea of the Loveless Motel as a metaphor for a man's loveless home life. He told me to send him the song when it was finished.'

'That's our song. Don't you be cutting me out on this,' Amy warned. In that moment, I imagined that if he tried anything underhanded, she would cut Our Willie's throat as she had sawed off the fringe of her shirt with my knife.

'He give you his home address to send the song?' I asked as a final test of Our Willie's story.

'No, but he gave his agent's fax number.'

It seemed that Our Willie might have scored.

Wouldn't it be ironic if Our Willie hit it in Nashville by coming through the Texas backdoor? Nashville and Austin have a slightly cantankerous relationship with regards to country music. Nashville's Music Row considers the Texas musicians as a little 'loose'. The Austin musicians consider Music Row's country as 'soul-deadening slick'. Yet, there is a great deal of commerce and musical exchange between the two camps. Nashville's record labels scout Austin's annual South-by-Southwest music showcase for new songwriters, singers, and material. Texas musicians record in Nashville because the facilities and resources are more diverse and plentiful.

The Flatlanders – Jimmie Dale Gilmore, Joe Ely, and Butch Hancock – are a good example of Texas coming to Tennessee, but without making concessions. Their legendary first album was cut in Nashville in 1972. Nearly 30 years later, the Flatlanders second album, *Now Again* (New West), was cut in Nashville over a three-year period, with the master being mixed in 2002. In those intervening years, the three musicians have had successful solo careers. Jimmie Dale has been the most visible of the trio, cutting numerous albums and touring. Joe Ely formed his own band in 1975. Country purists and punk rockers alike have mined his musical eclecticism and intensity. Butch Hancock, a storyteller and wordsmith, formed publishing and record companies and released a series of poetic albums.

The day after Our Willie bragged about his Texas connection, The Flatlanders came to Nashville's Tower Records for a release performance, where I caught up with Jimmie Dale.

'We always had this plan to get together,' said Jimmie Dale, explaining how the *Now Again* album happened. 'What finally catalyzed it, we were invited to do music for Robert Redford's film *The Horse Whisperer*. The three of us got together. We discovered that we enjoyed it a lot.'

Jimmie Dale and I once sat at the feet of the same guru and knew each other from years back. 'I never had the dislike of Nashville that is fashionable among the alt-country musicians,' he said as we talked among the record bins. 'Most of what I've recorded has been in Nashville. I did the second HiTone album here. *Spinning Around the Sun*, which is straight Nashville, was done over at Woodland Studios with Emory Gordy. It's not that I like Nashville itself, the city, so much. It has some of the greatest talent in the world and the studios and infrastructure are centered here.'

Texas country music has an identifiable sound different from Nashville country. Texas country is not as prissy. The musicians don't worry if every note is exactly perfect. Their lyrics are bolder, more clear-eyed truthful. A cow is a cow is a cow shitting on your boot, rather than Ol' Besty in the pasture doing her country thing naturally. Texas musicians, as a whole, like a little unpredictability. They seek an edge that bends a note a bit out of shape just because the musicians want to hear it. They tend not to fiddle on the soundboard to minutely adjust every flat and sharp to perfect pitch. They would rather be passionately in error than be heard as infallible.

'I do think that Nashville has bred more of a mercantile, rather than artistic, ethic in the music,' Jimmie Dale said. 'Some of the most crass commercial people make the best music. It's weird. I don't think that's happened in a long time but it has happened. It's a fluke of the world that it does happen.'

Jimmie Dale has remained a thin sparse man over the years, not gathering a middle-age spread. He's not tall but he seems that way on stage. His hair still comes down over his shoulders and he makes no effort to style it. There are a few strands of silver in the brown now. He has sharp angular features and warm brown eyes. His voice is unmistakable, that high lonesome twang of West Texas Lubbock, where he grew up with Joe Ely and Butch Hancock. Lubbock is also the hometown of the 'Big Bopper' Buddy Holly.

'Joe, Butch, and I were a creative nucleus for each other,' Jimmie Dale said of his life-long friends. 'Music was the bond between myself, Joe, and Butch, who I have known since seventh grade. In the first years, we were each other's only audience. We were interested only in the love of music. Then, we had no thought of music careers. Joe and I were the first men to wear long hair in Lubbock. We were seen as "strange kids", an image we cultivated. We were deliberately flamboyant. We were in reaction to the conservative, repressive attitudes of West Texas. When we did that first album, we were completely naïve. And the record people had no idea what we were about and the right way to market us. We were much more from a folk and rock background, although we had plenty of country influence.'

Jimmie Dale's father, Brian, was the director of the dairy industry plant at Texas Tech. He also played electric guitar in a western dance band and introduced his first-born son to the music of Bob Wills, Lefty Frizzell, Hank Williams, the Rose Sisters, the Maddox Brothers, and Ernest Tubb. Jimmie, named after Jimmie Rodgers, took up the fiddle in the fourth grade but switched to trombone so he could play in the school band. An uncle gave him an acoustic guitar and Jimmie Dale found his musical soul mate. He listened to pop, rock, honky-tonk, and the blues along with country music, influences still heard in his music.

He ran away from home during his senior year in high school, but his teachers would not let such a promising student escape and convinced him to return. While in high school, he met Terry Allen, the influential Texas songwriter/singer, who is also an accomplished painter and sculptor. They became friends and Jimmie Dale realized that he didn't have to wait until he was 'grown up' to become a musician.

Another seminal event for Jimmie Dale was when Joe Ely called him up and said, 'I've got a record I want you to listen to.' Joe had picked up a hitchhiker coming through Lubbock. On the short ride from one side of town to the other, Joe learned that the guy was a musician, too. When Joe dropped him off, the guy reached into his backpack and handed Joe an album he had cut. 'You've got to hear this guy Townes Van Zandt,' Joe told Jimmie.

Jimmie Dale got his high school diploma, married a fellow student less than a year after graduation and became a father. The marriage ended in 1970. He and his wife since 1988, Janet, an ex-teacher, live on a five-acre spread of scrub oak and wild flowers near Spice Wood in the Texas hill country near Austin.

As a teenage father, Jimmie Dale enrolled at Texas Tech, where he studied logic, linguistic analysis and philosophy. 'I learned to doubt in a very, very studied and meticulous way, but by temperament I'm a mystic,' he explained. These two forces, the rational and the mystic, have been fundamental to shaping his sensibilities and music.

'For years I struggled with which of those I should throw out, the rational or the mystic. The real truth is understanding those co-exist. They are not contradictory. That Townes Van Zandt record Joe played for me was a revelation because I heard folk music and country music in the same place. I didn't have to throw one out.'

In the 1970s, he began a serious study of Eastern philosophies and accepted the teenage East Indian Maharaji as his teacher. He gave up music and moved into Maharaji's Divine Light Mission ashram in Denver. For five years he worked as a janitor in a synagogue, became serious about macrobiotics, studied to be an acupuncturist and meditated on Maharaji's teachings. He moved back to Austin in 1980 and resumed his music.

'I don't think my music would work if I didn't express a longing in literal spiritual terms,' Jimmie Dale said. 'Expressing the spiritual is the point of it all. My aspiration is that the spiritual questing for understanding becomes the dominant component of my art. You know, Hank Williams personally had a very spiritual longing that was never satisfied. I think such longing is the basis of all suffering, even if it is expressed as broken-heart romance, or sexual problems, or drinking, or whatever.'

He may have put his finger on the very soul of country music.

'What attracts me to any song has been an intensity of feeling, whether in the lyrics or the sound, the musical structure. Some kind of passion is what I've always gravitated toward. I felt that quality in early country music and in the blues. They grab me emotionally, or with humor, and sometimes with both. The best have both. I love what they call old-time country music. That was my original love. Then the folk scene started happening and I discovered the roots stuff, the bluegrass, and heavy Delta blues, Lightnin' Hopkins blues, Mance Liscomb.

'Blues, for me, is the underpinning of everything I love the most. I've never been associated as a blues artist, but it's in my taste. It's the deepest root. I've discovered that all the country music I love the most has derived, as least partly, from the blues, the black music. But the blues influence sort of disappeared in the Nashville music.

'The passion is the music being made in a very personal sense, rather than of trying to make a hit record. When you take that personal route, you take a risk of not being financially successful. Most of my favorite artists haven't been financially successful. I left that criterion behind a long time ago. I have managed to survive. Some of my friends do very well. Some of my friends have died completely penniless, but still doing the kind of music they wanted to. That's the difference between my real peer group and the more commercial music.

'There are people who manage to do both, to be intensely personal and be commercially successful. Bob Dylan is a perfect example. He created genuinely creative revolutionary musical art. He was never successful in the sense of The Beatles or The Eagles or Paul Simon, but he managed to make a whole lot of money by going absolutely his own way. Lyle Lovett falls in the category of being artistically successful, moderately so because I don't think he's the greatest. He managed to have a following and to make some money. He pays good musicians to go on the road with him. That's a kind of success that can't be looked down on. Lyle is wonderful. He's a great artist.

'I don't consider myself a country performer or remotely an expert on it. My music is as different as possible from what they call country today. I came out of a country background but Top 40 country radio went in a different direction from my taste and background. I would have never remotely guessed that what has happened to country music would have happened. It has become watered-down pop music instead of country music.

'That comes from the Nashville system of making the music a product of the money, rather than the music being more a concern of art. Simple as that. Texas music has something to do with more concern for expressing personal interest and personal passion, rather than figuring out what's going to be a hit.

'Nashville is associated with country music the same as Hollywood is associated with movies. The real truth is that the things that have affected country music the most didn't happen in Nashville. Sun Records in Memphis, Buck Owens in Bakersfield, the attitude down in Texas, that's where the real things in country have happened. The performers who go to Nashville have probably already cast their lot with the homogenized music, rather than having an intensely individualistic approach.

'What is called Nashville is really more the product of radio. There is not really a Nashville music. The aesthetic of Nashville music is almost to sound like you're not really involved. The goal is to sing the note right, on pitch, in tune, with the right pronunciation and inflection, but you're not supposed to sound like there's much emotion behind it. That's the difference between Nashville country and Texas country.'

★

Buck Owens and his Buckaroos play their part-rockabilly, part-honky-tonk mixed with high-octane rock'n'roll primarily in the clubs of central and southern California. Owens is a central figure in country music but he is not of the Nashville sound or establishment. The Others' country sound, like Phil Lee and Hank 3, found their inspiration, in part, in Buck Owens. The electronic guitars of Owens and his partner, Don Rich, fashioned hard country music but kept strands of the honky-tonk style popularized by Ray Price and the Cherokee Cowboys of the 1950s. They amped up the traditional country instruments and added the G, F, D, C of rock'n'roll to the traditional country language that already included jazz and rhythm-and-blues phrases.

Buck Owens influenced The Flying Burrito Brothers, founded by Chris Hillman and Gram Parsons, Dwight Yoakam, the Detailers – who recently relocated from Nashville to the Northwest – BR549 and the Los Angeles 'cowpunks' who brought the aggressive edge, blasting rock'n'roll decibels and attitude found in punk.

Toni Price, who started her country singing career in Nashville, but moved to Austin for artistic self preservation, says that she didn't know who Buck Owens was until she moved to Austin. 'Nobody talked about him in Nashville,' she said in a phone conversation. 'To the country music people in Nashville, he was more or less a clown. In Texas, people worship Buck Owens. We have a yearly tribute to him. He's a very serious musician, but in Nashville all they gave us was the *Hee Haw* Buck Owens.'

Toni's opinion of Nashville is not uncommon among Texan country musicians. The danger about generalizations is that they are inherently wrong. Nevertheless, she said, 'What I see happening in country on the street level is a renaissance in old-country music. The country scene in Nashville has nothing to do with what's going on the street. It's a business, a machine.' Toni is a very popular performer in Austin, with a steady club gig. 'A lot of people are writing and playing with their hearts in country music. They're not trying to do all that bullshit that country music has become – cheesy. For me, country music is very simple. It's filled with emotion. It tells a story. It's not whiny. It doesn't have some corny play on words. Hank Williams was real. He could tell you of the saddest suffering and not be whiny. Willie is country. He's kept it alive with his extended family. He just keeps rockin'. He never cared what Nashville said, or what anybody said. He might be keeping it alive single-handedly since we lost Waylon.'

Ray Benson Siefert is another Texan musician who has recorded a dozen albums in Nashville but prefers Austin. As Ray Benson, he is the leader of the band Asleep At The Wheel that has kept alive the Bob Wills and the Texas Playboys tradition of Texas swing. Merle Haggard led the renewed interest in Bob Wills with his own special tribute in 1970. In 1973, some of the original Texas Playboys reunited to record. Wills was too ill to perform but he sat in on the session, adding his famous holler on some songs. When Asleep At The Wheel heard Haggard's tribute to Wills, the band changed, in 1974, from rock'n'roll and country rock to Texas Western swing.

The source of Asleep At The Wheel's music is threefold, according to Benson. 'We dredge up forgotten music, the old songs,' he explained. 'Thirty years ago we found the old 78s, listened to them and reinterpreted the music. Then, I write music sometimes in the form of 1939 western twang or 1948 hillbilly or 1951 R&B. And third, I just write whatever the hell it is that fits my voice.' Asleep At The Wheel first recorded 'Boot Scootin' Boogie' before Brooks And Dunn.

Benson makes a distinction between Texas swing and country swing. Country swing is George Strait; Texas swing is Bob Wills and the singers Hank Thompson, Red Steagall, Ray Price, and bandleader Hoyle Nix.

'Wills would never consider himself a country artist in the least,' Benson said in his deep Texan voice that completely obliterates his Philadelphia roots. 'His music is very western as opposed to country. His music is very big band swing jazzy but it is also rural root music with fiddles. That's why these different musics are considered 'country and western'. When they dropped the 'western' part, that pissed me off. To me, that's the biggest travesty that's happened to country music. Country musics, and there are many different kinds of country music, started out as rural music. Wills knew that his audience was rural. In the 1930s and the 1950s, there was a great shift of population from the rural to the city. But the music – bluegrass, western swing, honky-tonk, Jim Reeves country, whatever –

was rural music based on people's lives that were based on a rural economy. A big shift to the cities started in World War II as people left the rural areas to work in the war-time factories. By the '60s, the rural population in America had dropped to under ten per cent.'

Benson and Asleep At The Wheel did their own tribute album, *Ride with Bob, A Tribute to Bob Wills and the Texas Playboys*, recorded in Nashville in 1999. The album features Vince Gill, Clint Black, Tim McGraw, Willie Nelson, Lee Ann Womack, Lyle Lovett, Shawn Colvin, and The Dixie Chicks. The music is distinctly Texas western swing with the stalwarts of country music playing rural dance music that links both musics.

'The importance of that album for me was that we were able to do the music in a way directly related to the way it was supposed to be done, and has been done,' Benson said. 'Yet, it was updated to the year 2000. We brought the music into the present without it being a museum piece.'

So, if the rural population, the historical base fan group of country music, is now largely an urban/suburban population, what makes a country song?

'The term country is so widespread that's it ridiculous,' Benson answered. 'This is country music; you've got Bill Monroe and Ralph Stanley playing bluegrass; Doug Kershaw and Beausoleil play Cajun country; Willie Nelson, Johnny Cash, Merle Haggard have their country; you got Alan Jackson and George Strait; you got Jim Reeves and Patsy Cline; then you got Bob Wills and western swing.

'Is Lyle Lovett a country performer? Sometimes he is, but sometimes he's not. He's from rural Texas, still lives in his grandfather's house out in the country. Does he fit all the criteria of a country singer? Yeah, sometimes. George Strait is a genuine Texas rancher. His dad was a small town school principal. George is a real rancher and once taught agriculture extension classes at the high school. Does he fit the criteria of a country singer? Yeah, but he also has a mainstream commercial base. Same with Alan Jackson. Country, in its broadest terms, uses string instruments and is based around the basic blues chords, one-four-five. Bob Wills used saxophones, trombones, and woodwinds. Is that country? Yeah.

'What do all these kinds of country have in common? Nothing. Only, the thing that holds true is that it's a lyrical music. The lyrics are very important. The lyrics are very direct, very much plain spoken. They're not flowery. They're pretty much in the language that we use on a daily basis. The music is generally simplistic in its makeup. But don't get me wrong, it's not simplistic music. The harmonic simplicity and the melodic simplicity is inherent, still it's a complex music.'

Part of the complexity is found in the largely unspoken background of the music.

'Woodie Guthrie is thought of as folk, but that's country,' Benson said. 'Country of Guthrie's music has that little guy versus the big guy. That's inherent in the lyrics and the mythology of country music. But, in our time, the little guy has been co-opted by corporate America. There is this individuality dichotomy in country now. The strong individual with his or her own way and mind has always been an important figure in country. But then there's the "my country love it or leave it" mentality. How does that fit with the individual standing for what he or she believes? Nowadays, it's like you can't speak out against anything that is American without the risk of being called un-American, especially since the September 11 terrorist attack. Yet, the little guy has to speak out.

'Music, especially country and western, tends to be taken by political or ideological people and used for their political purposes. "Okie from Muskogee" by Merle Haggard comes out and it is used as a whip against the hippie war protesters in 1969. That was ridiculous. Merle Haggard was a pothead. But the song framed the whole political debate at that moment. It was used as a rallying point for the conservative "love or leave it" point of view when, in reality, that was not entirely true about the song.

'People identify their lifestyle and political beliefs by the music they listen to. I've always been against that because it's like a blanket. It's not for real. When someone says, "I'm a country music fan," that says, "I'm a conservative person, I believe in the flag, in America." That's true to a certain extent. But if you go deeper than that it's really not true.'

Benson's example of 'Okie From Muskogee' is apt. The title is a tribute to Haggard's father, James, according to Ace Collins' book, *The Stories Behind Country Music's All-Time Greatest 100 Songs* (Boulevard Books, New York 1996). The Great Depression and the Dustbowl forced James to sell his Oklahoma farm. He loaded his family in an old truck and joined the exodus of Okies going to California, where Merle was born. In California, he moved his family into an abandoned boxcar. He took whatever work he could find, as did thousands of others in the 1930s. James died poor, proud of being a workingman. Haggard recalls his father as a man of self-respect who was proud to be an American.

Haggard came out of that Okie culture and environment of John Steinbeck's *The Grapes Of Wrath*. He was, and is, an individual to the bone, to the extent of being a juvenile delinquent and doing jail time. Haggard wrote 'Okie From Muskogee' when on a tour of the farm belt with his band. They had stopped outside of Muskogee, Oklahoma, a small farm town in central Oklahoma. The musicians found themselves in a political discussion with some locals on the Vietnam War, President Johnson, civil rights, burning draft cards, the National Guard shooting the anti-war protest students at Kent State and marijuana.

According to Collins' book, someone joked, 'I bet that they don't smoke marijuana in Muskogee.' That was the trigger for listing a lot of things conservative Americans don't do. And what they didn't do was used to define what is a true American, sort of a reverse negative. Haggard and his drummer, Roy Burris, wrote down the list and finished the song in 20 minutes.

'Okie From Muskogee' can be read as a popular emblematic song of conservative America, or an ironic emblematic song of conservative America, which was Benson's point.

To keep on the point of the dichotomy in country music, Benson continued, 'The music is used as a white person's music. But this is also completely false because it has drawn on so much of the blues. That's why I love Bob Wills. He and his music was so much of a dichotomy. He was a white guy in the most racist society that American has ever seen, Texas in the '30s. Yet, he embraced Betsy Smith, Louis Armstrong, Dixieland, and Spanish music.'

Jim Bob Wills was born in Kosse, Texas in 1905. His father had a dance band and Wills was an accomplished guitarist by the age of ten. He ran away from home at 14 and began his individualist exploration of music. Early on, he was drawn to black music. He did blackface and fronted a medicine show as a comic. Over years of experimentation, the combining of black and white music sounds became his signature music. That extended to putting urban musical style with the western sound of rural Texas.

In the early 1930s, he formed the Texas Playboys and continued to perfect his 'western jazz'. He used drums and electrical guitars for long solos, when drums were banned from the Grand Ole Opry stage as not country. Electric instruments were heretical to country purists. His musical experimentation led to an entirely new sound in country music. His song 'Spanish Two Step', a Tex-Mex dance number, combined rural western, border Mexican, and New Orleans black jazz. The song sold well in Texas and Oklahoma, but the rest of the country wasn't listening. Wills gave the music of his rural Texas such a sophisticated sound that Irving Berlin published, in 1938, Wills' 'San Antonio Rose'. The song was a hit and continues to be a standard.

'You cannot overestimate the importance of race in this,' Benson continued. 'Sure, there is Charlie Pride. I used to work with a guy named Stony Edwards, a black country singer from Oklahoma. There is now Trini Triggs out of Louisiana. There are certainly black people who enjoy country music. But the preponderance of country fans is white. The preponderance of people who don't like country is non-white, non-rural, non-Southern, and/or highly educated. The generalization holds true for a majority, but they aren't the whole picture. If you're a black person trying to escape the racism of American, you're not going to embrace Ralph Stanley and bluegrass. As a generalization, the Southern bluegrass fans fly the Confederate flag at the shows and are proud of their Southern roots. They don't hate black people but their ancestors owned black slaves and, deep in the consciousness, both groups are aware of that.'

With all this diversity in country music, what makes for an authentic country performer?

'That's a tough one,' Benson admitted. 'I'm a suburban Jewish kid from Philadelphia. When I first started playing this music, I had a thing that I was not authentic. I wrestled with authenticity for years and decided to let peoples' ears do the deciding. Because I knew it so well and I lived it, I was it. George Strait grew up in the Western culture in south Texas of a Christian family. That's authentic. What he and I do is very similar. Is he more authentic than I am because of his upbringing? In one way, yeah, but in another way, no. My music is more authentic than his music. But he is more authentic from a sociological, cultural evaluation of his place. The authenticity, the purity of a Bill Monroe, even that's bullshit because it's all perception. Bill Monroe had an accordion player in his first band. How pure bluegrass is that?

'If someone came from Waco, Texas and did what I'm doing, would they be more authentic? In my judgment, yeah. But they couldn't do what I'm doing because of the cultural imperative. One of the reasons I am able to do my music is because my dad didn't like Merle Haggard and country music. The people I grew up with didn't like country music. But I thought the music had great merit based on its inherent qualities. I didn't have to go through the stage, "My Uncle Buford, a racist pig, loved this music, therefore I have to hate it", like many people from the South who came from a country background. I understood that there was great racism in country music, but I understood that there was great humanity in country music.'

18 Why Nashville?

Why is Nashville the capital of country music? Why not Muscle Shoals, Charlotte, Atlanta, Dallas, Cincinnati, Knoxville, San Antonio, Austin, Bristol, or Memphis?

Each of those cities has a claim on country music, some that predate Nashville. Several had considerable recording facilities in the 1920s and '30s, before Nashville had a decent studio. Hank Williams recorded 'Love Sick Blues' in Cincinnati in 1948, before Nashville was firmly established as the country-recording center.

Nashville won out because of money and location – and the insurance industry.

Muscle Shoals, Alabama, a three-hour ride south/southwest from Nashville, was in the music business long before Nashville. A small town in the hill-and-lake country, Muscle Shoals was a port on the Tennessee River. Rivers, especially the Mississippi, Tennessee, Cumberland, and Ohio, were main conduits for trading goods and music. The rivermen who worked the barges were walking songbooks and exchanged songs. They made instruments and traded them. Muscle Shoals was known as a musical instrument trading and manufacturing center since the time of WC Handy. Music instrument stores lined the riverfront along with the bars and hotels.

Good music, better music than that heard in Nashville some argue, is performed in Muscle Shoals today. Muscle Shoals' professional musicians enjoy a high reputation as sidemen and session players with their own style and sound, especially in the blues and R&B. Aretha Franklin is one of many singers who has recorded in Muscle Shoals specifically for the sound. Muscle Shoals players work on Nashville sessions, putting the edgier pop and the funk influence into Nashville country. Then they go home. Muscle Shoals has always been music before the business of music.

Bristol, in the northeastern corner of Tennessee, was where Ralph Peer first recorded the Carter Family, Jimmie Rodgers and the Ernest Stoneman Family. This is Appalachian Tennessee, a root source of old country music. But outside of the Bristol Sessions in the 1920s, the town never attracted the music business. Johnson City, a little south of Bristol, is becoming a local center of old-timey music. Bristol has had its moment in the country sun.

Austin and Nashville are state capitals; both are university towns; and both have a lively music and recording scene. It's an issue of attitude – and radio stations – that made the difference. Austin's attitude has been to enjoy the music. Nashville sought to turn music into a cash cow. And in the 1930s, Nashville was home to WSM radio, the home of the Grand Ole Opry, which broadcasted nationwide and helped to brand Nashville with country music.

The two cities have always had an ear for different sounds. Austin has been a musical stew of rock, blues, country boogie, folk, cowboy, honky-tonk, and Western swing. It was the center of Willie Nelson's Outlaw country in the 1960s and '70s. The Texas attitude is freer, perhaps more inventive and more open to ethnic and cultural pluralism. Texas was once Mexico and the Mexican influence is second nature to the place. Nashville never has had its own distinct sound, except that manufactured in the studios. In Texas, they raise cattle; in Tennessee, they raise show horses. That says it all about attitude.

Nashville and Memphis are both music cities: Nashville has Opryland and Memphis has Graceland. Both cities have faux monuments of antiquity: the Parthenon in Nashville and the Pyramid in Memphis. They are both river towns: Nashville on the Cumberland and Memphis on the Mississippi. Both cities have a long historical connection to music – but Memphis doesn't have a music industry and Nashville does.

Memphis and Nashville have always had different musical tastes. Memphis caught the flavor of the Delta blues as musicians from Louisiana and Mississippi followed the Old Man River up to Chicago. Blues-gospel-rockabilly country was the Memphis sound, and brassy horns. Jerry Lee Lewis, Carl Perkins, Elvis Presley epitomized the Memphis music that looked forward to rock 'n' roll. Nashville homogenized country into pop or perpetuated the nostalgia of a mythical country image.

Perhaps Memphis developed a music sound, rather than a music industry, because the city was more of a way station while Nashville was the terminal. Musicians traveling from New Orleans to Chicago, by train or highway, stopped in Memphis but were always moving on. The Memphis music industry never gained sustainable mass.

Memphis's biggest star, Elvis Presley, was sold to Nashville. Elvis first recorded at Sam Phillip's Sun Studios, at 710 Union in Memphis. The studio is a small storefront on a busy street not far from downtown Memphis. It looks very 1950s, the brick façade painted white, with two 4ft (1.2m) windows on either side of the door. It could have been a bakery. Next door, is the Walker Radiator Works. Above the entrance is SUN in red neon. Neon signs in the window read Memphis (in red) Recording (in blue script) Service (in red).

The place is as much a museum as a working studio, although U2, Ringo Starr, Bonnie Raitt, and Beck, among others, have recorded there in recent years. BB King recorded 'When Love Comes to Town' in the old Sun studio to capture the particular sound of the place.

In the small reception area is the secretary Marion Keiskar's original desk with its Remington Rand manual typewriter and clunky black phone. In the summer of 1953, Marion Keiskar, not Sam Phillips, recorded the 18-year-old Elvis's first demo, 'My Happiness'. The record was a birthday present to his mother, so the story is told. Keiskar reportedly thought that Elvis had a sweet tenor but was not generally impressed by him. Nevertheless, she kept a copy of the demo for herself.

A big plate glass window in the reception room looks directly into the recording studio, which has not been refurbished since the 1950s. A drum kit, an upright piano, and vintage guitars line the walls of original white acoustic tiles, the type often used as office ceiling. The beige linoleum floor tiles are the ones that Bob Dylan got down on his knees and kissed as sacred ground. The dark window of control rooms looks down from the back wall. The original standup mic with its big silver head that Elvis used is in the back corner. Elvis stood in that corner, in front of the mic opposite the drum kit in the far corner, for his last recording session at Sun. Elvis had a direct view of Carl Perkins making funny faces through the window in the reception area. On the original tape of the session, which is played as part of the studio tour, Elvis breaks up and says about Carl ruining his concentration.

In this studio Chester 'Howlin' Wolf' Burnett, Phillips's first artist, recorded. Ike Turner cut 'Rocket 88' in 1951. Jerry Lee Lewis recorded 'Whole Lot of Shaking Going On' and 'Great Balls of Fire' in the studio. In 1954, Johnny Cash recorded at Sun 'Hey Porter', a poem he had written while in the army. He did 'Cry, Cry, Cry' on the flip side and so began his music career. Until then, he was working as an appliance salesman in Memphis. He had approached Philips to record gospel songs but Philips rejected the idea because gospel albums didn't sell enough to cover expenses. Carl Perkins' 'Blue Suede Shoes' was Sun's first million-seller hit.

A year after doing Elvis's demo, Marion Keiskar called him and made an appointment for his first professional studio session. On July 5, 1954, he cut the blues-country-rockabilly 'That's All Right'. Released three days later on the local *Red, Hot, & Blue* radio show, the song was an instant hit. It was played 14 times during the three-hour show by listeners' requests. Elvis left truck driving and began his music career.

In 1955, Sun Studios faced bankruptcy. Phillips realized that he could not do Elvis's burgeoning career justice and he needed money to keep the studio in business. So he made a deal to sell Elvis's contract to RCA. Actually, RCA's Steve Sholes bought the contract from Elvis's manager, Colonel Tom Parker, who had purchased the option from Phillips for $5,000 (£3000), once Parker knew that RCA had guaranteed Elvis a recording deal. Sholes made a $35,000 (£22,500) high-risk, career-ending gamble on an unproven singer.

Sholes is a pivotal figure in Nashville's development as a music industry power point. Sholes recognized that Nashville had the potential to become the hub of country music before any other major label executive. In the same year he picked up Elvis's contract, he signed on Jim Reeves, Hank Snow, the Blackwood Brothers, and Arthur 'Big Boy' Crudup, a personal hero to Elvis. RCA's mainline acts at the time were Perry Como, Eddie Fisher, and Harry Belafonte. Sholes's artists were in the Specialty Singles Division, which was the dumping ground for blues, gospel, comedy, and kids' music.

In 1954, Sholes established RCA's own Nashville recording studio by leasing the Methodist Television Radio & Film Commission studio. He put RCA's mascot logo Nipper on the wall and hired Chet Atkins to run the operation. Sholes continued to work out the New York headquarters. Hiring Atkins proved to be another turning point for the Nashville music industry.

In 1955, the entire country music business was run by four men: RCA's Sholes, who came from Washington DC and whose musical background was classical; Decca's Paul Cohen, a Chicago native, and a former salesman who enjoyed classical music; Capitol's Ken Nelson, another Chicago native and lover of classical music; and Columbia's Don Law, an Englishman from London.

On January 10, 1956, Elvis arrived at RCA's Nashville studio for his first recording session. He cut 'Heartbreak Hotel', which climbed the charts to knock his last recording for Sun, reissued by RCA, 'I Forgot To Remember To Forget' out of the number one slot on the country charts. Sholes pressured RCA's marketing department to push Elvis as a country and pop singer. He wanted Elvis to be RCA's Bill Haley.

(Sholes, a vastly obese man with a rheumatic heart condition, died of a heart attack in Nashville on April 22, 1968.)

Haley started as a country yodeler and leader of a Pennsylvania cowboy band, the Saddleman, that played Western swing. He added drums and a sax, changed the band's name to the Comets, shamelessly borrowed (stole) tunes, licks, and beats from black artists and became the first big-time blue-eyed rocker. His hit 'Shake, Rattle and Roll' was a cover of Big Joe Turner's R&B classic. Haley's mega hit 'Rock Around the Clock' was derived from the blues song 'My Daddy Rocks Me With a Steady Roll'. Haley's version sold 25 million copies, the biggest selling rock single in history.

Bill Haley and the Comets toured with the Platters, the Drifters, and Bo Diddley. These billings sometimes turned his Southern concerts into riots and events of violence. Preachers condemned him, and his music, as a moral threat to teenagers. FBI Director J Edgar Hoover sent agents to dig dirt on Haley.

When he toured England in 1957, one Fleet Street editorial harrumphed, 'Bill Haley, music's Attila the Hun with guitar and drums, plans another path of destruction across Great Britain.' Despite the dire warning, Haley's sellout British concerts were peaceful. John Lennon, then 16, and Paul McCartney attended the Liverpool concert. Six years later, The Beatles would set off fan hysteria not seen since Bill Haley and the Comets.

Haley, crowned as Father of Rock, was the genre's first international superstar. He opened the door for Jerry Lee Lewis, Elvis Presley, The Everly Brothers, The Beatles, and The Rolling Stones. But after 1958, his career took a dive into divorce, tax problems, alcohol, money troubles, and self-exile to Mexico. He died in 1981, at the age of 55, in Harlingen, Texas.

Haley may have been the Father of Rock, but Presley became the King of rock 'n' roll. Like Haley, Elvis was influenced by black music, particularly Wynonie Harris, an R&B raucous shouter from Omaha. Wynonie did the hip thrust and curled his lips into a sexy sneer. Elvis went to Harris's concerts and studied his moves to the extent Elvis was called the 'white Wynonie'. But Elvis also saw the leg-shaking, shoulder-rolling moves in the Pentecostal church in which he was raised. Elvis covered Wynonie's 1948 R&B hit 'Good Rockin' Tonight'. Wynonie returned the favor by turning Hank Penny's country song 'Bloodshot Eyes' into an R&B number.

On December 4, 1956, Elvis was in Memphis on a holiday and visited Sun Studios, where Jerry Lee Lewis and Carl Perkins were hanging around. Sam Phillips called in Johnny Cash and got the local newspaper to take a publicity shot. After the photo, the musicians started to jam. The result, recorded by Phillips, was released as *Elvis Presley: The Million Dollar Quartet* on RCA. Of the 38 cuts, 13 are white gospel, ten are country (four of which are bluegrass), nine are rock 'n' roll, four are blues, and two are covers of pop songs. The music was more Memphis than Nashville.

★

Here's the short and sweet on Nashville, the city...

The city occupies part of what was once a game preserve of the local Native American tribes, which included the Natchez and Cherokee. The tribes agreed that no villages would be built in the shared hunting grounds.

In 1710, French fur traders set up a trading post near the area's salt spring. This low-impact intrusion continued for 70 years until the first permanent white settlement was established on Christmas Day, 1779. A party of 400 men, led by James Robertson, an experienced backwoodsman, crossed the frozen Cumberland River after a 300-mile (480km) trek from North Carolina. Their first act was to build a fort on the bluff overlooking the river to protect themselves from the Indians, whose lands they were expropriating. They it named Fort Nashborough, after Revolutionary War General Francis Nash. This expedition was a business enterprise to establish a commercial center for trading on the river. The region was also a hub for Indian trade routes.

A second group of 85 men, women, children and the elderly arrived in late April 1780. This expedition, led by John Donelson, spent four months on four different river systems to reach its destination. About a third of the original group died on the journey.

In 1781, the Indians tried to drive the whites away. They lost their last chance of reclaiming their land in the Battle of the Bluff, which the whites won by setting their dogs on the Indians.

Tennessee joined the Union in 1796 as an official state. Nashville was established as a city in 1804 and had a population of 2,000 in 1810. The Cumberland River gave access to the Mississippi, Ohio, and Tennessee river systems and Nashville flourished as a commercial center. Nashville has always been, since its inception, a business town. The network of railroads centered in Nashville made the city a pivotal re-supply town during the Civil War. As a Southern city, Nashville started in the breakaway Confederacy camp. Union forces captured the city in 1862 and remained for the nearly four-year duration of the war.

Nashville's justly deserved reputation as a center for higher education started with the founding of Vanderbilt University in 1873. The New York-born industrialist Cornelius Vanderbilt funded the school as a Methodist institution for 'strengthening the ties which should exist between all geographical sections of our common country.' Today, Vanderbilt is renowned for it medical and law schools.

Nashville calls itself 'Music City USA'. This tag did not originate in country music but rather with the Jubilee Singers of Fisk University, another Nashville historical educational institution. Founded in 1879, Fisk University was the first African-American university in the United States. Its choir, the Jubilee Singers, toured Europe in the 1880s to raise money for the fledgling school. They labeled themselves as coming from 'Music City USA' as Nashville was not an international name. The Jubilee Singers went on numerous successful national tours, which they continue to do today.

The full-size replica of the Parthenon in the city's Centennial Park reflects Nashville's pride as a seat of learning. It was originally built in 1897 as a temporary plaster-and-lathe building as part of the state's 100th anniversary celebrations. It was replaced by a 228ft (69m) long, 65' (20m) high cement version, complete with Grecian friezes and copies of statue body parts from the original Parthenon. Inside is a 415' (126m) statue of Athena. This is the worlds' only fully constructed Parthenon, from which Nashville claims the title 'Athens of the South'.

In the 1800s, three presidents came from Nashville: the seventh, Andrew 'Old Hickory' Jackson; the 11th, James 'Young Hickory' Polk; and the 17th, Andrew Jackson, the only president to be impeached.

Music is not Nashville's prominent industry. Christian publishing houses and insurance companies are the foundations of the city's wealth, and both have played determining roles in making Nashville the country music center.

Western Harmony, the first publishing house founded by Allen D Carden and Samuel J Rogers in 1824, produced a book of hymns and instructions for singing. Today, Nashville's gospel music industry is growing faster than the country music segment. The city is the headquarters of operations for Methodists, Presbyterians, and Baptists. There are reportedly more churches in Nashville than bars, and Nashville is not a prudish city about drinking, or drinking in strip clubs. Another tag for Nashville is the 'buckle of the Bible Belt' because it is a center of evangelical Christianity and Southern spirituality.

But it was the insurance companies, specifically National Life and Accident Insurance Company, that put Nashville on the country music map. In October of 1925, the company, whose slogan was 'We Shield Millions', set up a 1,000W transmitter on Seventh Avenue and Union Street in the National Life Building in downtown Nashville. The station, with the call signals of WSM, was a cost-effective means of publicizing the low-cost insurance peddled by National Life agents, primarily in rural areas. In 1926, the Life and Casualty Insurance Company started WLAC for the same reason. The stations, knowing their audience, broadcasted hillbilly music.

However, the Nashville stations were not the first to broadcast country music. WSB in Atlanta broadcast Fiddlin' Jack Carson on September 9, 1922. WBAP out of Austin broadcast the first barn dance in 1923, 90 minutes of square dance directed by old-time fiddler and Confederate veteran Captain MJ Bonner. Their signal, in times of non-regulation, could be picked up in New York and in Haiti, reaching thousands of listeners. Chicago's powerful WGN also broadcast a country music show.

The new program director at WSM, George D Hay, picked up the barn dance format and the home variety shows popping up on the newly formed commercial radio. Hay, a former broadcaster for WGN in Chicago and a former newspaperman for the Memphis *Commercial Appeal*, jumped on the hillbilly bandwagon. On November 8, on the 8pm show, he introduced the 80-year-old mountain fiddler Uncle Jimmy Thompson.

WSM's *Barn Dance* was so popular it expanded to three hours. One of the show's early headliners, and then the show's only black musician, was DeFord Bailey, 'the Harmonica Wizard'. In 1927, WSM's *Barn Dance* followed NBC's *Musical Appreciation Hour* with Dr Walter Damrosch, a highbrow classical music show that featured grand opera. On one show, after Bailey played 'Pan American Blues', inspired by central South's most famous train that ran near his home, Hays reportedly announced, 'For the past hour, we have been listening to music taken largely from the grand opera, but from now on we will present the Grand Ole Opry.' Another version of the quote is, 'You've been up in the cloud with grand opera, now get down to earth with us in a performance of Grand Ole Opry.'

From then on the show was known as the Grand Ole Opry, the longest continuously running radio show in the United States. The show has been of fundamental importance in spreading the popularity of country music. Hay copyrighted the name Grand Ole Opry, which is now owned by the Gaylord Entertainment Co, founded by Edward Gaylord. The corporation also owns Opryland, the 406-acre (164ha) entertainment/ hotel/shopping mall where the Grand Ole Opry relocated in 1974. Gaylord also has interests in Country Music Television, in Nashville's professional ice hockey team, the Predators, and the arena where they play.

DeFord Bailey, who learned the harmonica while bed-ridden with polio at the age of three, was considered one of the most influential harmonica players of the first half of the 20th century. He called his music 'black hillbilly music'. Dr Charles Wolfe, Grand Ole Opry historian and folk music expert, calls Bailey's music 'eclectic'.

'It was Southern roots music, a mixture of blues, of country, of old-time fiddle music, of vaudeville music and old-time pop music from the '20s,' Dr Wolfe told Ken Beck for an article in *The Tennessean* reporting a 30-minute documentary on Bailey's life, *A Legend Lost: DeFord Bailey*. The documentary raised the issue that Bailey has never been inducted into the Grand Ole Opry's Hall of Fame, although he has been a first-round nominee from 1999–2001. His exclusion has caused controversy. According to Dan Rogers, marketing director for the Grand Ole Opry, this might be due to the fact that Bailey didn't make many recordings – record sales are taken into consideration for entry into the Hall of Fame.

'If you sell one million records, you are not automatically in the running to be an Opry member,' Rogers cautioned. 'We want someone who will have a lasting career, so will have an impact on country music and be someone folks will want to come and see 20 years from now as much as this weekend.'

Who becomes a member of the Grand Ole Opry is a decision of Opry management. 'It boils down to two or three persons making the decision based on the artist appealing to the Opry crowd,' Rogers said. 'And a proven track record in country or bluegrass music. And a proven interest in becoming a member, committing to performing on the show and being an active part of the Opry family.'

Bailey was fired from the Grand Ole Opry in 1941. Frye Gaillard, in *Watermelon Wine: The Spirit of Country Music*, wrote that Bailey was 'dropped from the cast on the dubious grounds that he hadn't written enough new songs (a fact that hadn't disturbed the Opry's executives until after they bought stock in a new song-licensing company called BMI).'

In other words, producing revenue for the Grand Ole Opry was more important than producing and preserving country music, especially one as unique as Bailey's black hillbilly music. Rogers indicated that the same principle applies today in that members are selected, in part, for their ability to pull an audience to the Grand Ole Opry.

Dr Wolfe has written that Bailey was fired for complex reasons, including a feud between BMA and ASCAP, changing musical tastes and the increasing professionalism of the Opry.

After he left the Opry, Bailey, who also played the guitar, fiddle, and banjo, shined shoes for a living. In 1974, he was invited to make an appearance at the grand opening of the new Grand Ole Opry in Opryland. He appeared four times on the Grand Ole Opry in the 1970s and early '80s. In the documentary on his life, Bailey, who died in 1982, says, 'They got the goods out of me and turned me loose.'

Ed Benson, executive director of the Country Music Association, predicts that it is just a matter of time before Bailey will be in the Hall of Fame.

George Hay, who became the Grand Ole Opry's manager and chief announcer, was a major influence on the type of music, and the image of the music, broadcasted on the Grand Ole Opry – and his decisions were based in commerce.

Throughout the early 1930s, country music gained popular commercial appeal by playing up the hillbilly characteristics. Hay reinforced the stereotypes by giving names, such as The Skillet Lickers, to musicians who literally wandered in from the hills. He gave himself the appellation of the 'Solemn Old Judge' to stay in character, although he was neither old nor a judge.

Hays understood the concept of market branding. If country music based its authenticity on nature, of being the natural music of the natural country, then it had better look the part. Country music needed a dress code in keeping with its own identity of being rooted in the natural world. Suits and ties and vests had to go. Hay coaxed and cajoled musicians to appear on stage in denim overalls, no shoes, and play the hillbilly hick.

Even so, the most popular act in Grand Ole Opry in 1938 was The Vagabonds, a trio of college-educated harmony singers from Chicago. They appeared on stage in matching, casual, collegiate outfits and sung mostly well-known sentimental ballads, 'Red River Valley', and heart songs like 'When It's Lamp Lightin' Time in the Valley'.

That same year Roy Acuff and his Smokey Mountain Boys came to Nashville from Knoxville in eastern Tennessee. His recording of 'The Great Speckled Bird' and 'Steel Guitar Blues' put him in the top five in country sales for 1937. His 'Wabash Cannonball' was a number one country song and became his signature song when he joined the Grand Ole Opry. Acuff, called 'King of the Hillbillies', 'Backwoods Sinatra', and the 'Caruso of Mountain Music', dressed his band in casual hick mountain fashion. They won the lead spot on the Grand Ole Opry in 1939.

Acuff went on to become a fulcrum in why Nashville is the business center of country music. He was the artist/performer who laid the basis for the first generation of music executives. He regarded country performing as a business and a full-time career, not just an avocation to fill in between day jobs. Acuff saw the economic value of music publishing. He sponsored 15 minutes on WSM to sell his songbook. In the first week, he had 10,000 orders, at 25 cents (16p) each, and sold 100,000 copies in the first two months. But he eventually felt abused by the New York and Chicago-based music publishers. In 1942, he formed a partnership with Fred Rose, a skillful Tin Pan Alley composer of country and western songs, to create the song-publishing firm of Acuff-Rose Music, a major player in Nashville today.

In the early 1940s, Julian and Jean Aberbach (German Jewish refugees) established Hill Music and Range Music. These publishers of hillbilly music merged into Hill & Range. RCA's Steve Sholes, who brought Elvis to Nashville, worked closed with the Aberbachs. When an artist on his roster recorded a public domain song, Sholes always gave the publishing rights to Hill & Range, even though RCA had its own publishing company. Acuff-Rose and Hill & Range were cornerstones vital to the development of Nashville as the country music capital.

The Grand Ole Opry, in 1931, broadcasted on 50,000 clear-channel signals that could be heard from the Gulf of Mexico to the Canadian border, from the Rocky Mountains to the Atlantic Ocean. The show gained 'national feed' status from NBC Radio Network in 1939 and supplied many live music shows broadcasted nationally. The importance of the Grand Ole Opry in shaping the cultural program of millions of Americans cannot be overstated.

In 1934 another important piece to securing Nashville's position in country music fell into place. WSM established its Artists Service Bureau to book Opry performers for appearances outside of Nashville. The performers would go on the road during the week but had to be back for the weekend Opry shows.

Experienced booking agents soon set up shop, which gave Nashville an edge in attracting performers from other competing cities. The skilled musicians became the core of backup musicians, who became recording session players. A mass of highly skilled musicians gathered in Nashville, another asset the competing cities did not possess.

But a major component was missing from the mix of Nashville becoming the predominant country music recording capital – a good recording studio. That was rectified in 1946 when three WSM engineers – Aaron Shelton, Carl Jenkins, and George Reynolds – established the Castle Recording Company in downtown Nashville. The Castle, which took its name from one of WSM's self-devised slogans, 'Castle of the Air', was the beginning of organized, centrally located recording in Nashville. The business was based around many of WSM's stars. The Castle's success spawned other studios. Now it made good economic sense for the New York, Los Angeles, and Chicago labels to record the hillbilly musicians in Nashville, rather than bringing the musicians to the companies' home studios.

Decca's Paul Cohen recorded Ernest Tubb, Kitty Wells, and Red Foley. Williams' 'Your Cheatin' Heart' was recorded at the WSM studio. Capital and RCA soon opened a Nashville branch office.

In the 1940s, two music institutions added economic weight to Nashville's position – American Society of Composers, Authors, and Publishers (ASCAP), and Broadcast Music Incorporated (BMI). ASCAP was, and is, the performing rights organization that collects royalties for music publishers and songwriters for use of their music. In its early years, ASCAP was very exclusionary, ignoring and snubbing country music, blues, and most jazz composers. Those musicians had no way of receiving compensation for the use of their songs in public broadcast. BMI, incorporated to serve those excluded by ASCAP, opened the doors of American music to all composers. Many years later ASCAP adopted an 'open door' policy and most of the practises of BMI.

All the elements necessary for a music industry to flourish were in place; singing stars with a large national following, a weekly radio show to broadcast shows over a substantial part of the United States, several experienced booking agencies to schedule appearances, a recording studio, backup musicians, and publishing companies to sell the sheet music and arrangements. Nashville became the nation's fourth music center, behind New York, Los Angeles, and Chicago.

Another important event happened to country music in 1946 – Hank Williams. He was to country music what Coltrane was to jazz. It's hard to appreciate now how revolutionary he was at the time. Singers wanted to sound and write like Hank Williams, so we think of him as traditional country as it always was. But he stood apart from the other country crooners of his day. He wrote simple, piercing songs and had a distinct voice. Williams became a huge country and popular star. Perhaps his most important contribution to country music was the acceptance of his songs by pop artists and their appearance in the popular charts. In the 1950s, his songs were recorded by Tony Bennett ('Cold, Cold Heart'), Joni James ('Your Cheatin' Heart'), and Jo Stafford ('Jambalaya').

Williams died in the back seat of his car on New Year's Eve 1952 while being driven overnight to a gig.

Nashville's first hit record, in 1947, was not country but the pop song 'Near You' by Kermit Goell and Francis Craig, recorded by Craig's orchestra.

In the 1950s, Chet Atkins and Owen Bradley put their imprimaturs on Nashville music, and the way of producing that music, that still resonates today. Atkins and Bradley were musicians who became producers. Atkins (who came to Nashville in 1946 as a guitarist sideman with singer Red Foley) and Bradley were the first to directly manage Nashville major label divisions. Atkins was the head of RCA's A&R division and Bradley was the chief of operations at Decca.

As musicians, they had sensibilities in country and pop. As record executives, they were aware of country music's commercial potential. They understood how music could be an art form as an economic proposition. Their jobs depended on the creation of a system that kept control of the country record-making process in Nashville. They became the first producer/label division heads, which was unique to the Nashville music business. As local division executives, they were more knowledgeable, and had a greater comprehension of the music they produced, than their bosses in New York or Los Angeles.

Atkins and Bradley transformed the music producer from the person who mated song material with artists to someone who, as a musician, became more involved in shaping the sound and arrangements of recording. They were the prototype of the activist producer who began to control the artist.

The producer's role is now akin to a film director. He/she oversees the entire creative process of a record, including the choice of song material, the choice of recording, mixing and mastering, studio, and the studio musicians. The Beatles and their producer George Martin set the tone for 25 years in pop production, where the artist was the overall creative force channeled by the producer. In country music, the producer has retained far more authority over the record-making process than in pop or rock.

The ascendancy of the producer gave rise to the Nashville Sound, a combination of recording techniques and aesthetic sensibilities decided on by the producer. The Nashville Sound in the 1960s was country without twang, a new sweet sound of country records. It is also called 'Chet's Compromise'. He replaced fiddles with violins, added drums, fancy piano runs and melodious, creamy background vocals as heard in the Jim Reeves and Don Williams recording.

The Nashville Sound smoothed the rough edges off country music and gave it more polish.

The Nashville Sound was a successful attempt to put more pop into country. Don Gibson's 1958 sessions that produced 'Oh Lonesome Me' was, according to Atkins, the beginning of his efforts to consciously break the country mold. The song became Gibson's first country hit and a major pop hit.

Others working with Atkins to develop this sound were Owen Bradley, Don Law, Anita Kerr, the bassist Bob Moore, guitarists Hank 'Sugarfoot' Garland and Grady Martin, pianist Floyd Cramer, drummer Buddy Harmon, and saxophonist Boots Randolf.

Atkins explained that the Nashville Sound was created from necessity rather than from any desire to change or experiment for the sake of musical creativity. 'I wasn't trying to move country music uptown or anything like that. I was just trying to keep my job. I knew I had to make records that would sell.'

Nicholas Dawidoff in his *In The Country of Country, People and Places in American Music* (Pantheon Books, New York, 1997) quotes Atkins: 'Somebody interviewing me once asked me, "What's the Nashville Sound?" I was stumbling around for an answer and he got out some coins and shook them and he was right. People were in it to make a living. The Nashville Sound was just a sales tag. If there is a Nashville Sound, it's the Southern accent. You speak with it, maybe you play with it, too. I don't know if there is such a thing as Nashville Sound. We took the twang out of it, Owen Bradley and I. What we did was, we tried to make hit records. We wanted to keep our jobs. The way you make hit records is to incorporate a new rhythm feel or something lyrically different. In my case, it went more uptown. I'd take out the steel guitar and fiddle, which branded a song as strictly country. I tried to make songs for both markets.'

Atkin's influence carried on to Ray Charles's 1962 *Modern Sounds in Country & Western Music*, on which his biggest hit was 'I Can't Stop Loving You', a version of Don Gibson's 1958 country hit. The song won Charles a number one on the pop charts and his sixth Grammy. The following year, his Vol II of country won him a Grammy in R&B category for 'Busted' by Nashville songwriter Harlan Howard. Eddy Arnold, the Browns, Patsy Cline, Sonny James, and Jim Reeves scored country and pop hits with the Nashville Sound.

Atkins signed Waylon Jennings to RCA but it was the Nashville Sound, and the way of producing that music, that Waylon Jennings, Willie Nelson, Kris Kristofferson, Kinky Friedman and other Outlaws rebelled against. Waylon said, 'Awash in strings, crooning and mooning and juneing, the Nashville Sound may have been Nashville's way of broadening its pop horizons, but it was making for non-controversial, watered-down, dull music that soothed rather than stirred the emotions.'

There is one other important element in Nashville's success as a country music center: geography.

Nashville sits on the central plateau mid-way between Appalachian eastern Tennessee and blues/rockabilly western Tennessee. The I-40, the east-west superhighway that crosses the southern US, connects Nashville with Wilmington, North Carolina, Knoxville, Memphis, Little Rock, Arkansas, Oklahoma City, Albuquerque, New Mexico, California's San Fernando Valley, and Los Angeles. Alan Jackson and Travis Tritt (northern Georgia); Wynonna Judd (Kentucky); Garth Brooks, Wade Hayes, Reba McEntire, Vince Gill (Oklahoma); and Dwight Yoakam (California) grew up within 100 miles (160km) of the I-40.

A second interstate, the I-24, links Nashville to St Louis and Chicago to the north and to Chattanooga to the south. Nashville is connected to Birmingham by a third interstate, the I-65. Thirty states are within 600 miles (960km) of Nashville, the territory a bus can cover overnight. St Louis, Kansas City, Chicago, New Orleans, Atlanta, with their clubs and shows, are easily accessible via the highway network.

Musicians find Nashville to be a convenient home base.

19 Hope Or Heartbreak

Jill King had her showcase for record executives the other night. When I went to Tootsie's to ask her about it, she was still singing her set. Our Willie, Amy, and Hank sat at the usual corner table. I walked back, curious if Our Willie was still living on hope, or Amy was still impaled on heartbreak, or Hank was deeper in love with the image of his hat.

'How's it going?'

'Nothing like a rain storm after a hurricane to make you think things are getting better,' Amy answered.

'Is that like getting poison ivy after breaking a leg to make you think things are getting better?'

'Improving, improving,' Our Willie answered. 'Things are back on track.'

Improving from what? But perhaps certain snakes should be left peacefully underground.

'How's the song going?'

'That's what's improving,' Our Willie replied. 'Listen to this:'

I woke up again
A rented man sleepin' in my own bed
On a short-term lease in the Loveless Motel.
My baby pays for me on the installment plan,
One month at a time,
I'm a rented man waiting for the buyout plan.

He stopped and didn't look any of us in the eye.

'That's how it is, you know,' Our Willie said. 'When two people are suspended with each other, waiting it out. You're just making another payment but not sure what you're buying.'

Amy shifted in her chair and cleared her throat. 'Here's another way to saying it.'

She sang in waltz time:

I'm a rented man in the Loveless Motel.
She has the room number but I have the key.
She pays with love and kisses.
My baby thinks I made a down payment
But it's only a short-term lease.

'That's sounds like the man is being the jerk,' Our Willie protested. 'Like he's keeping one foot out the door and that's not how it is. He wants to be in the relationship but the woman keeps him guessing.'

'But the woman is always the one deceived,' Amy replied, a bit heatedly. 'She is left, hung out, living on hope and false promises. She wants a home, security, but the man is only going day-to-day.'

'Willie wants a song from the man's point of view,' Our Willie said.

'He wants a good song, that's all,' Amy shot back. 'A true song and the truth is the woman always gets the shaft.'

'Not always,' Our Willie answered, talking to the tabletop.

He might as well have burst a water balloon of sadness over the table. The silence, growing heavy with embarrassment, was broken when Hank asked, 'How many country singers does it take to change a light bulb?'

Amy and Our Willie didn't say anything, perhaps suspecting that they were the butt of the joke.

'How many?' I asked.

'Two. One to unscrew the bulb and the other to sing about how much he misses the old bulb.'

Amy smiled. 'Good ol' Hank. You know when to come through. You going to cut the demo for us?'

'You've got to ask.'

'I'm askin'. Isn't that right, Our Willie?'

'Yeah. I have a friend with a little home studio. We can do it there.'

'I'll think about it,' Hank replied.

'You come to Nashville to sing or to talk about singin'?' challenged Amy.

'You get your song written first,' Hank replied. 'You've got a long way to go.'

Jill finished her set and I excused myself.

Jill was buoyant. 'It went very well, thank you for asking, seein' that Randy was murdered. That kept the turnout down a bit, I think. A lot of people went to the memorial.'

Randy Hardison, a session drummer for 20 years and songwriter who had written for Garth Brooks, Lee Ann Womack, and Mark Chesnutt among others and scored with hits, had been killed a week ago. He was working with a young singer to get her started in the music business. It was, according to those who knew, strictly a professional relationship. Her jealous ex-boyfriend resented that they spent so much time together writing songs and cutting tape, so the hearsay said. Jealousy, especially male-ego fueled jealousy, is the most potent of bitter poisons. The ex-boyfriend allegedly sent two thugs to rough up Randy. They hit him over the head too roughly and he died of the injuries. Over 750 people from the Nashville music industry attended his memorial service held in the chapel on the Vanderbilt campus.

Considering that, Jill said, her showcase went perfect. The room was at capacity with 200 people, including five major labels, four independent labels, two talent agents, and several songwriters and influential people in the music community.

'We found two ol' huge cowboy boot planters, maybe 3' [1m] high, with silver spurs that really turned,' she said, still excited by the evening. 'We also got two huge torches, like Olympic torches with the flames coming out, only they were electric so the light looks like flame coming out, and they had candles all around the rim. We had the stage decorated with just the boots and the torches. Simple, just enough touch, I thought. There were also candles on all the tables.'

Jill, the soundman and the band had been on site since mid-afternoon doing the sound check. 'We had great sound. All the band had separate monitor mixes.' No detail was too small for her to recall with pleasure. 'We also had a great room sound guy who was in charge of just the room, so the music sounded good for everyone. Then we had a lighting guy.'

The band, T Graham Brown, was a coup for Jill. They've had the hits 'Hell and High Water', 'I Tell It Like It Used To Be', and 'Darlene'. T Graham liked her sound enough to offer his band's services.

'To start, the stage was completely dark.' Listening to Jill was like hearing a bride relive her wedding. 'A spotlight hit me standing alone center stage with only my guitar. I sang "I Can Not Love You Anymore", just vocals and guitar. The room quieted right down. It was really powerful. Very effective. I was singing good that night. My nerves were not what I had expected them to be. I felt great. I was excited. I had that adrenaline rush goin' but no nerves. No one left through the whole showcase. That blew me away. I was expecting some to leave, the busy industry types, from what you hear of industry showcases. I held the room. I felt incredible about that.'

Her dad and mom sat in the middle of the crowd with friends from Arab. He whooped and hollered and she grinned with pride. After the songs, Jill did a mingle-and-meet. 'I was completely swarmed by friends and industry people,' she said. 'The band from Tootsie's came and plugged in, so I got back up on stage for another hour of tunes. It was great fun.'

But was it all show and no reality results? 'Joe Galante's office at RCA called and asked that I submit a package of my work and recording to them. The booking agencies that approached me seemed really excited about booking me in places across the country. T Graham Brown invited me to open for him at his Fan Fair show. Then I did a solo with his band at a club gig. I did Bonnie Raitt bluesy meets country. T Graham Brown offered to help any way he could, so things are good.'

I glanced to the back of the room where Amy and Our Willie were wrangling and working with each other. 'Well, that's good, Jill. But where there's hope, there is heartbreak.'

'I've known heartbreak,' she replied. 'I've had my heart broken and I've broken hearts. I've had my heart broken because I wanted somebody to be in a place where they really weren't. I've had a lot of issues with unfaithfulness. I try to put heartbreak, going both ways, in my voice. When I've been going through those times of heartbreak, whether because my family wasn't approving or because some love relationship wasn't going the way I wanted, those times when I really needed to get my emotions out, then I listen to songs where I can tell the person has been through the same thing. I try to do that for people. That's why performing for me is so exhausting. If you really open up and make yourself vulnerable to those emotions, which you really should do to be an effective singer, it can be like a tidal wave in a note that washes over you. There have been times on stage when I've felt like breaking down. When I sing songs, it's almost like a landscape laid out before me. It's a mental landscape and a musical landscape. It's almost like having my life flash before my eyes. I see my life experiences playing out as I am singing and I experience how it feels. It can mess me up some days.'

I decided not to introduce her to Amy and Our Willie. A rainstorm, even after a hurricane, may not be her idea of an uplifting experience. 'Gotta run. Catch you soon for an update.'

Emma Fox had invited me to hear her at The Basement's monthly writers' night. 'I've got good news,' she said. 'I'll tell you there.'

The Basement is another small club almost deliberately hidden away. It is the basement of an office building; the entrance around the back reached by finding the unmarked dirt alley that is, for the first 30' (9m), a residential driveway.

Billy Block, who does the Western Beat Show from the Exit/In, hosts The Basement's monthly writers' night on the last Friday of the month. Writers' nights can be the best deal in town. You hear new material from seasoned singer/songwriters and from absolute newcomers whose hope and humbleness – and optimism – gives an edge and depth to their talent. In a way, they are true country, folks singing their lives, not aiming for a hit that night but hoping that their life in song will be a hit.

The Bluebird Café's Monday's open mic is the best known of the writer's nights. The small club, which has been going for 40 years, is in a strip mall. The ceiling is festooned with theater spotlights, mostly aimed at nothing in particular. Oversized black-and-white photos of well-known singers hang on the walls. Garth Brooks was given his break at the Bluebird. On Monday, each singer/songwriter can do one song only. If the owner hears promise in the performer, that person is invited back for a four-song set the following Sunday show. That show, hosted by an established songwriter, is more of a showcase, with a good chance of A&R people in the audience.

The Basement's writers' night was potluck, with every performer required to bring a dish and the audience invited to eat. The food was much like the performances, some quite good and some store bought. The atmosphere was homey and friendly, in part because the club seats 30 maximum and Billy Block set a front porch we're-all-family mood. George, who arrived in Nashville ten days earlier from Ohio, sang a humorous double-entendre song about a beer holder. James from Hamilton, Ohio, a skinny kid fresh off the bus, did a dead-on Willie Nelson right down to the red high-top tennis shoes. He wasn't an impersonator but a young reflection doing original lyrics. He got warm applause for his laudable songs.

Emma Fox was the night's headliner. She loses her English accent in song but she doesn't put on a Southern twang, except in jest. She has a strong voice with natural country inflections that makes her music believable. She loves rubbing against the audience with her voice. A bit of a torch singer heats up her country as she dips her body invitingly, seductive without vamping. She is very captivating, very come-into-my-arms open. This is what Don Cook saw in her, the gesture of love sung in a clear voice.

The surprise of the night was Raul Malo, formerly of the Mavericks, who performed his hit 'Every Little Thing About You'. Colin Linden, the eight-time Juno Awards winner, the Canadian equivalent of a Grammy, closed the set. He played on the *O Brother, Where Art Thou?* soundtrack and toured with the Down From the Mountain show. None of the acts at The Basement had been advertised. The performers were there for the music and whoever showed up to listen. That's a reason I found writer's nights some of the most rewarding shows in Nashville.

Afterwards, Emma sat at my table. 'How did you like the show?' I told her about my impression of her contact with the audience. She thought for a moment. 'You don't think it will put the women off, do you? Trying to show them up? Like I'm coming on to their man?'

I reassured her that the women took no offense and enjoyed her style.

'My sensual stage presence, my way with the audience, I like that. I'm open and engaging and tactile. I'm not scared to let people in. Maybe that comes off as seductive. I'm an old fashion romantic. I love love. I love wanting love as much as getting it. In fact, I think I love the wanting more than the getting.'

I couldn't think of a snappy come on, so asked, 'Well, what's the news?'

'Wednesday was my birthday. I'm 24.'

'Congratulations.'

'And I got a birthday present.' Her face was bright as a full moon and her smile big as a Cheshire grin. 'I got a publishing deal.' She fairly squealed with joy, as much as Emma can squeal. It was more a boisterous exclamation.

'God, I really wanted a publishing deal,' she said in a moan of mock ecstasy. 'I want to give my music full attention and the best effort possible. Doing that while working three jobs has been very hard. I get an advance but it's not like, wow, now I've got some money. I can't go out and buy a new car or anything. It's not a lot of money but it's enough. I'm giving up one job straight away. I'll keep the other two part-time. It's almost like a psychological comfort thing, like TS Eliot wearing his banker suit even when he was a poet. He didn't want to lose that feeling of turning up on the job every day. I don't want to forget that. I kinda like getting my hands dirty. I always want to stay real.'

Emma confided that she feels a bit frightened. Sony Tree is paying her to write songs and they expect results. 'Shit, this is real. People have put their money where their mouth is. There's a voice in me that says, "To hell with it, relax. You've been given this opportunity." At the very least, if they don't renew my option, I've got one year. It's a luxury. I've got a year to totally immerse myself in creativity.'

'Why do you want to write songs?'

'I want to touch people, inspire people. It's a passion to connect with people. Sometimes it's purely therapeutic for me, an exorcism of a situation or a feeling. Madonna once said that artists are emotionally crippled.

It's like a co-dependency kind of thing. The creative type is kind of solitary and hermit-like, but we need people so much, too. It's really contradictory. We need acceptance, to be liked. We want to be loved. We want people to like what we do.'

I reeled out my line about hope and heartbreak.

'I've had my heart broken. I give a lot, you see. I'm talking about this guy I like and he's scared to commit to any one person. He has a lot of girls around him and he's a bit of a bugger, you know. Yes, I've been really hurt in my life and sobbed and had heartbreak because I left myself open to love. I'm like my grandmother. She had four husbands and is single now at 85. She still believes in romance. She asked me if I ever regret giving up Claus, the love of my life in England. "What do you mean?" I said.

'"To music," she said, "giving him up for music."

'"I didn't give him up for music. I gave him up because it wasn't right. We gave each other up," I said. Sometimes I put barriers up with the wrong people, and take the barriers down to let the Casanovas in. I let this one guy in. I turned the angel away and let in the Scarlet Pimpernel. The Pimpernel is more exciting. I took the chance. I took the risk. That I will never change about myself. You have to remain open to stuff. I won't change any of that heartbreak. I loved it before it turned bad. Better to have loved and lost than never have loved at all. That's the way I see it.'

She paused, as if trying a new line for a song.

'It's been written,' I said.

'That's the only song there is, the love song,' Emma said.

She paused again in thought. 'A lot of men in Nashville are so self obsessed. You have to be fairly obsessed to do the music. There is so much music, so much talent here that people in the industry get jaded. That's the word, jaded. I know a songwriter who thinks that if he ever gets happy and content, he won't be able to write anymore. The musicians, they're on the road all the time. They've got girls admiring them. It's like a power trip. They seek the excitement as well. I do worry about a certain vicious aspect of the business. Of getting dropped. Maybe that's why performers feel lonely. You don't let people get too close to you. If there's just you, you can't be dropped.' Another pause. 'Sometimes it's a curse to be attractive. You get dismissed. People don't think you can be attractive and intelligent and powerful and creative. There is a lot more to me than an attractive package. Most of the time I don't feel attractive anyway.'

Her face brightened and she asked, 'Do you who I've been writing songs with? Jim Lauderdale.'

Jim Lauderdale is one of Nashville's esteemed songwriters. He records on the small independent label Dualtone but his name is gold. In May 2002, he released two albums simultaneously, *Lost In The Lonesome Pines*, with Ralph Stanley & The Clinch Mountain Boys and *The Hummingbirds*, an album of his original work.

'I like the fact that he is very eclectic,' Emma continued. 'He can write a straight-on country song, then he can go as experimental as you want. He's both commercial and independent creative. He has done commercial songs, but he never backs off a subject because Music Row or radio wouldn't like it. He's a great writer in the craft, a great melody guy, great guitar player. But he's a bit quirky with all the different influences. He'll give it that little slant, that little quirkiness that's cool as shit. I can relate to that. I have a certain quirkiness myself.

'You know why he's more successful in a business sense, a sales sense, a commercial sense than some of the other avant garde people? He has a good measure of quirky and commercial. That overflows into his music. That's why he gets the George Strait hits and still does cool creative stuff.

'There are lots of cars to drive down Music Row, so why should you drive a car everyone else is driving? Too many people have their passions beaten out of them, put away in boxes. Oh, that's not real. You can't do that. You have to settle down. You have to have kids. You have to have a real job. I want to drive an luminous pink three-wheeler down Music Row.'

Matt King introduced me to Bean Central, another Monday night writers' place to hear interesting quality music. The coffee shop is an airy, sunny cyber café by day and a come-be-surprised club by night. Matt King describes his music as 'slingblade'.

He spent most of the past two years as a hermit in his basement, where he built a home studio computer from scratch. ('I had no idea how to do it and even less money.') When we met, he looked pasty but seemed sane enough. He had recorded a couple of albums on a major label, the now-defunct Atlanta Nashville, the first in 1997. His duet with Patty Loveless is still talked about with admiration by musicians. *People* magazine gave him good reviews. The critics loved him. Then one day the head of the label called Matt into his office.

'He told me, "Son, you're fucked. When critics hate my artists, they all go platinum. But once the critics love my artists, we can't sell the records,"' Matt said in his nasal North Carolina accent. 'I did one more album where we tried to strike a commercial vein, really old-time country in a pop '80s market. I had been in a '80s pop band as a lead guitar player. I didn't want to go back there. The album failed miserably. The duet with Patty sunk because of no promotion. Everybody at the label hated each other. They were all just trying to hold their seats as the label was sinking. I had horrible management, and they'd probably say the same about me. I lost my deal.'

His self-imposed exile from the music business was an effort to strip himself to his artistic bare bones and start again.

'I went into exile to decide how I wanted to approach music. I didn't care what it cost me. It had already cost my health, a publishing deal, a record deal, marriage, sanity, sobriety. What I had worked for for 15 years went away in about three months. I had to lose everything. I had to have it kicked out from under me.

'I do believe, and will always believe, that a committed artist will continue to quietly work away like an alchemist in his lab, trying to find that philosopher's stone. Good music will emerge. Something bigger than us dictates that. It's defining who you are, having something to say, and then asking, "What price will it cost me and how far am I willing to take this?"

'Whatever it costs me, fine. This is what I do and this is who I am. I've had to face that in my own life. How much more will it cost me? At least I feel good at the end of the day about what I've done. I make a lot of mistakes. So what if it cost me a home or a car? I've been a broke musician all my life who had a day or two making a living at it. Right now I'm putting my own thing together. That's what we all say when we're unemployed.'

He had a steady gig at the Grand Ole Opry for a few months. Lately, he's been doing club gigs to test his new material. The response has been strong. Three labels have been doing the sniff and retreat, sniff and retreat. Matt's glad they're interested but he's not planning any life changes.

'One day the labels are lovin' you so much and when they love you, they love you so much,' Matt said. 'Boy, they just make you feel great. And then when it's over, it's like the morning after. They don't remember your name.'

Matt grew up in Hendersonville, North Carolina, a nice bedroom retirement community. 'It was really hard growing up there, especially as the hillbilly hippie, 'cos I was into hard rock,' Matt said.

His dad was a rock mason, an auctioneer, and a hunter and trapper for profit and trade. He'd dry, cure, and stretch out the animal hides in the family home's basement. Matt grew up with boys who skipped school to go up into the mountains and dig up ginseng (gin-SANG in Matt's accent) and sell it. There is a lucrative North American and Asian market for American ginseng. A flourishing cottage industry of collecting the roots exists in the Appalachians and in Missouri.

Great-grandfather Wright was a coal miner and part of the Devil Ance Hatfield clan. He was so mean that he beat his own son, Matt's grandfather, with a bullwhip. One night, when men took to shooting at each other in the house, Matt's grandfather decided it was time to change his situation.

'Grandfather was hiding in between the mattresses,' Matt said in recounting his family history, which includes bootleggers, preachers, and prostitutes. 'When the shooting was over, he crawled out, grabbed a pair of women's shoes out of the trashcan, knocked the heels off, laced them on, went to work and never came back. He was seven when that happened. My grandfather was a wonderful man. He was plasterer who couldn't read or write; yet he could use a slide rule. He helped plaster the Citadel, the military academy. His sisters had roadhouses and ran liquor stills. They were survivors. They loved the Lord a whole lot and they loved their liquor a whole lot. When hillbillies get wound up on corn liquor, they start talking about Jesus to forget how bad they've been. My song "Ezekiel's Wheel" is about a little boy who beat his father. I'm just drawing from an honest place there.'

Matt's dad, who left the family when Matt was 13, was a big fan of the old gospel, old country, and old traditional bluegrass. Matt grew up going to bluegrass festivals but as a teenager decided that playing hard rock would get him laid a lot easier than picking bluegrass. 'Of course, it didn't work for me. I was the skinniest, nerdiest, shortest guy,' he admitted somewhat ruefully.

His dad played bluegrass at a weekly jam over at a friend's house. One jam included Ralph Stanley, Ricky Scaggs, and the late Keith Whitley. 'People would snicker and made fun of Ralph Stanley,' Matt said. 'Now I hear his name in the most posh bars in town. I think it's horrible. I want to throw up on those people's shoes. I hold the mountain music and the heritage very dear to me because it was a lifestyle. I embrace it more as I get older. So I find myself going back to that well. I started researching where my family came from and how they lived and started writing about that. I try not to be ironic, not to twist it, not to sound like a songwriter but just tell some stories. I know what that lifestyle is like. I speak that language. It's very easy and I'm fluent. So after I tried all the other stuff, stuff I thought I was supposed to do in writing, I went back to that well.'

'What is slingblade music?'

'When I think of slingblade, it's a biting slice of reality about the type of culture I came from. It's that little thin membrane that runs between good and evil that's always being broken. It's the mountain people, a sect of America that's almost forgotten. Outsiders think of the mountain people as a Hatfield McCoy feud and a bunch of inbreds and stereotypes. That's absurd.

'There are a number of musicians who are really speaking for an area of the Southern culture that is not the Old South. One author who will make you wish you were a Southerner is Rick Bragg. When Ricky said that he got accepted to do some time at Harvard and he felt like a hog in a cocktail dress, that was sling blade.'

The Others are slingblade artists, according to Matt. 'There is a group of people in country who are speaking that language of honesty in a very real sense, like Hank the Third,' he said. 'They're putting out, "This is how I feel. I cut, I bleed, I heal, I heal crooked, I heal bowlegged, let me tell you about it. This is how I see love; it's great, it's wonderful, it's blissful, it's beautiful, it's opaque." But that music is not a benign innocuous little ditty that you can get onto the radio for two minutes.

'The traditional country symbols are still pertinent and are being given today's meaning by Robbie Fulks and countless others. Are they being acknowledged by the moneymakers? Hell no. Absolutely not. There's a façade and the façade is, "We're going to appear to be really sweet good guys on TV so we can appeal to 35-year-old soccer moms, while we're doing our best friend's wife in the back of the bus." That's what I hate. At least in rock 'n' roll, it is what it is. They didn't pretend to be otherwise.'

So, what about the power of the artist, like Robbie Fulks, who wrote 'Fuck This Town' about Nashville, or Steve Earle, who caused yaps of protest with his song about the treatment of John Lindh Walker, the American teenager caught fighting in Afghanistan for the terrorist mastermind Osama bin Laden.

'There is no power of the artist in the music business,' Matt scoffed. 'That's a total illusion. The power of the artist is knowing who you are and saying what you say and going home feeling good or not feeling good about it.

'There has been a disconnection between culture and commerce. I think it's more extreme than ever now. *O Brother* is a vote by consumers saying, "I've had enough of the slick and hollow." You have a lot of rich hillbillies trying to hold on to their executive leather seats. If the business model changes, their chair goes away and in comes the new guy. So they're not listening to the *O Brother* vote, except as a passing nod. They're trying to dance as hard and fast as they can around that. There are a few guys who do have those powerful chairs who really do want to effect change in a good way. But that is like trying to turn the Titanic around in a rubber swimming pool.'

The Others, the Risky Country as opposed to no-risk corporate country music, is where Matt, and a growing number of country artists, are putting down their money.

'To me, that's the marrow and heart of what is going to be the next big explosion in country music,' Matt said. 'I believe that with all my heart. But the price these musicians are paying is a lot. There is a lot of poverty. There is a lot of rejection. But, when they get that big opportunity, they are going to be a lot more savvy in demanding for themselves and their music. What are the labels going to threaten them with, poverty? We're not afraid of that.'

A community of like-minded artists is starting to happen, according to Matt. 'I'm seeing this sense of community in places like the Western Beat Show, in Lower Broadway, in the small clubs. I'm finding a few people being more direct, which is encouraging in this town where talking out of two sides of your mouth is a normal conversation. That Southern charm that you don't mean is getting old. There are successful songwriters who are starting to call other songwriters on their own crap. They're saying, "It's insulting to dumb down the music, it's insulting to the great songwriters who have laid a foundation." Artists are making $250,000 [£160,000] on their own selling records, which weans them away from the corporations. I think the machine is starting to smoke really heavily.

'For me personally, I'm going back to Southern roots in kind of a twisted way. I call it Hillbilly Gothic. My music is a combination of my two loves: mountain music and rock 'n' roll. I try to stop writing ego-driven universal thoughts, those ironic twists on old phrases. Instead, my music is about the well that has healed me and killed me. It's not all about me. It's about a heritage. I'm trying to the best of my ability to write from that vantage point of the world as I see it. It's more of a Kerouac kind of observation. It's not about dirt roads, moonlight, kisses, and naked in the pond. That worked when I was 16. That's not where I am at now. I juxtapose what I'm doing against a rock edge, almost punk. It's not whether the music has a steel guitar or a banjo. It's the content, that's what it's about. If I truly love my community, and I take songwriting as a craft and trade and work hard to do it, then good things will come out of it.'

20 The Garth Brooks Way

I wondered about Hank. Who was this guy and where did he come from? He insinuated that he wants to be a singer, but I never heard him so much as hum. Matt King went into his metaphorical cave and whittled on himself. Emma Fox came halfway around the world and landed a deal because she made people believe in her. Jill King formulated a business plan for her career and threw a showcase to launch that plan. Hank tells light-bulb jokes.

Is there 'right' way to climb the artist's career ladder? You can make all the plans in the world but, in the meantime, life happens.

Take Garth Brooks's career. He has a college degree in marketing. He's been accused of using that 'book-learned' knowledge to plan his career moves: get a big black cowboy hat to establish the country image; do rock 'n' roll moves, swing out over the audience, abuse guitars, set off flashpots on stage; make a controversial video, like *Thunder Rolls*; have a public private life, complete with a public act of contrition with the wife, and then appear with the lover; and at the peak of fame, do a peek-a-boo with retirement. Chart that out on a timeline and *voilà* – a music career.

Well, not quite. When Garth Brooks arrived in Nashville he worked as a cowboy boot salesman. He sang at writer's nights and he did demo work. Basically, he was another face in the crowd. He didn't have the profundo bass voice considered a prerequisite for a male country singer. He was chubby and had a weak chin. If he doesn't sound like a star, and doesn't look like a star, then he must not be a star, so the label executives' thinking went.

Every label in Nashville turned him down. One day, his manager called Allen Reynolds, one of Nashville's pre-eminent independent producers. The manager, Bob Doyle, asked Reynolds if he was looking for new talent. 'Not really, but I'm open,' replied Reynolds. 'Then I think you'll be interested in talking with a writer/artist I'm working with,' said Doyle.

Allen told me this story at his studio Jack's Tracks, which he had bought from another Nashville legendary product, Cowboy Jack Clement.

'So Doyle came over with some song demo tapes,' Allen said. 'I liked what I heard. I liked the songs and the voice and what Garth had to say. So I suggested that the three of us get together, and we did. I always want to talk to the artists. I want to know what they are thinking, what their head is like. I don't want to waste a lot of my time and energy if they are yo-yos. I liked Garth. He didn't say a whole lot but I like what he had to say. What he had to say included, "I'm country and I don't want anybody questioning that."'

Allen suggested that they do a limited amount of work and see how they got along. They might like each other but not work well together. The first and second sessions went well and everyone enjoyed them. They cut some songs that became number one songs on Garth's first album.

'Garth took risks,' Allen said. 'No record label that I can see is taking a risk now. Or what they call a risk and what I call a risk is not the same thing. When I started working with Garth, Lynn Schults was the head of A&R at Capital Records. Capital had turned Garth down once. Then Lynn heard Garth at a writer's night. He told Garth that he'd have to square it with his superiors but as far as he was concerned, Garth had a deal. Capital was a smaller operation than other labels and there was not a lot of pressure. So there weren't a lot of lawyers or a lot of hype going on. We had a measured amount of money and were allowed to go to work. No one bothered me about wanting to hear things as we went. Occasionally I'd tell Lynn, "This guy is good. We're doing some good work."

'We got some good fundamental work done and helped Garth find himself. It was during that time Garth was singing some song and I said, "You're not sounding like yourself."

'He said, "I'm trying to get that George Strait kind of thing."

'I said, "Look, we already got George Strait. We don't need another one. What we need is you, uniquely you." So we got to do this discovery process. He had a wealth of songs that he had collected or written or co-written that included "The Dance". Then, when he and I were through, I told him that I thought the record would get him on down the road a way. I talked to him like a Dutch uncle about the business, selecting people and all that. I said that when it comes to picking singles, he and I and his manager should be unified about what we want before it gets into the label's hopper. We picked the first single and the second single.

'By that time Jimmy Bowen, head of the label, wanted to ditch the album and move on. He wanted a new album in two months. I said, "Jimmy, we can't do that and measure up to our standards. Before you leave this album, you need to listen yourself. There is a song on there called 'The Dance' that will separate Garth from the other hats. When he does the song at his shows, people are loving it. You can hear a pin drop. I know Garth wants it as a single."'

Bowen promised he'd listen again. This was December. He asked if Allen could produce another album by June. Allen agreed and he and Garth started working on album two. They produced two more singles, both of which went to number one. The second single was 'The Dance'. The first single on the next album was 'Friends in Low Places'.

'That wouldn't have happened at CBS,' Allen said. 'It wouldn't have happened under a label head that personally selects the songs. You can cut something he doesn't approve of, but I'll guarantee goddamn ya it won't be in the album. I don't work with the major labels because I know those operations. I know more about songs than most record executives will know if they live to be 500. That's my job. They're not in there working with the artist. I'm an entertainer and they're not. And if they don't like hearing that, they can kiss my ass. But that's the truth. I've had good luck with artists because I've been able to have my own ship here. I've kept the record labels the hell out of here. Anybody that wanted to crowd me, I said, "Hey, I'm just not your guy."'

Garth Brooks is widely regarded in the country music industry as a very very smart guy. He controls everything, from his staging to his record marketing, everything that is done in his career. He even went to the retail chains himself and held meetings with Wal-Mart and Target, a chore most artists won't go near. He's very professional in the studio, laying down his tracks quickly. And he approaches his music the Texas way. He might hit a note that's a little sharp, or the track is a little bit sloppy, but he goes with it as opposed to tweaking the sound for days with the engineer. He doesn't record the song, he performs the song. That is a crucial distinction. The energy is much different, which is what makes him so popular with the audience. His vocals connect with the listener because he is singing to them, not to the recording apparatus. He doesn't over-analyze the music but just sings it, which is what Allen recognized and the studio executives missed.

Allen made a solemn vow in the mid-'80s to stay far away from record labels and work as an independent producer. He'd only go near them if they asked, but on his terms. He has kept the vow. But business turned so bad that he nearly sold the studio and returned to songwriting. He wrote 'Ready for the Times to Get Better' cut by Crystal Gayle, who also recorded his 'We Should Be Together' and 'Somebody Loves You'. Waylon Jennings had a big hit with Allen's 'Dreaming My Dreams' on his album by the same name, considered a watershed recording in his career. Don Williams has also recorded a number of Allen's songs.

But he decided to stay in his corner, work the cracks and crannies, and make the best music he can, whether anybody wants it or not.

'Most of my success came with smaller or weaker labels,' Allen explained, 'like United Artists or Capital Records or Mercury when they were small operations. I've never had any success at CBS or RCA. When I started with Kathy Mattea, Mercury was like a secret label. It was the sleepiest place in the industry. They just weren't watching that close. You get to work with the artists without the label executives wanting to be in the studio with you, which I've always refused. I try to find an artist I can work with. The record labels don't understand any of that.

'I regard record labels as enormously ignorant about what they have, where it comes from, and how it is created. Furthermore, I think they are the seat of arrogance. I've always felt that way about them. You can't tell them anything. Nothing seems to register with them. All they've got to do is open their ears. Pay attention. Hire some people who really love music and know what they are doing about it. But they just can't seem to do that very often.

'I've been sitting here for years laughing at the amount of money they're throwing at artists who have never done anything except sing in the choir at their church. These are scrubbed and buffed little yuppie kids who've come to town, "Oh, I've just always loved to sing." They don't know their ass when it comes to songs. They don't know how they want to present themselves because they've never done it. And the record labels start bidding wars about these new folks. Some kind of buzz starts and they're bidding over someone who has never done anything. This is amazing to me. Then they go, "Well, we have a million dollars [£650,000] in this act and we haven't had a hit." I say, "That's because you're so bloody ignorant."'

What is it that Allen dislikes so much about the sound produced by the major labels? The homogenized sound, he states unequivocally. Record labels are always trying to water down the music to the blandest common dominator so as to appeal to the largest number of people.

'For them, a record is not a success unless it sells mega units,' Allen stated. 'It isn't about music with them. My experience has been 180 degrees in the opposite direction. I've had the most luck with singers who don't want anybody questioning whether they were country or not, and that includes Garth Brooks. I would put his catalogue up as an example. Garth brought a more Western slant to Nashville. Nashville tends to get pretty Appalachian in its definition of what's country. Kathy Mattea told me, "I don't want to straddle the fence. I don't want anyone wondering what I am. I want to be country. I want to be acoustic." That was basically my starting point with Kathy. Artists who straddle the fence annoy the hell out of me.'

Mainstream commercial radio's influence in dumbing down the music also annoys Allen, as it does almost everyone in the country music business.

'Radio is peopled by personnel who don't even have a sense of what country is and don't give a shit,' Allen claimed. 'Radio and the labels are in lockstep. Radio is worse than it's ever been. Now it's pay for play. It's absolutely cookie cutter bullshit. It's obscene. It's so boring and so limited. Clear Channel (one of the four major corporate owners of the commercial stations) is saying, "Look, this is what we want for our country music stations. We want music that appeals to women from ages 34 to 50. We don't want anything else. If you bring us anything that we think doesn't fit what we're asking for, we don't care what you call it, it's not for us." Clear Channel has over 1,200 radio stations. They cover a lot of major markets. They alone can keep you from charting. If you don't chart, you don't get bought by K-Mart and Wal-Mart and Target. Those chains sell the major part of the tonnage of country music. They buy only the top 20 on the chart or the top 15. If you don't get that chart position, they're not going to put you on the rack.

'Now, if it should break through Target and Wal-Mart consciousness that they're missing out, that radio is so vapid that the top 20 is no longer the criteria for listeners to buy records, then maybe things will open up some. But I don't expect that.'

The artist, talent, and material are there for a new surge in country, according to Allen. But distribution channels to get the music out to the general public are almost nonexistent. Boutique labels, vanity labels, and independents, even specialized labels within major companies, like Lost Highways as part of Mercury Records, have a very limited reach to the public. Radio has always been, stretching back to the 1930s, a fundamental necessity to the success of commercial country music, which is the bread-and-butter of the artists. The only way to avoid the stranglehold of the commercial radio powers is for the artists to hit the road and perform in every club, every bar, every living room they can – which is the approach of the Others.

The Others movement is like an artesian well burbling under the surface, Allen agreed. Sooner or later, it will find its way to the surface. The media has ignored it and the labels don't think they can make any money off it. But it's a vibrant scene.

Allen sees analogies between the Others movement and the folk scene in the 1960s. They both came from the grassroots. The music's emergence has resulted in the formation of 'really super record labels to present it', Allen said. 'It's possible that country can be somewhat like that. There are a lot of people around Nashville who are hopeful and have a fair amount of evidence to base their hope on.'

One reason to hope is that artists are willing to take risks. But consider this analogy: 'What did the fish say when it hit a wall? "*Dam!*"' Artists are the fish and the record labels are the dam. Labels don't naturally like artists who are independent and strong and know what they want, Allen emphasized. Labels prefer less talented people who are more pliable. That's why Allen calls the label executives arrogant.

'They are the very home of arrogance,' he said with heat. 'The inexperienced artist, when they are newly signed to a label, they are overwhelmed by the label. The labels talk too goddamn much. And the people who are talking don't know what they are talking about. The label executives have never written a song, never performed on stage, never gone through that process. They are the wrong people to be talking it up. They see end results. They interpret yesterday's information and try to tell the artist what to do.

'Instead, they ought to be looking for people who are especially talented. But they are happy to take these kids who have never done anything but have a nice voice. One of the most abundant things in nature is a nice voice. It's far more rare to find a really good interpreter or a really good singer or somebody whose soul is giving you something.'

If a 'primary hero' walked into most record executives' offices, they would try to change him, Allen maintained. It's something about the apparatus of record labels. They did that to Ricky Scaggs. His first album on Columbia was fantastic. Before the second album was released, the label's public relations manager took him to Atlanta and had him custom fitted and coiffed. The same treatment was given to his music. Look at the second album cover and listen to the music, challenged Allen. It turned Ricky off and he left the label.

Today it seems it's increasingly possible, at least as a dream, for an artist to break out without the major apparatus. The labels always seem to be out of step with the times, today more so than ever, Allen pointed out. If someone is going to emerge, it would have to be through the grassroots movement, he said.

'There is a wonderful encouraging amount of talent like Alison Krauss, on an independent label. She has spurned all advances, and there have been loving and lavish advances made by all the majors in Nashville to the House of Krauss. She has said no thank you to all of them because she preferred to keep her artistic freedom and integrity. Bless her heart. She continues to do some of the most interesting work of any producer or artist around these parts. To me, she is a real example of what is possible. She is another business model outside the label system.'

It is possible that the next major figure in country might not come from the label's system, Allen was happy to say. But he is pessimistic at the same time.

'I see people who have potential get buried by the system all the time because they are trying to be good artists,' he said. 'No one is trying to get their potential out of them, encouraging that. No one is saying, "How do you feel about this?" No one is helping them get good fundamentals so they can go from there and know who they are. As an artist, you either hook up with someone who thinks that way or you go find it yourself in the clubs and real life. Then, when you get to the label, maybe you'll have enough going for yourself already. Like what Springsteen did. They don't mess with him too much.'

The fact that Waylon Jennings and Willie Nelson and the Outlaws (which includes Kinky Friedman, Steve Earle, Lucinda Williams, Alison Krauss), the Matt Kings and Hank 3s and Joy Lynn Whites of country music emerged and gained a following was an accident, in Allen's opinion. The industry is, as a structure, against them. Such artists are always praised if for no other reason than for making a viable career despite the demands of the commercial model. They are loved the same way eccentric uncles are loved, as colorful characters that add dash and spice but really don't contribute that much to the bottom line. If an efficiency expert were to prune the family tree, the colorful uncle gets the pink slip first.

'The labels saw Waylon as a risk,' Allen said. 'They want artists that behave themselves, pull their socks up real neat, button their shirt, and put on a tie. That wasn't how he was. He was a west Texas boy, so he was a little bit disturbing. His music didn't feel like a risk to him. The music he wanted to make rang true to him and the people around him.

'When Waylon cut the *Dream of My Dreams* album at Glaser Brothers studio, he had just won his freedom from the RCA situation. At RCA, you had to cut in their studio or you had to take a pair of their engineers to where you were cutting. The engineers' union had a lock with RCA, as they do with many big labels, which said, by contract, union engineers had to be used on all RCA projects. Waylon had struggles at RCA anyway on different issues. He was their mischievous boy. He finally won the privilege of going to Hillbilly Central and cutting his record, where Cowboy Jack Clement produced him. They did this great work and that was followed by more great work because Waylon was out from under RCA's thumb.

'When Waylon cut "MacArthur Park" with the Kimberleys, that song made some eyebrows to up in country music. I remember his reply: "Country's not the song, it's the singer. I'm country. I can sing anything I want."'

That is the heart of the issue for Allen and all like-spirited Other Outlaws: Who is country? The artists or the Music Row labels? Both. The shifting values within that alliance determine the sound and message of country music that the general public gets to hear.

After Allen finished his last Garth Brooks album, he decided to stand back and take stock. He found nothing in mainstream country inviting. He did an independent album with Shawn Camp, but no label has shown interest. He will work with a few artists that interest him. He's 'getting in touch with my songwriter self again', doing some singing, and spending a year catching up on personal matters. He tells people that he might retire.

But he never stops paying attention to what is happening out in the mainstream. In Nashville, Allen has the reputation of always being ahead of the curve, of having his sensitive finger on a pulse no one else detects. If he is thinking of retirement, does that mean there is no pulse, certainly no interesting pulse, in country music?

I called Richard Bennett for a second opinion. Richard Bennett is a 35-year veteran in the music business. He has played guitar for Liberace, Peggy Lee, and Gene Vincent. He was Neil Diamond's lead guitarist for 17 years. He was a top Hollywood session player before moving to Nashville in 1985 at the urging of Steve Earle, then-Capital's chief Jimmy Bowen, and Tony Brown. For the past eight years, he has toured with Mark Knopfler and is preparing for a second world tour with Knopfler.

He has produced 40 albums, including four for Emmylou Harris. He was on stage playing with Keith Richards, Willie, and Hank 3 when they played the Ryman.

We met at his house in a sylvan neighborhood, rural in its quietness and peacefulness. His downstairs den was a musician's lair. Framed gold records lined the entrance. An entire wall of built-in shelves was filled with vinyl records. Tapes and CDs filled a separate smaller room from floor to ceiling. His 14-year-old son's drum kit and numerous guitars stood around the large rectangular room, where we sat in easy chairs and chatted.

Richard is a good sounding board because he hears from the disenfranchised and the label executives within corporate music. And what does he hear? 'God, isn't it all shit,' he replied. He is a very soft-spoken man, not given to hyperbole. 'There are a lot of people, in and out of the business, who can't stand to listen to country music. They have lost Mr and Mrs America to a great degree. Everyone is saying that there's got to be something else. Let's do something else. I'm not just talking about the musicians saying that. I'm talking about everybody. There are people in the business who say, "I can't bear it anymore. I can't listen to country radio. I can't listen to what I'm making."

'I think they don't know how to make anything else. They are afraid to. Tony Brown has probably put more of his money where his mouth is than anybody else by doing Steve Earle, Nanci Griffith, Allison Moorer. He's had his ass handed to him a bunch of times. When you get that many people who are dissatisfied, including those who are running the ugly end of the business, it will change.'

But, he warned, there are some things that will not change.

'The record business has always been a money business, from Edison on,' he said, somewhat resignedly. 'The genre is immaterial. The record business is selling and it doesn't matter what they're selling. Record labels have always dictated to the artists. Mitch Miller was the first real dictator/producer. A lot of his artists hated him. He made Tony Bennett sing Hank Williams' song, but Tony fancied himself as a jazzer. What the hell was that all about? It was about Columbia Records making money for the company, that's what it was about. There have always been the artists fighting the label and that will always be. Hopefully, there is a little bit of middle ground of give and take. More and more artists are standing up for their opinion in the studio.

'From my viewpoint, being in the record business, Nashville over the years, has geared itself up to do one thing very well – marketing this music. Finding where it can get played and where that money comes from they do very well. They can't seem to deal with anything else.'

Nashville is very good at refining; it's not good at invention. 'Every once in a while, something will drop out of the sky and they'll go, "Oh, yeah, great the next big thing,"' Richard said. 'Then they'll analyze it, dissect it, and sanitize it. They are very good at working off a formula but not very good at invention.'

But there is always invention going on in Nashville music. That's the nature of the beast.

'Yes,' Richard agreed, 'but the labels are afraid of it at the major level. I don't know if it's a threat to them or what. Pop music has always prided itself on different is good. It's mandatory to be different in pop music. But country music has always been the opposite, probably because it's always catered to a traditional market place. Country music, as an industry, doesn't necessarily want to know about different.

'The record labels, and to a large extent the musicians, have always prided themselves on wanting to be something other than hillbilly. But they're like beaten stepchildren. "No, we're not hillbillies. We're pop." But they're not really pop. That's always figured into it. Take Shania Twain. She's not current enough pop to get on pop radio and, although she's played on country radio, many don't consider her a country singer nowadays. Country music has become this vast trashcan of almost pop, old pop, Eagles recycles, and the James Taylor disease piling on.

'Go back to 1957, when the first Nashville cosmopolitan record was cut, Furlon Husky's "Gone". A brilliant record. A blatant attempt at making a pop country record. For all the derision that country pop got, they did it very well up until 1963–4. The Jim Reeves and Don Gibbon records, things like that. When you listened to that music, you didn't want to go drink a beer but smoke a Kent and have a Manhattan. It was that type of country music because it came more from jazz than pop. Then that sound wore very thin. It was refined and refined and refined until by 1964–5 it was nothing but spit polish.

'I think the current mess going on is more an evolution of that syndrome. But they get the wrong elements of pop. They're doing 20-year-old pop. It's like bad '80s corporate rock with pedal steel. They should go scrounge around in the bins and find what's cool in 2002, but don't bring Journey into it. It's wonderful that Nashville has become so accepting of all these things and, yet, it's a whole bunch of nothing right now. I'm talking only about the country corporate music.'

The new voice will come from outside the corporate system, in Richard's opinion. It will come from a lifestyle, an outlaw, and will be so authentic as to be unmistakable. It will have the quality that gave enduring worth to the great hillbilly musicians. Their music was an honest expression of their lifestyle. The art was the expression of the lifestyle.

'Now it's life imitating art,' Richard said. 'It's country fakes in crap cowboy hats and plaid shirts who drive around in pickup trucks and live in a condo in the suburbs.'

A real change, a change that will take country music to its next evolutionary level, according to Richard. That change will do what The Beatles and Elvis did to pop music, or what Hank Williams did to country. Everything that came before him sounded old. Garth Brooks made country music sound hip new but he was not the next evolution.

'Garth Brooks bought a fuck load of money to the business,' Richard said, 'but there was no artistry in there. It made the business very healthy for ten years but now the business is very sick.'

What about the Others? He has produced Phil Lee and played cuts on Jill King's demos.

'The community of musicians is very supportive but I haven't seen much acceptance by the record companies,' he replied. 'The record companies love to talk that up but I don't see many recording it. However, there is a growing groundswell. It's fantastic that it's happening but I don't know if anything will come of it. It's been bubbling now for 10 to 12 years and nothing has shot up out of it yet. I would love nothing better than to have someone come out of that scene and give it a voice. I don't think it has a voice yet. It doesn't have a focal point, one person to say, 'Come along, look at this.' That's what it needs. Historical moments call forth individuals and that might be what we're waiting for.

'The blessing of that movement is the energy and passion of it. It also has a lot of crap music in it as well. Even so, I think this other country is far more honest and is more the true country music than what's coming out of Business Row, as Phil Lee refers to Music Row. I don't see any energy down on Business Row. I see manufacturing. That's all it's been for so many years.'

The next phase of country music may come out of two scenarios; either a real new voice is heard, one with the old hillbilly authenticity in terms of being honest; or a slow evolution that steals a little bit from the Others and very gently massages that style into mainstream music.

'Business Row is now trying to incorporate the Others' stripped down sound, like *O Brother*, into their slick corporate records,' Richard said. 'A more pure sound, simpler, is the chat on the floor. But when the record gets out from a major label, it still has everything plus the kitchen sink. It's spit-polished to a chrome gleam. But the labels are aware now that this approach is failing. I'm not sure if they are aware because of the little side avenue country music is going on, or because pop music has been having a tendency to strip down as well.

'It would be great that if these non-mainstream artists, if and when the big labels want them, can say, "Fine, but as I am. You're not going to change me." It's the old jazz scenario, isn't it? The struggling jazz musician, no matter how brilliant they are, even when they are successful, they are still struggling. Very few of them came into any kind of money. They plodded along dedicated to the art. That's how every artist ought to feel. But, of course, you have a bunch of musicians who are willing to be molded. The whole pop machinery has done that for years.'

He sat back in his chair and looked at the hundreds of albums in the room. 'The adventure is when the cauldron is bubbling under it,' he said with a smile. 'That's the creativity of things.'

21 Making An Artist

Tony Brown has gambled one million dollars (£650,000) and walked away without a dime – three times. Imagine going to Las Vegas with a million bucks, expecting, truly believing, that you'll come away with at least five million (£3.25 million), maybe ten million (£6.5 million). You enter the casino full of brio and understated bluster, the way John Wayne rode into town. You roll the dice again and again, and get snakebitten every time. You spin the wheel and the bouncing ball just misses landing on your winning number, every time. But your confidence is not shaken. You know you have the right touch, that feeling of faith, that on the next take, the next song, your artist is going to hit gold, if only you can get the album finished. And then if the right people at the radio listen to it. And if people buy many millions of units. It will happen. You got the goods. Just listen, you tell everyone, just listen. The artist's voice is the sound of cash. Hear it?

Three times at a million each. Three million dollars (£1.9 million). Down the tubes.

How do you do that? What does it feel like? How come you still have a job?

Tony invited me to his house to talk about it. He lives in a spacious neighborhood of big lawns and rolling wooded hills. Donna Summers lives down the street. Don Cook's house is over the hill. It's a residential version of Music Row. Tony and his wife, Antastasia, helped design their house, which resembles a downsized French château, the façade made of millions of small slates of Tennessee limestone assembled without mortar. The house looked substantial, yet delicate. The wrought-iron front gates to the circular drive were closed. A yellow tape, the kind used at crime scenes, barred the back drive.

I cut across the lawn to the front door and pressed the buzzer. No answer. I pressed again. 'Yes?' Tony answered somewhat tentatively. I announced myself.

Tony sat in the kitchen slumped down so his head was below the windows that formed two walls. Strangers milled about his backyard. 'It's really weird to be a prisoner in your own house,' he said. Tony and Antastasia had lent their landscaped lawn to a charity fundraiser. The strangers had paid to examine the flowers and scrubs, while studiously trying not to look in the windows of the million-dollar (£650,000) house. A few feet away a well-dressed couple skirted the swimming pool. We made fleeting eye contact. I slunk down next to Tony.

'Three million dollars [£1.9 million] on an article of faith,' I said. 'It's cheaper to give at church.'

Tony smiled. 'Yeah, but because they have a choir that doesn't make a record business.'

Losing millions of dollars of a company's money does not go unnoticed. The men in suits who keep the accounts invite you to meetings. They ask pointed questions. They question your judgment. They give advice, like DROP THE ARTIST. NOW! A MILLION BUCKS ON A LOSER WE CAN'T AFFORD. Only they say it in modulated voices, but with a polite edge, the way the manager of a casino might ask for your credit rating – and first-born son.

Tony defended his artists. He justified the gamble, which was like trying to convince bean counters that a cone of cotton candy can be transformed into a bar of bullion. How can you transfigure something as unsubstantial as a song, which is only vibrations and intuition, into a disc of gold? Through faith, Tony told the suits. Faith, desire, hard work, and luck. Those are not accounting terms. The suits had difficulty grasping Tony's story line. But, he was Tony Brown. He had delivered millions of dollars of hits. Maybe they can take the next record to the bank. But if you don't deliver, the suits warned, we'll talk again.

'When I bailed on an artist, I did so reluctantly,' said Tony, nearly lying on the banquette to avoid being seen by the strangers in his garden.

'When that happened, it was with artists who were a little bit different, an Allison Moorer, who I had a lot of money invested in at MCA. We never got a song over 60 in the charts. But I still believe in her and brought her to Universal South with me. When I had to bail, I'd tell the artist, "I can't pull this off for you, so I have to let you go."

'They usually said, "Hey, man, thanks for believing in me."'

When he dropped a mil of MCA's money, the company was the number one label in town. George Strait, Trisha Yearwood, Vince Gill, Reba McEntire were on the roster and selling millions of every record they put out. That was the salad days of the '89 boom. The prevailing modus operandi was 'make more music to make more money'. So Tony, the president of MCA, spent money to diversify his stable of artists. With the label making money, he could spend a million on an artist he believed in.

'This was the thinking,' he said. 'If you get an artist, a mainstream artist, who makes you money, then you can experiment with the other kinds of artists who are a little different. Different meaning like different to the left where they are eclectic and cutting edge. Or different to the right, where they are so commercial that it almost makes you sick. You want an artist in between, someone that has the sensibilities of a crass commercial artist but also has the integrity of a left-of-center type of artist.

'The crass commercial artist may sell a lot of records, but they are not the artists people keep in their record collection for a long time. You keep Bruce Springsteen and George Jones and Waylon Jennings and Neil Young and George Strait and Vince Gill. As a record executive, you want artists on your roster that will sell for the long haul. And often they are the left-of-center types, so you take the million dollar gamble.'

What can be done to increase the odds of success? How do you assemble the package?

'Chemistry is the whole deal.' I understood why the accountants rolled their eyes when Tony explained his approach to making music for profit. 'Like with Vince. He had some pretty good records for RCA but never hit. When I moved from RCA to MCA and started producing records again, I signed Vince to MCA. Then we had Vince's first big hit, "When I Call Your Name". That didn't mean that I was a genius or anything. It just meant that the chemistry of him and me together just clicked. The more relaxed you make the artist, the better chance for good work. So the chemistry has to be right.

'You want to keep the artist secure and confident so they'll have the verve to perform. Every artist is going to go through that period where creativity may take a dip. That happens to a lot of artists. When they take a dip, if the artist relationship is not good, they can fall apart. If the relationship is good, then you can turn it around. That happened this past year with Brooks And Dunn. They had an incredible run. Then everyone was saying that there was a problem between Ronnie and Kix. Basically, they just got a little bit stale. This past year they pulled it back together again and they're bigger than they've ever been.'

But first, the record label must find the talent, or recognize the talent when he or she walks through the door.

In part, Tony looks for talent in other label's trash. Some of his biggest and best artists were being dropped by other labels: Steve Earle from CBS, Vince Gill from RCA, Marty Stuart from CBS. Tony got three gold records from Marty when CBS couldn't get a decent line dance going. It's the chemistry, stupid.

'I've always looked at other labels whenever they bailed very quickly on acts and I thought they were doing the wrong thing,' Tony said. 'Part of the package is that the label has to believe in that artist. Everybody at the label, in the building, has to buy into the artist. Once you cut the record, promotion, marketing, the whole team has to believe that this artist is the next big thing. That's a key to a successful package.

'Ask any star, from Garth Brooks to George Strait to Reba to Brooks And Dunn, and they'll say it's a team effort. The artist believes they got the goods. Everyone at the labels believes that as a creed of the faithful. You go to radio with that undeniable faith and knowledge and radio believes the same way the sinner believes in redemption after hearing a good preacher. Then you're on your way. That team effort has to stay intact. If anybody starts falling by the wayside, from producer to label to radio, that's when careers come apart.'

A good number of country artists paid their dues for years and years before making their name. Ronnie Dunn was around forever as a solo act before being teamed with Kix Brooks. Reba McEntire had seven albums before she hit gold. Keep the faith and you too may find your heaven.

'Part of my job as a label head is to make sure that all the parts of the machine, all the members of the team, function as they should,' Tony explained. 'That's the deal. So instead of pointing fingers, I try to slide in there and fix it. The psychology of our business helps the music happen. If there is great music but the psychology is all screwed up, the artist will not perform, the music will not come out. It's a real fine line of how we get the artist to perform that great music and once they perform it, how do we sell it. But if they don't perform the great music, we can't sell it.'

Little stars can burn out after a short run. Big stars can implode. Established stars can start to fade because of the slightest misstep. Creating an artist as a successful act requires a touch of alchemy to make the ethereal solid. This past week Tony received two records from an act, a top act with big hits, trying to find that magic again. The band completed an album for the label where they had hits and former success. The label decided that they didn't like the group or the album and dropped them, although the record was finished. The act went to another label, cut another record, and finished it. By now years of work and hundreds of thousands of dollars have been invested. The head of that label decided he didn't like the direction of the record and wouldn't release it. The musicians have two finished albums on two different labels that aren't released.

The albums were pitched to Tony. He listened but he's not going to take either one of them. The act, a big name with a successful track record (Tony wouldn't reveal their name) must be wondering what's wrong, what's failing here and why. And they can't figure it out. They are excellent musicians. Millions of people have bought their music. What's gone wrong?

'When you get right down to it, if the music doesn't work, the responsibility lies with the producer and the A&R person,' Tony explained. 'In the case of this particular artist, they write their own songs. There is no objectivity. It's really sad. With two albums, we're talking about close to two and a half or three years gone. After two finished records have been rejected, you can't tell me that psychologically the act isn't disillusioned. It's hard to come back from that. It would be really hard for this group to come back.

'I'm thinking that since they write all their own songs, they don't have a clue what is wrong. If I get involved with them, I'd probably have to fight over the song selection. And if they don't have a clue, then I've got the same problem that RCA and Warner Brothers had.'

Tony figured he couldn't put the bow back on that package, so he won't fool with the ribbon. And the group's career is headed for the 'has been' file. But other mainstream artists have managed to get a firm grip on the slippery slope and climb back to the top. When Brooks And Dunn were spinning their wheels, the Merlins in the studio made their analysis and tweaked the package. Ronnie Dunn is one of the finest country singers in the business. So build on that strength. Find a track that showcased Ronnie's voice. Stay close to the honky-tonk that Brooks And Dunn fans like, but make it sound fresh. A new producer, Mark Wright, came in, twisted the sound a little bit and BOOM, Brooks And Dunn are going stronger than ever.

'Now Alan Jackson and George Strait, you can't do that,' Tony explained. 'Nobody wants them to twist it too much. The fans want them to sound the same. Certain kinds of traditional, like Alan, George Strait, George Jones, you just have to get better songs. Brooks And Dunn is contemporary music with a traditional slant but basically mainstream music. They can twist it one way or another. It would be the wrong thing to do for me to say to George Strait, "Okay, George, everybody's sick of the traditional music. Let's cut a contemporary record." That would be the wrong thing to do for George Strait. I wouldn't do it.'

Then there is the consideration to package the act either as a solo or a band. As a general rule of thumb, a solo act has a better shot at success than a band. Alabama was the only band in country that's hit it really big big in country. Diamond Rio is enjoying a run but there is not another group on the track with them. And the package is wrapped differently if it's a male or female performer. In the past, the male definitely had the advantage. Now, it's more of an even playing field for female performers.

'There's tons of female potential stars on the horizon,' Tony said, 'but there aren't many males that I consider real contenders. We need some new male artists. Some stars. I found out that, in 2002 like in 1989–91 when the, what we called the Big Flush happened, when all the new acts – Travis Tritt, Alan Jackson, Vince, Reba, all the big acts happened – that big boom, it's about to happen again. Radio wants some new blood, some new meat. So it's up to the labels to deliver the new stars.

'Now, the music is good but the artists are not stars. We haven't found those artists who can become arena acts. In '89 and '90, we found a bunch of male artists, like Clint and Alan and Vince, Brooks And Dunn, Travis. In between then and now, a lot of female artists came along – Shania, Faith, The Dixie Chicks, Martina McBride. Now, I think some male artists have to emerge. Basically, we need some big stars. We've got to do a better job of picking artists that we think are stars. That's a very intangible thing.'

An emerging artist, a primary hero, can come not only from the South but any region. 'It doesn't matter,' Tony said. 'There are rednecks in Oregon and Washington just as there are in Georgia and Mississippi. There are working-class people everywhere. Country is about the working-class people. Those people are in every state in America. The majority of the artists seem to come from the South because the music came from the South. The emerging artist could come from another country. We have the Russian country band, Bering Straits, who are really good. Three of the hottest new acts come from Australia, keith urban, Kasey Chambers, and Jamie O'Neal. The next country music star could come from any country in the world.'

What about that primary hero coming from the Others? Tony wasn't so sure. The Others have a different agenda than Music Row and Music Row, in the hard reality, produces the country music that gets radio play that begets rack space at Wal-Mart that results in sales and profits. Anything outside that box is welcome to exist, but outside the box.

'The country side of country is about making money,' Tony said. 'The punk side of country is really about making a statement. In country, if you make a statement you must make sure it's nothing that will rile anybody. Punk music has a fuck you kind of attitude. I don't think Hank the Third's agenda is to make money. I think he wants to be more famous so his platform gets bigger. Most country artists' agenda is to make money.

'When you make money, you want to make more money. When you make more money, you want to make lots of money. And if you keep doing everything that's right, you can make lots of money. Then you figure out how to keep making lots of money for ten years. I can make movies. I can make endorsements. There is no end to the money I can make if I just keep doing it right. That's the package for a successful Music Row artist. I think the punk attitude is not about money. It's about I have something to say by God and here I come. Making money is a by-product of them making their statement.'

Having a successful first album is a champagne occasion. But take a sip, set the flute down and get back to work. The hard part is still ahead. The pressure is to repeat the success but with greater sales numbers. You have to bang it home at least three times in a row, probably five, to become the flavor of the month, in Tony's estimation. If the artist grabs the brass ring on the first go around, but the next effort or two stops at ten or 20 on the charts, it's back to square one.

'You've got to do a home run on the first song on the second album,' Tony said. 'If you do it three times and you don't do it the next two times, the artist can go away in the public's mind. Once the record is number one and all over the press, then the marketing department re-releases the record and it goes back out to the retailers. You put a big sticker on the CD, NUMBER ONE HIT. You want that seen everywhere. When a person walks into Tower Records, you want them to see that record prominently displayed. But you have to pay to get your record up front. The space is like real estate, like shelf space in grocery stores. You have to pay a slotting fee. And that drives up the cost of producing an album.'

Realistically how much does it take to cut a record? If it's a home studio effort, a CD can be produced for $6,000 (£4,000) to $20,000 (£13,000). A downtown studio production can cost $150,000 (£97,500) to $500,000 (£320,000). Tony's fee as a producer is $40,000 (£26,000) up front, a reasonable expense for a good producer. Labels and studios with a union contract, which means all professional studios, are subject to union pay scale. The double-scale players, the most seasoned and skilled who therefore cost less studio time to produce the record, get $1,000 (£650) a session. Each session is three hours long and there are two three-hour sessions a day. Sessions are normally scheduled from 10am–1pm, 2–5pm, and 6–9pm to allow players time to get from one session to the next as they work on different projects. Demo players receive $180 (£115) to $320 (£200) per session.

So, it can cost $2,000 (£1,300) a day per player for a full-scale studio session. A standard country band has five to six players – a bass, drums, piano, acoustic guitar, electric guitar, standup bass, fiddle. That's $12,000 (£8,000) a day for the musicians for two sessions. A ten-song album takes a minimum of four days with experienced musicians, which is why double-scale players get the premium. So pencil in a minimum of $48,000 (£30,000) for the musicians to get the basic tracks down. An engineer gets anywhere from $800 (£500) to $1,000 (£650) a day and the second engineer is $300–500 (£200–300) a day. Studio rental is anywhere from $1,000 (£650) to $2,500 (£1,600) a day. Then there is the tape expense, food, and miscellaneous. And you're just getting started.

'I'm accustomed to an album costing me $150,000 [£95,000] and up to $300,000 [£190,000], depending how indecisive or slow I am as a producer,' Tony said. 'A George Strait album usually goes really fast and costs usually $175,000 [£110,000]. He goes in there and we just knock it out real quick. A Wynonna Judd record, where she takes her time, can cost $300,000 [£190,000]. Money spent on records is basically about time spent.'

The costs also depend on a studio's aspirations. A major label's agenda is to sell hit records. If the album, or artist, doesn't sell, to hell with 'em, get them out of here. The smaller independent labels are not under the same pressure to produce big profits to satisfy corporate headquarters.

'As an independent, you don't have to sell as many records to make money,' Tony explained. 'If you cut a record at the right price, which most independents can, you can break even or make money. So you can actually find music that you like. At our label, we approach the business with an independent spirit. The spirit of what we are doing is "don't think so mainstream that you might blow off someone off to the left." We may have the spirit of an independent but bottom line is we're thinking big. Most independents aren't thinking that big. There are a lot of independents that, if you go to them and ask if they want to sell more records, they'll say, "No, thanks, we're happy with the way we are." We might pick up records that are cut independently. We're thinking about buying up Rodney Crowell's new record. It's finished. I think we're going to take it.'

Once the record is cut, the next step is promotion. This can cost more than producing the record. In the Battle of the Promotion departments, the label with the deepest pockets has the advantage. A blitz is launched to get attention in the industry press and the mass media. The artist is offered up for interviews to the publications with the biggest circulations. The de rigueur video, which can cost an easy $200,000 (£130,000), needs to do a heavy rotation of Country Music TV and Great American Country. Coveted TV interviews are pursued with the zest of a CEO going after stock options. The competition is fierce. Not only are the various country acts competing with each other, but also going head-to-head with pop artists.

'If you're a pop act, you can get on Leno, Letterman, "Good Morning, America", the "Today" show,' Tony said. 'But country artists have real trouble getting on those shows. There are a lot of acts that have platinum or gold hits and cannot get on Letterman or Leno because the programmer doesn't think those audiences wants to hear country.'

Tony eased himself up and peeked out the window. Strangers in the backyard saw him and looked away. He settled back down with a sigh.

'You know what we need?' A beer, I thought. 'Instead of one primary hero, or five top acts like we have now, we need ten or 15. During the '89 and '90 boom, nine or ten new acts were discovered. In the past five years, we've had Shania, Faith, Tim McGraw, who emerged since he wasn't like a new act, Kenny Chesney, The Dixie Chicks. Now we need ten or 12 new acts for the format to once again explode. And it ain't happening, not yet. I think it may happen this year or next year.

'Right now feels the same as 1989–90. We're about to go through this creative cycle and out of this new crop of artists we'll find the acts. But about five or six of the established artists are going to bite the big one to make room. The format goes, "Okay, enough of you already. Let's make room for this new product."'

The jackpot question is: who or what is the next new product, the next hero of the sales chart?

That person, or sound, is already here, according to Professor Richard Peterson, who taught the course 'The Sociology of Country Music', until his retirement from Vanderbilt in 2002. We spent an afternoon on his back patio beneath an enormous shade tree speculating about country music, like pundits dissecting a political party. He had recently returned from Holland, where he gave a lecture on country music.

'It isn't after the fad that the new music comes,' Prof Peterson said. 'It's already there, maybe in inchoate forms and not identified with any one category found in the record store. It's been around for a while, only below the radar. It starts to happen when it gets noticed in a big way. In the mid-'80s, the more rootsy neo-traditional was noticed but that had been around before. So the question is: which of the things going on in country music is most likely to happen?'

New big moves in country music have come when lots of working-class type people are involved, Prof Peterson observed. The Americana alternative range of music is an obvious place to look. By alt country music, Prof Peterson means a new sound that comes out of people who are rock fans, or alternative rock fans, that push the music into country.

Prof Peterson finds much of alternative country music fairly intellectual, or middle class, or sort of folk music. It doesn't have the characteristics of a breakout. One characteristic of a new cycle is music that involves a new form of dancing, he noted. This holds true in pop and in country. Right now, nothing characteristically new is coming from country.

'The other thing is that the working class is dying out,' Prof Peterson pointed out. 'Many of the know-nothing types in our society have white-collar jobs. Those people often romantically look back to a time in the hills, a simpler time, and freedom and all of that. So there is a romance with bluegrass/country but it's different than what I think of the classical country music.

'One possibility is that you have to find new symbols of working class. What is it that brings these people together? The working class should be defined more by income than occupation, so blue collar and working class are not synonymous. After all, the income of a policeman or school teacher in Tennessee is just above the welfare line.'

What will music be like in five or ten years? Prof Peterson foretells several possible scenarios:

The country music industry will be owned by practically one company, which is an extended amplification of the existing situation.

Or the mega-corporations will leave the country music industry because they cannot make big profits. The advent of self-created CDs, of taking music off the Internet, and artists offering their music directly to the consumer via websites is eroding the profit base.

If the big firms get out, that leaves what Prof Peterson terms the 'mice', self-producing tiny things that breed like crazy and fill up the world. Independent labels will rush into the void and multiply.

Or big companies will stay in the part of the industry where they can make money. They will concentrate on middle-of-the-road music for an audience that really doesn't want to make choices. They will produce and control music that Tony Brown calls 'so commercial it makes you sick'. The creative music, the alt country, will be the providence of the independent micro-companies, the mice. Prof Peterson sees this bifurcation as a real possibility.

'There are a lot of people in the business of helping this along,' Prof Peterson said. 'Every October, Nashville is the site of the New Music Conference. Seminars on distribution, making CDs, all aspects of the business are presented, like how to make $100,000 [£65,000] without a major label deal. There is a developing service industry. It's all being formed, what the parts are and what the roles are. This is indeed a very exciting time because there are so many potentials.'

22 The Radio Play

Every Monday is Truth or Consequence for the labels' promotion departments. The weekly *R&R* and *Billboard* charts are posted on Mondays. Has the previous week's cajoling, arm twisting, sweet talking, dangling inducements, calling in favors and, if necessary, making threats paid off? A song's position on the charts is determined by how many spins a record got on the 152 reporting stations for the *R&R* chart and the 149 monitored stations for the *Billboard* chart. Upward or downward movement on the charts translates to more money or less money for a record company. Promotions, bonuses, house payments, jobs, even careers, depend on delivering the spins.

Bill Macky, vice-president of national promotions for MCA Nashville, places a conference call to his regional directors nationwide every Monday at 8.30am. He works the phone all day gathering information on spins, regional performance of a record, whether the record met its goal, and local market research for the record. He's looking for an edge, identifying the comers, and strategizing how to help stalling records from going into a tailspin.

On Tuesday morning, he calls his field managers to evaluate and adjust, if necessary, the coming week's plan. Tally is kept on which stations might add, or drop, a record. Tactics are discussed on how to push a record up the charts. Any problems, or potential problems, are sniffed out. Macky goes through this process with each regional director for every MCA song on charts.

The object is to grab the top spot(s) and hang on for as long as possible. This serves two purposes: you win and they lose. A carefully crafted and detailed strategy is necessary to play this game. Macky, the team captain, gets the chalkboard out, huddles the team, and a game plan is devised to move a song up the charts week by week. The effort to move a song to its goal may take many months, so the captain periodically gives pep talks to keep the team's morale high. Each week the team's performance is assessed and adjustments made. When the goal is reached, symbolic high-fives are electronically flashed around the country to the team members.

A superstar like George Strait can get into the top of the chart in 16 to 18 weeks. Macky and his team worked for 44 weeks to get Gary Allen's record into the top five. Allen, who is a platinum-selling singer, is still a building act, in radio's assessment.

We sat in his office and discussed the behind-the-scenes nitty gritty of pushing a record to the one number spot. Macky is a young man, casually dressed, intense in a coach-like way; that is, coiled with energy but not visibly caffeine wired. His conversation was sprinkled with sport analogies.

'You do whatever you can to manufacture spins,' Macky explained, as if to a new recruit. It's Wednesday, so his command central office is quiet. The large-screen computer is turned off. No lights blink on his phone console. Even the sound system is silent. Nevertheless, Macky exudes an impatient energy, as if he knows there is a marketing crisis somewhere in his network and he needs to rush out and deal with it.

However, he affably sketched out for me the Xs and Os of his playbook when plotting the arc of a song up the charts.

First thing needed is a buzz about the song and the artist. This starts before the record is released. Tidbits are placed in various publications' music columns about the upcoming release or the artist.

Six months in front of the release, the artist may be sent on a bus tour to play for the staff of radio stations. When that record comes out, the label wants name recognition, and a warm and fuzzy personal experience associated with the name. The artist's 'likable' factor becomes part of the music's appeal.

In addition to, or as an alternative, the label might fly key radio personnel, like the program directors and their wives, to a private showcase performance by the artist. The guests are wined and dined, and made to feel important. Hopefully, this will put them in a receptive mood to like the artist and the music. The showcase might be held in Hawaii, or an equally enticing resort locale, with a couple of days of golf and shopping on the schedule.

Keep in mind that every promotion department of every label is doing the same thing. The competition is fierce. War terms can easily be substituted for the sports analogies to describe the battle for the hearts and minds – and airplay – of the radio people.

Country music is as dependent on radio as a mistress's fortunes depend on her sugar daddy. But, as every sugar daddy knows, the mistress is not without assets. Without radio, the artists cannot be heard by the national masses. The labels acquiesce that radio has the power to break an artist out of the pack. Or, put in the graphic terminology of a label executive, radio can choke off a song as surely as an assassin garrottes a newborn. But without the record companies and their artists, radio has no product to play on the air. Radio has the power, claim the record companies. Without radio, we can't have a hit.

No, no, no, counter the radio stations. The record companies determine what is heard on the air. After all, they produce the music.

It goes both ways, as any sugar daddy and his mistress will testify.

'In country music, we have always been manipulated by radio,' Tony Brown once explained. 'Radio manipulates us, we react to them. That's the nature of our genre of music. In pop music, the label's A&R personnel can manipulate what is heard on the radio. The music changes from urban to alternative or to whatever slick boy band. Pop and A&R lead the charge and radio has to follow. When A&R gets sick of a type of music, like boy bands, these young A&R kids bring in a different kind of pop music. Then you start to hear that.'

Bill Macky agrees with Brown that country radio is more important to the labels than any other format. 'Radio is the number one avenue for us to get music out to the listeners and consumers,' he said during our playbook session. 'Rock has a lot of club scenes, a lot of underground things, Internet stuff. But in country, radio is really our pipeline to the consumer, more so than even the video channels.'

Clear Channel Communications, Infinity, Cumulus Broadcasting, and Citadel are the big four country radio networks, with Clear Channel dominating. Clear Channel also controls a large segment of the arena concert business, so it can pull the double whammy play. Artists are put on the stations' playlist and booked into the concert halls controlled by the radio network, if the record labels that make all the right kiss-kiss noises.

'Some of the radio companies do dictate the playlist,' confirmed Macky. 'Some have brand marketing managers that heavily suggest not necessarily what the playlist should be, but what the size of the playlist should be. The Cox chain has a very very tight playlist. A song has to be a top 20 record at least before most of those stations will even consider playing it. There's a lot of speculation about Clear Channel right now that a lot of their brand managers are cutting their playlist down to 25 songs per station. Infinity is still very very autonomous as far as letting each program director make decisions for their own stations. There are a lot of independent individual stations that work autonomously, with each station having its own authority.'

With fewer radio slots and increasing numbers of artists vying for the shrinking radio opportunities, battle plan rather than game plan best describes the promotion departments' exercises. Plus, there has been a contraction and consolidation of the number of country radio stations since 2000. Macky has noticed a new mentality in the industry. Terms like 'cluster management', 'program marketing managers', and 'format captains' may be harbingers of an increasing trend where managers choose the playlist based on business, rather than musical, concerns.

Okay, the record is released. Now the game begins in earnest.

'From day one, you line up your various syndication opportunities to help build your story,' Macky explained.

The story is the selling pitch to gain support from radio stations. It's not about the quality of the music, or the significance of the singer or band. The story is about how the product is behaving on the charts. The story line is taken from the *R&R* indicator chart, which tracks the smaller-market, more musically aggressive stations. These program directors are contacted almost daily for the latest report. If a record is actively upward on the indicator chart, the story is, 'Hey, look at this. We have an artist at 28 on the *Billboard* chart, but he is at 22 on the indicator chart. The record is moving up. Get on the bandwagon and help push. Give us a few additional spins and you'll be called an oracle.'

Then there is this wrinkle: *R&R* has different criteria than *Billboard*. On the *R&R* chart, each station is given a weight, that is points, based upon their audience size. The *R&R* chart is built on points as opposed to spins. KZLA in Los Angeles is the highest weighted station with a record given ten points for every spin.

'At the moment, I have a George Strait album sitting at eight on the *R&R* chart,' Macky said. 'There's a record behind it that has more plays. But because George is being played in bigger markets on more heavily weighted stations, he has more points. I'm winning.'

Syndications are a key element in Macky's strategy. They are package programs, a one-stop time and cost efficient way to get a song played on many stations. 'After Midnight' is a program on hundreds of stations, including 38 reporting stations that make up the chart. That show is heavily courted. Syndication programs are not necessarily the countdown shows – 'and now, number 20 on the charts this week…' – but also personally tailored shows, like 'Lela's Neon Nights' on 24 stations. Lela is courted.

'Myself and my national director will line up a syndication and track it and manufacture,' Macky said. 'I called it manufacture because you're kind of making the spins up that really won't be there. You do that by getting the syndication. Let's say you're a radio station. You have your playlist and it's playing X amount of time. But on Sunday morning from six to ten you carry a syndicated program because you don't have any jocks who will work on air at that time in the morning. So you put on a syndicated program. You're not programming that syndicated program. That comes from a national source that the radio stations get in the mail on disk. Listeners do love countdown shows and syndicated shows, so your records get a lot of spins.'

Then there are specialty shows, like auto racing, a big draw, where music can be placed. A niche song may get spins in that limited market, which helps push the song up the chart. But specialty shows are only a short-gain play. To pick up real yardage, the song must get into regular radio rotation – that is, scheduled to be played so many times per hour or per day. When you've secured that slot, the song is a contender.

In the pre-game planning stages, Macky predicts when his record will reach the top five. He sets goals for each phase, much like a quarterback calling a series of plays to gain ten yards. Ideally, the syndication is lined up for the entire march down the field, with the crescendo culminating for the touchdown push to number one.

But syndication can have a dangerous backspin, especially for a young artist, or for a record's life in the early stages. You place a record in syndication and you get 50 spins this week, Macky explained. The record gains a few notches on the charts. But the following week, a syndicated show may drop the record. You lose those 50 spins and that threatens your chart position. So you have to get those 50 spins from the individual radio programs. Otherwise, you'll lose your bullet because you've lost the spins from the previous week. You really have to learn how to manage and manipulate the syndication to get your record's momentum moving and get it up the charts.

A 'bullet' is a wingding on the chart beside the record's name indicating upward movement over the week. A 'bullet' signifies a 'comer'. To keep the bullet, a song must have at least one more spin from the previous week. To lose the bullet could signal the beginning of the slide off the charts. Game's over. Head for the showers.

Now, the record has been launched and is getting spins. The name of the game becomes how to get more spins. The publicity department, which at most labels is different from the promotion department, goes to work. The appropriate press, such as *Country Music* magazine, is contacted. Would they like an interview? How about a scoop? The story is worth a cover, don't you think? Or the main feature? Or a front of the book piece? How about putting the artist's name in bold face print? Anything in print about the artist and the new album is another yard down the field.

Then there's that $200,000 (£130,000) video to get in circulation. Calls are made to Country Music TV, regional shows, any and all shows that might show the video. If it does make CMTV's schedule, then the pressure is on to get the video in heavy rotation.

With a new act, or B level and C level act, the radio program directors must be convinced to play the record. Charm and salesmanship is ladled on as if icing a cake. With luck, some stations are willing to take a chance on a new artist. Track-proven artists like George Strait, Tim McGraw, or a top five act, is usually added to the playlist. However, well-known singers, such as Lyle Lovett or Merle Haggard or Wynonna Judd, may not be given an automatic spin. Different markets in different regions of the country have different flavors. Macky's national playbook is thick with the variation of variables on the best way to approach each market.

'Sometimes the artist will visit stations,' Macky said. 'Or we'll put the artist on the phone to talk with the station and do a satellite tour. In that scenario, the artist will talk in four hours to maybe 24 to 28 radio stations in five- to seven-minute increments. It's usually morning shows and those shows will usually play the song the artist is plugging. That's an extra play. So if you can do that at 59 stations in a week, you might get 50 spins you didn't have the week before. So you're building momentum for the record.'

The station might ask, or the label offer, that the artist do a 'Listener Appreciation' free show for the station. The artist is sent to the city and performs pro bono. The labels bear the expense to garner goodwill. The station reaps listeners' loyalty for throwing the free concert. This you-scratch-my-back, I'll-scratch-yours can produce extra spins for a record.

Macky has a staff of 60 field representatives who make personal calls on radio stations. He has a secondary marketing manager, a national director of promotion, and six regional directors who cover the nation.

'This is a very personal business,' Macky said. 'It's all about relationships with radio stations. A lot of the relationships depend on face-to-face meetings between the field representative and radio staff. Then you have a much better chance when you come back the next time. My national staff and myself go into places where they need help. They might be getting very close to having a record added and a call from the head of promotion could make the difference.

'Sometimes you go to a program director and say, "Look, I know you don't hear this record but you have to trust me on this. Give me the shot and I'll prove it to you." If you don't have those relationships with the radio stations, you never get off the ground. It's all sales when you get down to it. A sale is the sale that benefits both parties. At the end of day, if you keep giving a guy a stiff record and a stiff after stiff after stiff, he's not going to believe you anymore.'

All right. The machine is rolling, the rails are greased, everybody is on board the team train and you're headed for the playoffs. The record has climbed the charts, presumably because the listening public loves the music. Macky now has his eye on the number one slot. He fires up his staff to get the record on more stations and to push it into heavy rotation. Alternative versions of the record are released to freshen up the song and re-energize the radio guys and the listeners about the record.

'When you get a record in the top ten or five, it's very competitive,' Macky said. 'In order to get into the top ten, you're in heavy rotation with the majority of the radio stations in the nation. You're on every syndicated countdown show. You go for the other shows you can use to help generate spins. Then it gets down to promotion and research how the song is testing locally. The stations will do local call outs to test how a record is doing with their audience. You research how it is doing nationally. There are four major consultants that deal with the majority of the radio stations. What are the consultants doing with the record? There is independent promotion. There are all kinds of things you can do to help generate more airplay at radio stations. Everyone at the top of the charts is doing the same thing. You try to find something nobody else has thought of this week.'

But some times no matter what is done, no matter now many personal phone calls are made, or how many trips are offered or other deals cut, a record can't crack the top spot. An example is George Strait's last single 'Run' and Alan Jackson's 'Where Were You When The World Stopped Turning?'

MCA had released Strait's record three weeks after the World Trade Center terrorist attack. It was a career record for Strait and immediately went screaming up the charts. Then RCA released Jackson's song.

'Alan came up with one of the most amazing songs in the history of music, as far as touching people emotionally,' Macky admitted. 'It literally exploded and went to the top. All of our syndication was lined up to take George into number one early in December. Alan's song came out in mid-November. So all our syndication was in place and we couldn't pull the record and wait for a better time, perhaps when Alan's record cooled off. We did everything we could to get George up there but Alan was so strong. It was such an amazing record. I don't know if anyone could have got around him.

'Alan's song went there because the public wanted to hear it. We had been fighting and fighting for so long to get Alan out of there. That fighting was calling up the radio stations and trying to convince them to play our record. We didn't tell them to drop Alan's record, just to give ours a chance. Our team doesn't do a lot of negative promotion. We finally ran out of gas with George's record.'

He added somewhat ruefully, but with the grace of a coach who lost a close game, 'You may stay at number two and get nearly as many spins as number one, but it doesn't feel successful.'

The average time of a record in the *Billboard* top ten is currently 22 weeks. Macky finds the top a little bit weak at the moment.

'Everything is young or it's not testing so well,' he explained. 'We've seen records stay on top of the charts for five, six weeks because there was nothing strong enough to take the spot, not necessarily because the top record was that strong. When a song has been top for so long, radio thinks that it's time to move it out. We help them think that way, especially if it's not our record. "Hey, come on, give us a shot."'

If an MCA song starts to drop on the charts, before its time or not, Macky has a counter strategy. If a major station drops a song, he's on the phone, the regional directors are calling and the act's manager is calling. On occasion, Macky has gotten the chairman of the company to call a station's program director.

'We'll go to the general manager of a station if we have to,' Macky said. 'We'll to the regional vice-president of programming to get the song back on their playlist. We'll do everything we possibly can to make sure a station doesn't drop a song. If they do, then every effort possible is made to get that song added back on the list. We'll bring up research, sales, any little piece of information we think will give the station confidence to get back on the record. Usually, when a radio station, especially in a major market, drops a record it's because the record is not testing in their call out research. Or, they've played it so much they need to get off it. When you get 500 to 600 spins, you're on thin ice, unless it's an amazing kind of record. With the Gary Allen record, during the 44-week campaign, many stations played that over 1000 times. That's a massive amount of spins for country.

'Again, it's about relationship. If a station is going to drop a record, we should have a week or two weeks advance notice because we've been talking to that radio station. When we see it coming, our regional director, the national director of promotion, the vice president of promotion starts working with the station's program director saying, "What can we do?" Sometimes we'll do a promotion to generate listener excitement about the song. If it's a big artist and a big station, maybe we do a promotion where we'll fly a couple of people from the radio station to see that artist in concert someplace.'

But the bottom line is bad music doesn't sell.

'If it's not a hit record, it doesn't matter how much money you throw into it, it's still not a hit,' Macky conceded. 'It doesn't matter if you dump $5 million [£3.2 million] in promoting a song. We don't release the album until 20 to 24 weeks into the life of a single. We've invested hundreds of thousands of dollars, especially with a new artist, of taking that artist to radio, promoting that artist, taking that artist out to do free shows for listener appreciation shows at stations, advertising, manufacturing of the album, art work, recording costs. We've got this huge investment and we don't know until that record hits the stores what the return might be. That's the gamble.'

Then he admitted, 'In our format, probably more than any other format, sales don't have that big of an impact in the equation of adding records, moving records up, or taking records to the top. A lot of country program directors don't even use sales in their decision-making process. Some do, especially the really good ones. Our format has a history of having a lot of radio records.

'Radio records are records that test very well. They're nice and safe. They are not going to offend anybody. But they're not going to move the meter at the turnstiles for concerts. They don't move product out the door. A lot of money is spent getting a record out and moving it up the charts but, at the end of day, if the album isn't selling, it doesn't do the record companies any good.'

Tony Brown and Tim DuBois went on a tour of radio stations along the East Coast, from New England down to Maryland, that report to *R&R* and *Billboard* charts. They hired a bus, the type used by bands on the road, and set out to introduce themselves and their new label to program directors.

'Being on the road to radio stations, if you're a record executive, is pretty humbling,' Tony said when he returned to town. 'Some of the radio people were nice and some were quite standoffish. We actually got stood up at one place. The person we had come to see went to lunch just before we pulled in. That was to tell us that he held the power. Our whole entertainment industry is about egos. If you can control your ego, then there is no end to what you can do. Like Garth Brooks, George Straits and Reba McEntire, three good examples of people who are huge stars and have ego control.'

Tony and Tim were looking for feedback on what kind of music program directors would play.

'As of late, the music industry has been picking on radio, saying they are one of the reasons for the trouble we're in. We discovered people in radio who feel embarrassed by what radio has become, in that they won't play various records. It used to be you'd have a station in a region, say the Southeast, which would play a record that wasn't played anywhere else. That doesn't happen anymore because Clear Channel, Cumulus, Infinity, Citadel, several chains control most of the airplay. Clear Channel decides what all their stations are playing. It's not a mandate but they suggest the playlist and most stations follow suit.'

That was a known. But what pleasantly surprised Tony were the few program directors who still believe in the old way. They were willing to play a new act not on the company's playlist. 'There are people who play by the corporate book,' Tony said. 'But there are still people at the big stations who are mavericks and still believe that music has power.'

Radio deregulation has been bad for the record business, in Tony's opinion. A result has been fewer people making decisions about what gets played in entire sections of the country. Before deregulation, there might be a maverick jock in Dallas and one in Atlanta and LA who would go out on a limb for an artist they liked and start playing the record. Because they played the record, other DJs started and a buzz got going.

'Now the network stations have a playlist that is delegated by consultants,' Tony said. 'So all the stations are mandated to play the list. If the DJs stray from that, I don't know the consequence. They get fired or chastised. Clear Channel and Infinity chains control so many stations that it rarely happens a maverick jock can break a record.'

Nashville has a DJ, Carl P Mayfield at 103FM, who has stepped out several times. When nobody else on radio would play George Jones's song 'Choices', Mayfield did. He said on the air, 'I'll play George and the rest of you are cowards.' He called George live on air and said, 'George, I'm playing your record. Why do you think everyone else in Nashville and the United States are cowards?' AP picked up story and soon a few other stations added the song. The song became a hit. Alan Jackson was on the CMA Award show during the time the song was being put out. On stage, Alan stopped in the middle of his own song and started playing George's song.

'He was just giving the finger to radio,' Tony said with satisfaction. 'Deregulation has made it really hard for us to break artists. We have to go to the chain stations and pitch to the chains. They dictate our business strategy.'

So, how do you develop a counter-strategy?

'I don't know,' Tony answered. 'If we can figure out a way to put deregulation back in the box, we'd definitely do that. We just deal with it. Basically, we just have to deal with the chains. The majority of the big stations are in the chains. That's not only in country but in pop, too. We can put artists on the road doing shows to build a ground swell but it's expensive. But not all artists are good entertainers in the beginning. They can go out there and not make an impact. Garth was a monster on the road. That propelled his fame. If an artist does a good job on the road, that helps. But you got to get on the radio.

'Another thing about deregulation. Why would a Clear Channel AC (adult contemporary) station want to play a country song that was crossing over. They want country fans to stay with their country station so it remains high in the ratings. So Clear Channel wants their AC station to sound a bit different. If they start crossing everything over, then their country station doesn't have a sound and their AC station doesn't have a sound.

'In the old days, if you had a crossover record, you'd go to the AC stations. If they thought it was a hit, they'd play it. They wanted the country listeners too. Deregulation has messed that up. It has made the promoting of records a harder thing to do. This doesn't affect the songs you record but it does affect your ability to get it on the radio.'

There is an alternative to the commercial radio networks. The Americana network is an alternative loose affiliation of small stations. Americana music is a term coined for the country music that the mainstream country national labels and country radio left behind in lieu of the more pop-sounding country, according to Al Moss, a music promoter and a founding member of the Americana network. He has been on the board of directors since its beginning in 1995.

The Americana Music Association was created in 2000 by a group of 32 people interested in the music ignored by mainstream labels and stations. Independent labels, such as John Prine's Oh Boy and Rounder Records, promoters, publicists, and booking agents formed the trade association. The intent was to promote the music by pooling their collective resources and energies. The goal is to build a platform to give the artists a better chance, strength in numbers sort of thing, Moss said.

The Americana umbrella covers a broad spectrum of music. The range can be bluegrass, a folkie singer/songwriter, an edge band that is rock but with country elements, a real hardcore honky-tonk, a Western swing band, or James Taylor. The Others are favorite artists on Americana.

'We've taken those radio stations around the country that play varying degrees of that kind of music,' Moss said. 'We are pulling them together and creating a trade chart to reflect what is being done in that kind of music. There are a lot of non-commercial stations that play the music. Some have a specialty show for bluegrass or old-time country. Some are National Public Radio-type stations. Some Triple A rock stations incorporate certain of the Americana artists that lean toward the rock spectrum, such as Lucinda Williams or Steve Earle or Delbert McClinton. Then there are some country stations that play mainstream pop country but will incorporate some other elements of more traditional country.'

For producers and label executives like Tony Brown, Americana is a place to promote Rodney Crowell and Jimmie Dale Gilmore. 'Where else we going to park them?' asked Tony Brown. 'It doesn't look like the Americana network is going to get much bigger. There are about 200 Americana stations and 2000 country stations. The 200 stations, they are scattered around, their signal is not strong and they are probably the least popular station with the advertisers. But they are playing good music. I don't know if Americana will succeed. I wish it would.'

One record executive quipped, 'Americana has more artists than it does listeners.'

23 Personal Songwriter

I spent an afternoon and evening in the Greyhound bus station, a couple of blocks up the hill from the Country Music Hall of Fame. I wanted to see the raw meat in its natural state before being reshaped into wholesome, healthy and tasty-looking specimens wrapped in a bright package with decals telling me how new, improved and better it was after being processed. I was feeling cynical, now that I better understood how country music, and the country star, is manufactured.

At least one, often two or three, people got off the long-distance buses carrying a guitar case. A young hunk with steer-wrestling shoulders and a freshly starched Western shirt looked straight off the ranch. He tipped his cowboy hat goodbye to a fellow female passenger, shouldered his duffle bag and strode out onto the street, his guitar case held as if a vanquishing sword.

There was a young woman in a full-length skirt, the kind worn by hippie flower children, with long flowing brunette hair. She had a mandolin case in one hand and her suitcase the other. She tried to look confident as she asked directions to the YWCA, or any Christian group that might take her in.

Off a late bus stumbled a dust devil in black, his face smeared with a three-day beard. His wore an unsuccessful pompadour that stood up and bent over simultaneously. It reminded me of a top-heavy sunflower, perhaps because the dye job was telephone directory yellow. His guitar case was a gnawed dog bone buried and dug up one too many times. He glanced around like, 'If you've seen one bus station, you've seen them all.' He saw me watching and ambled over.

'Where's Tootsie's? I need a drink.' He wasn't Texan, maybe east Oklahoma or southern Nebraska or Brooklyn by way of Possum Springs. The country nasal twang is so well traveled that it's hard to pin down. Listen to foreigners sing country and you'd swear they're from Yonder Mountain, KY. Like Mari, the young Japanese singer who recently cut her album *Hear My Heart*, produced by Charlie McCoy. McCoy is a Nashville big-timer who has worked with Dylan and Baez and hundreds of other music greats, so Mari must have the chops. Wood Newton, who co-penned the hit 'Riding With Private Malone', wrote a song on her album. Will she be one of the primary heroes riding out of the rising sun to boost country's sagging sales? Or this rag of a fellow, trail weary and thirsty, standing in front of me?

'Come on,' I said. I hadn't seen Amy and Hank and Our Willie for several days and wondered what they had been up to. I thought about telling this fellow all I had learned about how to be a star in Nashville. And offer to buy him a ticket, right then and there, out of town. But he looked like a man fond of gathering experiences, so let him have his Nashville story.

When we got to Tootsie's, he stopped on the sidewalk and leaned on the small end of his guitar case. Music came out the open door. The male singer had good sound – the keening of Marty Brown, George Jones on a soulful day, and the steady reassurance of Johnny Cash. My bus-station buddy cocked an ear and listened. Then he straightened up, took a deep breath, and said to himself, 'I do better,' and walked into the bar. My three pals weren't at their usual table, which wasn't surprising. They prefer the afternoons, when Tootsie's isn't full of tourists. I thought about rejoining my nameless friend and coaxing out his story, so I could write some jaded commentary on disillusionment, art and commerce, the lamb, and the high priest. But trudging down that road was like walking a mile at high noon on a hot day with a load of manure on my back. There was a better way to spend my time. I decided to call in the invitation to visit Gretchen Peters at her home.

As a songwriter of status, Gretchen doesn't need to package herself. She doesn't wear logos and slogans or practice bending with the wind. She doesn't look at country music from an office window. I wanted her to tell me how country music could still be a drink of cool water, appreciated simply for the good taste.

Gretchen and her husband Green and their teenage daughter live on the outskirts of Hendersonville, a 30-minute drive from Nashville. Many country stars live around Hendersonville's large lake, where they keep cabin cruisers. Gretchen and Green live in the opposite direction, on the wooded side of Hendersonville. Their house, hard to find if you don't look close, is tucked down a hillside of tall trees.

Gretchen's home studio is a free-standing structure next to the main house. The compact, self-contained studio/music workroom is airy and light, with big windows to let in the green of the trees. Two keyboards were placed so she could play both, one with each hand. Several hand mics and mic stands stood at the ready. Two guitars were in the upright position. A squeezebox lay on the table. Headphones were casually draped as if waiting for an interpreted conversation to resume. A computer with software for working on songs sat on the desk.

In a corner stood an adult-sized stuffed Bugs Bunny holding an outsized purple crayon, a gift from Warner Brothers Records for her number one hit 'Secret of Life'. Gretchen's company, which holds the rights to her music, is Purple Crayon, taken from 'Harold and the Purple Crayon'. On a wall, next to a full-sized cut-out of Elvis, were her gold records and other discs celebrating her songs with Bonnie Raitt and Martina McBride.

'I call this room the Chamber of Horrors,' she said with a laugh as we settled on the settee. 'When I come in here, I'm all alone with my mind, and your mind can be your enemy. When I'm in here, it's all about shutting down the mind. Most of the stuff your brain tells you is wrong and not useful to a writer. The mind is a hindrance. That's a huge part of the battle for me, shutting down the intellectual mind so the creative mind can have its say.'

Paul Simon, one of the more cerebral songwriters, wrote a song about over-thinking called 'I Think Too Much'. When he finished one version, he couldn't stop thinking about it, so he wrote another song about the problem of thinking too much. Many artists resort to physical activities to avoid over-thinking a creative problem. Gretchen likes to garden to relieve the cerebral pressure. Sewing is another non-cerebral joy in her life.

'Writing is never going to be easy.' Gretchen sounded like a person looking at a 300-bench press. Even though the weights are lifted every day, 300lb (140kg) is always 300lb and a strain to heft. 'In fact, writing may get harder,' she said, not sure whether to be amused by her insight or not. 'For me, it has gotten more difficult. It's like approaching infinity. It may seem that you get closer to whatever you're after, but it always remains far away. That's the fascination. When I sew something, it's done. I hold it in my hand and it's concrete. It's such a non-intellectual activity. It's really a relief,' she said with a laugh.

The idea of short-circuiting the creative process, of devising a methodology and manual to songwriting, offends her. That's flabby artistry. That kind of thinking is one symptom of Music Row's illness, in her opinion.

'I hate this idea in songwriting workshops that you can teach the creative process, that you can intellectualize and analyze the creative process to the extent you give instructions. There are these workshops all over Nashville, everywhere actually. Put a different rhythm scheme in the chorus than in the verse; lift up the chorus melodically by at least a third to make it really pop. I instinctively know that stuff but I could have never told you how I do it. The idea that you can train someone to do it must suck the life out of his or her creative process.'

There are those who accused Alan Jackson of penning a knee-jerk, flag-waving country song to cash in on easy sentiments with his hit, 'Where Were You When', about the September 11 attack on the World Trade Center. The song is so well crafted that it appears formulaic, the way a novel may appear formulaic because the reader is taken effortlessly from point A to point B. Gretchen sees Jackson's song through the well-tuned ears of a fellow songwriter.

'I think that song was a completely authentic honest reaction of who Alan is,' she said. 'He wrote an artistically successful song because it was so honest and real. That's who he is. That's why people responded to it. I think people who really don't know about country music have this one-dimensional idea that it's all about Mama, trucks, flag waving, I'll-kick-your-ass-if-you-don't-get-off-my-land kind of thing. There is so much more, so much longing and regret and ambiguity and darkness.

There is a lot of shading that people don't understand unless they dig a little deeper. If your stereotypical view of country is "Oke from Muskogee", then go listen to Kris Kristofferson and some of Tom T Hall's Vietnam era songs. Or the songs of John Prine. Go listen to his "Your Flag Decal Won't Get You Into Heaven Anymore".'

Dolly Parton is another artistic reference for Gretchen. Parton is a skilled songwriter and a poet of an authentic culture.

'Her words come from some place very deep and she doesn't think about it too much,' Gretchen said in admiration. 'A lot of my favorite country songwriters are that way. When I heard Dolly's "Down from Dover" about a girl who is pregnant and unmarried, it was like lightning struck. It's a very dark and haunting mountain ballad. This I sink my teeth into, this is really some stuff. It's part of a huge tradition that has been, unfortunately, discouraged by radio. God forbid, we can't sell tyres if you're going to be singing about death. Nobody wants to hear that.

'I've always been in the camp that music is cathartic. It's much more compelling and interesting if you talk about the dark things. Happy music that's happy all the time is very oppressive. If you don't feel happy, and that's all the music you're hearing, you can feel like the loneliest person in the world. Whereas, if you can hear something about someone in pain, and you are also in pain, it's like, to paraphrase CS Lewis, "We read to know that we're not alone." I think of music in the same way. If you're in a place that's dark, sometimes the most heartening thing you can hear is music that says you're not alone. I love the gothic side, the killing side. I love that. The death songs are the best. That's my place. The Irish have the same sense of doom.'

Gretchen's music has many of the traditional themes of country music – independence, freedom of the road, loneliness, spirituality, home, and self-reliance. But she doesn't simply repackage the old chestnuts, the way it's done in the song factories on Music Row. Those songs always sound the same, despite the bright new ribbon of pop, or the wrapping of a fad that faded two years past.

Gretchen is too singular to be of the Others, but she comes from that sensibility. She thinks that country music is a very American music, arguably more so than jazz. The national psyche is more clearly heard in country music because the plain language is more accessible. Country is not as contorted or self-referential as much of punk rock or as clubby as hip-hop. Country music, in the hands of Gretchen and a select few other songwriters, applies the traditional themes of country music to the present day without the bromides often used in one-dimensional writing.

'We, as a people, are as lonely and isolated now as the old cowboy songs suggested, but in a totally different way,' Gretchen observed. She writes of the individual's longing for the connection to humanity, with all the attending sorrow and joy. She writes without the nostalgia of longing.

The open road, the going for the hell of it, the freedom of leaving, the quest for traveling is another big theme for Gretchen, as it always has been in country music.

'I yearn to get in a car and go somewhere,' she said. 'That's an expression of the idea of freedom for Americans, hitting the road. That's part of our psyche, part of our identity, the going to some place. Because we have such a big, wide-open country, we think nothing of driving a couple of hours to get someplace. It's a very American idea to get in your car and drive across the desert just for the hell of it. The mother road, Kerouac on the road, *The Grapes of Wrath*, all that is in our psyche. Americans internalized that so much that songs about it resonate, even if the people never drive further than the mall. We feel that it is our right, as part of our identity as Americans, to drive not only into the horizon, but over the horizon.'

If you've ever traveled the American plains that stretch from the Mississippi Valley to the Rocky Mountains, that swath of grasslands from the Canadian border to the Mexican border, you'll understand the visceral thrill of the American road experience. The horizon is so huge you can literally see the curve of the earth. When you start west out of the wooded hills of the Mississippi Valley, you drive uphill for 900 miles (1,440km) on an incline that tilts you ever so slightly back in the car seat, as if in a plane lifting off. There is nothing but space in front of you and around you. Everywhere you look there is a great empty space of land and sky. You have truly left the East. The country physically changes and people's attitudes adjust to that change. There is an 'Omigod' exhilaration of what can be created in all that space, and, at the same time, a humbling fear of what the forces of that space can do to you. So people try to conquer, to control, to make that space their tame backyard. Otherwise, they'd curl up in a fetal position, afraid for their life. That choice, strive or die, has always been part of the American experience. All the subtle emotional and psychological shadings in that choice are expressed in well-written country music.

Leaving implies there is a place to leave and in country music that place is usually the home. In the songs, home is often viewed from a distance. It's viewed nostalgically and with fond memories. The romanticization of home and family, and what all that means, is a constant theme in country music.

'I bristle at the whole idea that country music is about family values in the Republican Party sense,' Gretchen said. 'In country, the home songs are about longing. The people are in some way down-and-out. They've moved to a big city and are lonely. That's a human thing. The songs are sung to people who have seen both sides. It's about family and home being good. Not being home is an emotional negative. But it's not black and white.

'As a songwriter, leaving home is a device used to underscore a person's isolation and loneliness. The protagonists in Kris Kristofferson's songs aren't the guys who are going to settle down. They are not going to stay in the same town for the rest of their lives. He's a guy who can't and won't and didn't, but has regrets about it. He has a feeling of isolation and loneliness.'

Religion in country music has always been more Old Testament than New Age. But that attitude is only one wire in the American piano of spiritual view values. Country music still plucks that wire but Gretchen, like Leonard Cohen, is more interested in the subtleties of the full chord. Gretchen is a literary writer, an elegant stylist comparable to Leonard Cohen. 'He's a master, number one on my list,' she said. 'There are a lot of his songs that I would give anything to have written. Just to have some of the ideas.'

Cohen once lived in Nashville and worked as a country songwriter. His song 'Closing Time' gives a feel for his countryside. In his song 'Tower of Song', Cohen claims to have talked to Hank Williams about the trials of being a songwriter, but Hank didn't answer.

'I totally understand "Closing Time",' Gretchen said. 'I played bars in Boulder for ten years, starting in high school before I was legally old enough to be in such places. When you're playing crummy bars, your only friends sometimes are the waitresses and maybe the bartender. The owner is trying not to pay you. The audience could not give a shit. The waitresses mothered me and watched out for me so nothing bad would happen. I remember one waitress who was getting older and waitressing was all she had done and would do for her working life. It's very hard work. She was very proud and would never admit defeat or admit that she had chosen the wrong life. There was a proudness about her. She had a little disdain for a woman just married who sat back and was a housewife. That's who that woman in "Closing Time" was.'

Cohen's 'Joan of Arc' is Gretchen's favorite song 'ever. The imagery in the song is so powerful it takes your breath away,' she said. 'I use a lot of religious imagery in my songs. I find it incredibly evocative. If you are ever short of song titles, go to the Bible. The metaphoric content of religion stirs us in a very deep way. I'm not particularly religious, but I understand the power of the words and images. I know that I have a soul. I can feel it like I can feel my foot is there. Can you really separate the soul from whatever clothes the religion wears? That's my problem with organized religion. It's a construct made to define something that is indefinable.'

Her song 'Like Water Into Wine' has the line, 'we are miracles of science, we are accidents divine/we're just water, baby, just water into wine.'

Gretchen grew up in a left-wing liberal agnostic family. The only religion in the house was the bemoaning of crimes committed in the name of religion. But she understands the heart emotion of religion, and that is in her songs. 'If you're really a serious writer, you have to deal with the spirituality or religion or whatever you want to call it,' she said. 'You can't not because it's about the spirit, the soul, one of the big questions. And religion is part of our common mythology as being a basically Judo-Christian people. It's part of our background. Just like gospel music is part of the background of country music. It's a foundation, one of the building blocks, one of the underlying blocks of country music.

'For me, there are five cornerstones of country music; mountain music, bluegrass, cowboy songs, gospel, and the Jimmie Rodgers common-man kind of thing. In the South, white gospel and black gospel aren't that separate in a fundamental sense. If you grew up in the rural South, you heard both. Blacks and whites knew each other's music. That's is part of what makes country music a Southern art form.'

Gretchen is a Northerner who came to the South because she fell in love with the place and its music. 'It's not my sibling, it's my love,' she freely confessed. 'There is a Southern sense of humor, a Southern mentality. Part of the Southern mentality is having lost the Civil War. I think that a group of people who had lost a war is forever changed. That event is forever imprinted on the psyche of that people. There was a deep and widespread physical poverty, for the blacks and the whites, in the South after the Civil War.

'Think of the sadness and poignancy that comes out of a culture that has lost something great, something large. A lot of Southern literature and music comes from that deep sense, I think. The writers and songwriters say, "This is part of me. Here's the story. This is what happened, let me tell you." That's part of country music, a mental and emotional place it grew out of.'

Back in Nashville, Alice Randall agreed to talk with me about country music as a Southern art form. She is a Detroit native, a Harvard graduate, an intellectual in the high sense who became interested in country music 'through the early American metaphysical poetry and the English poet John Donne. That poetry, and country music, presented metaphysical strategies in the modern world,' she explained over coffee at Fidos.

She has had 20 country songs recorded, including the hit 'Xs and Os'. She wrote, with Mark O'Conner, videos for Reba McEntire. But she is best known as the author of *The Wind Done Gone*, a novel that tells the *Gone With the Wind* story from a female house slave's point of view.

The executors of Margaret Mitchell's estate, the author of *Gone With the Wind*, sued Randall and her publisher, Houghton Mifflin, to stop publication. Lawyers for the Mitchell trust argued that Randall appropriated characters, scene, setting, plot, and some passages straight from *Gone With the Wind*. Randall countered that *The Wind Done Gone* was a parody protected by the First Amendment.

But the novel was far more than a knock-off parody. 'It's a parody in the sense that the cakewalk dance was the black slaves' parody of the white's quadrille,' Alice explained as we sipped coffee. 'The whites thought that the blacks were doing the dance poorly, but they missed the parody. If you read my book the same way, you'll miss the parody. You'll also miss the deeper oblique references to Brontë, Wadsworth, and other literary references, including *Gulliver's Travels*.'

The book presents a view from the oppressed, the underclass, in which Randall includes women today. 'I was scheduled to give a reading at a community center in a small town deep in rural Mississippi,' she said. 'It was a Saturday and the weather was poor. I thought no one would come. But a large number of women arrived, white and black, to tell me how much the book meant in their lives. To them, it wasn't the retelling of a story set in the Civil War. It was about the class issues they faced daily.'

The Civil War, from the Southern perspective, was all about the rights of privileged people, Randall pointed out. The vast majority of Southern whites did not own slaves. The Civil War was fought acting out the ideas and issues of privileged white Southerners in conflict with privileged white Northerners. Steve Earle has a song about a Confederate soldier who says, 'I don't know what I'm fighting for/I ain't never owned a slave.' It was not his war, not his fight.

'Country music is class music,' Randall said. 'It is the music of the Southern white underclass. It is not the music of the aristocrat class. Roots country came out of poverty. The common connection of the black and white underclass is poverty. My favorite country song is Merle Haggard's 'Mama's Hungry Eyes'. It's about a father and mother who cannot provide adequately for their children. The mother has negative feelings about the father who cannot provide for the family. That is very hard class music about poverty and the destruction of interpersonal relationships by poverty, which is very much a country music subject.'

The Wind Done Gone, published in 2001, was on the best-seller list for weeks. After a year of legal battles, an out-of-court settlement was reached in which Houghton Mifflin agreed to make an unspecified contribution to Morehouse College, a historically black school in Atlanta. In return, Mitchell's estate agreed to stop trying to block sales of Randall's book.

'The language of the book was how to express the Southern common themes of love and betrayal and loneliness and being denied,' Alice said. 'Those are the themes in country music. I think that country music definitely is a Southern art form. But I see fundamental country music being essentially Afro-Celtic, where we have black blues, gospel, and Celtic, those Appalachian story songs, ballads. It's that combination. Even bluegrass has a tremendous black influence. The banjo is an African instrument. The place where the African-Scottish-English-Irish influences intersect is the South and in the South's root country music.'

The African influence eventually emerged as rock 'n' roll. Rock 'n' roll was an evolution of country music. Boogie-woogie, honky-tonk, heavy metal, and punk rock derived from the Afro-Celtic root of rock 'n' roll. Chuck Berry, Little Richard, and Elvis Presley understood themselves as country artists. People like Mick Jagger were more in touch with the blues aspect of it than the Celtic aspect. However, Keith Richards and Ringo Starr are very much into the Celtic side. The Beatles were not particularly a country act, but in the sense of the Afro-Celtic-English, they're in that same genre and therefore part of the continuum.

'Country music is very much survival music,' Randall pointed out. 'The Dixie Chicks' song "Goodbye, Earl" is true survival music. I love that song. It's a truly important modern song about the two women who kill the abusive Earl and wrap him up in a rug and drop him off. Earl had to die. These women were cooking food for him, canning food, and selling it at a roadside stand. This is very country and in these countrywomen are the underclass. They don't have a lot of options, even when dealing with violent men. So it is true survival music. They had to do something and what they ended up doing was very desperate. Killing was something that a privileged person would never do. For the most part, that kind of voice and message has been washed out of top 40 country radio.

'But, on the other hand, Johnny Cash's song from Fulsom Prison says, "I shot a man in Reno just to watch him die." This is music of the really dispossessed outlaw, the underclass person who is not involved with the system. The prison experience is part of country. That experience is part of rap. In country and rap, it's not so much a romanticism but fear of prison, fear of lack of freedom, a fear of entrapment. In country, lack of freedom is equated with hell.'

The relationship between hip-hop and country interests Randall. Hip-hop and country are, for her, storytelling forms, a literary form, sung poetry.

'Hip-hop and country have a common theme of violence,' she said. 'One of the main themes of earlier country, even in the '50s and '60s, was violence and murder. Violence is a theme in hip-hop/rap, particularly gangsta hip-hop, which is about the underclass fighting out of poverty.

'Hip-hop and country are much further out than punk ever was. Punk comes from a suburban non-tribe life. Most of punk comes from suburban boredom and self-inflicted hate. If you are in desperate circumstances, you don't have time to be bored. Punk is about time and abstract metaphysics as opposed to narrative or theology.'

How is country expressing urban poverty, which is a theme in hip-hop and rap?

'That's very interesting. I don't think the country music heard on country radio really addresses the issue of urban poverty. It should be an issue of country music. Rural poverty was an issue in early country, like Merle Haggard, or even Dolly Parton. A lot of what we hear on country radio is not country music. Country needs to become more psychological. The country experiences of our lives are psychological now, not rural. Fundamentally, country music is about tough times. The under-the-radar country is talking about tough times. It is direct and in-your-face.

'I am really interested in country music about inner life, which I think country does so well. Country music is perhaps the only aesthetic form that takes under consideration that some people don't evolve or progress. There is no change but death. There is the song about the man saying, "I'll love you until I die." And the hook is that he stopped loving her on the day he died. That is the profundity and irony of the song. It's beautifully ironic.'

24 Company Songwriter

Nine out of ten employed songwriters in Nashville work for a publishing company. They clock in regular hours at an office building. A typical company songwriter's cubicle has a keyboard, computer, appropriate software to create music, and perhaps a mini-soundboard. Sometimes there is a real guitar, but it's not necessary. The floors on which they work are unusually quiet for a music-making place. People do not stand around a piano brainstorming chords and choruses. There is no piano.

When I visited with Troy Tomlinson, senior vice-president of Acuff-Rose Music Publishing, I had the same reaction Our Willie did to Music Row – it's awfully silent and somber and without the crackle of festival one associates with music. Acuff-Rose is one of the founding firms of the Nashville country music industry. Acuff is Roy Acuff, a sanctified name in country music. Known as 'The King of Country Music', he was one of the most popular stars of the genre during his prime in the 1930s and '40s. He was so popular that he made several tries to be elected governor of Tennessee. He won the Republican primary in 1948 but lost the general election. He was the first country performer to take his show overseas to entertain the troops. In 1949, he took his show to Berlin during the airlift face off. He performed for the troops in Korea during the Korean War and in the 1970s he entertained the troops in Vietnam.

His publishing partner, Fred Rose, was never a country performer, but he was a major influence on country music. He taught pop to country. When he settled in Nashville in 1942, he showed country songwriters how to use Tin Pan Alley techniques in their music. And he introduced country into the pop world. He convinced Tony Bennett, the crooner who regarded himself as a jazz singer, and Patti Page, who sang swing with big bands and pop ballads, to record country songs.

Rose was a self-taught musician who survived a hard-knocks childhood worthy of a country song. He was born in 1898 in Evansville, Indiana into a dysfunctional family. Plus, he had the handicap of being seriously cross-eyed. His Scottish-Irish father and his Texan mother lived in a union of discord. Rose and his younger sister, Effie Mae, were sent as children to the mother's relatives in St Louis. When his mother died in 1904, the father dropped out the children's lives. Rose's eye problems made reading difficult so he stopped going to grammar school by the fourth grade. He spent his days around taverns making money running errands and shining shoes. By the age of ten, he was singing for tips in saloons and mastering the piano by listening to barrelhouse musicians.

He went to Chicago in his teens and played the gin joints, jazz clubs, bawdy houses, anywhere that had a piano and would pay him. He worked vaudeville (his first act was as a singing newsboy) and minstrel shows. He learned to drink. His was not a brawler but he got along in a rough-and-tumble world of blues singers, bar-rooms and after-hours joints. All the while he worked on his music. He recorded piano rolls for the Brunswick label and performed on the Chicago stations KYW and WBBM.

He was a well-regarded jazz pianist and played with the Paul Whitman and Fata Waller orchestras. But songwriting was his forte. Joe 'King' Oliver recorded Rose's 'Sweet Mama, Papa's Getting Mad' in a popular jazz style. Sophie Tucker made his 'Red Hot Mama' her signature song. Crooner Gene Austin scored a top-selling hit with Rose's 'Deed I Do'. Rose was still in his early 20s.

By his mid-30s, Rose was in demand enough to be traveling between Chicago, New York, and Nashville, the hometown of his future wife. Unfortunately, he was nearly blind from untreatable cataracts.

In 1938, he moved to Hollywood, where he spent four years writing a string of hits for Gene Autry and his cowboy movies, like *Gold Mine in the Sky*. He had known Autry from WLS in Chicago. He penned the popular Western song 'We'll Rest at the End of the Trail'. Autry, Roy Rogers, and other cowboy movie musicians regularly went to Rose's house for Sunday brunch because his wife was such a good cook. They brought their guitars and indulged in jazz jam sessions. Autry and the others modeled themselves on pop vocalists, singing distinctly and from the chest, and shunned hillbilly twang. Rose used pop structures and conventional love themes for many of his Western songs to accommodate their styles.

His wife grew homesick for Nashville and campaigned for a relocation. Rose's good friends from Chicago, the Vagabonds, a popular quartet on the Grand Ole Opry, threw their support behind the Nashville move. In 1942, Rose made the move and the Vagabonds gave him a crash course in country. He quickly figured out how pop vocal stylings and marketing could sell country music. He wrote country music under several pen names, including Bart Dawson and Floyd Jenkins, in the belief that country-sounding names would give credibility to his songs. Acuff recorded Rose's (under the name Floyd Jenkins) 'I'll Reap My Harvest In Heaven.' The newly minted song sounded like it came out of a 100-year-old Protestant hymnal.

Rose wrote 'Blues Eyes Crying in the Rain', a hit for Willie Nelson. Ray Charles went to number one with Rose's 'Take These Chains From My Heart'. Other well-known Fred Rose country songs include 'Deep Water' and 'Low and Lonely'.

Acuff, as good a businessman as he was a musician, made a good living as a performer. But he knew that publishing was the gold mine. He offered to put up $25,000 (£16,000) in seed money if Rose would become his partner. In 1942–3, Acuff-Rose Publications opened its doors for business. Acuff-Rose acquired a vast number of copyrights, including those of Hank Williams Sr and Ernest Tubb.

Rose talked the composers Pee Wee King and Redd Stewart into selling the copyright to their song 'Tennessee Waltz'. The song became Tennessee's official state song and generated millions of dollars in airplay and sales revenues.

King was born Julius Frank Anthony Kucynski, son of a violinist, in Milwaukee, Wisconsin, in 1914. He was performing at the age of 14 and went to Louisville, Kentucky, where he got a job on the Gene Autry radio show. In 1934, he changed his name to Frankie King and the following year formed his band, the Golden West Cowboys. One of the people he hired was Redd Stewart, a Kentucky native.

One night driving back from a gig, they heard Bill Monroe's popular 'Kentucky Waltz' on the radio. If Kentucky can have a waltz, why not Tennessee? To pass the hours, they reworked the song, substituting Tennessee for Kentucky, and set it to King's theme song, 'No Name Waltz'. Stewart, singing the lead vocals, recorded the 'Tennessee Waltz' in 1948. It stayed on the charts for 30 weeks. Rose knew a keeper when he heard one. In the '50s, he convinced Patti Page to record the song. Her version sold 4.8 million copies, earning Acuff-Rose $330,000 (£214,000). Rose had purchased the copyright for a reported $50 (£30).

Rose died in 1954 but his son Wesley, an accountant, brought to Nashville by his father to straighten out the company's books, assumed a leadership role. Gaylord Entertainment bought the company and recently put it on the block as Gaylord consolidated its core business.

Acuff-Rose established a way of doing business that was unique to country music's needs. They signed writers and developed them, as well as developing recording artists. This arrangement remains the basic model in Nashville song publishing. Limited partnerships are formed – performing rights organizations (PROs such as BMI, ASCAP and SESAC), production, and record companies. The business of the publisher and the record label has become so intertwined that the right hand and the left feed the common mouth.

When I spoke with Troy Tomlinson in his office, he went into detail on how the system works. He was an affable young man who started in the business as a song plugger. Now he helps to determine a singer's or songwriter's career.

'We sign a writer and set them up with a co-writer, one of our other guys, building relationships,' he said. 'But, sooner or later, you have to depend on the writer to bring you in something where you didn't set up a co-write, something you didn't plan on.'

Acuff-Rose maintains about 20 staff writers. Some, Skip Ewing and Dean Dillon and Donny Kees, do nothing but write songs for a living. Then there are the developmental artists, the 'start-up folks'. They are given an advance against future earnings so they can focus on writing and not have to work at McDonald's to make ends meet. The money is not a salary but a loan. They are like sharecroppers funded by the landowner until the crops come in, and then it's payback time. Jennifer Hanson, a new young artist scheduled to release her first album on Capital, and Clint Daniels, another new artist coming out on Sony, are part of the Acuff-Rose farm team.

And there are the veteran writer/artists like Rodney Crowell and Kenny Chesney.

'With Kenny, he was parking cars over at a restaurant on Music Row,' Tomlinson said. 'Clay Bradley, who worked at BMI, a friend of mine, called me up. "Hey, there's this young man. He's parking cars but he's a good little writer. Why don't you meet with him?" We met with Kenny and loved him. Two days later, we offered him a publishing deal. We believed that whether we got him a record deal or not, we could get his songs recorded by other people. But it became obvious that he was the artist after going into the studio with him twice making demos to pitch to other people. He first went to a small rather independent label, Capricorn, which closed their country division after a year or so. But he had gained enough exposure through that label that BNA, an RCA label, signed him.

'In that case, we had an active hand in the Capricorn and the BNA deals. It is to our advantage to get one of our songwriters a record deal. When they cut some of their own songs, it makes my job easier in placing the songs we own. Sometimes we see that our writers have artist potential and I'll call up a label head, say Joe Galante at RCA, and say, "Joe, we got this new writer/artist over here and you ought hear him or her. They're pretty cool."

'He'll go, "Bring them on by." If he loves them, he'll sign them. They'll write for me, record for him, and go out and get themselves a manager, agent, etc.'

That's how the business works. How much independence within this system does the songwriter have to write what they want?

'We do encourage the songwriters to write things that give them greater odds of getting recorded,' Tomlinson answered. 'It doesn't do any of us any good to write a bunch of artsy things that never get recorded. We, as pluggers and publisher, can objectively sit back and say, "What seems to be the trend? What seem to be the hits? Is there a common denominator?"

'It doesn't take long looking at the charts to realize a couple of basic things. First of all, the majority of number one records are mid- to uptempo. The majority of the biggest songs in country music are ballads. A lot of writers have a reputation for liking to write ballads. But to have radio success, which is where the real money is, they need songs that go to the top of the charts, which are mid- to uptempo songs. There are ballads that go to number one but if you look at a five-year period, you see that the vast majority of the top five songs tend to be mid- to uptempo.

'So we encourage our writers by giving them information like that. If a writer determines that he or she is going to write what they write no matter what the odds, we support that and try to get them cut. But if you walk by our board back there where the writers work, there's probably a sign in huge magic maker letters that says, "UPTEMPO PLEASE."'

Uptempo songs are happy songs.

Are the writers given direction, useful information, on what subject matter best suits the market?

'There is subject matter that is best avoided but that changes with the times,' Tomlinson replied. 'We just had a song recorded that touches on an abortion issue. We've had two songs recorded in the past few years on abortion. To me, the jury is still out on that whether it will be accepted. Things like drinking go in vogue and out of vogue. Right now, you could probably get away with a little drinking, whereas not even five years ago it didn't seem like we could. There are certain subjects that tend not to be as palatable.

'If you are an artist desiring to say what you want to say, and make the music you want to make, and commercial success is not how you grade success, you can say anything you want to say. If you're an artist who says, "I want to touch a million peoples' lives. I want to get into the homes of a million plus people," then there are obviously things that just don't get said. But there is no censorship. The song "Little Girl" by John Michael Montgomory is about a child in an abusive home who is eventually rescued into a loving family. Kenny Chesney's song, "That's Why I'm Here", is about an alcoholic.'

However, it is tactfully acknowledged that songs about homosexual lifestyles do not get airplay on mainstream country radio. So what's the point of writing them? Gretchen Peters has a song called 'Eddie's First Wife'. Clueless Eddie comes home one day and his wife tells him that she's found the love of her life, and 'she's a good old-fashion girl'. It's a fun, humorous song that would never come out of Acuff-Rose or any other Music Row publishing house. Other hard social issues – drug use, drive-by shooting, an economic system that increasingly creates a division between the haves and have-nots in terms of real power – are not subjects of Music Row songs.

'There are people like Aaron Tippin who are very serious that their music reflects the people they know who are out there in mid-America,' Tomlinson pointed out. 'He is very serious about making music for people like him, an American Southern boy. He has a personal mandate to make music that reflects that. Other folks feel like they can make music that is positive, uplifting, fun, puts a smile on your face and whether or not one calls that sugar coated really doesn't matter to that artist.

'Those artists say, "If a guy gets in his truck and his girlfriend is on his back and his job's not going well, and he gets in that truck that afternoon after work at 3.30 from a factory, and he's tired and worn out and dirty and he has to go home to this relationship that's not happenin', if it means that he turns on the radio and my song plays and it's a lighthearted fun song that's not going to change the world but it makes that ol' boy smile, then I have written America's music. At that moment, for that man, I was what he needed."'

Let's say an artist gets a hit. How is the money divvied up between the record company, the publisher, and the artist?

'On a million units sold by an artist, the amount the label is going to pay the writer and publisher on one song is approximately $80,000 [£52,000],' Tomlinson answered. 'That's 8 cents [5p] per copy sold. That 8 cents does get adjusted periodically. It recently went up to 8 cents from 7.057 [4$\frac{1}{2}$p] or so. But it literally takes an act of Congress to adjust the copyright law. If that song is released as a single and goes top five on the charts, then the writer and publisher are going to make about $500,000 [£325,000] between the two of them on performances. Then, if that song is used in a film or national advertising campaign or television they will get an additional negotiated fee.'

When an advertiser wants to use an Acuff-Rose song, they pay a for-use fee to the publisher. If the artist performs the song, that deal is done with the artist.

'For example,' Tomlinson said, 'if Mabelline wants to use "Pretty Woman" in a television ad, they contact the publisher first for the rights to the song. Then they'd go to the record company for the rights to the master recording. In the best-case scenario for advertising a product, you want to use the song with the voice that made it popular. If you can't do that, or you don't have the money to do that, or you want a different sound, then you get the rights to the song and have someone else record it for a lower fee.'

The fees are set according to what the market will bear and the result of complicated negotiations, especially for film and television. Variables include in what territories the film will be shown; how long is the license, one year, two years; how many seconds will it be used in the film; is the song used at the beginning or ending credits; is it an 'exclusive use'; is there talk over the top of the song or just the song playing.

'The talk over the music doesn't so much determine the fee but rather tells us what's going on in the piece of work while our song is being played,' Tomlinson explained. 'There are times when we don't want our song being used in a particular way because it is inappropriate for our song. We're very careful about associating our song with products that might damage our copyright. Areas in which we are cautious include hygiene products, alcohol, tobacco, firearms, or sexually explicit material. In a film, we want to know in what scene our music will be used. We get a script so we know how the song will be used in context.'

A song may be strongly identified with a product, perhaps for a very long time. So when negotiating, Tomlinson is careful is leave a backdoor open for future resale of the song.

'I want our songs to be used in such a way that a year later the song can be used for a totally different product,' he said. 'If we've allowed our song to be used in some not so cool way, it might damage me a year or two or three later from being used in a different product. We don't want to get a song branded to lawnmowers, for example.'

What if the songwriter doesn't want his song associated with a product or film? Do they have any say in the matter?

'In some cases, according to the success of the writer, some writers will have a greater degree of say in the use than others do,' Tomlinson answered. 'Some of our writers have attained such success that they can say if they don't want songs used in certain types of uses. With younger writers who are just dying to get activity, usually we, the publisher, have the full right to decide how to pitch their songs. That usually isn't a huge issue. We desire to protect the songs as much as the writer does. Usually there is not a rub. A true publisher wants to protect the song because it means money to them as well as the writer.'

From a publisher's perspective, what's the condition of the country music industry?

'Through the '90s, when there was a money machine on Music Row and money was flowing everywhere, we had a lot of people come into this town to get into this business for the wrong reasons,' Tomlinson said. 'They were okay talented, they sang okay, wrote okay, but they weren't the craftsmen that this town had been built on. Therefore, a lot of our music began to be just okay. At the time, it sold well because country was in vogue.

'As country's popularity began to slip, that okay stuff began to be repulsive to people. It wasn't even okay any more. It got weeded out. A lot of folks have had to go home. A lot of folks that came here for the wrong reasons who were okay have had to go back wherever they came from. My hope is, and I think it's reflected in the record companies, that maybe this is a good settling out, sifting, that has happened in our industry. Maybe a lot of the okay stuff has been sifted out and we're back to a smaller business model that reflects more quality than quantity.

'We can make the assumption that we are going to see consistently more quality. I believe that we've bottomed out, seen the worst of the dive. It's worth remembering that in the early '80s, when sales stunk in country music, if we were at the letter Z and climbed to letter A in the mid-'90s at the peak of country music. We've not fallen back to letter Z. We may have fallen to letter M. The fall has stopped, the sifting has happened, and we're already starting to see more focused artists who realize that they don't need five buses on their debut tour. We're seeing record companies beginning to understand they have to have a smaller business model to make it work financially. It causes us all to get real again.'

The big publishers, such as Acuff-Rose or Sony Tree, are not the only game in town. In the 1970s, there was an explosion of smaller publishing houses in Nashville. These independents became an important outlet for singer/songwriters that wanted more artistic freedom than that granted on Music Row. Such publishing houses are where you find the Others.

The Welk Music Group (WMG) is one of the important independent players. Larry Welk, the founder, is the son of the bandleader Lawrence Welk of polka fame. Years ago, Welk Publishing was the largest independent in Nashville, with 55 songwriters on their roster. The company was sold to Polygram. Then Larry Welk and his friend Bob Kirsch started WMG from scratch as an alternative to the big mainstream publishers. WMG's offices are in a renovated house located miles away from Music Row, which may be a telling statement.

Bob Kirsch showed me into his spacious upstairs office. 'I wanted to work with people who were left of center by Nashville standards, and that's what we've done,' Kirsch said. 'It's a tough road. The whole music business, but particularly in Nashville, has changed drastically since 1999. Radio lists have gotten much shorter. They don't play oldies any more. An old song is six months old. They don't play Tom T Hall.

'I don't know if it's optimism or a flight of fancy to put our emphasis on the other country music that the majors ignore, for the most part. I really think our music has a shot that's good, slightly different, with a lot of energy put into it and a marketing game plan. My artists probably have as much, or better, shot than a brand new act at a major label, where the odds are terrible no matter how good the singer or how good the label. But I have the same problem of getting my artists noticed. Amy Rigby gets four-star reviews. She's invited on national talk shows. But no sales, no hits. Artists like Joy Lynn White or Gregg Trooper get remarkable reviews but the records don't sell because people aren't aware of them. But our act Nickel Creek has been a huge public success.

'These alternative artists think of themselves as true country, and I think they are correct. A lot of what is considered alternative today is really traditional music. It was once mainstream country music. But today's mainstream country is so different from that, so away from that base, that the traditional-based music is considered alternative. What these artists are doing is country music as we know it historically, only they're doing it in a modern way.

'The record-buying kids like it. They can tell who's phony and who isn't. Merle Haggard just played New York to a sold-out crowd of mostly 20- and 30-year-olds. Merle Haggard hasn't been on country radio in 15 years. He records on a little company, Anti, which is part of Epitaph, a punk label in LA. He's put out two albums, both of which sold over 125,000. So we know that a market exists outside of mainstream commercial country.'

An infrastructure for the Others music is in place. Publishers and producers like WMG, VFR, Audium, HiTone, Dueltone, Artemis, Blue Water, Shanachie, and many more get the music out. Booking agents keep the artists touring a circuit of small clubs and house concerts. The alternative Americana radio stations play the music. Occasionally the mass media notices. Many record executives would not be surprised if the next big movement came out of the cadre of Others. So how valid is this moment in the real world of music business?

Rick Cady is a talent agent for the Third Coast Artists Agency in Nashville. He once managed the Exit/In club. He books acts around the country. It's his business to know the music business. What does he think about what's happening for the Others movement?

'It's very valid,' he said over drinks. 'It has the same infrastructure that exists for the mainstream rock industry for the most part. A lot of the Americana acts, or alt country, are playing in the same venues as up and coming rock acts on a major label. There are a handful of agents like myself around the country that have this niche that represents these acts. There are some rooms that predominately cater to these acts.'

Seattle, Minneapolis, Houston, Nashville, Washington DC, Cleveland, Ann Arbor, Chicago, Los Angeles, and Dallas are developing as hubs for the alt artists. Nevertheless, Cady thinks the horizon for the Others is limited.

'I think it is what it is,' he said. 'The bookings have been at a plateau. The number of non-commercial country acts is fairly stable, again relative to the act and the market, but not growing much. That commercial country is going down reflects that radio listenership is down, unit sales are down, and payments for shows are down. But overall the alt country numbers are drastically less than commercial country. Alan Jackson, Vince Gill, Faith Hill, Tim McGraw will go into arena shows and sell 8,000 to 15,000 on average. The alt country acts sells 1,800 to 2,000.'

The house concert circuit is not a career-building opportunity in Cady's opinion.

'The house concerts have very little to do with creating a ground swell effect for the artists,' he said. 'Usually the people holding these house concerts are college educated, professionals in the community. The people coming to the concerts are those people's friends being loyal fans. Sometimes those people will actually pay to see the artist in a club. But seeing the acts in their living room or backyard has spoiled them. I don't think in the big scheme of things that those 50 people add up to a movement.

'I'd rather be winning over a 20-year-old college kid who sees the artist in a club in his town and tells five of his friends of the act. The next time that act comes to town, that friend and his five friends go to the club and they all buy a CD. In turn, they tell five of their friends. At the same time, they are establishing buying habits. They are very impressionable at that age. You are winning over a fan for life. Usually with the house concert people, they do a no-show at the clubs. So based on that, I don't consider, in my experience, house concerts as a factor in the growth and development of an artist's fan base.

'Radio is going to make the difference, whether you're commercial or non-commercial country. There are plenty of non-commercial radio stations, like in Carbondale, Colorado, which serves the Aspen area. That can have more of an impact in a wealthy market than a house concert. If the artist gets airplay in the market, then they can use that as a starting place when they come play a local club. Maybe they'll get 50 people at that show. Hopefully, those people buy the CD and the station gives some more airplay and you come back six months later to hopefully play to 100 people.

'That said, the movement is valid because people trickle through to the mainstream. This movement as I describe the 20-year-old college kid is exactly how the Dave Matthews Band started. Now they play to sold-out amphitheatres and walk out with a million dollars [£650,000] a night. They started out as a non-mainstream college bar band. So it's possible. That's all, just possible.'

25 Country Gospel

Paul Cory Sparks started his music career as a rocker. He played guitar on Neil Young's 1972 album *Journey to the Past* and toured with REO Speedwagon. He had the same manager as the Eagles, played with the hot bands, and stayed on the road. He recorded solo on a label out of West Virginia and went to Hollywood to be a movie star, all before he was 20 years old. He had a rock 'n' roll life of drugs, music, and getting it on the run. Not bad for a skinny little kid from Covington, Indiana, who played trumpet in the high school band.

In Hollywood, he landed a main part in the *Last Picture Show* and was ready to upgrade his lifestyle. The night before shooting was to start, Cory's life turned upside down.

'I got saved and became a Christian,' he said as we sat in a tiny studio at Nashville's radio station WNAH on Music Row. 'I had to decide which road I wanted to go and I went the road with the Lord. Most of my life was rock 'n' roll music. I met some of the big ones, like Jim Morrison, who at that time was my idol, and I'd seen him live with The Doors.'

After he was saved, Cory stayed in Hollywood hoping to lead others to the Lord's path. One day, in the early winter of 1970, he was passing out gospel pamphlets on Hollywood Boulevard near the Strip. He saw Jim Morrison approaching, his idol, his Musician on the Mountain Top, walking down the sidewalk like any mortal with long hair, coming right to Cory. Cory stuck out his hand and Morrison shook it.

'I said, "Here you go, Jim, take this little pamphlet I got here. We've got a little church right across the street, Crescent Heights here. Jesus is coming soon. We're going to perish." Morrison took the pamphlet.

He got this weird look on his face. He put that pamphlet in his mouth and ate it.'

Cory paused his story, as if still trying, after all these years, to make sense of Jim Morrison eating the pamphlet, the whole thing, as if a hungry communicant gobbling a holy wafer. 'He took a lot of drugs at the end of 1970,' Cory continued. 'He tried to cough them up and actually choked to death. I'm not saying that's got anything to do with it. But I'm saying you don't mock God. That's one thing I noticed from Jim's concerts. He'd always talk in a foul way about God and everything like that. It's going to come out in the end.'

Cory's half-hour evangelical show, 'Cory on the Half', was scheduled to go on air in five minutes, at 12.30pm. He thumbed through his King James Bible looking for appropriate passages and then played chords on the piano to test the tuning. Radio had an important influence in spreading gospel music nationwide in the 1930s, as it did for country music. I had met Cory at Western Trials, a clothing store on Lower Broadway where he was a salesman. He once had his own company, Dangerous Threads, and, as a designer, custom-made clothes for the country stars. He and Manuel pretty much had the town sewn up, if you'll forgive the pun.

'I've met about every country singer there is,' he had told me. 'I made clothes for a lot of them. I got to see the legends at their homes and talk with them. George and Nancy Jones, very wonderful people. Waylon Jennings, Billy Cyrus, Tammy Wynette, I could just go right down the line. Gospel is an important theme in country and all of those people were into gospel, perhaps more than country.'

Barbara Mandrell has publicly testified to her salvation at the age of ten and her upbringing as a Pentecostal Christian. Loretta Lynn, Bill Monroe, Johnny Cash, Elvis Presley, Merle Haggard, Chet Aktins, Reba McEntire, Garth Brooks, nearly anyone who calls themselves a country singer sings gospel. Cash wrote a novel, *Man in White*, about the disciple Paul and has spoken from the stage about his deeply held beliefs. Dolly Parton's autobiographical 'Appalachian Memories', in the gospel tradition, incorporates evangelical faith and keeping the faith with the past.

Willie Nelson, a former Sunday school teacher, recorded 'In the Garden' and 15 other traditional gospel hymns on his 1976 album *The*

Troublemaker. The troublemaker is a rambler with long hair and sandals who leads a group of unemployed disciples from town to town inciting the youths to reject the establishment.

'I had a powerful spiritual urge. My inner voice told me the Methodists and the Baptists didn't have a hammerlock on God,' he was reported as saying in T Walter Herbert's essay, 'The Voice of Woe, Willie Nelson, and Evangelical Spirituality.' 'I went to the Fort Worth Public Library and began reading every book on religion I could find.'

Evangelicalism teaches that the matter of the soul is directly between the person and God. In country music, that relationship can be found in the honky-tonk. In gospel, the church, or the revival tent, can be the honky-tonk.

It was once de rigueur that country albums include at least one gospel song. Country singers had a gospel song in their live shows. Gospel remains only one song sheet away in most country performances. Gospel songs have been regular staple on the Grand Ole Opry since the earliest days. The pleating of country and gospel would make a waterproof basket, if the music were reeds.

Cory found two passages in the scriptures and marked the pages. 'I really believe the Gospel,' he said, taking the countdown cue from the engineer behind the plate glass window. 'I believe there is a heaven and a hell. I don't want to go to hell. I feel a calling on my life in the Lord to sing. I'm not a preacher. I'm a gospel singer. I've seen the Lord heal people and touch people. I'm doing this because I feel like the Lord is behind it.'

The red ON AIR sign flashed on. Cory leaned into the mic and thanked people for tuning in his show. He is a small, slight man, soft spoken, and, for the most part, wears a serious demeanor. Yet, his eyes seem to smile all the time. He has a spot on the corner of his mouth that flickers, as if a laugh was always tugging on his lips to better climb out. He's an attractive man with dark hair and childhood around his eyes. That shine of being entertained by life masks some of the pain of adulthood, but not all the pain. The knowledge that he, all of us, are sinners, and he will have to work with the fall from grace all his life, that palimpsest of true gospel is seen faintly in the corners of his eyes.

'I fell away, to be honest with ya,' he admitted when we talked earlier. 'I made a rededication to God. I know what's it's like to be away from God and what it's like with God. I want to be with Him. It's a very empty feeling to not have God in your life. One time I said, "Lord, what do you want me to do? I don't have a lot of money, I ain't like these other people who have all this stuff."

'He said, "My people hurt. There's a lot of people out there on the streets that don't know God or that they are God's people. Somebody has to tell them. Without a preacher, how are they to know?"

'So I got this little evangelical radio program.'

He spoke to his unseen radio audience as if to a friend. He quoted scripture but he didn't preach. He didn't tell people they were sinners and he knew how they could be saved. No fire and brimstone here. Cory's most attractive characteristic was his sincere humility. I'm not here to convince you of anything, he told his listeners. I'll tell you only what I know, and that is how the Lord Jesus has made a difference in my life. Take it for what you will. Then he accompanied himself on the piano while he sang a hymn.

It's easy to deride and mock fundamental believers like Cory. They're all emotions and no analytical thinking, sneer the intellectuals. They're so self-righteous and simple minded, proclaim those who embrace the universal spirit. They're narrow-minded bigots who want to impose their 'we're right, you're wrong' morally on everyone else, even trying to legislate their morality into national law, claim the civil libertarians.

'Evangelical means to evangelize and that's to talk to people about the Lord and let them have an experience with Him,' Cory explained. 'The Bible said, "If you confess with your mouth and believe in your heart that Jesus is the Son of God, that He rose up from the dead, thou shalt be saved." After that you've got to get yourself a Bible. There comes a time when you get old, when people don't care any more no matter how famous you had been. A lot of people, when they get to that certain old age, they want to get to God because they know something is going to happen to them pretty soon. The thing is, when you feel a calling for your life in God, you've got to go ahead and do it. If you don't, you'll be miserable. I'm the guy who knows that.'

Evangelical religion preaches that sinners, fornicators, and the broke and desperate drunks have only themselves to blame. It also teaches that God will not despise a contrite heart. Humbleness and piety are at the heart of evangelical tradition, although not so apparent in the country tradition. However, salvation, which requires a show of humbleness and piety, no matter how original in expression, is a shared pew in which country and gospel kneel in prayer.

'In country music, misery loves company,' Cory said. 'Patty Loveless has a song "Holding On to Nothing but the Wheel". Patty comes from a deeply religious family. In the song, the singer, she led her life. She got left. She's driving out of Texas or somewhere and all she's got to hold onto is the wheel. I'm here to tell people that there is more to hold on to and it's eternal, something that can make you happy and give you peace.'

Cory came to Nashville in 1993. The next year he won a Best Country Singer contest. He gave that road a try but quit.

'There is so much politics in country music. There is more politics in Nashville than there is in Washington DC,' he said. 'I couldn't handle that. Besides, my manager got on cocaine and crack and couldn't even function. So it's good nothing really happened for me. I didn't really want to be a country singer. That's not where my heart is at. I'm just a gospel singer who has this little half hour radio program and that's what I'm going to do until He says not.'

Country music and gospel are siblings in many ways. Both musics are about the heart. They speak plainly about the fundamentals of the human condition. They express the loneliness and fear and love and joy of sensing that the divine spirit is the seed of the human spirit. Both musics sing about making a journey, whether on the path of Lord or on the lonesome highway. In country music, the road represents conflicts between the free-ranging individualist and the dear ones at home. In gospel music, the path to the Lord usually brings into conflict an individual's ego's desire to exert itself and the need for that ego to surrender to a higher authority. In country and in gospel, the individual is a pilgrim for better or worse. The metaphorical road trip is a spiritual journey: an important theme in both musics.

'Lonesome Highway', written by Leon Payne and made popular by Hank Williams, is an example of country gospel. In the song, a wayward soul wanders down the lonesome highway lost in vice and temptation without the solace of family or belief in the loving grace of the Lord. One of Williams' signature songs, 'I Saw the Light', was his personal testimony of being set free by the Lord's love and now not afraid of death. He wrote 20 other gospel songs, 15 per cent of his total output as a songwriter.

'I Saw the Light' was inspired by Albert E Brumley's gospel standard 'He Set Me Free'. Brumley is a pivotal figure in the crossover between gospel and country. He began his 50-year-long songwriting career in the late 1920s and wrote over 600 songs. Many of his songs became mainstays in country and bluegrass, while appearing in gospel hymnals. He claimed never to have written a country song but was evangelizing through music.

His song, 'Turn Your Radio On', invited listeners to 'get in touch with God' by tuning into gospel music. The song was written for the Stamps All-Star Quartet, the family group where Tony Brown started his career in music. The Stamps were forerunners in 1928 of the gospel/country blend in their syncopated 'after beat' style, taken from the field blues call-and-response, where the lead bass vocal was answered by the other three voices. Their song 'Give the World a Smile Each Day' was a significant departure from the traditional gospel form and put a catchy rhythm in the music. Their jazz-influenced piano player, Dwight Brock, added secular music color to the gospel, broadening its appeal.

Pentecostal music, the Stamps' home base, hillbilly and old-time gospel were voices in the same choir during the 1930s. The shared influences have stayed in the music. The old-gospel was both white and black. RE Winsett, a music publisher and founding member of the largest Pentecostal denomination, the Assembly of God, was the first white publisher of songs by Thomas A Dorsey. Dorsey was an African-American musician/composer in Chicago who launched the black gospel song movement. Two of Dorsey's best-known songs are 'Peace in the Valley' and 'Precious Lord, Take My Hand'.

The Negro spiritual is also Southern gospel. The African-American writer and social philosopher WEB Du Bois called spirituals like 'Road to Heaven' 'sorrow songs' of 'an unhappy people [expressing] their unvoiced longing toward a truer world.' These songs are a foundation stone of Southern gospel and a fundamental part of Southern country music. Country music has been described as the soul music of the white South.

Harland Howard, the esteemed songwriter, is quoted by Nicholas Dawidoff in his book *In the Country of Country, People and Places in American Music* on the subject of spirituality and morality in country music: 'Good is good, bad will suffer and your cheatin' heart will make you weep. Most people don't understand that Hank Williams was preaching to them just as fervently as a Baptist preacher on Sunday. I like that thread – good is good, bad will get your ass kicked. I believe it.'

Home, whether in the bosom of the Lord or in front of the hearth, is a central image in gospel and country. In both cases, the home is idealized to an unattainable paradigm. In the songs, the feelings of yearning and desire for such a place become a sweet pain.

Rebellion, redemption, and retribution; sinning and praying for forgiveness, and sinning again; and begging for the mercy of salvation are themes in gospel and in country. Being saved, or not saved, is a chord heard in both musics. Rebellion and sinning is active striving, the source and subject of good country songs. Praying and beseeching forgiveness is passive expectation, the source and subject of good gospel songs. Saturday night and Sunday morning, hedonism and piety, give country and gospel songs their juice and pathos. Sin and salvation is a country song put in an evangelical framework. In country, you raise hell; in gospel, you give your life up to Jesus – just one degree of separation. In country music, that one degree is often a good woman working to save her man from domestic turmoil and the temptations on the road. She is a stand-in for the Lord in gospel music. Same salvation motif, different saviors.

It's not surprising that many country singers came out of gospel music.

'Country is okay but a lot of it's sad,' Cory said as we left the studio after his show. 'It's about lives that happen to people and happen all over again. Unending pain. Bluegrass is the saddest music. They have songs like, "Don't send me no flowers when I'm dead, send them to me now." I imagine somebody bringing me a bunch of flowers. "Here," they say, "I want to bring these to you before you die." Now, that's not a happy gift.'

★

The early-18th-century northern British fairs along the Scottish border were the seedbeds of Southern gospel. These 'holy fairs' of music and praise were the forerunners of the fundamental evangelical camp meetings held by Scots-Presbyterians who settled in Appalachia. Southern gospel further developed out of 19th-century evangelical revivals and shape-note singing schools. Shape-note singing schools taught melodies using shapes, such as diamonds or squares, to indicate relative places of notes on the scale. Anyone without musical training could read the music, making it more accessible and popular.

Christian/gospel music has become so popular that nearly 50 million albums were sold in 2001. In terms of album sales, the Christian/gospel music industry is at least two-thirds bigger than country music, according to the Gospel Music Association.

Casting a wide net bolsters Christian/gospel album sales numbers. *O Brother, Where Art Thou?* and the New Age Mannheim Steamroller Christmas album are tallied in Christian/gospel sales. The best selling rap/metal foursome POD is also counted in the sales figures. The Christian-oriented music magazine *CCM* listed *O Brother, Where Art Thou?* as number one on its charts, followed by POD's *Satellite* (Atlantic Records). Neither *Billboard* or *R&R* listed the albums in their Christian category. SoundScan, which tracks sales of records sold at Christian and mainstream retail, reported that 500,000 POD albums were sold in Christian stores alone.

POD might seem a bit incongruous with the Christian image. The band members' tattoos and the stare-down look carry the vibe of the tough neighborhood where they grew up in San Diego. They play blistering music from the mosh pits rather than the pulpit, which makes them a big hit when they perform on Ozzy Osbourne's Ozzfest tour. Osbourne, the former vocalist for Black Sabbath, is infamous for biting the heads off doves on stage and for his non-reverential wit, intentional or not, often aimed at Christian sensibilities.

POD – Wuv Bernardo, Sonny Sandoval, Traa Daniels, and Marcos Curiel – chaff under the rubric of Christian band. They consider themselves foremost as musicians who have a positive message. 'I don't want to come off as, "Hi, I'm Christian Sonny,"' Sandoval once told a reporter. The band has been nominated twice (2001/2002) for best artist and group at the prestigious Gospel Music Association's Dove Awards. They refused to attend the ceremony both years.

'It's all politics,' Sandoval told Keith Cartwright, a reporter for *The Tennessean*. '[This] year, we'll just say, "Thanks, but we really don't want to be part of this little, it's almost like a secret, society-type thing."'

Sandoval has been blunt in his assessment of the Christian/gospel industry's claim to help the band break into the mainstream. 'Let's be honest with ourselves,' he said in an interview. 'That's not your [industry executives'] hearts' intention. You're just selling records. Whatever link you have to this [POD and its music], it looks good on your plate.'

Country music artists make the same accusation in their industry.

Nashville is the headquarters for both music industries and the parallels do not stop there. As Christian/gospel music grows in popular and commercial success, it faces some of the same issues that country music experienced.

Corporations are buying into gospel big time, as they did with country music. Warner/Chappell Music Group, BMG Songs, Sony, EMI Christian Music Publishing, DreamWorks, Columbia, Interscope, and Capital are the major secular corporations looking to cash in on gospel music, whose market share is growing faster than country music. They compete with well-established Christian-based publishing and recording companies like Sparrow Label Group, New Spring Publishing, Creative Trust Entertainment Management, Integrity Inc, INO Records, and Word Label Group. Consolidation is happening within the Christian/gospel music industry, as it did in country music. This leaves room for boutique and independent labels. Country has gone through a boom of independent publishers and small labels. Big labels are buying up gospel independents and tucking them under the corporate umbrella, as happened in country. Mercury Records has its Lost Highways; Sony sponsors its quasi-independent Lucky Dog label. Now EMI is part owner in the Christian/gospel label Gotee Records.

Gotee Records is one of the most successful Christian/gospel independent labels, known for its grassroots approach to business and its eclectic roster of musicians. EMI Christian Music Group bought a 25 per cent stake in Gotee and promised Toby McKeehan, Gotee's founder, that he will retain creative control. This is not much different from the relationship Tony Brown and Tim DuBois at Universal South have with their parent company, Universal.

Those within the industry welcome the significant influx of secular corporate influence in Christian music. The corporations' name and money will attract more qualified people, so the reasoning goes. The result will be a better produced, marketed, and publicized product. This in turn will expand the fan base and, the assumption goes, lead to making the music better. That has been the model in country: take the music into the mainstream pop market. And with that business model came focus groups, market surveys, target markets, and, critics claim, a general dumbing down of the music – the backlash which the country music industry is currently experiencing in declining market share and sales.

'The audience today demands excellence in the art and truthfulness in the message. In the past, our audience has tolerated inferior art because of the heart behind the communicator,' Jeff Moseley, president of INO Records, has been quoted. Hillbilly and old-timey country music was once seen as inferior art tolerated because of its authentic heart. That music didn't make the big bucks until it slicked down the cowlick and adapted the pop commercial sound. In the country music business, excellent music got confused with excellent marketing.

The Christian/gospel has similar ambitions. In recent years, the marketers have pushed hard to place the records in big retail outlets like Target, Wal-Mart, and Best Buy, where country generates most of its sales. There is now official Dove Awards (the Christian/gospel equivalent of the Grammys) point-of-purchase in 7,000 retail stores. Record chains, such as Tower Records, no longer dump Christian/gospel in the miscellaneous bin. Christian/gospel has its own category, same as country.

Christian/gospel relies heavily on radio to increase its market, as does country. Forty new Christian stations have come on-line since 2000 in markets like LA, Atlanta, Chicago, Dallas, and Cleveland. The intent is the same as in country commercial radio; attract a larger audience share so the stations can charge more for advertising time. The corollary is selling more records so the record companies and publishers make more money. Radio and the Christian/gospel music industry are doing the commercial two-step, known in country as dancing with the devil.

The Christian/gospel industry is targeting the youth market. Country went that route, too, and it has proven less than stellar business strategy. In the 1990s, the country music industry skewed the music into what appeals to the 13- to 21-year-old audience, with particular attention to the female consumer. Christian music is starting to use younger acts to appeal to a younger audience, according to Frank Breeden, president of the Gospel Music Association (GMA), not to be confused with the Country Music Association (CMA). 'The younger acts are breaking faster at a higher selling pace. They're going gold sooner,' Breeden was quoted in an interview in *The Tennessean*.

J David Huffman, chief operating officer of Creative Trust Entertainment Management, has stated that 'it is getting harder to develop new acts into brands, while the cost and competition continue to intensify.' He sounds like any country music industry executive. The music and artists have become marketing terms; the music is described in accountant's terms. 'We need to continue finding talent that speaks to the 13- to 21-year-old buying audience while providing faith-provoking, transparent, high-quality entertainment,' Huffman said.

Barry Landis, president of the Word Label Group, supports that viewpoint. 'Today's teenagers are looking for sounds that equate with everyday lives – things that fit in with their culture,' he stated in *The Tennessean*. 'That means Christian music has to relate and respond to what is going on in the mainstream.'

That is the same corporate-values clapper that rang country's bell. Go mainstream to make more money. If the music has to be tweaked to appeal to the greatest common dominator, well, that's business. Christian/gospel is already well tweaked. The sound of many bands is identical to mainstream rock, or hip-hop, or country groups. And, like country, Christian/gospel see female consumers as a rich consumer vein to tap. Superchick, a popular Christian group, can stand right alongside The Dixie Chicks. The Girls of Grace tour went on the road with the mission 'to send positive messages to a culture about women, to show

how important women are, to build them some self-respect and to counter all of the forces that come against women in our culture,' according to GMA president Frank Breeden.

Songwriter Kim Patton-Johnston has a foot in the gospel camp and a foot in the country camp. She has received two Dove Awards, gospel music's equivalent of a Grammy, the latest in 2002. Country stars such as Tim McGraw, Trisha Yearwood, Pam Tillis, and the Judds have recorded her songs. She is a member of the GMA and the CMA.

She thinks of country and gospel as sister genres. Country music, especially in its roots, tells stories of life lessons. It's real music about real people. That's how she sees gospel music. Jesus taught by telling stories and gospel music does that. In Southern gospel songs, verse one sets up the story, the chorus makes the point and the second verse applies the story to life today. Country music tends to do that. 'It's very honor my father and mother, mom this or mom that,' she said as we sat in her office at Jody Williams Publishing and Worley Publishers. She is also a writer for Sony/Tree.

Kim pointed out that a lot of the sound in gospel and country is stylistically similar. The close block harmonies, almost hymn like but with a hand-clapping feel. The Sunday go-to-meetin'-dinner kind of thing, as she said. Real down home. That is a connection between gospel and country.

'By and large I just write what comes out,' she said. 'I dabble in soulful pop alternative. I love to write groove tunes. I just write. I don't really separate my categories. The industry does that for me.' She has been a professional songwriter for 14 years, since 1986. Gospel and country came naturally to her. In her Greensboro, North Carolina home, her mother listened to gospel and her father tuned in Jim Reeves. The Oak Ridge Boys, who spanned gospel and country, was a shared enjoyment.

Southern gospel and early country were so similar to her that she started writing gospel while listening to country radio. Kathy Mattea's 'You Are the Power' was a 'total God song for me', she said. 'Another country song that was scripture for me was "Untasted Honey". I didn't see a division between gospel and country. I thought, "Great, country music likes spiritual things." To me it was the same music with the hand-clapping feelin'.'

The similar shared feeling in the musics has become stronger, in Kim's opinion. 'Southern gospel seems to be right now very influenced by country music,' she said. 'The sound, production, feel is very country. When I turn on my Southern gospel station, I think of country music seven or eight years ago. Some of the drum sounds, harmonies, phrasings, rhythms, choice of words in the lyrics. Real country.

'Country music is known for its Southern pride. There was a song "You've Got to Stand for Something or You'll Fall for Anything". That's a real theme of country music, that strength, that conviction. In that regard, it is evangelical. Evangelical is straightforward and simple. Country shares that trait. I love you and you broke my heart. There's no beating around the bush. It is what it is.'

Like country, contemporary Christian/gospel music is defined in several sub-categories: Southern gospel, contemporary gospel, rap, rock 'n' roll gospel, adult contemporary, inspirational. There is even a link to folk country. Amy Grant's first big hit was 'My Father Dies', a folk acoustic country song. Contemporary Christian is very pop.

'The hip new gospel, rock 'n' roll gospel, upset a lot of the fundamentalist church goers but it gave a lot of us a new expression,' Kim said.

The tone of gospel music has been influenced by all the new translations of the Bible, according to Kim. The early hymns, 'Amazing Grace', 'I Come to Jesus', 'I Come to the Garden', and other traditional hymns have a King James flavor. The words and phrasing are antiquated and not as conservational as we use today.

The Southern gospel stays more specific to the Bible but finds a new twist on a Bible story. The language is not as King Jamesy as the old traditional. Contemporary gospel uses more everyday language than Southern gospel. That's the influence of the NIV Bible (New International Version). The NIV has brought gospel music closer to country, in that country music is so conversational.

'It's like you're sitting in your kitchen with the neighbor from the farm next door,' Kim said, 'and talking about how the green beans are going to sprout this year. There is still that element to country music, even with all the pop influence.'

At the same time, country music is coming back to a spiritual aspect, Kim observed. People are awake to that sort of thing. A lot of the artists are open to cutting the kind of song that has something deeper to say, something meaningful, especially after September 11. There is also a reaction against the slick pop trend in country for the past decade.

'Country is not going to go back to its most traditional basic basic roots,' she said. 'But it does seem to want to become more real, more earthy. How do you do that in a way that lets the music grow and become something new? To do so, the music must draw from its traditional roots and, in doing so, have a deeper meaning. It finds something more to say about life lessons and telling the stories that matter. I think that is an aspect of country that nobody wants to lose.

'The record labels are open to more spiritual music. That's my personal experience with the songs that I'm writing. I tend to cross the lines back and forth a lot. A song that I find is country, others find it gospel. On the flip side, songs I thought were blatantly gospel had interest from the pure country.'

Kim performs on the gospel version of the house circuit, playing in churches in Texas, Oklahoma, Tennessee, North Carolina, and in Canada. She leads a Bible study and prayer group every Tuesday night in Nashville.

'Every human being walking the planet has a spiritual need,' she said. 'There is something that makes us want to take our next breath that we can't explain. It is beyond the physical. Music is such a gateway to tapping into that. Country does that better than any, sometimes better than the gospel seems to.'

26 Blue Country

Jefferson Street is the historical blues heart of Nashville, as well as the line that defines the black community from the white community. It was once a thriving main thoroughfare with businesses, banks, restaurants, and theaters. Then, in the late 1960s, Interstate 40 was built to bisect Jefferson Street, dividing the community with eight lanes of cement and thousands of 60mph (100kph) cars. The neighborhood went into decline, businesses closed, and the once-bustling Jefferson Street looked in need of a trim and bath.

The Jefferson Street United Merchants Partnership is spearheading an effort to revitalize Jefferson Street. New businesses are moving in and the blues, which never left, is being heard. In the early '60s, more than a dozen legal clubs, and even more after-hours joints, were open 24 hours with 12 hours of live music along Jefferson Street. Now the street's premier blues club is the Ebony Room tucked in the back of Sir Pizza. Sir Pizza's owner, Fred Westbrook, opened the Ebony Room four years ago with the idea of bringing blues back to Jefferson Street and to provide entertainment for the older crowd. Every Friday blues is played in the back room while Fred makes pizza out front for customers. Tuesday nights are reserved for Bible study and poetry readings are held on Wednesdays.

Jimi Hendrix played the Jefferson Street clubs when stationed in the army at nearby Fort Campbell. He was nicknamed 'marble head' by the Jefferson street regulars, who thought he was crazy with his early '60s acid rock. His house, since demolished, stood where I-40 West crosses over Jefferson Street. The Music City Blues Society plans to mark the site with a commemorative plaque.

The Nashville blues scene is small but active. Blues can be heard in a dozen venues around town, including Harvey Washbangers Eat Drink & Do Laundry and Fate's Pig and Pie, a terrific barbeque place on the edge of town. The Bourbon Street Blues & Boogie Bar in Printer's Alley is the city's quintessential blues bar. Other clubs in the short, dead end alley are the Steel Guitar Bar, Lonnie's Western Room, Lonnie's Karaoke Bar, and the Brass Stables, a bar featuring 'exotic showgirls'. Once the center of Nashville's printing industry, Printer's Alley is now a historical landmark.

Black blues and country are musical cousins related by raw, soulful, dolefully humorous, and double entendre lyrics – and three chords. They are storytelling musics, different in form but similar in content. Blues and country germinated from rural roots and were nourished by blacks and whites that lived with poverty, injustice, and discrimination.

Poor whites were neighbors to poor blacks. They listened to each other's music. Country music was part of the rural Appalachian blacks' musical background as much as the blues. As a boy, Ray Charles listened to the Grand Ole Opry's Saturday night broadcasts. His album *Modern Sounds in Country and Western Music* is his R&B interpretations of old-time country songs. The fusion of African-American and Anglo-American made Southern music different from other regional musics. The blues and jazz influences gave Southern string bands their punch and driving syncopated rhythm.

Hank Williams, AP Carter, Johnny Cash, Brenda Lee, Bob Wills, Elvis Presley, Jerry Lee Lewis, and Buck Owens all learned licks from black musicians. Buck Owens once said, 'If Chuck Berry had been white, he'd have been a country singer.'

Bill Monroe learned from the black musician Arnold Schultz. 'If you listen to my work, you see that there's blues in it,' Monroe has pointed out. Schultz was a freight hauler when Monroe met him at a dance near Rosine, Kentucky. The syncopated licks heard in Monroe's 'Rocky Road Blues' came from Schultz's guitar.

Jimmie Rodgers, the father of country music, grew up listening to the black music. He was born in the village of Pine Springs, Mississippi in 1897 but claimed Meridan as his hometown, where he was raised by his Aunt Dora after his mother died. Meridan is on the Alabama border where north, south, east and west railroad lines crossed. Union General William Tecumseh Sherman razed the transportation center during the Civil War.

Rodgers' father, Aaron Rodgers, was a section foreman on the Mobile and Ohio line. Young Jimmie occasionally hauled buckets of water to the 'gandy dancers', the black work crews repairing the tracks. Rodgers' youth can be heard in his line, 'Hey little waterboy, bring that water 'round/If you don't like your job, set yo' water bucket down.'

Gandy dancers did the hard heavy work of replacing worn ties and damaged rails. To better coordinate lifting 100lb (45kg) steel rails, the workers set a rhythm by chanting a cadence 'sung' by a caller, usually the foreman. Young Jimmie soaked in this music, along with music of the local vaudeville theater and the opera house. He heard harmonies in the barbershops and jazz and parlor music in the town's hotel lobbies. As a musician, he adopted the plaintive rhythms and bluesy lyrics of black popular music into his music.

Rodgers worked as a brakeman, flagman, and baggage handler on the railroads, until he traveled up to Bristol, Tennessee and sang for Ralph Peer in 1922. That's when 'America's Blue Yodler' started his music career. It was a short career. He suffered from tuberculosis, which he sang about in his song 'TB Blues': 'I'm fighting like a lion, look like I'm going to lose/Cause there ain't nobody ever whipped the TB Blues.' He died from the disease in 1933 in the Taft Hotel in New York, two days after making his final recording.

People said that Rodgers was a white man gone black singing nigger blues. He was not the only musician to sing the 'white country blues'. Instrumental work, lyrics, and vocal techniques of rural black blues are in the earliest country music recordings. Rodgers, along with Riley Puckett, Frank Hutchinson, Cliff Carlisle, Emmett Miller, and Tom Darby laid the foundation that Hank Williams, Elvis Presley, Jerry Lee Lewis, and the Rolling Stones built upon.

'Boarding House Blues' by Henry Glover, the black R&B musician and composer, provided the melody to the Delmore Brothers' 'Blues Stay Away from Me'. Wayne Raney, the country harmonica player and vocalist, wrote the lyrics to 'Blues Stay Away from Me' over Glover's music.

Country pianist Moon Mullican and the black bandleader Tiny Bradshaw had a crossover hit 'Well Oh Well'. The R&B 'Finger Poppin' Time' has become a bluegrass song performed by Ralph Stanley and others.

Bluesman Keb' Mo sings 'I'm So Lonesome I Could Cry' on the *Timeless* tribute album to Hank Williams. Beck, Sheryl Crow, Ryan Adams, Mark Knopfler and his band, and Hank 3 also perform on the album.

Colin Linden is another bluesman at home in country. A Canadian, he is a seven-time winner in the blues category of the Juno Award (the Canadian equivalent of the Grammy), receiving the last one in April 2002. T Bone Burnett hired Colin to teach Chris Thomas King to play the song he performs in the *O Brother, Where Art Thou?* film. Colin played the instrumental on the soundtrack and performed on the Down From the Mountain Tour. He moved from Toronto to Nashville in May 2001. We met over coffee to talk about the blues in country.

'In the country and blues, so many of the songs are the same, so many of the ideas are the same, so many of the people are similar people,' Colin said. 'I got to meet Ralph Stanley, the greatest guy, an amazing musician, on the Down From the Mountain Tour. I found that Ralph Stanley as a person is very similar to a lot of the older blues guys I knew as a kid coming up. For starters, they have the wisdom that comes from playing music for a really really long time. They understand the quiet strength you get from doing something that's timeless. A lot of the greatest artists in the blues and in country, probably all kinds of music, when you've been playing music for a long time, a lot of the artist as a person comes out. There is a tremendous amount of grace, and a tremendous amount of humility and humor and wisdom, from that kind of life.'

Colin is a short man with a close black beard who habitually dresses entirely in black, including a black fedora. He started playing the guitar as a kid and got into rock 'n' roll. As a teenager, he played lead guitar in country and blues bands. He signed with the Nashville publisher Warner Chappell in 1987 as a songwriter. He and his wife made frequent trips to Nashville and fell in love with the place, in part for the like-minded people Colin met.

He was a close friend to Rick Danco of The Band. 'I worked with The Band a lot and Rick was very close to me,' he recalled of his friend.

'He grew up in a house without electricity until he was about 12 years old. As soon as he got a radio, he'd listen to the Memphis stations playing the blues and the Nashville stations playing country. He developed a great love for the music. It was fascinating to him. It was from a different place, like from outer space. There is a great love that a lot of Northern people have for Southern culture. I've felt that my whole life. There is a kinship that we north of the 48th parallel feel for the people south of the Mason-Dixon line.'

To hear the blues in country, you have to listen to the roots in the country music, according to Colin. But commercial country radio doesn't offer the roots connection. There is more Celine Dion and Toto on country radio than Hank Williams or Merle Haggard or Loretta Lynn.

'I hear blues in almost all country artists who are traditional artists,' he commented. 'I hear it in some of the contemporary guys who, even if they are mainstream, have deep roots, like Gary Allen.'

The blues' one-four-five chords are usually heard in country songs like Hank Williams' 'Honky-Tonk Blues' or 'Prison Blues' by Johnny Cash. Merle Haggard also works with the blues form. Country doesn't use the straight 12-bar blues, but close enough to be a kissin' cousin to the blues.

'You hear blues things all over country from a musical point of view,' Colin said. 'The type of singing, the blues notes, the sevenths and neutral thirds, minor sevens that are major sevens. A lot of it comes from the musical language, the type of singing, the type of grooves and rhythm patterns that are all over the blues and country music.

'The great soul singers, like Percy Sledge or Arthur Alexander, if they had a different look and used steel guitars and fiddles on their records, they'd be country singers. Same with Chuck Berry. There is a lot of country in his music. A lot of the old blues artists loved country and were familiar with it, and vice versa.

Colin identifies his music as rootsy but closer to the blues root than anything else.

'I've always been able to interface with folk and country music,' he said. 'In the grand scheme of roots music, I try not to divvy things up too carefully. I like to be inclusive, rather than exclusive, because so much has changed in the blues and country. The most interesting blues artists are the ones who expand the boundaries of the genre. Country music is a little different because commercially it's taken off as such a big business. Traditional country artists are the exception as opposed to the rule. In blues, it's sort of the other way around. What non-commercial country and blues share in common is that they haven't stripped away the human emotion.'

Some artists, such as Colin's friend, blues performer Keb' Mo, are breaking down barriers between blues and country. That whole thing between black man blues and white man blues, those terms exist for people who make divisions, people who have to define, according to Colin. The term 'white man's blues' to describe country music, anything from mountain music to bluegrass to country music in the contemporary sense, comes from identifying the same kind of honesty heard in blues.

Blues and the country of Hank Williams' era shared a sense of humor with double entendre and subtle word play. Contemporary country has, for the most part, lost that sense of humor. Blues is also, to a degree, a coded language carried over from slaves delivering messages to one another they didn't want the master to understand. There is an element of coded language in the older country music that came from the isolated Appalachian society.

As we finished our coffees, Colin told me about an interview with Nigerian musicians. 'They were talking about the roots and influences of their music. Some acknowledged the influence of James Brown. Several said Jim Reeves influenced their music. Just goes to prove that what goes around comes around.'

Taj Mahal, early in this career, won contests as a bluegrass banjo picker. In the 1960s, he learned licks from Bill Monroe and played with the Whites – the White Family, father and daughters – a long-standing traditional country act that regularly performs on the Grand Ole Opry. He's old friends with Emmylou Harris, Janis Ian, and Linda Ronstadt. He played three California dates on the Down From the Mountain Tour, where he performed with Alison Krauss.

'I love the purity and the clarity of the bluegrass music,' Taj said as we talked before a gig. 'I would have loved to be out for the whole tour.

It was just pure acoustic beautiful music. The mics picked up every note and 6,000 people could clearly hear each note.'

The recent upshot with *O Brother, Where Art Thou?* was the best thing that has happened to the music scene, in Taj's opinion. 'It didn't take country music to do that,' he said in his distinctive gravel bass. 'It took getting the music to the people. The people were like the desert. They were parched. For the past 30 years, people have been playing attenuated music. It's all highly processed and here comes this pure moving sound. There was no argument with people on that. It's still no argument. The music industry is trying to ignore it. That's that old empire idea – if we ignore them, they'll go away. Well, in some cases they do. But, I think, that's always the downfall of an empire.'

The circle of country music and blues is turning back on itself, according to Taj. The two musics were close to each other before the turn of the 19th century and into the early 20th century. Basically, everybody was dipping out of the same bag.

'Where it starts to differ is, where the older slave plantation lifestyle faded and the slaves were less exposed to Celtic music through fiddle tunes,' Taj said. 'Then, you might hear a different kind of swing from it if you hear an African fiddler play the same thing because of the different kinds of rhythmic concepts. But essentially, it's the same melody in the different types of tunes and dances. The music ping-ponged back and forth. If a development happened in the Celtic style, it would be picked up in the African style. And evolutions in the African style would show up in the Celtic playing. So you had influences moving back and forth from what we call now country and blues.

'Plus, everybody lived in the environment. If you were playing blues on the street, you had your ear to other music on the radio. You heard, and could play, Hank Williams songs. So, if somebody came up and said, "I'll pay you $5 [£3] to play a Hank Williams tune," you could roll it out. Hank leaned more towards the honky-tonk and bluesy sound and he had big heapin' of the Louisiana sound in his music.'

The music also blended in the recording facilities, where blues, gospel, and country music mixed, whether people wanted it to happen or not. The gospel people, from both black and white traditions, the black and white musicians playing blues and country, you find a lot of this happening, like in the Sun Studios in Memphis.

'The white musicians knew that the music they heard wouldn't be acceptable across the board if played by a black musician. If they could find a white musician to play that, or add some semblance of the black sound into the white music, then they could get it into the broadcasting.

'You can't draw a line down the middle and say, "This is white man's blues and this is black man's blues." Sometimes they blend. Basically, Elvis was singing black man's music. Chuck Berry took the articulateness of country music and goosed it with some blues and rock 'n' roll and created a whole other way to get across that line between black man and white man music. He was coming back the other way, so the circle was complete.'

White man's blues or black man's blues, there is no difference in the subject matter. Heartache is a human condition. That's why people feel it all over the world. But country and the blues delivery is different, according to Taj. The notes are bent differently between blues and country blues, even city blues, or between *the* blues and country music. Lines are dragged longer. A lot of times, the blues story style will swing over into country. But the delivery in country didn't have an African tune or bent notes. It was like a straight set of three chords that delivered the same thing.

'Country bends notes, we're not talkin' that they don't bend some notes,' Taj exclaimed. 'They learned some notes, like James Burton down in Austin. James from years ago was one of my favorites. He's one of those Texas country guys. He's a really good guitar player. He synthesized a lot of stuff between country and blues. Listen to his 'Susie Q'. And don't leave out writers, like Dan Penn. Penn was basically a country songwriter but found R&B and blues artists to record his songs, like 'Dark End of the Street'. He saw a market for country songs in the R&B style. If you start going for Dan Penn songs, you'll be going forever. He was very important.'

Country and the blues share a common emotional source. As Taj colorfully put it, 'Any one man plowin' behind mules tryin' everyday to keep his family together, they're hearing the same thing no matter what direction it's coming from, and I'm talking more than just music. The majority of African-Americans in the United States doesn't recognize that there is a tremendous amount of poor white people in this country. The blacks need to acknowledge that they aren't the only ones who had to plow with mules, and suffer through having to see the kids go without, and not having the smarts or means to go down to tell the people at the courthouse about it.

'That was one of the things that the whole folk music scene in the '60s opened up even more to me about the human condition. I learned a lot about the people in Appalachia because the music was a similar situation, whereby the music was something that helped them get through the hard times. The music for getting through those times was something they brought over from Scotland and England and Ireland. Hard times are not a white man/black man situation. Or even a geographical situation. And neither is the music.

'The thing was, the Europeans brought their musical traditions, whereas the Africans were forced to leave theirs behind, or, more accurately, were forced by the slave owners to abandon their instruments and musical traditions. Drums were outlawed because the slave owners feared that the "talking drums" carried coded messages. And they were right. So the Africans had to graft themselves onto a tradition that existed here, a musical tradition brought from Europe. But they swung the music in a different way.'

The blues will come back into country, Taj predicts. Not only that, country will finally come back into country. 'The present-day country music is maybe a lot closer to modern blues, I'm talkin' from the '30s on,' he said. 'The bottom line is that the people know the real music. There's no excuse why this music can't come back around. The only reason they say it can't is because of the money, not because of the music. The music is timeless. The problem with the country music industry is that they are waiting for that next 'primary hero'. They're not pro-active. You get musicians like the Whites and Hank 3, they're about music. They're into the music. They're on the road. They're playing wherever they can, whenever they can.

'What's going on on this planet is just the latest installment. We're here because of all the other people before us. And that can be heard best in the music. It's all about the music.'

27 Bluegrass Country

There is another blue in country: bluegrass.

The white bread conception of bluegrass is of nice people playing hot music, but leaving it on the stage. Not like the rock 'n' roll delinquents who believe that a rowdy life is necessary to play fast-paced music. Fast music doesn't mean life in the fast lane in the bluegrass world.

But keep in mind that The Grateful Dead started as a bluegrass group.

Truths about bluegrass:

Bluegrass's heartthrob is Death. It loves to scare itself with the Grim Reaper. It will even sharpen the blade for the visceral thrill of being so close to the cut. Ralph Stanley's 'Old Man Death', that he sang *a capella* on the Down From the Mountain Tour and became the signature song for the tour, is all about the fear of death.

Violence is bluegrass's dirty secret, or as secret as can be when sung for thousands of people. Bluegrass songs have a morbid fascination with stabbing people, hitting them over the head, and drowning. Blowing people up is too modern for bluegrass and not personal enough. Bluegrass likes to get its hands bloody.

Death and sex have a close relationship in bluegrass. They go to concerts together and hold hands – and do the suck face for an ultimate climax. In many bluegrass songs, women are drowned, bludgeoned, beaten, and dragged around by their hair by men. These are sorrowful songs, often in waltz time, in which the men are portrayed as misguided romantics.

Betrayal is a favorite pastime in bluegrass. Often the man kills the woman for making him feel bad. The old English ballad and bluegrass standby, 'Barbara Allen', is about betrayal and its companion, revenge.

The woman rejects the man. He feels betrayed because she did not submit to him. Then he dies. Her punishment for being 'hard hearted' is death. They are buried side-by-side. A rose grows from his grave, symbolizing the gentle male nature. A briar grows out of her grave, symbolizing the jabbing thorns that gave Jesus his final headache. In the song, the rose twines around briar, not in a loving embrace but to dominate in a lover's knot. The man strangles the woman even from the grave.

There is more murder in bluegrass than in most slasher films, and bloodier the better. But what would you expect in a music seeped in violence, death, betrayal, and sex, which is another form of death in bluegrass.

Ghosts, destruction by the wrathful Old Testament God, doom, and a world of darkness are preoccupations of gothic bluegrass. Death is not portrayed as a homecoming embrace of a loving God but as a cold, cold grave. The religion is fundamentalist with a moral. Men who kill women are executed and sent to Hell. But they keep killing women in song after song. Women didn't kill the man until The Dixie Chicks came along and gave Earl his due.

Bluegrass has a relatively small fan base, compared to pop or even country, but they are ardent fans. Bluegrass fans consider country music to be corrupted by pop, by the dollar, by people running out the door chasing stardom. The fans cherish the myth that bluegrass was spawned by 'real' folks who never left their roots, never abandoned the coonskin cap for the cowboy hat. Bluegrass considers itself less tainted by commercialism than country. It's proud to be a niche market, pretending that it doesn't have aspirations for a greater audience. But bluegrass has always been a commercial music.

Bluegrass portrays itself as the little cabin on the hill, a refuge from the false values of the consumer society and the crass vulgarities of commercialism. Never mind that the little cabin on the hill in Monroe's song was a place to lick the singer's wounds after a failed love affair. Bluegrass, more than country music, has nurtured the idealized time of one-room schoolhouses, the country prayer meetings, and the community of unpretentious folks enjoying a tune and chaw on the front porch.

Bluegrass thinks of itself as America's truest form of country music coming from Mother Appalachia.

But players like Alison Krauss, Laurie Lewis, Tim O'Brien, Sam Bush, Bela Fleck, Kathy Chiavola, and Doug Green ('Ranger Doug' of the cowboy trio Riders In The Sky and a former member of Bill Monroe's Blue Grass Boys) use a traditional style upon which to create new forms. They have given old-time bluegrass a new sound without stabbing it in the back. They play the classic bluegrass instruments to infuse classical, jazz, pop, and the blues into their country bluegrass. Stephane Grappelli and Tommy Jarell are their sources as much as traditional Celtic songs.

Tim O'Brien is a founding member of the Grammy-winning progressive bluegrass band Hot Rize. He is the president of the International Bluegrass Musical Association (IBMA) and does guest appearances with Phish. O'Brien is a traveler of several different musical roads. He sells songs to country radio. He plays to the folk crowd, knows his Irish music, and performs at the traditional bluegrass outdoor festivals. He appears with his old band Hot Rize when they reunite for special performances. He also plays The Beatles and Bob Dylan.

'The Beatles were so much of what I cut my teeth on musically,' he said as we settled on the back porch of his Nashville home. 'They're the reason I played the guitar. They are my roots just as much as the old country music and bluegrass fiddle tunes. So I didn't want to leave that out.' His version of 'Norwegian Wood' is becoming a classic. 'I was looking for something that would fit the traditional instruments. Also I think that's a great song. Somebody said that's the best Bob Dylan song that he didn't write.'

O'Brien's 1996 Grammy-nominated *My Red on Blond* album is a direct allusion to Dylan's *Blond on Blond*. Tim is Irish in complexion and reddish in hair. 'It was a good way to make an entry into new places through the association of the great Bob Dylan,' he said. 'My record takes the music out of the stereotype of Dylan, the nasal singing, loud and brash, and political protest. My version just says, "Here's some music. Listen to it." I thought it was a natural fit for anyone playing traditional music to play Dylan's music.'

Dylan, The Beatles and Chuck Berry songs have become part of bluegrass repertoire since the 1960s. The Charles River Valley Boys put out an album called *Beatle's Country*. Jim and Jesse did an album covering

Chuck Berry songs, *Berry Picking*. The Country Gentlemen introduced folk and pop into their bluegrass. The Dillards and many others beside O'Brien made Dylan a bluegrass crossover.

'Bluegrass has sort of been country's embarrassing cousin,' Tim said. 'In the last ten years, bluegrass has evolved into country music's venerated cousin. Now it's a nice cousin, a prestige thing, part of country's heritage. It's to be valued but not taken seriously as a commercial form. That's probably a good, fair assessment of how it is.

'Stylistically, mostly when you say country, you're talking about a market. That's what country radio means anyway. Bluegrass has been much less influenced, infected some say, by the need to be saleable. In fact, it's almost designed not to be saleable. In the '60s, when country became more pop, bluegrass really got shoved to the side. Meanwhile, Flatt and Scruggs were selling lots of tickets to shows and lots of records. Bluegrass was going strong but it was pushed out of radio and the main part of the marketplace.'

O'Brien shares the opinion of many others that country music has become a marketing campaign more than anything. The labels decide what's the one thing they can sell the most of, then they go there and leave everything else out. 'It's like whole wheat flour versus bleached white flour,' Tim said. 'I think the country music executives are going to change their tune. There is a movement to let country be country. The industry concurs that they blew it by trying to market to youth. The older audience is the one who has stood by the music, is still the base of the market, so they're going back to that. They marketed Shania Twain and Garth Brooks to the youth, but only after those artists took hold with the older bread-and-butter audience.'

It's true that bluegrass doesn't have to make the compromises of country music, Tim conceded. Despite bluegrass's non-commercial attitude, a marketplace has developed, primarily through bluegrass associations, festivals, blocks of radio programs, and the periodic revivals, like that ignited by the success of *O Brother, Where Art Thou?* Bluegrass now has its own radio chart.

When the music industry puts a dollar value on chart positions, it will invariably invest money in securing the top chart positions. Getting a chart position means getting radio airplay and getting airplay means appealing to program directors. Bluegrass must instrumentally sound like bluegrass to get airplay, but with concessions. Strict instrumentals are not very important anymore, Tim noted. A song without vocals is a drawback from airplay. Also, there is a trend to have a gospel song or two on bluegrass records. Bluegrass is getting a little homogenized, Tim acknowledged. Commercial concerns have drifted into the music.

Bluegrass still claims the high ground it staked out in the folk boom of the 1960s. When the rock festivals, like Woodstock, happened, bluegrass festivals advertised no drugs, no motorcycles, no alcohol, and no pets. The hardcore bluegrass fan didn't want to align with the rock movement. Some hippie folk fans went to bluegrass because they considered it a form of country music closer to the original folk songs. The music was designed not to be too popular. It could stay free of the taint of commercialization, like an organic commune could somehow remain free of the vulgar ornamentation of a consumer society.

The bluegrass festivals are family events with very little boundary between the performers and the audience. Pete Seeger said that he didn't have fans, he had friends. O'Brien sees the same people at different bluegrass events year after year. He'd know their names, their kids' names, and where they are from. They are familiar. Those loyal fans expect to be treated as family. They expect O'Brien and other performers to be available, to mingle, and to sit down and chat.

The outdoor bluegrass festivals retain the ambience of a revival tent camp meeting. Old-time religion is the True Cross in bluegrass. There is more heart-of-Jesus gospel in bluegrass than in country. That's perhaps because the average bluegrass fan, or musician, is a convert, being neither born to Protestant fundamentalism or the working-class South. Converts are more fanatical than those born-to. Listening to or performing the 'pure' bluegrass is a way of affirming the depth of one's conviction. It's a bit like Martin Luther posting his 99 condemnations of the Catholic Church as a declaration to a purer, brighter faith.

The influence of church music is plainly heard in bluegrass. The long, drawn-out note, the country call, has been traced back to an early period of medieval church singing. In church terms, the country call was the *jubilus*, Latin for 'joyful call' or 'country cry'. St Hilary wrote in the fourth century 'the jubilation of the voice is heard through the emphasis of a long drawn out and expressive rendering.' The *jubilus* is found in the psalm-song, the oldest form of Christian worship, which was adopted from the Jewish ritual at the dawn of the Christian era, according to scholars.

The etymological root of *jubilus* is the Hebrew *yobel*, ram's-horn trumpet. The blast of the trumpet announced the sabbatical year, a year-long celebration held every 50 years in which all bondmen were freed, mortgaged lands were restored to the original owners and land was left fallow.

It is tempting to say that the high, lonesome sound of bluegrass is a descendent of the ancient *jubilus*, but solid scholastic work does not conclusively support the claim.

The 'shouting' style of bluegrass singing belongs to the folk church. The high-pitched bluegrass singing found in eastern Kentucky, Bill Monroe country, is associated with hymns of the Primitive Baptist, who may have taken literally Isaiah's (58:1) admonition to 'lift up thy voice like a trumpet'.

Bluegrass singing employs the West African and the Celtic traditions of high pitches, vocal tension and a declamatory style. Black influence appears in the shortened phrases, a more careful matching of pitch with speech sounds and syncopation. The song 'Shortin' Bread', once routinely taught in grammar schools, is a typical example.

Cecil Sharp wrote in his book *English Folk Songs from the Southern Appalachians* (Ed. Maud Karpeles, London, 1932) that 'the mountain singers sing in very much the same way as English folksingers – in the same straightforward, direct manner, without any conscious effort at expression, and with the even tone and clarity of enunciation with which all folksong collectors are familiar.'

'But bluegrass singing, even more than its hillbilly and country cousins, seems to have drunk deeply from the black well,' states Robert Cantwell in his book *Bluegrass Breakdown, The Making of the Old Southern Sound* (Da Capo Press, New York, 1992). 'Like blues singing, bluegrass singing is undeviatingly rhythmical – a rigorous, clattering, indignant delivery, which seems to favor groups of three or four syllables tied to a strong accent but which in any case leaves no syllable of the lyric rhythmically untouched… But the sheer effort required to sing in this style imparts a passion and a drive to the singing that is simply unparalleled in country music.'

The bluegrass Appalachian 'old Southern sound' is very much an Afro-American sound, Cantwell pointed out. The black music came with the minstrel shows on the riverboats, then with the railroads, and then with radio and the phonograph. Blues and early jazz are the modern influences on bluegrass precisely because they have preserved the enduring traits of black tradition, Cantwell stated.

The banjo is the most obvious African instrumental influence on bluegrass. Captured West Africans sold into slavery brought the early form of the instrument to the New World. The African version was usually a hollowed gourd or calabash with a hide stretched over the sound hole and fitted with a long fretless neck. The strings were vine, gut, silk, or wire. The instrument was noted on the West Indies island of Martinique in 1678. By the mid-1700s, the banjo was common on the Southern plantations among the slaves, where it was called various names, including 'merrywang'.

'The banjo is a drum on a stick,' Tim O'Brien said. 'The melody is the musical structure of the Celtic fiddle as played in Ireland and the British Isles. But in the United States, the music evolved to where the chords and rhythm sections are as much of the structure as anything. That's the Afro-American influence.

The guitar makes the one- and three-rhythm section and the banjo subdivides, making a grid for the melody to go across. That helped to bring about improvisation, where you don't have to stay with the melody as much. The rhythm section became as important as the melody and that influence came from African music. The African cross-rhythm found a companion in the off-beat accentuated gait in Scottish song, a rhythm pattern favored by Irish fiddlers. The fiddle and the banjo are the duet of Europe and Africa.

'The church music and country music of the South owes a lot to the black culture. And there is the minstrel show tradition, where the blacks are imitating the whites and the whites are imitating the blacks. It keeps reflecting back and forth until you can't tell where it started.'

Musically, the Celtic and the African musics shared the major pentatonic. The fourth and the seventh is excluded in the gapped scale but the third and fifth made sweet and resonant. Singers of blues, spirituals, jazz, country, and bluegrass use the 'blue tonality' in the third and seventh degrees of the scale. The blues singer 'bends' a note, typically a sharp or minor third, toward the major. Bluegrass musicians do the same, as heard in Bill Monroe's 'Uncle Pen'.

The major pentatonic has been called the 'African' pentatonic because it is so common in spirituals, such as 'Swing Low Sweet Chariot' and 'Nobody Knows the Trouble I've Seen'. The majority of bluegrass songs are in the pentatonic, like 'Old Susanna'.

The African influence was why the industrialist Henry Ford actively promoted Appalachian music. He considered the Celtic version as pure untainted American music. He thought that the African-influenced ragtime and jazz was corrupting America's youth.

Ford, a virulent anti-Semite and an early admirer of Hitler, believed that a Jewish conspiracy lay behind the degeneracy of 'Africanized' music. He financed the magazine *The Dearborn Independent* as his mouthpiece to express concern about the threats to the 'pure' Christian America. He actively promoted American music by sponsoring old-time fiddle contests though Ford dealerships in various cities. He also financed a book of dance instructions and sponsored a dance orchestra that revived old instruments and dance music he enjoyed as a youth in rural Michigan.

Ford brought musicians to Detroit in 1926 for a national fiddle competition. The winner was Uncle Bunt Stephens from Tennessee who played 'The Old Hen Cackled'. Ford's effort, if not his politics, struck a chord with many Americans who longed for the simpler society before assembly lines and factories. Ironically, he became something of a folk hero in the rural South for raising the national awareness of old-time fiddle styles.

Bluegrass is a new music. Bill Monroe, the acknowledged father of bluegrass, created the form in the late 1930s. Innovative musicians such as Lester Flatt, Earl Scruggs, Chubby Wise, Don Reno, and Jimmy Martin further developed the style in the '40s. Bluegrass did not become a distinct genre until the '50s. The term 'bluegrass' was inspired by Monroe's band, the Blue Grass Boys, named after their home state, Kentucky, the bluegrass state. In late May, for about two weeks, tiny blossoms tint the rolling pastures of the horse country around Lexington a hazy blue.

Bluegrass projects an image of being the last vestiges of the authentic real music that came from the distant past. This is achieved, in part, through the makeup of a conventional bluegrass band – guitar, five-string banjo, fiddle, mandolin, and acoustic upright bass. The drums, electric guitars, and keyboards that country has incorporated are not allowed in a traditional bluegrass band. This is largely Monroe's lingering influence. His intention was to play country music 'as it should be sung and played'. He wanted to keep a heritage of old-time music untainted by the electrification of instruments.

The only concession to modernity in the lineup was the introduction of the dobro in 1955. The dobro is named after the Dopyera Brothers. John Dopyera, a Czech immigrant in Chicago, invented in 1928 a wood-body resonator guitar with a metal cover plate over the sound hole and an aluminum cone for amplification. Dobro is also the Slovak word for 'good'. The innovation was the metal-cone-amplification of a slide guitar.

The dobro has won its place as a bluegrass instrument and the master of the dobro is Jerry Douglas. The Grammy winner has recorded with Ray Charles, Yo-Yo Ma, Paul Simon, Garth Brooks, and James Taylor. He has recorded regularly with Alison Krauss and Union Station since 1998. When he was 13, Douglas started playing in bars on weekends with his father's band. His father, a native of West Virginia, had moved the family to Ohio, where Jerry was born, to find work in the steel mills. When Jerry was 17, members of the highbrow bluegrass band, the Country Gentlemen, heard him play and invited him to join them on the road. He never looked back.

He has expanded the instrument's repertoire in texture, rhythm, tonal clarity, and content. He has done for the dobro what Bela Fleck has done for the banjo, expanded the versatility of the instrument and taken it to new levels. He is the dobro icon.

The core of Bill Monroe's early band was Chubby Wise, Lester Flatt, and Earl Scruggs. Wise, from Florida, played a bluesy soulful fiddle, a perfect fit for Monroe's love of the blues sound. Flatt, the rhythm guitar player and a good singer, and the young banjo player Earl Scruggs gave the band a fast-driving base sound for Monroe's mandolin to float across. Scruggs was the Eddy Van Halen of the banjo. Like Van Halen on the guitar, Scruggs played the banjo like no one before him, introducing his three-finger picking style when he joined Monroe's band in 1945.

Flatt and Scruggs chafed under Monroe's firm hand. They left to form their own band, which Monroe saw as a betrayal and didn't speak to either man for years. While Monroe and other traditional players, like the Stanley Brothers, stayed in the music of heartbreak, loss, and death, Flatt and Scruggs introduced novelty tunes, gospel, lighthearted and funny songs into gothic bluegrass. They took the music in a more commercial major third direction and left behind much of Monroe's blues sound.

Scruggs confounded bluegrass fans and angered purists with his early 1970s country-rock band, the Earl Scruggs Revue. The revue was largely a nod to the music of Earl's sons. But it wasn't a one-off aberration. In 2002, he came out with his first album in 17 years, *Earl Scruggs and Friends* with rock superstar Elton John on the first track, 'Country Comfort'.

Bluegrass can be roughly divided into BBM (Before Bill Monroe) and ABM (After Bill Monroe).

'He was a watershed in the evolution of bluegrass,' according to Laurie Lewis, who performed on the 1996 Grammy-winning album *True Life Blues, The Songs of Bill Monroe*. Tim O'Brien produced one of her 13 albums and she is a producer herself. She was twice voted as the IBMA female vocalist of the year, and her recording of 'Who'll Watch the Home Place' was voted song of the year.

'Bill Monroe took aspects of this music that were floating around him – the church music, blues, gospel, old-time fiddle tunes, the early country songs, and the old-time ballads that were all around the hills where he grew up – and he made something very personal out of it,' Laurie said from her home in Berkeley. 'The importance of Bill Monroe, besides his revolutionary way of playing the mandolin, was that he made bluegrass personal.'

BBM bluegrass was mostly event songs, the broadcast ballads that retold events. Monroe shifted the public event to the singer/songwriter event. 'He talked about himself and his feelings,' Laurie said. 'He might be talking about them in a stoic way but he moved the emphasis from the impersonal news event to the personal event. His "Can't You Hear Me Cryin'" is one of the best-known early bluegrass songs of this nature and is now a songbook standard. It's about him and Bessie Lee Mauldin. He called these songs of the personal nature his "true songs".'

As country music went more towards pop, bluegrass was perceived as 'too country'. It represented the 'wrong kind' of country music to attract the new audiences. The music was de-emphasized by major record labels and the Country Music Association. Bluegrass on country radio was in steady decline throughout the late 1950s and '60s. The only outlet was on college and public stations, on the left side of the FM dial.

The recent surge of interest in bluegrass has less to do with the soundtrack *O Brother, Where Art Thou?*, which is old-timey country rather than bluegrass, and more to do with the music of Alison Krauss, Nickel Creek, and the Yonder Mountain String Band.

Bluegrass is tinged with what commercial radio wants to hear, a more pop sound.

'The songs Alison chooses to sing do not sound like bluegrass songs to me,' Laurie observed. 'But, they retain the same instrumentation. Alison is very lucky in that her personal tastes and what she musically wants to do coincide with the pop sensibilities of the market. She has proven that you can play pop music with bluegrass instruments. I won't say that she is trying to do something more commercial. She is naturally more attuned to what is more commercial. She has had an enormous effect, especially on other women. Her style of singing has become one of the ways for women to sing in bluegrass.

'I see an opening up of lyric content in bluegrass being brought about to a large extent by the number of women getting involved in the music,' Laurie said. 'We're not going to choose to sing ballads about women getting killed or you've done me wrong, you left me for another man sort of thing. We've got to find our own material. We have to write our own songs or turn to the modern writers.'

The current hotbed of bluegrass is, somewhat surprisingly, San Francisco and Portland, Oregon. The San Francisco scene evolved around David Grisman, a long-time resident of the city. 'He's had a huge impact on bluegrass with his music,' Laurie explained. 'He has taken the musical composition a couple of steps further and his various bands and quartets have spawned so many great players, like Mike Marshall and Tony Rice.

'In Portland, there are so many young people playing the old-time string band music that those bands play in rock clubs. Jam festivals that are bluegrass based are becoming really popular. There, the music is taking a Grateful Dead direction, like you hear in the Yonder Mountain String Band. This is even happening at the traditionalist Merlefest, the largest bluegrass festival put on by Doc Watson in memory of his son Merle. A part of the drawing card is musicians jamming together. A lot of young people go there for that reason. They don't know who they are going to hear playing with whom, or how the songs are going to be played.

'Bluegrass is a tradition based on messing with tradition. It's okay that you bring new stuff to the music. That makes it a living and vibrant tradition, rather than something that's dead in the museum.'

28 The Loveless Motel

In Nashville, I lived on the elbow of West End Road, right where it bends to avoid running into the McCabe Golf Course. That bend is the nexus of the neighborhood, with its coffee shop, two grocery stores, a dry cleaners, and the A Squeeky Clean Coin Laundry. Russian immigrants ran the Amoco gas station, but the mechanic was a Nashville native. There are four restaurants in the mix: the McCabe Pub, Park Café, Caffe Nonna, and the Sylvan Park. The McCabe was voted best neighborhood pub in Nashville for 2002. The Park Café is an upscale place packed on the weekends. The Caffe Nonna is ranked as one of the finest Italian restaurants in the city. The Sylvan Park is a straightforward meat-and-three place.

The restaurant is a white clapboard box of a place, plain and without pretension. It is run by women with the attitude that if you are there to eat, they are there to put the food in front of you. No need to chat about it or wish you a good day. Whether your day is good or bad is up to you. They don't have time to hear about it. Ten tables crowd the small room. The daily menu is set with Southern standards: fried chicken, creamed corn, mashed potatoes, green beans, corn biscuits, coleslaw, jello, and a meat dish. A Coke machine stands in a corner. Next to the cash register are tracts promoting fundamental Christianity. The Sylvan Park, famous in Nashville and beyond (it has been featured in in-flight magazines) for its down home Southernness, is Tompall Glaser's favorite restaurant.

Tompall is one of the Glaser Brothers – with siblings Chuck and Jim – that started as Marty Robbins' backup group. They became a well-known act in their own right and were also songwriters who branched out into publishing. The Glasers' best-known songs were John Hartford's

'Gentle on My Mind' and Tompall's own 'Streets of Baltimore'. Tompall played with Gram Parson and the Byrds. He was friends with Kris Kristofferson and Billy Joe Shaver.

But most importantly, Tompall was an Outlaw. Waylon Jennings called his pinball playing partner and coke snortin' buddy Tompall 'best friend'. With publishing profits, the Glaser brothers built a recording studio at 916 19th Avenue South, which became the famous Hillbilly Central, where Waylon and Willie made *Wanted: The Outlaws*. The album cover shows an old, tattered, Wild West 'wanted' poster of unshaven Willie, Waylon, and Tompall looking like fugitives under their badass cowboy hats – and an unsmiling Jessi Colter.

I invited Tompall to lunch. I waited outside the Sylvan Park and watched him approach slowly among the parked cars. He has gained a lot of weight over the years, which makes him uncomfortable. His parabolic belly increases the stress on his knees, making it physically awkward for him to move. He's always been conscious of his appearance, and he doesn't like how he looks now. He calls himself a recluse who doesn't often leave his house, where his wife looks after him.

Inside, we sat at a back corner table. Tompall wears big glasses and has a shock of white hair. He never removed his ball cap during the meal. Our conversation was a mumbled shambling affair between bites of food.

'I didn't do the Outlaw thing to make money. I did it because I thought it should be done and that's all there was to it.'

We pulled apart the fried chicken breasts with our fingers.

'RCA didn't pay me for two years for using the studio. But I had plenty of money.'

We paused when the waitress brought our ice tea.

'I didn't want to get a stable of guys and try to make everything go the same way. I wanted them to do what they wanted to do. I just let Waylon do it and I sat there.'

Tompall spoke inside his mouth and down into his chest. We ate slow but steady.

'I had to sue Waylon. He was an uneducated man. He just couldn't get anything through his head. I never knew him sober. I was into that, the booze and coke, too.'

We slathered butter on the steaming corn bread biscuits.

'Would I start recording people again? Well, the mind set has to be there. All I did for Waylon was open the doors like a good producer does. A producer didn't go in and tell Waylon how to make a record. I just put him up in the studio and said, "There's no lock. Take as long as you want. Work it out with your guys and come out with a hit." I'm retired now, or semi-retired.'

Corn biscuit crumbs littered our shirtfronts and caught in Tompall's white beard.

'Some of those sounds that came up in the Outlaws had been around for years. Willie had old stuff from RCA that they dropped because they didn't want it anymore.'

We wiped up the gravy with slices of white bread.

'Bluegrass is going to run its course. It's about done. Look at *O Brother*. Where did that come from? It wasn't out of Nashville. The soundtrack came out of LA or New York.'

The waitress brought desserts, ice cream for me and a slice of cake for Tompall.

'What's next in country music? I think the next thing will probably be country with a Latin American beat. It hasn't been exploited yet. Johnnie and Jack did country with a Latin beat back in the '50s "Ashes of Love". Johnnie Wright married Kitty Wells. Jack died with Patsy Cline in her plane crash. I like that new kid, Ricky Martin. Some of those Latin writers write beautiful lyrics, kinda of like country used to be. That's why I think it's a good possibility. Raul Malo, he has a good voice and writes good songs. The crop of writers we got in country now is just writing last month's top ten. I don't even listen to country music anymore. Haven't for years.'

Outside, I thanked Tompall. I noticed for the first time that he has a sweet smile. He waved goodbye and ambled to his car.

The connection between Latin beat and country is not a stretch. Brooks And Dunn's hit 'My Heart Is Lost to You' has been translated into Spanish. The songwriters, Brett Beavers and Connie Harrington, wrote the words in English but the chord progressions sound Spanish. Beavers, a Texan with an ear for the Tex-Mex rhythms, suggested they add a little steamy sultry Latin feel. Harrington, also a Texan, wondered what the words would sound like in Spanish. Neither speaks Spanish, so they called Alex Torres, Beaver's publishing partner who works with Emma Fox. A Texan of Mexican parentage, Torres contacted his grandmother, who gave her translation. That translation was checked with waiters at a Mexican restaurant in Nashville.

The link between Nashville and Mexico is short indeed.

The link between Nashville and Cuba is even shorter.

Raul Malo lives in Nashville. He became a country star as the lead singer for the now defunct Mavericks. He had a hit, 'Every Little Thing About You', on his solo album *Today* (2001). Four of the 12 tracks on the album are in Cuban Spanish.

Raul was born in Miami after his parents fled Castro's Cuba. He grew up comfortable (his father is a banker) and had no romantic yearnings to be a cowboy, or to sing like a cowboy. He has the clear, clean romantic sound of a natural balladeer. The Mavericks were formed in Miami, where every sound was Latin or pop. To catch the ear of club owners, they needed a different sound, so the band went country ballad with a touch of be-bop and honky-tonk. Their manager also managed Marilyn Manson. The rock-bashing ghoul Manson and the American-Cuban singing seductive country songs shared gigs in punk clubs.

'The kids with the Mohawks and the dog collars loved the Mavericks and what we were doing,' Raul said. 'We were right there on the edge. It was a great way to hone your craft and skills in crowd control.'

Raul asked that we meet at his studio out of Hillsboro Road on the edge of Nashville. His family home, wife and three children, was 3 miles (5km) further down the road. The area is one of mini-Versailles mansions complete with shooting fountains and acres of rolling lawns. Amidst this grandeur, I found the gravel lane leading back to Raul's studio, a modest brick house. His road racing motorcycle was parked by the back door.

Black-out curtains on the windows made the living room dim and vague. Glowing red and yellow lights from the recording equipment gave a sci-fi effect, like we were in the cabin of a space vehicle. As my eyes adjusted, I saw guitars in their stands, an upright bass lying on the floor, several keyboards, a drum kit and, over the unused fireplace, a painting of Elvis.

Raul directed me through the kitchen and past the room his wife uses as a painting studio, bare of furniture but with an unfinished piece on the easel. We settled in the sitting room, a small, sunny space with two comfortable overstuffed armchairs and another portrait of Elvis.

Raul and the Mavericks moved to Nashville when Steve Earle, Nanci Griffith, Dwight Yoakam, Kelly Willis, Lyle Lovett and Randy Travis were putting a new twist to country. The Mavericks toured with Trisha Yearwood and cut albums for MCA. But Raul never left his Cuban heritage behind. The title track of The Mavericks's first album was 'From Hell to Paradise', about the plight of Cuban immigrants. The last Mavericks studio album in 1998, *Trampoline*, had a heavy Latin flavor. The label didn't know how to market it, so it received little airplay. But the band toured and made it a success with the fans. In Europe, the album 'went through the roof', in Raul's words.

'Funny, but now we're hearing that country is going Latin,' Raul mused. He is an outgoing, gregarious man, always with a smile. 'Marty Robbins did Latin in country before we did it. He was a huge influence in my life. I loved Marty Robbins. A lot of Mexican music is very similar to American country. There are a lot of similarities, like waltzes and two beats, which has nothing to do with geography, or your social background. The music is intertwined. That's the beauty. But the intertwined music can be difficult in a business. It confuses the market. That's a shame because the music suffers. It all starts to sound the same after awhile.'

Latin music has always been in country, Raul pointed out. Along with the Appalachian influence, there has been the Western sound. The West was settled, in part, by Mexicans and other Latinos. Country and Latin musics blend well because of rhythm patterns and lyrical content.

'A couple of years ago, the Mavericks did a song with Flaco Jeminez, the Mexican accordion player,' Raul said. 'That was our highest charting single in the States, 'All You Ever Do Is Bring Me Down', our only top ten hit. When we toured, especially in California and the Southwest, the Latin contingent in the crowd was growing everywhere we went. Here was a country band singing in Spanish and people were hootin' and yollarin'. They loved it. Right now I'm producing Rick Travino. He had success in the '90s and recently signed with Warner Brothers. We're using

Latin influence in country and using the traditional sounds instruments, including the Cuban *tres*, a guitar, in new ways. It will be interesting to see what Warner Brothers does with it.'

Raul grew up listening to traditional Cuban country *son* music. He is experimenting with ways to align American country with *son*.

'I find the heart-felt, emotionally wretched singing styles of Hank Williams and Bill Monroe and Ralph Stanley very similar to the Cuban *soneros*,' he explained. 'When you hear Bill Monroe sing, you believe what he's singing. He's seen the dark side. He's seen the other side of the mountain. He's been to it and knows what it's like. That's very similar to the old Cuban singers, like Benny More, one of the great *soneros* of Cuba. They sing with nasal-cutting-through-everything vocals. You can hear it through thick walls. The emotions of those old country songs are very similar to the emotions found in Cuban music. It's just different languages and rhythm patterns. *Son* is uniquely Cuban. Bluegrass is uniquely Appalachian. Both musics are born out of similar conditions. The best stuff we have as humans comes from really poor downtrodden people, foods, music, styles, and rhythms.'

Raul records with Higher Octave, a Los Angeles label, and with BMG Gravity in Europe.

'They've given me complete freedom,' he said. 'Originally, I had a whole collection of Latin songs that were going on a full-on Spanish album. But we left MCA so it never happened. Now, I am free to record whatever I want. I love incorporating different styles of music and throwing it all together, like the Nortec Collective out of Tijuana does. Los Cadillac is perhaps the best-known group coming out of that. The Beatles mixed different styles all the time. If you listen to their albums from beginning to end, you'll hear ten styles.

'We should not become rigid in our expectations of artists so they have to do the same thing over and over and over again. That's what the record companies do. If the artist has success in one thing, they want you to keep doing it. There are people, audiences, out there that appreciate different stuff. The records companies are not catering to them. The labels go for the common denominator. There is a whole segment of the population that is not being catered to, not being attended to by the labels. What's coming out of the major labels is getting more and more stale, more and more dull and boring.

'What could be happening in Americana and country is what happened in rap years ago, when the major labels weren't touching rap artists. So the rap guys were selling the records out of the trunks of their cars, basically. That's how Dr Drie got to be worth $200 million [£130 million] or whatever he's worth. They worked and worked and when they started to get success the labels said, "Hey, we need to make them partners." So you got Innerscope. There is a whole group of musicians in Nashville that is under the radar of the label powers. That's where the new music comes from and the Latin. You'll be hearing a lot more Latin influence.'

I made a round of calls to Jill King and Emma Fox and Matt King for news. Perhaps they were taking Spanish lessons.

'I'm real excited right now,' Jill King told me. 'I'm going into the studio in four weeks to record an album for Blue Diamond Records. We're doing the song selections now. I got real traditional country players and a great producer. We've got a full promotion staff and national distribution. I'm going on a club and radio tour in a couple of months, starting November 15. We'll put the single out to the stations in January and release the album in March. This is a career record. I feel good about this. That's when the magic happens.'

What happened to opening for Brooks And Dunn at county fairs over the summer?

'That didn't happen and I really don't know why. The road manager for Destiny's Child, who was Brooks And Dunn's and Reba McEntire's road manager, he was suppose to set it up. I was all ready to go but as the date got closer he got wishy-washy. Finally he stopped returning calls. You can only count on what you can control in the music business.'

She was still playing down at Tootsie's. A&R people for a couple of major labels have been in to hear her. 'Word is out that I want to be a contender,' she said. 'We're going to shop the album to the majors. My lawyer has contacts with Universal, Sony, and MCA.'

She was totally buzzed about her gig at Tootsie's the night before. 'I was singing good and the band was really on and we were having a great time. The tips were big. Some guy went next door and bought me a cowboy hat. Another guy who could yodel got up on stage and he was real good. This 11-year-old boy who could drum anything, he sat in. People were having such a good time. I said to myself, "This is why I'm doing this."'

Emma Fox was as determined as ever to conquer Nashville in double time. She had just finished her official four-song demo for Sony. 'I've been experimenting so we spent more time than usual,' she said. 'I have developed a sound that's like a female Chris Isaac/Linda Ronstadt that I like. I've been writing a lot of songs with Don Cook and been demoing them in the studio. He's invited me to sing at this big BMI affair, sort of a cross between a showcase and a golf holiday.' She was working only one part-time job. Plans for her own showcase in a couple of months at a Nashville club were fermenting. She had increased her gig load and was writing, writing, writing. 'It's still the romantic melancholy with hooky melodies that I've always done,' she said. 'I'm deeper into the cool groove of black music with real country. I want two things by Christmas, in three months' time. I want someone to cut one of my songs and I want a record deal. I've already got my two front teeth.'

Matt King sounded gothic optimistic. He had filed for bankruptcy, had health problems, and had been told 'you're not a mainstream act.' But, what do you expect, he said. I've been working towards that.

'My music has gotten better. It's extremely challenging. I've been getting lots of positive feedback from people and a few nibbles. I hope to get a publishing deal. I have new management and we're working on a college tour. I'm planning a new album, kind of a Woodie Guthrie approach. I'm going to take a cross-country trip by car and stop in factories and working places and talk to people about their lives. The album will be based on those conversations. Things are going exactly like I thought they would. I'm poor, writing good music from the truth, and getting ready to go on the road.'

Loveless Motel, the real Loveless Motel, is located 20 minutes outside Nashville. The place started, in 1948, as the Harpeth Valley Tearoom.

Lon and Annie Loveless, a name as common as Smith in the region, bought the eatery in 1950 and built the eponymous motel. The McCabe family took over in 1973 and made the restaurant famous for its biscuits, smoked ham, and peach preserves. The motel section closed in 1987 and now houses the Sunday buffet room.

Sunday morning brunch at the Loveless Motel is a favorite place to famous people watch. Alan Jackson or Vince Gill and Amy or Wynonna Judd or any number of recording stars have been spotted there. During Paul McCartney's 1974 Nashville stay, his whole family regularly ate at the Loveless Motel. McCartney spent six weeks in Nashville and cut 'Sally G', 'Bridge Over the River', 'Hey Diddle', and 'Junior's Farm'. McCartney and his family stayed on a farm owned by the rocker Curly 'Junior' Putnam. 'Junior's Farm' became a number three hit in 1974.

I thought it appropriate to invite Our Willie, Amy, and Hank to my farewell breakfast at the Loveless Motel. I found them at our regular Tootsie's table. To my surprise, Hank immediately bought a round of beer.

'I have a toast,' he announced. 'To my friends.' He nodded to each of us. 'To Nashville.' He lifted his beer bottle towards the singer on the stage. 'To my departure.' He drank deeply. We sat stunned.

'You're giving up,' Amy asked in disbelief. 'You're quitting!'

'No,' Hank answered calmly. 'My vacation time is over. I'm going back to my job.'

'What?!' I exclaimed. 'What job?'

Hank set his bottle down on the table. 'My name is Henry Wolly. I'm a cattle buyer for a meat packer. I live in Laramie, Wyoming.'

Hank explained that he grew up on a ranch. He knew how to handle a horse before he could write a sentence. By the age of ten, he was helping his dad and their four hands in the annual roundup. He branded cattle, gave them vaccinations, helped with the birthing, and rode out in blizzards to rescue cows. In high school, he was an offensive and defensive end on the football team. He competed in bronc riding and steer wrestling on the rodeo team. He went to college on a rodeo scholarship.

He sang a little on weekends in bars. 'People told me that I was good,' he said. 'I can sound just like Wade Hayes or Clint Black. I earned enough to buy myself a new pickup.'

He flirted with the idea of testing himself in Nashville before settling down to a real life. But, just after he graduated with a degree in business, his dad took sick. It wasn't a hard choice for Hank to take over the ranch.

'That lasted six years before drought and market prices drove me out of business. I moved to town, worked in an insurance office and tried to get married. But I missed the ranch and the kind of men I grew up with. We were cowboys, real cowboys who sat around campfires and sang songs and loved our horses. I quit my job, broke my engagement and found a job that connected me back to ranch life.'

He spends more time on the range than in the office, going from ranch to ranch checking on the meat supply. Actually, he explained, he didn't have to visit the ranches. But he needed to, so he convinced his boss that buying cattle from the ranchers was more cost effective than buying from feed lots.

'I listen to a lot of country music on those long drives from ranch to ranch,' he said. 'Small stations in small towns that don't pay attention to the top 40. They play the real corny stuff, songs about the life their listeners live every day. There is great satisfaction in that music. Nevertheless, I was always curious about Nashville, the capital of country music. So I came to check it out.'

'Why you going back?' asked Our Willie.

'There is a bar near Gillette where I like to sit and listen to the songs. When I'm at Pine Tree Junction, people ask me to sing and they seem to genuinely like me. I know a steakhouse/bar at a crossroads that's the only building for 60 miles [100km] in any direction. It's my favorite place to sing. It's my Tootsie's, so I'm going home.'

Bibliography

CANTWELL, Robert: *Bluegrass Breakdown – The Making Of The Old Southern Sound* (Da Capo Press, New York, 1992)

COLLINS, Ace: *The Stories Behind Country Music's All-Time Greatest 100 Songs* (Boulevard Books, New York, 1996)

DALEY, Dan: *Nashville's Unwritten Rules – Inside the Business of Country Music* (The Overlook Press, Woodstock & New York, 1998)

DAWIDOFF, Nicholas: *In The Country Of Country – People And Places In American Music* (Pantheon Books, New York, 1997)

FEILER, Bruce: *Dreaming Out Loud* (Avon Books, New York, 1998)

HINTON, Brian: *Country Roads – How Country Came To Nashville* (Sanctuary Publishing, London, 2000)

LOMAX, John III: *Nashville Music City USA* (Harry N Abrams, New York, 1985)

MALONE, Bill C: *Don't Get Above Your Raisin' – Country Music And The Southern Working Class* (University of Illinois Press, Urbana and Chicago, 2002)

MASSEY, Sara A (editor): *Black Cowboys Of Texas* (Texas M & M University Press, Austin, 2000)

TICHI, Cecelia: *High Lonesome – The American Culture Of Country Music* (University of North Carolina Press, Chapel Hill and London, 1994)

TICHI, Cecelia (editor): *Reading Country Music, Steel Guitars, Opry Stars, And Honky-Tonk Bars* (Duke University Press, Durham and London, 1998)

Index